ISRAEL'S LONG WAR WITH HEZBOLLAH

ISRAEL'S LONG WAR WITH HEZBOLLAH

Military Innovation and Adaptation Under Fire

RAPHAEL D. MARCUS

Washington, DC / Georgetown University Press

The publisher is not responsible for third-party websites or their content. URL links were active at time of publication.

Library of Congress Cataloging-in-Publication Data

Names: Marcus, Raphael D., author.
Title: Israel's long war with Hezbollah : military innovation and adaptation under fire / Raphael D. Marcus.
Description: Washington, DC : Georgetown University Press, 2018. | Includes bibliographical references and index.
Identifiers: LCCN 2017058064 (print) | LCCN 2018012278 (ebook) | ISBN 9781626166127 (ebook) | ISBN 9781626166110 (pbk. : alk. paper) | ISBN 9781626166103 (hardcover : alk. paper)
Subjects: LCSH: Israel. Tseva haganah le-Yiâsra®el—History. | Israel—History, Military—20th century. | Israel—History, Military—21st century. | Hizballah (Lebanon)—History. | Israel—Military relations—Lebanon. | Lebanon—Military relations—Israel. | Operational art (Military science)
Classification: LCC UA853.I8 (ebook) | LCC UA853.I8 M358 2018 (print) | DDC 956.05—dc23
LC record available at https://lccn.loc.gov/2017058064

♾ This book is printed on acid-free paper meeting the requirements of the American National Standard for Permanence in Paper for Printed Library Materials.

19 18   9 8 7 6 5 4 3 2   First printing

Printed in the United States of America

Map by Chris Robinson.
Cover design by N. Putens.
Cover image by Alex Lerner/Shutterstock.com.

CONTENTS

Acknowledgments   vii

Abbreviations   ix

Introduction   1

Part I. Strategic Adaptation

Introduction to Part I   31

1   IDF "Routine Security" and the Evolution of Hezbollah (1985–92)   37

2   Deterrence, Guerrilla Warfare, and the Establishment of the "Rules of the Game" (1993–99)   54

3   A Change in the Strategic Equation: The IDF Withdrawal from Lebanon (2000)   75

4   The Erosion of Deterrence, the 2006 War, and the Dahiya Doctrine (2000–2017)   90

Conclusion to Part I   113

Part II. Operational Adaptation

Introduction to Part II   121

5   The Origins of the RMA in Israel   127

6   The RMA in Action: IDF Operations in Lebanon and Hezbollah's Adaptation in the 1990s   141

7   The Rise of the IDF's Operational Theory Research Institute and Systemic Operational Design   162

8 The 2006 Lebanon War: Military Adaptation and
   Counteradaptation   185

9 The Blame Game: A Reappraisal of the IDF's 2006
   Operational Concept   214

   Conclusion to Part II   237

Conclusions   245
Afterword: Back to the Future: IDF Force Planning and
   Hezbollah's Military Adaptation in Syria   263
Chronology   285
Selected Bibliography   289
Index   315
About the Author   331

ACKNOWLEDGMENTS

I AM DEEPLY INDEBTED to many people who helped me throughout my odyssey of completing this book. At King's College London, my PhD supervisor, Prof. David Betz, provided excellent mentorship and guidance throughout the project's development. Thanks to my secondary supervisor, Prof. Sir Lawrence Freedman, for his kind assistance and for reading over the final draft of this study as a doctoral dissertation. I appreciate the helpful comments of Prof. Theo Farrell, Dr. Ahron Bregman, and Lt. Col. (Ret.) Dr. Frank Hoffman over the years. Dr. David Parker and Dr. Joana Cook also deserve mention for their friendship and support throughout our times as stressed doctoral students.

Field research in Israel and Lebanon was no easy task, and I am appreciative to those who helped facilitate interviews and meetings. I am deeply thankful to each and every interviewee who candidly spoke with me, on and off the record, during my research trips to the Middle East. It goes without saying that any errors, omissions, or mistranslations from Hebrew or Arabic are my responsibility alone and are not the responsibility of any of the interviewees.

I acknowledge the financial support of the Department of War Studies, the Faculty of Social Science and Public Policy, and the Graduate School at King's College London, which enabled several field trips to the Middle East and my participation in international conferences where I presented my research. I am also grateful to the Allan and Nesta Ferguson Charitable Trust for their generosity.

For my trip to Lebanon, Prof. Norton Mezvinsky gave much helpful advice in the earliest stages of doctoral research, and I am appreciative of the collegiality of Dr. Mohsen Saleh of the Al-Zaytouna Center for Studies and Consultations in Beirut. In Israel, Dr. Eitan Shamir provided friendly guidance and much assistance during my trips. Dr. Ofra Graicer was especially generous with her time in our meetings, and her patience was appreciated when trying to help me understand the nuances of Systemic Operational Design. Thanks also to Brig. Gen. (Res.) Meir Finkel, Dr. Eado Hecht, and

Carmit Valensi for their insights and interesting discussions along the way. Special thanks are due to my great friend Dr. Eytan Debbi and his family for generously hosting me in Israel on my numerous trips. Throughout the publication process, the team at Georgetown University Press, especially Don Jacobs, Kathryn Owens, and Don McKeon, have been a pleasure to work with, and I thank them for all their efforts toward making this book a reality.

I would like to dedicate this book to the memory of my dear grandmother, Sylvia Marcus, for her passionate commitment to lifelong learning and ardent support of education. I would also like to dedicate it to the memory of Prof. Joseph "Yossi" Kostiner, scholar, teacher, and mentor, who instilled in me great enthusiasm for Middle Eastern studies and provided the original inspiration for this research project.

I would not have been able to complete this odyssey without the warm and enduring support of my dear family, cousins, grandmother, and family friends in London, who provided a home away from home during my years working on my research. I am very grateful for the encouragement from my family, friends, and loved ones in New York, especially during the difficult home-stretch. I am deeply indebted to my parents and sister for their steadfast encouragement, support, humor, boundless patience, and continued belief that I would somehow eventually be able to complete this project.

All views are strictly my own.

ABBREVIATIONS

ATM	antitank missile
COS	chief of staff (IDF)
DOD	Department of Defense (US)
EBO	Effects-Based Operations
FBIS	Foreign Broadcast Information Service
GFC	Ground Forces Command (IDF)
IAF	Israeli Air Force
IDF	Israel Defense Forces
IED	improvised explosive device
IRGC	Islamic Revolutionary Guard Corps (Iran)
ISIS	Islamic State of Iraq and Syria
LIC	low-intensity conflict
MI	Military Intelligence Directorate (Israel)
MOD	Ministry of Defense
MP	member of Parliament
NSC	National Security Council (Israel)
OTRI	Operational Theory Research Institute (IDF)
PLO	Palestine Liberation Organization
R&D	research and development
RMA	Revolution in Military Affairs
SAMS	School of Advanced Military Studies (Fort Leavenworth, Kansas)
SLA	South Lebanon Army
SOCOM	United States Special Operations Command
SOD	Systemic Operational Design
TRADOC	Training and Doctrine Command (US Army)
UAV	unmanned aerial vehicle
UN	United Nations
UNIFIL	United Nations Interim Force in Lebanon

INTRODUCTION

War is nothing but a duel on a larger scale. Countless duels go to make up a war, but a picture of it can be formed by imagining a pair of wrestlers. Each tries through physical force to compel the other to do his will; his immediate aim is to throw his opponent in order to make him incapable of further resistance.

—CARL VON CLAUSEWITZ

THE THREE-DECADE SIMMERING conflict between Israel and the Lebanese Shi'ite militant group Hezbollah burst into the global spotlight upon the outbreak of war in 2006. The Second Lebanon War, as officially named in Israel, or the July War (Harb Tammuz), as referred to by Hezbollah, erupted on July 12, 2006, after Hezbollah infiltrated Israel's northern border and launched a surprise operation on a patrolling reservist unit, kidnapping two Israel Defense Forces (IDF) soldiers and killing three others in the initial attack. Amid the perception of disappointment with the IDF's performance during the thirty-four-day war in Lebanon, the Israeli government appointed a commission of inquiry to investigate the failings, led by Justice Eliyahu Winograd, a retired Supreme Court judge, whose findings were published in Hebrew as the Winograd Commission Report.

The 617-page Winograd Commission Final Report released in January 2008 (henceforth the Winograd Commission) assessed many aspects of the IDF's war effort. Much has been written about Israel's mediocre performance during the 2006 war, the major criticisms being the setting of unattainable and unrealistic objectives by politicians, a lack of strategic and operational direction, reluctance by senior generals to wage a large-scale ground campaign, and the subpar performance of undertrained ground units. Both the Winograd Commission and the prevalent academic scholarship gave much scrutiny to describing *what* the IDF did wrong during the 2006 war, but far less has been offered as to *why* the IDF chose to operate as it did. Maj. Gen. (Ret.) Giora Eiland, a senior IDF commander and former national security adviser, noted that in both the Winograd Commission and internal IDF investigations, "despite the criticisms, insufficient attention was given to *the causes* of these lapses."[1]

To establish a fuller understanding of the IDF's mode of thinking behind its strategy and operational decision-making during the war, this book examines military innovation and adaptation of the IDF throughout its protracted conflict with Hezbollah in Lebanon. It assesses how the IDF adapted "under fire" throughout the conflict with Hezbollah since the emergence of the group in the early 1980s, focusing on broad processes of strategic and operational change. Primarily, it examines the evolution and adaptation of the IDF's conceptual understanding of Hezbollah, its strategy and preferred means for dealing with Hezbollah, and the development and application of its operational warfighting concept in the four-decades-long conflict in Lebanon, which includes the 2006 war and the tumultuous decade since the war.

The great military theorist Carl von Clausewitz wrote, "War is nothing but a duel on a larger scale." Strategic and operational change by the IDF often triggered innovative responses from Hezbollah, whose own continuous learning, adaptation, and development as a potent militant force is discussed in tandem. As if to illustrate Clausewitz's point, Hezbollah's secretary-general, Hassan Nasrallah, revealed in a televised interview that his group was studying and scrutinizing Israel's own lessons learned from the 2006 war: "No doubt the publication of the [Winograd] Report, although it was a partial one, is a very important and big event that requires close examination, study and deep contemplation, rather than celebration."[2] To gain a complete understanding of the dynamics of protracted conflict and the underlying processes of learning on both sides, this book also examines the organizational evolution of Hezbollah and its capacity to militarily adapt and innovate throughout the conflict.

The ensuing chapters tell the story of the Israel-Hezbollah conflict since 1985, after the Israeli invasion of Lebanon when the IDF officially established its "security zone" in southern Lebanon. It covers the evolution of the conflict, including the IDF's long counterguerrilla warfare campaign, the 2000 Israeli withdrawal from Lebanon, and the road to the 2006 Israel-Hezbollah War, and concludes in 2018, more than a decade after the 2006 war.

Part I of this book examines strategic adaptation, focusing on the IDF's evolving conceptualization of the threat from Hezbollah and how Israel sought to deal with Hezbollah by adapting its traditional policy of deterrence, long a central pillar of Israeli defense thinking. The IDF's deterrence policy, while consistently remaining a doctrinal priority, was adapted throughout the conflict with Hezbollah and frequently challenged in Lebanon. It also discusses the evolution of Hezbollah organizationally and militarily and highlights processes of learning by the group as it adapted its own strategic posture vis-à-vis Israel.

Part II examines operational adaptation, focusing on the evolution of the IDF's operational concept for warfighting and analyzes the drivers and shapers of change related to IDF defense planning and its preferred means of fighting in Lebanon. This incremental and evolutionary process to adapt its "way of war" over three decades of conflict culminated in the operational concept of the IDF in the 2006 Lebanon War. Its approach to warfighting was deeply influenced by a variety of "revolutionary" military concepts and technological and societal trends that had a transformational effect in the years before the war. This section also provides an analysis of the development of Hezbollah's own unique military concept for warfare and highlights important operational lessons it learned as it developed innovative counteradaptations to the IDF's methods throughout preceding decades.

This book is the first academic study in English to delve into the military development, strategy, and operational conduct of both the IDF and Hezbollah from the origins of the conflict in the 1980s up to and including the 2006 war and its aftermath. It uses the existing body of literature related to military innovation and organizational learning as a general framework to examine sources of military change in the IDF, the shapers and drivers of change, how specific military innovations were initiated and implemented, and how IDF performance in Lebanon was affected. The book's aim is to tell the military history of the Israel-Hezbollah conflict while highlighting important processes of organizational learning and adaptation by both sides that have dramatically shaped the progression and trajectory of the conflict. The concluding chapter summarizes the factors that enabled or hindered IDF strategic and operational learning and adaptation in Lebanon since the 1980s and also provides a unique mode of analysis for understanding the evolution of Hezbollah as an adaptive military force.

THE 2006 LEBANON WAR AS "THE HARBINGER OF FUTURE CONFLICT"

Despite a general lack of attention to the Israel-Hezbollah conflict from the academic and military community over three decades, the 2006 Lebanon War garnered interest because of the perception of a surprisingly mediocre performance by the conventionally superior, technologically advanced IDF confronting well-trained Hezbollah guerrillas. As described in published US Army and UK Ministry of Defence assessments, Hezbollah's adaptive means and methods provide a fairly clear picture of how the West thinks the future of warfare will look, and the group has been labeled as an archetypical adversary on the future battlefield.[3]

The 2006 Israel-Hezbollah War, identified by the US Army as a "harbinger of future conflict," exemplifies the adaptive nature of irregular adversaries and their ability to marginalize conventional military superiority. From the British perspective, the Ministry of Defence's *Future Character of Conflict* assessment affirmed the importance of military adaptation and highlighted Hezbollah's mode of warfare and the group's ability to delegitimize aspects of Israel's war effort for special attention. Elsewhere, the esteemed British general Sir Rupert Smith highlighted Hezbollah's ability to operate "amongst the people"—that is, within the civilian fabric of the battlespace—to be paradigmatic of the associated operational difficulties that make attainment of decisive victory increasingly challenging for Western militaries.[4] The current emphasis of Western military organizations on force agility and adaptability highlights the relevance of this book's primary focus on Israeli military learning and adaptation in the decades prior to the 2006 war and in its aftermath. This book also elucidates the evolution of Hezbollah's unique mode of warfare by describing the adoption, adaptation, and refinement of its military principles throughout the conflict and illustrates how Hezbollah's military approach, perfectly tailored to the operational weaknesses of the IDF, was able to circumvent Israeli conventional military superiority.

The timely debates within the US and British defense communities on how to balance current threats from diverse sources while preparing for tomorrow's wars, without compromising conventional security and ongoing campaigns, mirrors IDF experiences in Lebanon and underscores the significance of military adaptation. Learning from the IDF's adaptation under fire in protracted conflict and its battlefield performance against Hezbollah is valuable in this regard. The explosively destabilizing nature of the Israel-Hezbollah conflict has geostrategic implications for the greater Middle East and takes greater urgency with Hezbollah's involvement in the Syrian Civil War. An analysis of military adaptation on both sides of the Israel-Hezbollah conflict is valuable not only for understanding the past and the events surrounding the 2006 war but also for understanding the ongoing progression of the conflict and future trajectories.

FRAMEWORK OF THE BOOK: MILITARY INNOVATION AND ADAPTATION

This examination of the Israel-Hezbollah conflict provides an original contribution to the growing field of study on military innovation, which seeks to understand how military organizations learn, innovate, and adapt. To carry out a nuanced and holistic analysis of military change, elements from a number of schools of thought related to military innovation are utilized, each with direct relevance to the IDF.

There are lengthy, unresolved scholarly debates over differentiating between types of military change—namely, innovation and adaptation. For this book's purpose, a military innovation can be defined as a major change in the conduct of warfare that produces a significant increase in military effectiveness as measured by battlefield results. An innovation is novel, and significant in the scope of its impact, changes the way the military functions in the field, and increases military effectiveness.[5] More precisely, innovation "involves developing new military technologies, tactics, strategies and structures," while adaptation "involves adjusting existing military means and methods."[6] Notably, adaptation should not be considered "less significant" than innovation, as adaptation "can add up to significant change in a military's capabilities or approach to operations."[7] Multiple adaptations may (but need not) accumulate into an innovation over time and can lead to the evolutionary adoption of new strategies, tactics, means, or methods.[8]

As one leading scholar pointed out, it may not be "feasible or fruitful to draw too fine a distinction between adaptation and innovation. Indeed, it may be more helpful to think of the two as points on a sliding scale."[9] It is important to note that innovation and/or adaptation may occur at the strategic, operational, or tactical levels of war, and each can trigger related change on higher and lower levels of warfare. Therefore, it is better to not get bogged down with definitional semantics but rather to simply recognize that since change in war is evolutionary, processes of innovation are certainly influenced by previous adaptations, and identifying the "adaptive moment" is often not possible or productive.[10] This book assesses the development of Israeli military thinking, strategy, and operational preferences in Lebanon by analyzing processes of adaptation and identifying important milestones that contributed to the momentum of these evolutionary changes.

Militaries are generally viewed as conservative, bureaucratic institutions that, like the humans who operate within them, prefer to keep order and are not inclined to change battle-tested norms and routines. This is understandable given the risks in carrying out change in the face of incalculable friction in war and the ensuing horrific chaos that could result from inappropriate change. However, if militaries remain rigid and do not adapt, they are likely to suffer even more greatly in both blood and treasure in the long term.[11]

While some broad trends within the military innovation literature may be identified, instances of innovation that occurred throughout the Israel-Hezbollah conflict are based on a host of setting-specific and case-dependent factors that require a unique layer of contextual understanding of the conflict.[12] Three broad, interrelated schools of thought have been identified that have specific relevance to the Israel-Hezbollah case study. These schools of thought are best viewed as complementary and interdependent, rather than distinct and competing.

First, sources of military change can result from dynamic interactions of civilian and/or military leaders who drive through change. Second, competition or rivalry, both externally (between competing military forces) or internally (within different branches of the military bureaucracy), can impact processes of change. Last and most important, the organizational culture of the military deeply affects its willingness and ability to successfully adapt and carry out innovation. Organizational culture also affects the nature of civil-military relations and the sensitivity of the defense establishment (or parts thereof) to both internal and external rivalry.

Civil–Military Relations

The role of political leaders and their interactive relationship with military officers is an oft-cited factor that effects military change. In his seminal work, Barry Posen attributes change in military organizations to external sources outside the military—namely, from civilian reformers within government, often with the assistance of cooperative military officers ("mavericks"), who together push change through. Driven by realist fears of military incompetence, failure, or defeat, politicians intervene to force militaries to adopt more effective fighting methods.[13] This school of thought views civilian intervention as necessary for innovation, as militaries are viewed as inherently conservative bureaucracies that strive to protect their own organizational interests, prestige, autonomy, and access to resources and innovate only when faced with defeat or failure.[14]

The military leadership is strongly conditioned by civilian institutional oversight and past choices of the civilian leadership, which promote certain policies and standards and create an institutional bias, which strongly influences the military's operating procedures and responses.[15] Threatening shifts in enemy military doctrine that affect the strategic environment may alternatively trigger a response from the military among officers who are concerned for the security of the state and the prestige of their organization vis-à-vis the rival military, regardless of the degree of civilian intervention. However, civilian leadership intervention can also trigger innovation, by either pushing change through forcefully or by building coalitions of like-minded reformists within the military and subtly influencing innovation.[16] Since change is evolutionary, others argue that enduring innovations are dependent on a concerted organizational focus over time, rather than the actions of civilian or military individuals over a short time period.[17] However, numerous examples illustrate that bold individual leadership can act as a critical enabler of innovative processes of change and adaptation.[18]

Stephen Rosen provides an alternative view to Posen and argues that civilian leaders lack the expertise, and military mavericks lack the clout, to bring about genuine change. Rather, new enemy strategies may trigger a process that is internal to the military organization, independent of civilian meddling in military affairs. Instead, innovation is often driven by "visionary officers" who create a new theory of victory and new types of missions, offering a pathway to promotion for low- and midlevel officers. These visionary officers may receive some support from political leaders. By inspiring a generation of younger, "fresh" officers who view the adoption of the innovation as a means to promotion, the continuity of the innovation is protected.[19]

The impact of civil-military relations on innovation is particularly relevant in the case of Israel, which has a complex political-military dynamic. As a former Israeli deputy national security adviser wrote, Israel's civil-military relations are complicated by an idiosyncratic, improvised, highly politicized decision-making process that resembles "semi-organized anarchy."[20] The prestigious role of the IDF in Israeli society affords the military great leverage over many aspects of national security, political and internal planning, and decision-making processes. Critics complain that the political echelon often does not have clear, well-formulated goals or directives, lacks high-level professional staff work, and overly relies on the IDF for its superior intelligence collection and systematic modes of analysis.[21] Military meddling in civilian affairs is common, as senior military commanders often enter politics within a few years of retirement and often influence political and military planning and policy.[22]

Since Israeli politicians gain popular legitimacy through military service or with military support, and politicians aid the transition of retired military elites into political appointments, it has even been argued that a "security network" of members of the defense establishment, retired military officers, political elites, and defense industry officials unduly influences Israel's security policies and the IDF's priorities.[23] However, despite the strength of the military establishment, there have been notable cases in which determined Israeli civilian leaders imposed their will on a resistant IDF. For example, the Israeli defense minister forced the IDF, much to its objection, to establish a separate Home Front Command following the 1991 Gulf War. More recent examples include the Defense Ministry's overruling the IDF to financially support research and development for the Iron Dome missile defense system that, surprisingly, was initially resisted by the IDF.[24]

Deep but informal ties between active-duty military elites and their political counterparts may sometimes enhance the ability of the IDF to innovate, which enables rapid and flexible decision-making.[25] The IDF's dominance sometimes allows for rapid change or decisive action, without political obstacles or internal wrangling. Complicating the decision-making dynamic further, civilian leaders often make strategic decisions without consulting their official advisory committees and without carrying out proper staff work, instead relying on private advisers who lack an official title in government.[26] The Israeli cabinet's own inability to deal with complex defense issues without adequate policy staff and the weakness of Israel's National Security Council (NSC) vis-à-vis the IDF, combined with highly idiosyncratic, personalized decision-making processes, make adaptation on all levels of warfare a challenging process.

Organizational Rivalry and Competition

Rivalry among competing opponents is an obvious and evident factor that spurs a continuous process of reactive innovation, out of fear of being outmatched or defeated by an enemy.[27] On the other hand, emulation of allies is a common trigger for military innovation, especially those strategies or tactics that have been successfully battle-tested and proven effective.[28] Emulation of friends (or rivals) causes "competitive isomorphism," as the mimicking of perceived "more professional or legitimate" militaries and their organizational forms and practices is often a means for the imitating military to legitimate its own practices.[29] The frequency of allies' emulating one another is made possible by the transmission of knowledge facilitated by the commonality in available technology, ease of diffusion of information, common sources of military education, and large professional officer networks.[30] However, universal appeal of a strategy or tactic does not translate into universal instrumentality for all military organizations.[31] Many smaller militaries, including the IDF, have often sought to emulate the US military regarding doctrine and technology, despite the strategies' being inappropriate for the specific circumstances.[32] However, Israel's own homegrown military innovations have diffused externally to both large and small states in which the innovations have been partially or fully adopted. This illustrates how military willingness to emulate is deeply dependent on regional context and a variety of institutional, local, and cultural factors.[33]

Competition within a military organization between its branches over material resources, reputation, or prestige can result in rivalry and power struggles that trigger or hinder change. Rivalry also exists between military officials and civilian policymakers, which creates institutional hurdles that impede adaptation.[34] Interservice competition over finite resources remains a consistent factor that affects the preferences of the military to favor expensive innovations, thereby augmenting military (or branch) prestige and resource allocation.[35] While representatives of each branch in the IDF's centralized General Staff are generally encouraged to lose their distinctive service identity, rivalry and competition still affect innovation, as institutional relationships are often hinged on highly personalized relations between decision-makers. Egoistic and self-serving rivalries between civilian and/or military leaders over prestige, influence, or personal fulfillment commonly hinder innovation in any organizational structure.[36] The peculiar nature of Israeli parliamentary politics makes it possible for political rivals to be partners in a governing coalition, which has led to competition for resources and influence.[37] However, close personal relations (and often, geographic proximity) between politicians, military officials, and the private defense-technology industry does facilitate rapid development and implementation of innovative technology into the IDF.[38]

There is overt rivalry over resource allocation and funds for military purposes versus domestic purposes amid the continuous debate over the role of the IDF in Israeli society. The degree that society prioritizes the military deeply affects its prestige, budget, influence, and propensity for change. This was illustrated in the 2011 large-scale summer demonstrations throughout Israel in which protesters demanded that part of the defense budget be diverted to alleviate the high cost of living, and it arises annually amid the internal debates over the IDF's budget. It is well known that domestic considerations and societal pressure trigger military change and shape military choices, but how governments and militaries compete with or balance domestic concerns when adapting is far from uniform.[39]

Organizational Culture

Most important, organizational culture sets the context for all military innovation and affects other factors that influence adaptation, including civil-military relations, leadership style, threat perceptions, organizational structures, and institutional dynamics.[40] Culture consists of "beliefs, symbols, rituals, and practices that give meaning to the activity of an organization" and influences perceptions of "the optimal means to fight wars." It shapes organizational norms and choices, impacts preferences and actions, and sets the context for how organizations view problems and establish solutions.[41] Most successful innovations are those that are compatible with the self-identity and organizational culture of the military.[42]

Much of the literature highlights military change as driven by the political or military leadership and "pushed down" through the organizational hierarchy. Change is implemented in doctrine and strategy first by the leadership, who set organizational priorities, cultural norms, avenues of promotion, and so forth, which eventually affects tactical conduct.[43] The literature on military innovation has focused on change originating at the highest echelons that diffuses from the top down, highlighting the gap in our understanding of innovation that originates at lower levels.[44] This in turn sparked a growing interest in understanding "bottom-up" military adaptation, including enabling factors, processes of diffusion, and ultimately how learning mechanisms can be implemented "at the bottom" to improve battlefield effectiveness. Several important studies have greatly expanded our understanding of military adaptation as an organic process that starts with units in the field intuitively dealing with specific battlefield challenges.[45]

Tactical innovation and adaptation of commanders on the ground has the potential to trigger the adoption of new standing operating procedures, which if successful can lead to fundamental changes in formalized military doctrine.[46] It has been noted that even if change is triggered from the bottom, organizational adaptation can still be slow, as critical time is lost as the new ideas slowly diffuse "vertically" up the hierarchy. It has been argued that military adaptation is effectively enabled by the passing of knowledge between lower- and mid-level units, as such "horizontal" learning occurs more rapidly between units based on shared experiences, rather than via a central directive.[47]

The IDF's experience highlights several organizational traits that help facilitate bottom-up learning, innovation, and adaptation, which is most likely in an organization with a weak central doctrine, informal networks between officers, a versatile organizational structure with flattened, informal hierarchies that promote "mission command", a lack of "ownership" of ideas, and a nonpunitive, collaborative learning culture. Mission command, the command philosophy whereby officers grant significant autonomy and operational independence to subordinates to achieve the overall mission set out by the senior command, is a critical enabler of bottom-up innovation.[48] The IDF's "organizational learning capacity" is enabled by its culture, its decentralized command-and-control system, its mechanisms for learning, and a means to disseminate lessons, which together promote officer initiative and autonomy, creative thinking, improvisation, and adaptation.[49] By institutionalizing bottom-up learning through formalized battlefield lesson-learning and knowledge-management systems, modern militaries are increasingly able to learn and adapt at a rapid pace.[50] Moreover, if bottom-up adaptations are not formally institutionalized within the organization, these hard-earned lessons are lost and will have to be relearned again in the future, often at a higher and bloodier cost.[51] There is a seemingly artificial tendency to bifurcate top-down and bottom-up innovation, yet most effective innovation, including in the IDF, is the result of a dynamic interplay of top-down and bottom-up processes.[52]

Strategic culture and the ethos of the military has a paramount impact on organizational norms, leadership choices when approaching change and innovation, and the willingness of a military organization to emulate an ally or rival and adopt new technologies, doctrine, or organizational forms.[53] The successful adoption and diffusion of an innovation is often dependent on the military's institutional capacity to implement change without being blocked by bureaucratic obstacles; the critical task focus of the military, its commitment to experimentation, the innovation's financial burden, and organizational age and rigidity each contribute to this capacity.[54] While domestic politics may set certain restraints, culture has an independent explanatory power for analyzing innovation, decision-making, and the preferences of civilian or military leaders who operate within their respective subcultures.[55]

Successful adaptation is more likely if a military emphasizes a balanced military doctrine that takes into account diverse types of warfare, flexible force-planning, technological versatility, and officer education grounded in a military culture that promotes agile thinking.[56] Lt. Col. (Ret.) John Nagl identified organizational traits that characterize military "learning institutions": the propensity for learning at the top and bottom, the ability to question superiors, a responsive senior staff, cultivation of local training and doctrine development, and a willingness to challenge basic assumptions.[57] The criteria outlined are wholly applicable to the IDF's open and informal military culture, which cultivates the resourcefulness of individual "maverick" commanders who are encouraged to confront their superiors, personifying the classic Israeli cultural attribute of "chutzpah" (which derives from Hebrew as "audacity" or "gall").

The IDF, known as an army of "doers," maintains a cultural affinity for action based on mission command and an intuition-led, hands-on approach that favors immediate practical results, historically out of operational necessity and survival.[58] The legendary experiences in the IDF's formative years of bold, young commanders leading from the front, learning on the go, improvising under fire, and autonomously creating new tactics from the bottom up are imbued within its strategic culture and organizational memory.[59] IDF learning capabilities in this regard are reliant on its flexibility as an organization and the qualitative edge of the individual soldier, grounded in distinctive Israeli cultural values that emphasize initiative, out-of-the-box thinking, and tenacity.[60] Personifying these valued cultural traits, Gen. Moshe Dayan famously said, "I prefer excessive initiative and action, even if it involves some mistakes here and there, to the passivity of 'sit and do nothing' and covering yourself with paper and seven authorizations for an operation before its execution."[61]

Complex social interactions like military innovation do not work in a mechanistic or deterministic manner but rather comprise the nonlinear "interplay of thousands of independent variables" and are "more of an art than a science. . . . involving myriad actors, complex technologies, and uncertainties of conflict and human relations."[62] Therefore, like other studies in the military innovation field, this book avoids "reductionist" reasoning to understand complex human processes and recognizes that none of the schools of thought above are sufficient alone to explain the innovation process.[63] Scholars are increasingly blending elements of existing theories and schools of thought to better gain a nuanced picture and holistic understanding of military innovation.[64] This book will capture the complexity and messiness of military change in the Israel-Hezbollah conflict by flexibly integrating elements of the various schools of thought behind the drivers and shapers of adaptation.

A GAP IN UNDERSTANDING THE ISRAEL-HEZBOLLAH CONFLICT

A theoretical and historical gap is filled in the two disciplines in which this book is grounded. From a theoretical perspective, no study exists that examines processes of military change by both the IDF and Hezbollah from an organizational learning perspective. It is worth emphasizing that the drive for a military to adapt is inherently influenced by the changing nature of its enemy, yet most of the existing literature that analyzes military innovation during "long wars" or counterinsurgency fails to adequately elaborate how insurgent-group learning and adaptation impacts change in the military organization.[65] This is a critical shortcoming in assessing the innovation and adaptation of terrorist and insurgent groups in protracted conflict that scholars are only beginning to respond to.[66] Within the context of understanding IDF military adaptation throughout its odyssey in Lebanon, this book contributes an in-depth case study on Hezbollah related to insurgent-group learning and adaptation.

From a historical perspective, in the literature on the Arab-Israeli conflict there is surprisingly no authoritative military history chronicling the IDF's involvement in Lebanon. No book exists in English that systematically examines the Israeli army's campaign in Lebanon from 1985 up to the 2000 withdrawal and through to the period after the 2006 war. A rigorous, focused examination of IDF involvement in Lebanon is an underresearched area both inside and outside Israel. Most previous studies on innovation and adaptation focused on the IDF's conventional wars in 1967 and 1973.[67] IDF low-intensity conflict (LIC), or "routine security" as it is referred to in Israel, was frequently neglected for systematic analysis when appraising Israeli national security, the reason cited often being that such threats do not constitute an existential threat to Israeli security.[68] This trend within the academic community mirrored sentiment within the IDF itself, largely because of the IDF's own doctrinal and conceptual inertia in dealing with low-intensity threats that were historically viewed as not worthy of rigorous intellectual or operational attention.[69] This trend shifted slowly over the last two decades, triggered by the critical threat posed by Palestinian suicide terrorism; hence, when scholarship did focus on LIC, it often focused on Israeli counterterrorism, especially during the intifadas.[70]

The Lebanon conflict generally did not receive rigorous academic attention before the outbreak of the 2006 Israel-Hezbollah War.[71] In Israel, this is because the Lebanon conflict, sometimes dubbed "Israel's Vietnam," is viewed as a significant trauma partially because of the sustained military losses during the occupation period (1985–2000) but more because of the sociological and psychological implications of the prolonged conflict on Israeli society. The Lebanon conflict also remained on the periphery of academic and military discourse owing to pressing concerns associated with the outbreak of the Second Palestinian Intifada, which erupted less than six months after the withdrawal from Lebanon. With a few exceptions, there remains little written material in English that systematically examines the military history of the IDF in Lebanon since the 1980s, especially after the establishment of the security zone in southern Lebanon in 1985.

Because of the complex sociological and psychological effect of the conflict on the "Lebanon generation" of IDF soldiers, only a handful of IDF officers who served in Lebanon have published memoirs in Hebrew that provide fascinating personal accounts of their experiences.[72] Following the 2006 war, several top commanders involved published memoirs in Hebrew, though these were more defensive personal accounts justifying their actions during 2006.[73] Soldiers in the field in 2006 have also begun writing about their wartime experiences.[74] This "opening up" and increasing focus on the Lebanon conflict has continued slowly in a new wave of critically acclaimed Israeli films focusing on soldiers' experiences in earlier decades in Lebanon.[75] The first memoir in English of an IDF conscript in Lebanon during the 1990s was published in 2016. The author of the poignant memoir noted, "My intention here is not to get bogged down in historical explanation. I would rather suggest the title of a comprehensive history of these years of the Lebanon security zone in the 1990s for those interested in background. . . . Unfortunately no such history has been written."[76] No work in English to date has yet to take advantage of this gradual "opening up" within the IDF. This book fills this gap and makes a contribution to telling the story of the IDF in Lebanon by offering a detailed military history of the Israel-Hezbollah conflict based largely on primary sources and interviews.

With world attention attracted to the Israel-Hezbollah conflict by the 2006 war, a flurry of military assessments surfaced of varying quality and depth examining the war itself. Excellent journalistic books provided accounts of the IDF's experience during the 2006 war.[77] Detailed military analyses focused on relevant lessons learned by the IDF in 2006 that were implemented during Israel's 2008 Gaza War.[78] Other works assessed various milestones of the conflict in historical and comparative perspective.[79] Analysts in the defense community scrutinized Hezbollah's operational capabilities in 2006 and its "hybrid" mode of warfare.[80] While important for understanding Hezbollah's operational approach in 2006, these studies often neglected a thorough examination of the two decades prior to the war and failed to adequately examine how experiences in the 1980s and 1990s influenced both the

IDF's and Hezbollah's actions in 2006. Technical monographs that did discuss the 1985–2000 period often did so too briefly.[81] Within the existing scholarship on the Israel-Hezbollah conflict, there are seminal histories published from 1985 to 1989 on the opening stages of the 1982 First Lebanon War, which set the stage for the emergence of Hezbollah.[82] However, to date there is no systematic study of the IDF military experience in Lebanon from the formal establishment of the security zone in 1985 to the present day.

A moderate amount of literature exists on Hezbollah.[83] Most focus on the general history of the group and its origins and development during the civil war in Lebanon.[84] There are a number of solid histories of Hezbollah, often relaying similar narratives and reaching similar conclusions, but which neglect a correspondingly thorough analysis of the IDF.[85] Important works focus on the historical and theological issues surrounding Hezbollah's emergence and the sociological role Hezbollah plays in Lebanese Shi'ite society.[86] There has also been a keen interest in the group's ideological adaptation regarding its entry into politics and the advancement of its social services capability.[87] Other seminal works document Hezbollah's kidnapping and terrorism campaign in the 1980s and Iran's influence and training during Hezbollah's formative years.[88] Hezbollah's terrorist activity globally has also been rigorously documented, highlighting another important identity of the group.[89] Nicholas Blanford provides one of the best assessments of the development of Hezbollah organizationally and militarily, though it is from a journalistic perspective without rigorous sourcing of data.[90] These works often neglected a correspondingly thorough analysis of the IDF. Overall, very little literature methodically deals with Hezbollah's military development since the 1980s and its processes of organizational change in relation to Israel's own military adaptation and shifts in strategy throughout the four-decade conflict.

Hezbollah's political and military identities have been deeply studied, and scholars have debated Hezbollah's shift from a militant-centric identity toward a more "moderate" political identity as part of its attempt to broaden appeal in Lebanese society ("Lebanonization") throughout the 1990s and 2000s.[91] This book's focus on Hezbollah's military development does not downplay the importance of its political identity, but it is beyond its scope to detail Hezbollah's entry into politics and political evolution.[92] Arguably, one of the most significant innovations in Hezbollah's history was its groundbreaking decision to participate in Lebanese parliamentary politics in 1992. But while political and social identities are indeed important elements of the group, this book primarily focuses on Hezbollah's military evolution. A Lebanese scholar sympathetic to Hezbollah wrote, "Hezbollah defines itself first and foremost as a 'jihadi movement' or a 'party of resistance' whose paramount function is the liberation of Lebanese territory from Israeli occupation by means of armed resistance." She argued that it is difficult to extricate its political activities from its militant identity, as Hezbollah "is more akin to an army with administrative and combative departments."[93] Interestingly, Hezbollah deputy secretary-general Naim Qassem highlighted the unified leadership of the multifaceted Hezbollah and the false dichotomy between the military and political echelons: "Hezbollah has a single leadership. . . . All political, social and jihad work is tied to the decisions of this leadership. The same leadership that directs the parliamentary and government work also leads jihad actions in the struggle against Israel."[94]

Nasrallah said on record that "this military resistance requires political backing. . . . Our entry into the ranks of parliamentary politics gives us the opportunity to defend our resistance on the political plane." He also stated that politics should be utilized to defend Hezbollah's weapons and military capabilities, while other Hezbollah figures have openly noted elsewhere that the group's primary identity is that of a military organization.[95] Given the centrality of Hezbollah's military identity, this book maintains a primary focus on military adaptation.

METHODOLOGY

This book conveys the story of the Israel-Hezbollah conflict by recounting both major and lesser-known events through the use of primary sources, explaining the importance of events, and analyzing and assessing processes of learning and adaptation on each side. Information on strategic and operational adaptation in the IDF and Hezbollah was obtained through more than three dozen interviews conducted in Israel and Lebanon by the author with senior IDF decision-makers and commanders in top planning and operational positions, IDF officers with combat experience in Lebanon, a Hezbollah media official, United Nations (UN) diplomatic and peacekeeping officials based in Lebanon, and senior British diplomats based in Lebanon. Personal interviews are bolstered by the use of hundreds of primary-source interviews, speeches, press briefings, and lectures given from the 1980s to the present day by Israel's military and political leaders and Hezbollah's secretaries-general and senior officials. Most of these interviews and speeches were published in Hebrew on Israeli television and radio or in Arabic on Hezbollah's own Al-Manar television station or its various radio stations or official websites. Others were published in the international press or scholarly volumes or were archived by official IDF sources, the Israel Ministry of Foreign Affairs, academic institutions, or, most notably, the Central Intelligence Agency's Foreign Broadcast Information Service (FBIS). Several IDF doctrinal documents were analyzed, as were dozens of articles published in Hebrew in the

IDF's official military journal *Maarachot* (Campaigns). Memoirs of IDF commanders who served in Lebanon, as well as Hebrew articles and books penned by key figures involved in Israeli decision-making in Lebanon, have been utilized for overall greater depth and quality when assessing adaptation in the conflict. To ascertain greater on-the-ground context, the author visited some of Hezbollah's areas of support in southern Lebanon, Hezbollah's Dahiya stronghold in southern Beirut, and a former military site in southern Lebanon that Hezbollah has turned into a "victory museum" with military displays and where access to primary-source information was available. The author also conducted an interview with a Hezbollah spokesperson who is a senior official with its Public Relations Bureau.

Compared to the relatively open nature of the IDF, the limitations are obvious regarding conducting academic research on an active militant group that is also a designated terrorist organization. The methodological short-coming of not interviewing a greater number of Hezbollah officials has been largely overcome by a deep and systematic examination of hundreds of speeches and interviews by Hezbollah's secretaries-general, Subhi Tufayli, Abbas Mussawi, and especially Hassan Nasrallah. Writing about method-ological issues, a veteran journalist noted that in public addresses "Nasrallah unveiled only what the party wanted the public to know about its positions and internal deliberations" but concluded that "Nasrallah's record provided the best repository through which to explore what Hezbollah really wanted."[96] Admittedly, like all studies that examine Hezbollah, the methodology is imperfect, but primary interviews, field research, and a detailed examination of four decades of Hezbollah leaders' statements do provide some illuminat-ing insights into processes of learning and adaptation vis-à-vis the IDF.

SETTING THE STAGE: ISRAEL'S INVOLVEMENT IN LEBANON AND THE ORIGINS OF THE SECURITY ZONE

What precipitated Israel's involvement in Lebanon? Until 1982, Israel's pri-mary focus in Lebanon throughout the decades was centered on ways to deal with Palestinian cross-border attacks, which often resulted in limited reprisal operations by the IDF. It is beyond the scope of this book to provide a detailed account of the 1982 Israeli invasion of Lebanon and the political and social factors that contributed to the emergence of Hezbollah, as several aforemen-tioned works published in the 1980s already provide rigorous historical accounts of the 1975–85 period.[97] Before beginning our story of military adaptation in the Israel-Hezbollah conflict, selected historical events will be briefly recounted to contextualize how and why Israel established the Leba-non security zone in 1985.

The PLO in Lebanon and Operation Litani

Israel has a long and complex history with Lebanon. Several regional issues led to increased Israeli involvement in Lebanon in the 1970s, which set the stage for the invasion in 1982. First, the expulsion of the Palestine Liberation Organization (PLO) from Jordan in 1970 during "Black September" and the establishment of the PLO's base of operations in Lebanon led to increased attacks against Israel. Second, within the context of the Lebanese Civil War (1975–89), in which there were bloody clashes between Christian (Maronite) and Palestinian forces, various Maronite leaders reached out to both Israel and Syria, external powers in the region, for support during the chaos. Israel was approached through secret channels to assist Maronite forces, which marked the strengthening of a quiet but long-standing Maronite-Israeli alliance.[98] Third, Israel felt threatened when Syria entered Lebanon in 1976, ostensibly to provide security for various loyal factions but more to exert influence over Lebanese affairs and solidify its control.

The IDF launched Operation Litani in March 1978 in response to a number of particularly gruesome terrorist attacks perpetrated by Palestinian militants from Lebanon. The operation involved thousands of troops supported by armor, artillery, and air assets, which led the IDF to temporarily occupy a portion of Lebanon south of the Litani River to target PLO terrorist facilities. A secondary goal of the operation was to extend the territory under the control of a local Christian militia supported by the IDF, the Free Lebanon Army, led by Maronite Lebanese army officer Maj. Saad Haddad, who sought to keep PLO militants out of his area of influence in southern Lebanon. In turn, Israel sought to secure Major Haddad's enclave so that it could act as a security buffer from attacks on the Israeli-Lebanese border and link various dominant Christian positions in southern Lebanon into a coherent strip. This strip would eventually become part of the future security zone in 1985, and Major Haddad's militia would evolve into the South Lebanon Army (SLA), Israel's proxy militia in Lebanon tasked to patrol the zone. Brig. Gen. (Ret.) Ephraim Sneh, a commander of this security strip (1981–82), described the goals of the Free Lebanon Army: "I worked personally with Maj. Haddad. He was a tough guy, extremely loyal, a genuine patriot of Lebanon, a true friend of Israel, and a man with dignity. . . . He wanted to maintain the security zone and to fend off the Syrians and, of course, the Palestinians and to maintain this security zone as a relatively safe place for his community."[99]

Operation Litani remained limited in scope, partially owing to an unspoken understanding with Syria, part of a complex "deterrence dialogue" between both sides following the 1973 Arab-Israeli War (also known as the Yom Kippur War).[100] Rather than expand the operation and move deeper into Lebanon, Israel chose to accept UN Resolutions 425 and 426, which outlined a cease-fire and an Israeli withdrawal from Lebanese territory. The resolutions also established a peacekeeping force, the United Nations Interim Force in Lebanon (UNIFIL) to assist the Lebanese government in exercising authority (which ineffectually patrols southern Lebanon to this day). While several hundred Palestinian militants were killed in Operation Litani, it failed to totally drive Palestinian militants north of the Litani River, did not prevent Palestinian rocket fire against Israel, nor did it deter future attacks, highlighting the inherent limitations of Israeli military force against nonstate actors and the difficulty of operating in Lebanese territory.[101]

Amid escalating confrontation in April 1981 over the downing of two Syrian helicopters in Lebanon by the IDF, Syria stationed antiaircraft missile batteries in Lebanon. This Syrian "missile crisis" triggered great alarm in Israel regarding Syrian intentions and severely increased tensions between both sides.[102] A two-week escalation in rocket fire by the PLO in July 1981, which emptied the northern Israeli town of Kiryat Shmona of residents (an ominous lesson learned by militants in Lebanon on the utility of rocket fire), led to a US-brokered cease-fire on July 24, 1981. The PLO interpreted this cease-fire as forbidding attacks launched from Lebanon against Israel but permitting PLO attacks launched from outside Lebanon against Israeli or Jewish targets.[103] The escalating conflict with the PLO after this two-week clash led Israel to believe that Palestinian terrorism had to be "solved at the root" by attacking its havens in Lebanon.[104] Ariel Sharon, appointed Israeli defense minister in August 1981, subsequently drafted several operational plans to deal with Palestinian militant groups in Lebanon.

The 1982 Invasion of Lebanon

Under the pretext of an assassination attempt by Palestinian militants in London, which critically wounded the Israeli ambassador to the United Kingdom, Shlomo Argov, Defense Minister Sharon initiated the 1982 Israeli invasion of Lebanon. Known as Operation Peace for Galilee, it sought to finish the job started in 1978 and destroy the PLO as a coherent political and military force. It was claimed that the assassination attempt violated the July 1981 cease-fire agreement between Israel and the PLO. However, the perpetrators of the attack were later revealed to be from the Abu Nidal Organization, a PLO rival, which highlights the extreme manipulation of information by the Israeli defense establishment and the murky pretext of initiating war in Lebanon.[105]

The goals and objectives laid out by Sharon during the 1982 operation remain a topic of much controversy and debate. Decision-making processes in 1982 were dysfunctional, politicized, and unduly influenced by key personalities in the defense establishment.[106] The cabinet was not adequately involved in war planning and was seemingly misled as to the operation's length, duration, and ultimate goals. Sharon, along with Prime Minister Menachem Begin and IDF chief of staff (COS) Lt. Gen. Rafael Eitan, influenced the cabinet to believe that the utility of the limited reprisal operations of the past decades had been exhausted and that a "replay" of Operation Litani would be of little efficacy.[107] Sharon was accused of manipulating the defense establishment in pursuit of much more ambitious political and military goals than those approved by the government, particularly regarding engaging PLO militants in Beirut, targeting Syrian military installations throughout Lebanon, forcing a Syrian withdrawal from Lebanon, and creating a Christian enclave in Lebanon. These goals were intermediary steps to achieve Sharon's chief aspiration—in his words, "a new political reality in Lebanon," where a pro-Israeli regime would be installed under the helm of Maronite (Phalange) militia leader Bashir Gemayel.[108]

The first phase of the 1982 Operation Peace for Galilee was an offensive campaign waged from June 6 to August 31, 1982. This conventional phase, which involved fifty-seven thousand troops and a thousand tanks, was waged successfully against the PLO's conventional brigades and Syrian forces in the Bekaa, Chouf, and coastal regions. The devastating "siege of Beirut" resulted in the departure of Yasser Arafat and the PLO to Tunis, Tunisia, and the ousting of five thousand Syrian troops from West Beirut and marked an achievement of one of the IDF's goals.[109] Sharon's "new reality" began to unravel immediately following this period, as Lebanese president-elect Bashir Gemayel was assassinated in September 1982, and Phalange militiamen angered over the assassination carried out a massacre in Sabra and Shatilla against Palestinians (in which the IDF was indirectly implicated). This mess contributed to the IDF's withdrawal from Beirut in September 1982.

Following a series of failed political negotiations in May 1983 with Lebanese president Amin Gemayel (Bashir's brother), the IDF became a persistent target of Iranian- and Syrian-sponsored militant attacks. Subsequent clashes between Christian and Druze factions in September 1983 in the Chouf region led to the IDF's phased pullback from surrounding areas to positions south of the Awali River.[110] When the IDF invaded Lebanon in 1982 to remove the PLO from Lebanon, many Shi'ites did not express solidarity with the PLO, largely because of Shi'ite resentment of Palestinian hegemony in southern Lebanon.[111] Surprisingly, the Shi'ite militia Amal tacitly welcomed the IDF invasion in 1982 and *initially* remained bystanders to Israeli operations. Moshe Arens, the defense minister at the time, recalled his in-depth talks with Amal commander Muhammad Ghaddar in 1983: "I said to him, we want to get out of Lebanon. We can make a deal, we can help his militia, train them, arm them, so they'd be the biggest militia in south Lebanon. Just one thing: Amal has to make sure there are no attacks against Israel. . . . He didn't say he didn't *want* to do it, but that he just *couldn't* do it." According to

Arens: "I told Ghaddar at the end that if you don't make a deal with us, we're going to have to fight, and you know the IDF will be victorious, so why don't you want to make a deal with us? He said to me, 'You forget one thing. We, the Shi'ites, enjoy suffering.'"[112]

With the breakdown of further talks at Naqoura that occurred from November 1984 to January 1985 to try to craft an Israeli-Lebanese security arrangement, the IDF ceased to be an initiating force in Lebanon and was forced into the defensive posture against increasing guerrilla attacks. Col. (Ret.) Reuven Erlich, an IDF military intelligence (MI) officer who became the Ministry of Defense's deputy coordinator for Lebanese Affairs in 1985, reflected that as Israel was negotiating under fire, "the IDF continued to sink into the Lebanese swamp."[113]

Following the breakdown of talks, the new defense minister, Yitzhak Rabin (1984–90), sought to withdraw the IDF unilaterally from Lebanon. Rabin convened several working groups to issue recommendations on the IDF's future in Lebanon. Three main viewpoints emerged. The first team, led by the hawkish Maj. Gen. Moshe Bar-Kochba, a well-known Armored Corps commander, argued against any withdrawal from Lebanon and sought to keep the IDF stationed up to the Litani River. Another team, led by Maj. Gen. Ehud Barak, head of IDF MI (1983–85), forcefully argued for a full withdrawal from Lebanon. The third team, led by Maj. Gen. Amir Drori, head of Northern Command (1981–83), advocated for establishing a security zone in Lebanon. Brig. Gen. (Ret.) Ephraim Sneh recalled his role on General Drori's team: "As the Lebanon expert, I was on this team, and I drew the line of the security zone which was actually accepted."[114]

Fierce debates ensued within the IDF General Staff surrounding the 1985 decision to withdraw from Lebanon. Moshe Arens, a minister in the government at the time, recalled that "there was a degree of schizophrenia in the defense establishment" since Rabin wanted to withdraw, but when it was clear that the SLA was not capable of maintaining security alone, he was forced to bolster IDF involvement in Lebanon.[115] Barak was apparently one of the lone voices of dissent in the IDF General Staff regarding a withdrawal from Lebanon in 1985. In a transcript of a March 15, 1985, General Staff meeting, Barak implored, "The SLA doesn't have a chance of being an efficient security filter . . . [and] will turn into a target [for Hezbollah]," and "we will reach . . . a dangerous [situation] where we will have to intervene more and more in order to protect what we have already sent inside."[116]

In the same March 1985 meeting, Barak had a heated exchange with the head of Northern Command, Maj. Gen. Ori Orr, shouting, "I want it to be recorded . . . we don't realize what's going to happen [if we stay in Lebanon] . . . Lebanon with all its entanglements and complications. . . . we've got to get our forces out of there!"[117] Barak's impressions as a young general at this time are important to keep in mind when he assumes political leadership a decade and a half in the future.

After considering dissenting views, Rabin sought to withdraw the IDF from various sectors in Lebanon in three phases. The Israeli government had declared on January 14, 1985, that it would withdraw from Lebanon but would establish a "temporary'" security zone to protect the Galilee, as advocated by Generals Drori and Sneh. The security zone was to be manned by SLA troops led by former Lebanese army general Antoine Lahd, who succeeded Major Haddad after his death in 1984. The IDF would "support" the SLA until "quiet" was achieved for Israel's northern towns still being attacked from Lebanon.

Ramifications of the Israeli Invasion of Lebanon

Operation Peace for Galilee marked the first time Israel initiated a "war of choice" in which its survival was not at stake and without national consensus. Because the IDF was known as the "people's army," this war drastically altered societal perceptions, fostered the notion of a military that had lost credibility and integrity, affected society's willingness and resilience to bear the burden of protracted conflict in Lebanon, and lessened international legitimacy for future operations there. Pivotally, in 1982, Israel lost (and has never reclaimed) the title of a professed status-quo state that would theoretically only embark on defensive wars of survival.[118]

After the January 1985 decision by Israel to establish the security zone, Maj. Gen. Ori Orr, head of IDF Northern Command (1983–86), ominously reflected on the future: "The withdrawal from Lebanon [in 1985] is, for me, only the end of a chapter, rather than the end of the book. The end of the book will be when there is calm in the north. . . . The problem of Lebanon is still not solved."[119]

The establishment of the security zone in 1985 marks the beginning of a "new chapter" in the IDF's protracted conflict in Lebanon and sets the stage for this book.

The Emergence of Hezbollah

Israel remained in Lebanon from 1982 to 1985 in an attempt to achieve some semblance of security and inadvertently fomented massive local Lebanese opposition.[120] Numerous secular and religious Lebanese "resistance" groups emerged, and, having overstayed its welcome, Israel soon found itself facing a bloody conflict of attritional warfare. The most effective militant organization that emerged was Hezbollah. While the immediate trigger for the emergence of Hezbollah is often attributed to the continued presence of the IDF in Lebanon, this is a gross oversimplification, as Shi'ite militarization and resistance against the IDF was only the immediate manifestation of a monumental process of Shi'ite communal empowerment that had been developing in Lebanon and the greater Middle East for at least the previous two decades.

The historic political, social, and economic marginalization of the Shi'ites of Lebanon eventually led to a Shi'ite "awakening," largely a result of the influence of key clerics who studied in the theological seminaries in the holy cities of Najaf in Iraq and Qom in Iran. These seminaries are where many in Hezbollah's future leadership met and were exposed to the teachings of respected Islamic jurists who called for a transition from historic Shi'ite quiescence and political passivity to communal activism and clerical leadership. The prominence of these "activist" clerics was enhanced by the weakening amid the civil war of the traditional patronage networks and feudal leaders in Lebanon (*zu'ama*) that had contributed to the historical marginalization of the Shi'ites. This "awakening" was coupled with the migration of poor Shi'ite families from the southern Lebanon hinterland to the urban centers in search of greater economic opportunity amid a process of social and economic transformation.[121]

This Shi'ite awakening gained traction in Lebanon with the arrival in 1959 of Musa al-Sadr, an influential Iranian cleric of Lebanese descent. The impact of al-Sadr on Shi'ite political consciousness in Lebanon cannot be understated, as he sought to transform the ingrained notion of provincialism and passivity among the Shi'ite clerics and urged that they should become active community and political leaders.[122] Al-Sadr rallied the Lebanon Shi'ite population through his Movement for the Deprived (Harakat al-Mahrumin), established in 1974, which was created as a mass protest movement to pressure the Lebanese government to address the community's marginalization. In response to the perceived need for self-protection of the Shi'ites amid civil war, Amal ("Hope" in Arabic and an acronym for Afwaj al-Muqawama al-Lubnaniya, "Lebanese Resistance Detachments") was created as an adjunct militia to the Movement for the Deprived but eventually subsumed it militarily and politically.[123] The formation of Amal marked the rise of Lebanese Shi'ite militancy. The shocking disappearance of the iconic al-Sadr while on a trip to Libya in 1978 reverberated throughout Lebanon and further energized the community. (Al-Sadr's unknown fate attracts significant political and media attention in Lebanon to this day.)

The 1979 Iranian Revolution, referred to as "the earthquake" by the Hezbollah ideologue Mohammad Hussein Fadlallah, is the most significant catalyzing event of the period and acted as a potent and inspirational model for realizing Shi'ite empowerment and revolutionary activism. The abstract ideals of a Shi'ite Islamic state became a realization as Ayatollah Ruhollah Khomeini swept into power on a "wave of popular revolutionary fervor."[124]

Hezbollah initially emerged as a loose umbrella for radical Shi'ite militancy from 1982 to 1983 but formally announced its existence in its 1985 manifesto, known as the "Open Letter Addressed by Hezbollah to the Downtrodden in Lebanon and in the World." It outlined the group's fundamental goals and objectives, which included Israel's "obliteration from existence" and the departure of "imperialist powers"—namely, the United States and France—from Lebanon. Hezbollah also sought to replace the unjust and oppressive Lebanese sectarian system by establishing an Islamic system in Lebanon and urged a strong allegiance and adherence to Iran's supreme leader, Ayatollah Khomeini.[125]

In Shi'ite dogma, the martyrdom of Ali, the prophet Muhammad's cousin and son-in-law, and Ali's son, Hussain, are cornerstones of the faith and signify the importance of the need to resist oppression and the reverence of self-sacrifice. Hezbollah's ideology, heavily influenced by these sentiments as well as the teachings of Khomeini, is grounded in the Shi'ite theological concept of *wilayat al-faqih* ("guardianship of the Islamic jurist"), which implies that the cleric acts as the absolute authority in religious, judicial, and political matters and led Hezbollah to view Iran's supreme leader as the arbiter of spiritual and state affairs and as the ultimate "source of emulation" (*marjah al-taqlid*).

When Israel invaded Lebanon in 1982, it did not fully comprehend the dramatic currents simmering within Lebanese Shi'ite society. While some, like Maj. Gen. Ehud Barak, warned of the risks of Israel's deployment in the Lebanese security zone, Israel's continued presence provided a fitting focal point for the massive militant energies that had been fomenting in Shi'ite society. As Israeli defense minister Rabin lamented in a 1985 speech, Israel's involvement in Lebanon "let the Shi'ite genie out of the bottle."[126]

STRUCTURE

This book is divided into two parts that tell the story of the Israel-Hezbollah conflict: part I (chapters 1–4) chronologically analyzes its *strategic* aspects, and part II (chapters 5–9) analyzes its *operational* aspects. As will be explained in their respective introductions, the book is divided along these lines because it correlates to the way in which Israel's Winograd Commission structured and defined the elements of warfare after the 2006 war. The concluding chapter assesses which schools of thought on military innovation were most influential in enabling and hindering military change in the IDF, ultimately illustrating that innovation and adaptation are driven and shaped by an interdependent and interactive dynamic of diverse factors. An afterword follows, which discusses IDF force planning and Hezbollah's military adaptation since the outbreak of the Syrian Civil War.

NOTES

Epigraph: Clausewitz, *On War*, 75.

1. Eiland, "IDF," 31.

2. Nasrallah, interview, May 6, 2007.

3. Department of the Army, *Army Capstone Concept*, 10–12; Ministry of Defence, *Future Character of Conflict*, 13–19.

4. Smith, *Utility of Force*, 262–65, 380–81.

5. Grissom, "Future of Military Innovation Studies," 907.

6. Farrell and Terriff, "Sources of Military Change," 6.

7. Farrell, "Military Adaptation in War," 6–7.

8. Russell, "Innovation in War," 619–22; Farrell, "Improving in War," 568–70; Farrell and Terriff, "Sources of Military Change," 6.

9. Farrell, "Military Adaptation in War," 7.

10. Ibid., 8.

11. Murray, *Military Adaptation in War*.

12. Griffin, "Military Innovation Studies"; Grissom, "Future of Military Innovation Studies"; Farrell, "Figuring Out Fighting Organisations."

13. Posen, *Sources of Military Doctrine*, 57–59, 174–75.

14. Ibid., 45–47; Farrell, "Figuring Out Fighting Organisations," 123; Pahlavi and Ouellet, "Institutional Analysis and Irregular Warfare."

15. Avant, "Institutional Sources of Military Doctrine," 413–14.

16. Zisk, *Engaging the Enemy*, 4–13.

17. Murray, "Innovation: Past and Future."

18. For example, see Naveh, *Operational Art and the IDF*.

19. Rosen, *Winning the Next War*, 20–21; Rosen, "New Ways of War."

20. Freilich, "National Security Decision-Making in Israel," 642; Freilich, *Zion's Dilemma*.

21. Michael, "Military Knowledge," 40–41; Michael, "Classical Dilemma of Civil-Military Relations," 523; Freilich, "National Security Decision-Making in Israel," 650.

22. Peri, *Generals in the Cabinet Room*.

23. Barak and Sheffer, "Israel's 'Security Network'"; Etzioni-Halevy, "Civil-Military Relations," 411–12.

24. Anshel Pfeffer, "Israel's Iron Dome Is the Hero of the Hour, but Bigger Challenges Lie Ahead," *Haaretz*, November 23, 2012.

25. Freilich, *Zion's Dilemma*; Etzioni-Halevy, "Civil-Military Relations," 411.

26. Eiland, "Decision-Making Process in Israel," 25–31.

27. Zisk, *Engaging the Enemy*, 4.

28. Farrell, "Dynamics of British Military Transformation," 781; Farrell, "World Culture and Military Power."

29. Farrell, "Culture and Military Power," 412.

30. Goldman, "New Threats," 63.

31. Farrell, "Culture and Military Power," 414. For an IDF example, see Demchak, "Numbers or Networks."

32. Demchak, "Technology's Knowledge Burden."

33. Hoyt, "Revolution and Counter-Revolution."

34. Ucko, *New Counterinsurgency Era*.

35. Posen, *Sources of Military Doctrine*, 49; Farrell, "Dynamics of British Military Transformation," 782.

36. Catignani, *Israeli Counter-Insurgency*, 38.

37. Michael, "Military Knowledge," 41.

38. Finkel, *On Flexibility*, chap. 5; Demchak, "Coping, Copying, and Concentrating," 351.

39. Farrell, "Military Adaptation in War," 10–12. For other examples, see Merom, *How Democracies Lose Small Wars*.

40. Farrell, "Dynamics of British Military Transformation"; Adamsky, *Culture of Military Innovation*.

41. This definition draws from Legro, "Military Culture and Inadvertent Escalation," 109; and Farrell, "Culture and Military Power," 410–11.

42. Terriff, "Warriors and Innovators," 238.

43. Grissom, "Future of Military Innovation Studies," 920.

44. Ibid.

45. The literature on bottom-up adaptation is small but growing fast. For example, see Russell, *Innovation, Transformation, and War*; Farrell, "Improving in War"; Catignani, "Getting COIN"; Marcus, "Military Innovation and Tactical Adaptation"; and Marcus, "Learning 'Under Fire.'"

46. Serena, *Revolution in Military Adaptation*; Russell, *Innovation, Transformation, and War*.

47. Foley, "Horizontal Military Innovation."

48. Ibid.; Farrell, "Improving in War," 572–84; Shamir, *Transforming Command*; Russell, "Innovation in War," 621; Horowitz, "Flexible Responsiveness," 192; Finkel, "Flexible Force Structure," 792–95.

49. On organizational learning capacity, see Hoffman, "Wartime 'Learning Gap.'" For an IDF example, see Marcus, "Learning 'Under Fire.'"

50. Foley, Griffin, and McCartney, "Transformation in Contact"; Mains and Ariely, "Learning while Fighting."

51. Catignani, "Coping with Knowledge."

52. Marcus, "Military Innovation and Tactical Adaptation."

53. Farrell and Terriff, "Sources of Military Change," 8–10; Adamsky, *Culture of Military Innovation*, 98; Goldman and Eliason, "Introduction."

54. Horowitz, *Diffusion of Military Power*, 34–38.

55. Kier, "Culture and Military Doctrine," 67–69; Goldman, "Cultural Foundations of Military Diffusion."

56. Finkel, *On Flexibility*, 2–4.

57. Nagl, *Learning to Eat Soup with a Knife*, 10.

58. Hasdai, "'Doers' and 'Thinkers' in the IDF."

59. Marcus, "Learning 'Under Fire,'" 11–12.

60. Horowitz, "Flexible Responsiveness," 191–99; Shamir, *Transforming Command*, 82–95; Adamsky, *Culture of Military Innovation*, 110–25; Katz and Bohbot, *Weapon Wizards*.

61. Quoted in Ben-Shalom and Shamir, "Mission Command," 105.

62. Murray, "Innovation: Past and Future," 52.

63. Murray, *Military Adaptation in War*; Farrell, "Military Adaptation in War"; Goldman, "New Threats"; Farrell, "World Culture and Military Power," 486.

64. For example, see Berman, "Capturing Contemporary Innovation"; Russell, *Innovation, Transformation, and War*; and, despite flawed conclusions, Pahlavi and Ouellet, "Institutional Analysis and Irregular Warfare."

65. For example, Nagl, *Learning to Eat Soup with a Knife*, does not discuss insurgent innovation at all.

66. Adamsky, "Jihadi Operational Art"; Jackson et al., *Aptitude for Destruction Vol. 1*; Rasmussen and Hafez, *Terrorist Innovations in Weapons of Mass Effect*; Brun, "While You're Busy"; Dolnik, *Understanding Terrorist Innovation*; Giustozzi, "Military Adaptation by the Taliban"; Moghadam, "How Al-Qaeda Innovates"; Ranstorp and Normark, *Understanding Terrorist Innovation and Learning*; Serena, *It Takes More Than a Network*.

67. Recent studies on adaptation in the 1967 and 1973 wars include Murray, *Military Adaptation in War*, chap. 7; and Finkel, *On Flexibility*, chap. 8–9.

68. For one such example, see Bar-Joseph, "Introduction," 3–4.

69. Cohen, *Israel and Its Army*, 47–48; Kober, "Israeli Military Thinking as Reflected in *Ma'arachot* Articles."

70. Byman, *High Price*; Catignani, *Israeli Counter-Insurgency*.

71. Exceptions include Jones, "Israeli Counter-Insurgency Strategy"; Jones, "Reach Greater Than the Grasp"; and Sobelman, *New Rules of the Game*.

72. The most notable memoir is Tamir, *Undeclared War*. See also Eiran, *Essence of Longing*.

73. Hirsch, *War Story, Love Story*; Haloutz, *At Eye Level*. Due to variations in transliteration from Hebrew, Gen. Dan Halutz's last name is spelled "Haloutz" in his authored English-language publications. Throughout this book, for consistency, "Halutz" is used, except in source citations and the bibliography to match his previous publications.

74. For a memoir on the war published in Hebrew in 2008, which was translated in 2016, see Lubotzky, *From the Wilderness*.

75. For example, see Folman, *Waltz with Bashir*; Cedar, *Beaufort*; and Maoz, *Levanon*.

76. Friedman, *Pumpkin Flowers*, 19. For a comedic memoir that covers the late 1990s, see Chasnoff, *188th Crybaby Brigade*, 211–47.

77. The best journalistic accounts are Harel and Issacharoff, *34 Days*; Rapaport, *Friendly Fire*; and Shelah and Limor, *Captives of Lebanon*. For the shortcomings of such accounts, see Zisser, "Israelis Confront the Second Lebanon War."

78. Johnson, *Hard Fighting*; Lambeth, "Israel's War in Gaza," 8.

79. For example, see Catignani, "Israeli Counterinsurgency Strategy," and other chapters in Jones and Catignani, *Israel and Hezbollah*.

80. Hoffman, *Conflict in the 21st Century*; Biddle and Friedman, *2006 Lebanon Campaign*.

81. For example, only eight pages are spent on the 1985–2000 period in Helmer, *Flipside of the COIN*, 52–60. Matthews, *We Were Caught Unprepared* devotes five pages (7–11).

82. Schiff and Yaari, *Israel's Lebanon War*; Friedman, *From Beirut to Jerusalem*; Yaniv, *Dilemmas of Israeli Security*; Rabinovich, *War for Lebanon, 1970–1985*; Evron, *War and Intervention in Lebanon*.

83. For a thematic literature review, see Marcus, "Hizbullah."

84. For example, Norton, "Hizballah and the Israeli Withdrawal from Southern Lebanon"; Deeb, "Shi'a Movements in Lebanon."

85. Jaber, *Hezbollah: Born with a Vengeance*; Palmer-Harik, *Hezbollah: The Changing Face of Terrorism.*

86. Shanahan, *Shi'a of Lebanon*; Kramer, "Oracle of Hizbullah"; Ajami, *Vanished Imam*; Nakash, *Reaching for Power*; Norton, *Amal and the Shi'a.*

87. Hamzeh, *Path of Hezbollah*; Alagha, *Shifts in Hizbullah's Ideology*; Alagha, *Hizbullah's Identity Construction*; Ghrorayeb, *Hizbullah*; Palmer-Harik, "Between Islam and the System."

88. Ranstorp, *Hizballah in Lebanon*; Kramer, "Hizbullah"; Ranstorp, "Hizbollah's Command Leadership"; Ranstorp, "Hizballah Training Camps of Lebanon."

89. Levitt, *Hezbollah.*

90. Blanford, *Warriors of God.*

91. For example, see Norton, *Hezbollah*; Norton, *Hizballah in Lebanon*; Hamzeh, "Lebanon's Hizbullah"; and Hamzeh, "Lebanon's Islamists and Local Politics." For critical perspectives, see Ranstorp, "Strategy and Tactics"; Zisser, "Hizballah in Lebanon"; Zisser, "Hizballah: New Course or Continued Warfare"; Azani, *Hezbollah.*

92. For a literature review surrounding Hezbollah's political participation, see Marcus, "Hizbullah."

93. Ghrorayeb, *Hizbullah*, 112–17.

94. Qassem, interview, April 13, 2009.

95. Nasrallah, interview, February 13, 1993; Fadlallah, interview, autumn 1995.

96. Cambanis, *Privilege to Die*, 193. This methodology was also used in Sobelman, "Learning to Deter."

97. See note 82.

98. On the origins of the Maronite-Israeli alliance, see Zisser, "Maronites, Lebanon, Israel"; Eisenberg, "History Revisited or Revamped?"

99. Author interview with Ephraim Sneh.

100. Evron, *War and Intervention in Lebanon*, 74–76.

101. For a short overview, see Bregman, *Israel's Wars*, 147–51. On how the operation impacted future war planning, see Schiff and Yaari, *Israel's Lebanon War*, chap. 3. Note: For semantic reasons, the term "rocket" will be used henceforth but is intended to include missiles as well.

102. Schiff and Yaari, *Israel's Lebanon War*, 31–37; Evron, *War and Intervention in Lebanon*, chap. 3; Yaniv, *Dilemmas of Israeli Security*, 59–61; Rabinovich, *War for Lebanon*, 118–20.

103. Erlich, *Road to the First Lebanon War*, 9–10.

104. Ibid., 6.

105. For details on the Abu Nidal–PLO rivalry in the lead-up to 1982, see Schiff and Yaari, *Israel's Lebanon War*, 98–100.

106. Freilich, *Zion's Dilemma*, chap. 5.

107. Yaniv and Lieber, "Personal Whim or Strategic Imperative?," 183.

108. Amir Oren, "Revealed: The Deceptions by Sharon, Begin and Eitan, behind the First Lebanon War," *Haaretz*, May 5, 2014.

109. For a concise account, see Bregman, *Israel's Wars*, 160–76. For a detailed account, see Schiff and Yaari, *Israel's Lebanon War*, 109–229.

110. Yaniv, *Dilemmas of Israeli Security*, 213–17.

111. Shefi Gabay, "Shi'ites Say Majority Oppose Terrorism," *Maariv*, March 28, 1985, Foreign Broadcast Information Service (hereafter FBIS).

112. Author interview with Moshe Arens.

113. Erlich, "When Did the First Lebanon War End?," 9.

114. Author interview with Ephraim Sneh.

115. Author interview with Moshe Arens.

116. Quoted in Bregman, *Israel's Wars*, 254.

117. Ibid., 255.

118. This section draws from Horowitz, "Israel's War in Lebanon," 88–92; Van Creveld, *Sword and the Olive*, 353–56.

119. Orr, interview, April 13, 1985.

120. An expanded version of this section appears in Marcus, "Hizbullah."

121. Shanahan, *Shi'a of Lebanon*.

122. Nakash, *Reaching for Power*, 117; Ajami, *Vanished Imam*.

123. Norton, *Amal and the Shi'a*; Shanahan, *Shi'a of Lebanon*, 107–8; Deeb, "Shi'a Movements in Lebanon."

124. Kramer, "Oracle of Hizbollah," 101.

125. For the full manifesto, see Norton, *Amal and the Shi'a*, 167–87.

126. This oft-cited quote can be first attributed to Yitzhak Rabin, speech, February 15, 1985.

PART I

STRATEGIC ADAPTATION

INTRODUCTION TO PART I

THE WINOGRAD COMMISSION critiqued numerous aspects of the IDF's war efforts, including intelligence, logistics, tactics, training, budgetary issues, its operational concept, and, most critically, its political-military strategy. In what ultimately contributed to the resignation of several senior IDF officials as well as the prime minister and the defense minister, the commission scathingly noted the "absence of a strategic view of the political and military echelons alike" and faulted both echelons for poor strategic dialogue with each other. The commission highlighted serious deficiencies in Israel's decision-making processes and discussed the poor formulation of strategy, the inappropriate conceptualization of the nature of Hezbollah, and the inadequate understanding of the challenges of asymmetrical conflict against nonstate opponents.[1] To understand the context of Israel's strategic outlook and the reasons behind the inconsistent formulation and haphazard application of fundamental strategic principles during the war, the following chapters centrally examine the IDF's evolving conceptualization of the threat from Hezbollah since the origins of the conflict, which deeply affected how the IDF's core concept of deterrence was adapted and utilized in Lebanon. It is critical to note that the adaptation of Israel's deterrence concept is inextricably linked to the IDF's evolving conceptualization of Hezbollah as an asymmetrical opponent throughout the conflict.

While the Winograd Commission has generally been praised inside and outside Israel (including by Hezbollah!) as a sign of IDF transparency, self-criticism, and self-improvement, one IDF colonel noted that one of the commission's major shortcomings is that "it isolates a single manifestation (summer 2006) and removes it from the wider context of the overall struggle" with Hezbollah, leaving an "anemic report that is in part irrelevant."[2] While the Winograd Commission noted the importance of events that occurred between the Israeli withdrawal from Lebanon in 2000 and the outbreak of war in 2006 as crucial for understanding the IDF's approach during the war, it is also necessary to examine the strategic adaptation of the IDF over the fifteen years prior to the IDF withdrawal to contextualize and fully understand Israel's strategy and evolving conceptualization of Hezbollah throughout the conflict.

The military theorist Clausewitz wrote, "War, however, is not the action of a living force upon a lifeless mass (total nonresistance would be no war at all) but always the collision of two living forces. . . . Once again there is interaction. . . . He dictates to me as much as I dictate to him."[3] Hence, the strategic evolution, military adaptation, and organizational development of Hezbollah are discussed in tandem. Notably, Israel's postwar learning process had a significant impact on Hezbollah, which deeply studied the Winograd Commission's reports. Secretary-General Hassan Nasrallah described its importance on Hezbollah's strategic learning after the war: "The [Winograd] Final Report, in my view, tackles the most important aspect, and that is the background for the decision to go to war. . . . But who actually made the decision? What is the background behind the decision to go to war against Lebanon?"[4]

Part I of this book answers Nasrallah's question about the strategic context surrounding Israel's decision-making on the long road to the 2006 war. The Winograd Commission highlighted "serious failings and shortcomings" in the political and military echelons related to decision-making processes, army preparedness, and strategic planning, which it noted can be adequately understood only by examining the IDF's strategic adaptation in historical context: "These weaknesses resulted in part from inadequacies of preparedness and strategic and operative planning *which go back long before the Second Lebanon War*."[5]

Illustrating the importance of contextual history in understanding both the IDF's and Hezbollah's learning and adaptation, Nasrallah said in a 2012 speech, "We are before thirty years of full experience . . . and the developments since June 1982 until this very day. . . . If one is a reasonable human being, he learns from his experiences and the experiences of others. . . . If we lock out this past, we will make wrong evaluations and comprehensions."[6]

Given the importance of past learning experiences and historical context in shaping the Hezbollah leader's current strategic assessment, part I also recounts the strategic development of Hezbollah, focusing centrally on its organizational adaptation and the evolution of its deterrent posture.

The evolution and adaptation of IDF strategy is analyzed in four broad time periods of the conflict that loosely structure part I chronologically. Chapter 1 covers the IDF's conceptual understanding of Hezbollah in the first decade of the IDF occupation of Lebanon, from the "formal" emergence of Hezbollah and the IDF's creation of the "security zone" in 1985 to the ascension of Hassan Nasrallah to the position of secretary-general in 1992. This period is an era of major organizational growth for Hezbollah, which slowly adapted and refined what was its relatively ineffective approach for confronting the IDF. Chapter 2 covers the adaptation of IDF strategy in Lebanon and the application of Israel's deterrence policy in the second decade (1993–99), which was adjusted to contain Hezbollah after the establishment of a set of understandings that laid out the "rules of the game" regarding "accepted" responses during the conflict. It also highlights Israel's shift in focus toward counterguerrilla warfare. The 1990s were pivotal for Hezbollah's evolution as it underwent an innovative and intensive period of strategic learning, organizational refinement, and military advancement under the command of Hassan Nasrallah. Chapter 3 deals with decision-making surrounding the dramatic decision by the IDF to withdraw from Lebanon. The military developments of this period, coupled with widespread popular protest within Israeli society, culminated in an eventual IDF withdrawal from Lebanon in May 2000, which resulted in a major shift in the strategic equation. Chapter 4 deals with IDF strategic readjustment in the decade following the 2000 withdrawal, which includes the erosion of deterrence and the road to the 2006 war. It discusses Israeli and Hezbollah strategy during the war and the strategic recalibration that has occurred in the war's aftermath, which has resulted in an equation of mutual deterrence between both sides.

ISRAEL'S STRATEGIC DOCTRINE

It is important to note that historically (until 2015) Israel did not publicly release an officially approved strategic doctrine. The doctrine of the IDF since its inception was more accurately a collection of concepts based on "learning by doing," institutionalized by the military's founding fathers. As the legendary IDF tank commander and strategist Maj. Gen. Israel Tal wrote, "Over the years, it has become clear that Israel's military thought, to this day, is little more than a series of footnotes to the doctrine which crystallized in the 1950s. . . . Although in the course of time changes and refinements were made, not always for the better, these foundations were preserved."[7]

The foundation of the IDF's "traditional" doctrine is centered on a number of important principles.[8] The IDF's limitations regarding its strategic environment are immense: geographic vulnerability and limited strategic depth, demographic inferiority compared to its Arab neighbors, and a vulnerable economy as a result of mobilizing IDF reservists from the working-age population. Israel crafted a doctrine that sought to overcome these realities by emphasizing early warning, a qualitative military edge, a tradition of initiative and self-reliance, and decisive, rapid operations. The

IDF also emphasized the "indirect approach" and offensive operations often launched preemptively, which would become its hallmark.[9] Defensible borders, intelligence superiority, and air force supremacy would allow Israel to maintain its deterrent posture, which consistently remains of paramount importance in Israeli strategic thinking.[10] During its engagement in Lebanon, the IDF slowly adapted its major strategic and operational principles in ways that challenged traditional concepts underlying Israeli security.

Historically, the IDF framed its security threats into two distinct categories. In Israeli security jargon, conventional threats from neighboring Arab militaries, termed "fundamental security" (*bitachon yisodi*), have been the main preoccupation.[11] By contrast, border infiltrations by Arab guerrillas (*fedayeen*) throughout the 1940s and 1950s, and continual terrorist and guerrilla incidents since, have been termed "routine security" (*bitachon shotef*).[12] Because of the existential danger to the state, the IDF has understandably focused on fundamental security throughout its history, a trend that continued even into the 1990s despite the primary operational focus from the mid-1980s onward on routine security in Lebanon. As will be illustrated, the adaptive shift in focus away from fundamental security toward routine security and the reconceptualization of the threat from Hezbollah would have large-scale implications on IDF strategy and deterrence.

Given its inability to sustain protracted conflict and its professed role as a state that seeks to maintain the status quo politically and territorially, Israel historically sought to utilize deterrence, persuading opponents that the costs or risks of a given course of action would outweigh its benefits.[13] Deterrence is the cornerstone of the IDF's strategic doctrine, historically utilized to prevent large-scale conventional war with its Arab neighbors, but it has also been utilized historically against LIC threats, often in the form of severe reprisal or retaliatory operations.[14] Because Israel's enemies have recognized their own operational limitations and have sought to avoid conventional war and instead engage Israel in protracted LIC, the IDF has relied on the concept of "cumulative deterrence," defined recently by Maj. Gen. (Ret.) Doron Almog, former head of IDF Southern Command:

> Cumulative deterrence works on two levels. On the macro-level, it seeks to create an image of overwhelming military supremacy. On the micro-level, it relies on specific military responses to specific threats or hostile acts. . . . Its effectiveness is measured in terms of number of victories accumulated over the duration of the conflict, which we can think of as "assets in a victory bank." . . . Over time, these victories produce increasingly moderate behavior on the part of the adversary and a shift in his strategic, operational, and tactical goals until there is a near-absence of direct conflict.[15]

The IDF has historically utilized exemplary force to convince its asymmetrical opponents to refrain from escalation of hostilities; it has set "red lines" that act as casus belli and has clearly defined "rules of the game" that connect "a series of acts of force to create and maintain general norms of behavior" throughout extended conflict.[16] Israel's qualitative military edge, together with the aggregate impact of Israel's displays of force, complements its overall deterrence posture.[17]

Historically, Israel sought to deter its Arab neighbors from attacking by both minimizing Israeli vulnerability through "denial" and inflicting "punishment" to imminent threats.[18] Deterrence by denial involved denying the enemy any military or territorial gains while carrying out limited disarming operations and maintaining a robust civilian homeland defense system. This includes air-raid sirens, bomb shelters, gas mask distribution, and an advanced, multitiered missile defense system, which together suggest the futility of striking Israel. Deterrence by punishment involves inflicting sharp, rapid strikes in response to enemy belligerence to dissuade further aggression. Both forms of deterrence may be insufficient individually, hence Israel sought to consistently display the futility of enemy hostility through the IDF's superiority, qualitative capability, and indefinite willingness to ensure its own security and survival as part of its cumulative deterrence strategy. As illustrated in the following chapters, Hezbollah's military development would both challenge the IDF's historical conceptualization of "routine security" and lead to an adaptation in its use of deterrence to cope with such threats.

NOTES

1. Winograd Commission, final report, chap. 18, paras. 21–22.
2. Siboni, "Victims of Friendly Fire," 84–88.
3. Clausewitz, *On War*, 77.
4. Nasrallah, interview, May 6, 2007.
5. Israel Ministry of Foreign Affairs, "English Summary of Winograd Commission Report," para. 12 (emphasis added).
6. Nasrallah, speech, November 11, 2012.
7. Tal, "Israel's Doctrine of National Security," 44.
8. This section draws from Dayan, "Israel's Border and Security Problems"; Allon, "Case for Defensible Borders"; Ben-Horin and Posen, *Israel's Strategic Doctrine*; Luttwak and Horowitz, *Israeli Army*; Van Creveld, *Sword and the Olive*; Schiff, *History of the Israeli Army*; and Tal, *National Security*.
9. Bond, "Liddell Hart's Influence."
10. Tal, *National Security*, chap. 9; Allon, "Case for Defensible Borders."
11. *Bitachon yisodi* alternatively translates as "basic security."
12. *Bitachon shotef* alternatively translates as "current security" or "ongoing security."

13. Tal, *National Security*, chap. 8.

14. Dayan, "Israel's Border and Security Problems"; Allon, "Case for Defensible Borders"; Vardi, "Pounding Their Feet."

15. Almog, "Cumulative Deterrence," 9.

16. Rid, "Deterrence beyond the State," 141–42.

17. Bar-Joseph, "Variations on a Theme," 151–57; Allon, "Case for Defensible Borders," 52.

18. This section draws from Ben-Horin and Posen, *Israel's Strategic Doctrine*, 13–14; Levite, *Offense and Defense*, 125.

CHAPTER 1

IDF "ROUTINE SECURITY" AND THE EVOLUTION OF HEZBOLLAH (1985–92)

One thing is clear: no fourth winter in Lebanon, not at any price.

—Defense Minister Yitzhak Rabin

Despite its intelligence capability, the Israeli enemy does not yet understand the truth about the makeup of Hezbollah or the nature of what it is facing.

—Sec.-Gen. Hassan Nasrallah

Following the opening high-intensity phase of 1982's Operation Peace for Galilee against the PLO and Syria, the IDF's primary operational focus in Lebanon from 1983 onward was low-intensity warfare against the plethora of hostile militant groups. However, the IDF remained conceptually focused on conventional warfare and focused its training and force structure on "fundamental security" for possible confrontation with Syria related to the Golan Heights and its presence in Lebanon.[1] Hezbollah in the 1980s was viewed on the same level militarily as Palestinian militias, as a "routine security" threat not worthy of major conceptual or operational attention, which could be dealt with by low-intensity security operations. The IDF's conceptual understanding of the nascent Hezbollah remained relatively static throughout the first decade of the IDF's security zone in Lebanon because of the low threat perception of the group. Hezbollah embarked on an era of major organizational growth in the early 1990s as the group slowly adapted and refined what was its relatively ineffective approach for confronting the IDF. Israel, focused on conventional threats, was slow to adapt to the rising threat from Hezbollah as the IDF became further entrenched in Lebanon.

THE IDF IN THE 1980s

After the trauma of the 1973 Arab-Israeli War, the IDF massively expanded its size and capabilities for conventional warfare to respond to "Yom Kippur War–style" existential threats, and as a result LIC was strategically and operationally sidelined. COS Lt. Gen. Dan Shomron said in 1988, "Despite the grief, the real threat comes not from terrorism or disturbances in the territories. The real threat to our existence is in the form of war against regular armies."[2] A Golani Brigade officer stationed in Lebanon from 1984 to 1988 recalled the low threat perceptions on the ground from Hezbollah, the ease at which the IDF targeted the group in the 1980s, and the IDF's wide freedom of movement throughout Lebanon. He facetiously described his service in Lebanon, with its bucolic terrain, as "like being in Switzerland . . . with its lovely views. We did some operations in the area, but some of the best times of my service were in Lebanon. It was a quiet border."[3] Illustrating the initial weakness of Hezbollah and its tactical inferiority vis-à-vis the IDF, another officer reflected on his combat experience in Lebanon in the late 1980s: "It took Hezbollah time to learn. For example, Hezbollah barely even knew that we had night-vision equipment. We used to shoot them down in nighttime raids, and they would have no idea where the shots were coming from." However, the officer lamented that "IDF tactical successes kept us from understanding our entanglement in Lebanon."[4]

While the threat from Hezbollah would slowly evolve, it took the IDF time to recognize Hezbollah's adaptive capability and the increasing challenge it would represent. Maj. Gen. (Ret.) Giora Eiland, former head of the IDF Operations Directorate, explained: "We still treated Hezbollah in a similar way to the way that we treated the Palestinian organizations that were fighting against us in the late 1970s from south Lebanon. It took some time to understand that this is a much more professional and much more committed organization and also enjoys the full support of the Shi'ite population in south Lebanon. And this created a real big challenge for us."[5]

While the IDF occupied a larger part of southern Lebanon from 1982 to 1985, the political leadership grappled with how to fully extricate the IDF from Lebanon. Illustrating the IDF's strategic dilemma, Defense Minister Yitzhak Rabin explained in a televised interview just after the phased Israeli withdrawal into the newly declared 328-square mile security zone in 1985:

We hoped that with the cabinet decision to redeploy the IDF along the international border, and with the beginning of the [1985] withdrawal, some of the Shi'ite motivation to act against us would be eliminated. This did not happen. . . . However, if our desire to live and let live is reciprocated with terrorism, we will defend ourselves. . . . The [1982] war in Lebanon did not eliminate the threat of terrorism against Israel from Lebanese territory; it may even have created a terrorist potential that was even worse than before. . . . However, we are on the way back home. But there is still one phase we have to go through.[6]

The first phase of the IDF's 1985 withdrawal was from the Sidon area in January and February, and the second phase in March was the withdrawal farther south from the Tyre and Nabatieh areas.[7] In hindsight, this final "phase" of withdrawal described by Rabin, which would involve withdrawing from the security zone back into Israel, would take the IDF and its allied SLA proxy militia on an eighteen-year odyssey in Lebanon and place the IDF in a political and military quagmire. According to an IDF military intelligence officer on the ground at the time, the IDF's strategic misunderstandings started early on as "from Hezbollah's inception, the IDF didn't understand Hezbollah at all and had major misunderstandings of the nature of the situation in Lebanon." By remaining in the security zone, "the IDF consolidated the necessary conditions for conflict with Hezbollah and gave Hezbollah the best possible political rationale it needed to exist and continue to fight us."[8] Israel's overall lack of strategic clarity was evident, as when COS Lt. Gen. Dan Shomron discussed the IDF's options regarding remaining in the security zone in 1988: "It would be better if we were not attacked from Lebanon. . . . Of all the alternatives we have, this one will be pursued, as I cannot see a better answer at the moment."[9]

THE EVOLUTION OF HEZBOLLAH IN THE 1980s

In the early 1980s, Hezbollah slowly solidified organizationally from amid the plethora of militant groups of all denominations that convulsed Lebanon during the civil war. Like-minded radical Shi'ite fighters coalesced from secular Palestinian militant groups, leftist militias, Shi'ite groups, and Iranian-linked groups to form Hezbollah, with its original support base in southern Lebanon and the Bekaa Valley. Hezbollah's guerrilla tactics in the 1980s were fairly ineffective, as the group was attempting to synthesize the various streams of knowledge and expertise that it had. Sec.-Gen. Hassan Nasrallah reflected that "at that stage, the Resistance did not pose a strategic threat or a threat to the very existence of the enemy entity at all. . . . [The Israelis] were yearning to stay, to occupy, and to consolidate the fait accompli, had it not been for the Resistance following 1985."[10]

Early on, Hezbollah militants were involved in the kidnappings of Western journalists, academics, and diplomatic staff in Lebanon, as well as IDF soldiers, which were relatively easy to do and did not require major organizational knowledge or learning processes, only needing basic reconnaissance and small arms.[11] Hezbollah was ideologically extreme and eventually expanded its kidnapping campaign and also carried out several highly publicized hijackings, terrorist attacks, and bombings. The kidnapping crisis throughout the 1980s was partially influenced by the broader regional conflict between Iran, Syria, and the West, as well as internal rivalries between Lebanese militant groups.[12]

Hezbollah pioneered suicide bombing in 1982, the use of which was justified theologically by leading Shi'ite religious ideologues such as Iran's Ayatollah Khomeini and Lebanon's Sayyid Mohammad Hussein Fadlallah. Hezbollah members were responsible for several notable attacks, including the November 1982 suicide bombing of an Israeli military government building in Tyre, which killed 91 (the first suicide attack for which Hezbollah officially claimed responsibility); the November 1983 suicide bombing of IDF headquarters in Tyre, which killed 60; the April 1983 suicide bombing of the American embassy in Beirut, which killed 63; and the nearly simultaneous October 1983 truck bombings of the US Marine Corps barracks in Beirut, which killed 241 US servicemen, and of the French army barracks, which killed 58 French soldiers.[13] The group was also linked to the 1984 abduction and murder of CIA station chief William Buckley, the 1985 skyjacking of TWA Flight 847, and the 1988 abduction and murder of Lt. Col. William Higgins, a US Marine serving as chief of a UN peacekeeping group in southern Lebanon.[14] According to Col. (Ret.) Reuven Erlich, at the time deputy head, Ministry of Defense (MOD) Coordinator for Lebanese Affairs, Hezbollah's utilization, with guidance from Iran, of suicide bombing against Western and Israeli targets was their "original innovation," which would soon be replicated by militant groups in Lebanon and globally.[15] Hezbollah's use of suicide bombing was based on clear cost-benefit calculations and was adopted because of early lessons learned of its propaganda value and its effectiveness in achieving both political and military goals.[16] Illustrating the calculated rationale for suicide bombing, Sayyid Fadlallah said in 1985, "We believe that suicide operations should only be carried out if they can bring about a political or military change in proportion to the passions that incite a person to make of his body an explosive bomb."[17] As they evolved in the early 1990s, Hezbollah would eventually move away from its strategic orientation as a clandestine militia using terrorist tactics and suicide bombings.

In its earliest years, Hezbollah was initially led by a cadre of key figures, most prominently the outspoken, hard-line Subhi Tufayli, hailing from the village of Brital in the Bekaa Valley, who would formally become Hezbollah's first secretary-general (1989–91). Hezbollah operated in a disjointed, slower-tempo manner in its early years, as the group was still organizationally solidifying and was hindered by the IDF's ability to easily counter routine security threats. Tufayli responded in a 1986 interview to a question seeking explanation for the low number of Hezbollah attacks in the mid-1980s, which was partially the result of the IDF's successful operations. He retorted, "On the contrary! The Resistance is calculating daily. If you mean there are no daily operations, it is because there is a pause between one operation and another, and that is the nature of military action. The Resistance is developing qualitatively faster than most people imagine."[18]

Hassan Nasrallah, the current secretary-general, reflected on Hezbollah's strategic posture in the 1980s: "A new phase started after 1985. It was when the popular resistance ended and the organized armed resistance began."[19] He said elsewhere, "We were a young movement wanting to resist a legendary army . . . despite the huge military and fighting imbalance of power between them." He described Hezbollah's earliest years, its campaign to mobilize the Shi'ite population, and its organizational solidification: "The main effort at the time went into mustering and attracting young men and setting up military camps where they could be trained and organized into small groups capable of carrying out resistance attacks against the occupying force. There were no institutions like now, no large organization or specialized departments."[20]

Hezbollah's ideological extremism was exhibited by its leadership's overt and fanatic commitment to Iran and Ayatollah Khomeini throughout the 1980s. Subhi Tufayli declared in a 1987 speech, "When Imam Khomeini speaks, others must keep silent. He orders us to struggle against America, Israel, the al-Saud family, and others, and we will obey," while Abbas Mussawi, a senior commander at the time, who would later succeed Tufayli as Hezbollah's second secretary-general, said of Khomeini that "he spells out the movement's line and issues directives of Hezbollah because he is the only spiritual chief capable of reflecting on any subject."[21]

Secretary-General Tufayli, known originally for his close ties with Iran, boasted of the military relations between Iran's Islamic Revolutionary Guard Corps (IRGC) and Hezbollah in the mid-1980s. Overtly confirming the IRGC's military support, he said, "Their role is to teach the young Lebanese the lessons of the Islamic Revolution and provide them with the military expertise they will need to fight Israel."[22] He said elsewhere, "To deny the Iranian aid issued to Lebanon's Hezbollah would be like denying that the sun provides light to the earth. Who can deny such a thing?"[23] Tufayli would frequently call for the dismantling of the Lebanese state and the establishment of an Islamic republic in Lebanon, another stance that Hezbollah would notably tone down later as part of a process of making the group more appealing to all Lebanese.[24]

To summarize Hezbollah's early development, according to longtime UNIFIL official Timur Goksel, who has been working in Lebanon since 1979: "Until 1988 they were very paranoid, very unkind to foreigners, too suspicious and secretive, impossible to talk to and communicate with, and extremely, unrealistically, fundamentalist. . . . They were very amateur, foolhardy in many ways, but very brave."[25]

Illustrating Hezbollah's awareness of its own shortcomings, after a successful kidnapping operation of two IDF soldiers from the security zone in February 1986, the IDF responded swiftly and temporarily reoccupied areas north of the zone to target Hezbollah militants in larger operations. Hassan Nasrallah, who was then a young military commander in the group, said that the IDF "wanted to teach us a lesson, namely, that anybody who even considers launching an operation against Israel would invite a violent response. This places many obstacles in the Resistance's path."[26]

Throughout the 1980s, the IDF still maintained tactical and operational superiority vis-à-vis Hezbollah. During this period, Hezbollah carried out large-scale (but ineffective) "hill-storming" operations, which entailed fighters openly charging the IDF's hilltop fortifications and were partially inspired by Iran's tactics during the Iran-Iraq War. An incident in February 1987—a frontal assault on IDF positions at Beaufort Castle in which Hezbollah was easily targeted by IDF forces and suffered eight casualties—exemplifies Hezbollah's ineffective early military strategies and tactics. Following this failed assault, the head of IDF Northern Command, Maj. Gen. Yossi Peled, said, "All indications show [Hezbollah] panicked and ran away, according to the large amount of arms and equipment found. It's clear that . . . painful failures, like this morning's, will bring about rethinking (by the guerrillas)."[27] General Peled's words proved to be ominously visionary.

According to Col. (Res.) Eitan Azani, the IDF Lebanon Division's senior intelligence officer at the time, Hezbollah's continued losses in these ineffective assaults pushed the group in 1987 to refine its tactics and move away from targeting IDF posts in large frontal ambushes, which sometimes involved fifty or more militants, toward an expansive antitank missile (ATM) and improvised explosive device (IED) campaign. He described a second "milestone" incident at Beaufort: "I recall it like it was yesterday—the milestone [April] 1987 attack near Beaufort Castle. After Hezbollah lost over eighteen fighters in the assault, Hezbollah made the decision that they are not yet fit to attack the IDF utilizing such bold tactics. This is a turning point, where Hezbollah starts to develop the capability of using ATMs instead of these direct ambushes."[28]

The April 1987 attack was a massive Hezbollah assault on two IDF positions in the central sector of the security zone, involving intensive rocket-propelled grenade and small-arms fire, which, according to the Hezbollah statement released on its clandestine radio station at the time, prevented the IDF from using attack helicopters against them.[29] However, despite these tactics, the assault was rebuffed by the IDF and resulted in serious Hezbollah casualties, the seizure of a significant amount of Hezbollah weapons, and no fatalities on the IDF side.[30]

This marked the point when Hezbollah began to move away from its "human-wave" attacks that involved storming IDF positions in the open, as well as larger, poorly coordinated assaults, where they were easily cut down by IDF troops positioned in defensive fortifications. In the late 1980s, senior UNIFIL official Timur Goksel described Hezbollah's activities: "There were twenty to thirty casualties a day for Hezbollah during these days, charging up a hill in a human-wave attack like the Iranians did during the Iran-Iraq War. The IDF was waiting for those kids. There was a lull for about six months, then a major change."[31]

The unsuccessful nature of Hezbollah's hill-storming led to a short-term increase in the tempo of suicide vehicle-bombings, which peaked in the late 1980s but whose use was generally curtailed by Hezbollah by the mid-1990s.[32] The suicide bombings were meant to vividly illustrate Hezbollah's strength and dispel the notion of an erosion of the group's capabilities amid clashes with rival Amal and the IDF and were also a result of differences with Iran regarding levels of support. From 1985, suicide vehicle-bombings became more widespread by all militant groups in Lebanon, though still rarely effective, with sixteen attempts in 1985 alone that were generally repelled by the IDF.[33]

Overall, according to IDF statistics, despite the short-term prevalence of suicide vehicle-bombings against IDF convoys, the tactic overwhelmingly favored by militants in Lebanon (Shi'ite and Palestinian) was roadside IEDs, with 178 IED attacks in 1988, compared to twenty-five infiltration attempts, twenty-three "clashes," and eighteen short-range rocket launchings.[34] Despite the increasing number of attacks, the IDF did not view any major changes in the threat from or capability of Hezbollah from 1987 to 1988, other than noting the marked decline in frontal assaults.[35] This was confirmed by statements by General Peled in an interview following another series of attacks by Hezbollah in mid-1987: "The situation is not deteriorating. . . . I do not see any change in the scope of the attacks on our troops in the area. I would like to emphasize that in almost all incidents in which Hezbollah squads were fired on, they quickly ran away."[36]

General Peled's statements reflect the thinking of the IDF more broadly, as the IDF still maintained operational and tactical superiority, despite the slowly increasing effectiveness of attacks by Hezbollah. In response, the IDF only made small-scale tactical adaptations to deal with the escalations. For example, in response to Hezbollah's increased use of suicide vehicle-bombs in the late 1980s, the IDF banned lone persons from driving cars in the security zone.[37] The IDF also improved the protective capability of its defensive fortifications in southern Lebanon in response to increased Hezbollah assaults in the summer of 1987, reflecting the IDF's passive and static mode of operation.[38] While the single-driver ban was at best partially effective, no major strategic reconsiderations were triggered in light of the IDF's military dominance overall.

In the mid-1980s, Hezbollah was developing its still modest abilities to operate in small teams and would target IDF troops by using primitive explosives.

They would carry out relatively unsophisticated ambushes with small arms, especially against lone vehicles, and launch rockets occasionally against Israeli border villages. But from 1989 to 1990, Hezbollah's strategic posture shifted, as it began operating a greater number of combat elements, including several thousand highly trained fighters carrying out more advanced guerrilla operations that included daytime and nighttime assaults. This was partially because of professional training from the IRGC, which involved explosive demolition, field intelligence, reconnaissance, and other military skills, as well as its own innate organizational learning.[39]

It is important to note that Hezbollah was largely preoccupied in the late 1980s with fighting rival Shi'ite militia Amal in what was known as the "War between Brothers."[40] During this time, Hezbollah's attacks against the IDF were still relatively ineffectual, as Secretary-General Tufayli explained in 1991: "The Resistance was affected by the fighting between Amal and Hezbollah over the last two years. Now, following resolution of the problems between ourselves and Amal, I believe the Resistance will be operating more effectively than it has before."[41]

In response to slowly increasing militant activity from Hezbollah (and Palestinian groups), the IDF launched in May 1988 a notable larger-scale operation against Hezbollah outside the security zone. While the majority of Operation Law and Order targeted Palestinian militias, the IDF also targeted the Hezbollah stronghold of Maydun on May 2, 1988, in a ten-hour assault involving hundreds of paratroopers, helicopters, artillery pieces, and tanks, resulting in forty Hezbollah killed and three IDF dead. The deputy IDF spokesperson at the time declared that the operation was meant "to enhance our deterrence in the ongoing struggle" since "we thought it's about time to issue that message . . . in order to deter Hezbollah from its creeping movement toward our border."[42] Gal Hirsch, a general during the 2006 war, reflected on his service as a company commander during the Maydun operation: "We were fighting in ditches and bunkers and in face-to-face combat inside houses. At some point, the penny finally dropped and we realized what was becoming evident as the battle's chronology unfolded. . . . It used to be a village once, but now it was a fortress, a citadel."[43]

The 1988 Maydun operation is important because it reflects the IDF's increased utilization of airpower and artillery beyond the security zone. It also acts as an early indicator of the incremental advancement of Hezbollah's urban warfare skills. It illustrates the group's proclivity to fight while embedded within the civilian population and its growing ability to develop fortifications and defenses in Lebanese villages—methods Hezbollah would perfect in ensuing decades.

Illustrating the importance of deterrence and the underlying goal of this operation, COS General Shomron, mentioning Hezbollah's forty casualties in Maydun, said, "These forty men will not come from any other outpost [to attack Israel] anymore. At the same time, the deterrence regarding other places will, no doubt, have a future effect as well."[44] Later in May 1988, the IDF targeted the Hezbollah stronghold in Luwayza, killing twenty fighters, which illustrated the IDF's increased entrenchment in southern Lebanon and highlighted its escalating response and willingness to confront Hezbollah in reactive, higher-tempo operations outside the security zone.[45]

Following a successful suicide car bombing in October 1988 by Hezbollah, the IDF responded with a number of air strikes against militant targets. An Israeli official said at the time, "The main purpose of the air raids was deterrence, to ensure that everyone in Lebanon gets the message that since a successful attack like the car bomb is likely to become a model for imitation."[46] Uri Lubrani, the MOD's longtime coordinator for Lebanese affairs, elaborated on the role of deterrence: "[IDF-initiated action] is an unavoidable method of deterrence. . . . We saved ourselves an erosion in our position vis-à-vis Hezbollah by initiating actions against them. . . . We send the air force on bombing raids deep into Lebanon not to show them that we exist, but as a deterrent and to interfere with various processes."[47]

However, such air strikes had a limited deterrent effect on Hezbollah's slowly growing capabilities, as Subhi Tufayli retorted, "What Israel could do is mount blitzkrieg operations or launch intimidation campaigns, but this does not frighten us. In fact, it would promote more friction with Israel, and so increase and expand the chances of fighting it."[48]

The IDF's willingness to engage Hezbollah outside the security zone with more intensive operations posed a challenge for the still young Hezbollah. Illustrating Hezbollah's difficulty in confronting the IDF's increasingly escalatory operations and Hezbollah's early reliance on Iran to operationally improve and adapt, Abbas Mussawi, a seasoned militant and cleric hailing from the Bekaa Valley, who succeeded Subhi Tufayli as secretary-general in 1991, said in an interview, "There has also been a great transformation—both qualitative and quantitative—in terms of Israel's threats against the Lebanese arena. Therefore, we and our brothers in the Islamic Republic [of Iran] conducted a comprehensive review of the need to bolster our oppressed arena in Lebanon, and we sensed from the brother officials in the Islamic Republic a growing realization of their responsibilities in this arena. . . . God willing, its practical results will provide conclusive confirmation of my words."[49]

HEZBOLLAH'S INNOVATIVE DEVELOPMENT IN THE EARLY 1990s

The "practical results" of Iranian assistance did lead to qualitative improvements in Hezbollah's military effectiveness. Throughout the early 1990s, while the number of Hezbollah attacks against IDF forces did not increase, the quality of the attacks and Israeli casualties did, partially owing to Hezbollah's new rigorous planning and training regimen, which emphasized careful preparation, sophisticated tactics, and better usage of terrain.[50] However, while Nasrallah is often credited for qualitatively improving the organizational capabilities of Hezbollah, this process of reform had been set in motion earlier by the second secretary-general, Abbas Mussawi, prior to his assassination in February 1992.

After Mussawi succeeded the more hard-line Subhi Tufayli as secretary-general in 1991, his short tenure was innovative and groundbreaking for Hezbollah. According to the IDF Lebanon Division's head intelligence officer, Mussawi enhanced Hezbollah's military apparatus: "In the late 1980s, Abbas Mussawi builds something new. . . . He organized the Islamic Resistance as a separate and specialized fighting force within Hezbollah. . . . Mussawi was in a unique role to carry out such changes, as he was part of the first course given by the Iranians in the Baalbek, and, based on these experiences, he designed further training courses and regimens for Hezbollah fighters."[51]

Such organizational adaptation was possible because of Hezbollah's new dominant role in Lebanon following its triumph over rival Amal and maintenance of its armed capabilities in contravention of the 1989 Taif Accord, which ended the civil war. This enabled Hezbollah to concentrate on strengthening its military posture against Israel. A profound insight from Col. (Res.) Giora Segal, a battalion commander in Lebanon in 1990, aptly sums up the development of Hezbollah: "After an organized Hezbollah assault on an IDF post in Nabatieh, we examined intelligence obtained from a militant, and I realize in hindsight that those were the first signs of Hezbollah's changing form. It was a window into their line of development, their ability to direct multifaceted assaults, and also their advanced command-and-control capabilities."[52]

Hassan Nasrallah reflected on Hezbollah's military evolution at this time and the ascension of Abbas Mussawi into a leadership position:

> At that stage, our leader, Sayyed Abbas Mussawi, who was a leading Hezbollah member from Baalbek, chose to head for southern Lebanon to manage operations. He used to supervise and take part in planning, be present in operation rooms, mourn martyrs, say farewell to mujahedeen, and move from town to town. . . . He sought to consecrate the organized and concentrated armed resistance system, giving this absolute priority in the culture, ideology, movement, performance, plans, programs, and behavior of Hezbollah, especially when he shouldered responsibility as Hezbollah's secretary-general. . . . This enabled the Resistance to develop in quality and quantity.[53]

In a decision made on February 16, 1992, in response to increased Hezbollah activity, the IAF targeted Sec.-Gen. Abbas Mussawi in an Apache helicopter strike, killing him as he traveled in his car in southern Lebanon. Highlighting the lackadaisical thinking in targeting Mussawi and an overall lack of strategic foresight on the implications of such a strike, Lt. Col. (Ret.) Roni Amir, former head of the IAF Doctrine Branch, revealed in an author interview that "when Mussawi was targeted, he wasn't actually supposed to be killed. The operation was just a rehearsal for the air force to see if we could actually target him, and then we saw the opportunity."[54]

Illustrating the improvised decision, in response to an interview question on the day of the Mussawi strike inquiring if the strike was planned, Defense Minister Moshe Arens responded to a reporter, "The attack was designed to strike Hezbollah. Presumably, the fact that he was killed was not entirely coincidental."[55] Arens later recalled that the IDF presented a short "window of opportunity" to target Mussawi: "The army came to me and said if you don't decide right now, we'll miss it. It was done under considerable pressure, and I didn't have too much time to consider it." The decision to carry out the assassination was made within a matter of hours, which allowed little time to consult intelligence assessments on repercussions of a strike or on Mussawi's possible successor. Arens lamented, "In retrospect, it is clear that one thing that was not considered was what would Hezbollah's reaction be— and Hezbollah's reaction was to blow up the Israeli embassy in Buenos Aries" in March 1992.[56]

Hezbollah deputy secretary-general Naim Qassem reflected on the IDF's incorrect assessment that assassinating Mussawi would damage Hezbollah:

> Israel, like many others in this world, thinks that the assassination of the first symbol and prominent leader will cause a state of panic and depression, which weakens the movement. But what they noticed is that Hezbollah is very different. Every time Hezbollah loses one of its leaders, it holds responsibility in a more comprehensive way and works on filling the gaps that occurred. . . . We have to prove to the enemy that we are more developed, more concerned, and stronger every time we give away martyrs who ascend to heaven.[57]

Echoing this in his eulogy for Abbas Mussawi in 1992, Hassan Nasrallah declared that the assassination marked "the beginning of a far-reaching spiritual, moral, and jihadist transformation that no one had expected, not even those who murdered him."[58] In another interview two weeks later, in response to claims that Hezbollah was organizationally damaged, Nasrallah said,

> Despite its intelligence capability, the Israeli enemy does not yet understand the truth about the makeup of Hezbollah or the nature of what it is facing. . . . So they thought: If we strike at Abbas Mussawi. . . . [it will lead to] further weakening and dividing Hezbollah. . . . Yet frankly, this caused only more alertness, stimulation, awareness, enthusiasm, unity, and cohesion around the

Resistance and animosity toward Israel than Sayyid Abbas al-Mussawi would have achieved in a lifetime![59]

On an author field trip to a Hezbollah site in southern Lebanon, one official informational sign described the evolution of the conflict in the early 1990s: "After the martyrdom of Sayyid Abbas [Mussawi] in 1992, a stage called 'the war of the brains' began between the Resistance and the Israeli army, requiring genius leadership that can administer the war, tactics, countertactics, new deterrence equations that can protect civilians, along with unprecedented weapons and techniques."[60] This "genius leadership" came with the ascension to secretary-general of Hassan Nasrallah, who promised "continuity of action" in the wake of Mussawi's assassination. Upon assuming leadership, he outlined Hezbollah's major objectives in a 1992 interview as "the creation of a state of popular awakening through acts of resistance" and the continuation of "a war of attrition against the enemy."[61] Nasrallah accelerated the process of strategic adaptation set in motion by Mussawi and noted, "we find that enemy Prime Minister Yitzhak Rabin, who always tries to appear as a strong, able man, is pressured by his society to do something."[62]

Describing Israel's slow adaptation to Hezbollah's increasing militant capabilities, Maj. Gen. Moshe Kaplinsky, commander of the Golani Brigade (1993–95), which was highly active in Lebanon, reflected, "We felt that the resistance had ended when the [Lebanese] Civil War ended [in 1989]. Then it started with an attack here and there, but we didn't change our attitude. We were too conservative. We slowly realized between 1990 and 1993 that we were facing a guerilla war. It took us too long to adjust our behavior."[63]

Nasrallah illustrated a shrewd understanding of this slow adjustment and adaptation within the IDF, the static strategic thinking, and the lack of creativity in Israel's Lebanon strategy, as he astutely said in a 1992 radio interview, "From what they say, we believe that Rabin and [Yitzhak] Shamir, Labor and Likud, are two sides of the same coin. There are no differences in the strategic constants, dreams, and aspirations. Consequently, we are not expecting anything new or any radical or drastic change in the Israeli policy. . . . Some aspects or forms of the tactics might change, but in the general framework, Israeli policy will remain as before."[64]

As secretary-general, Nasrallah continued the process of organizational adaptation started by Mussawi and embarked on an effort to improve operational security. UNIFIL official Timur Goksel described the changes:

Before Nasrallah took over, Hezbollah was taking many casualties needlessly because their field security was very weak and they had too many "cheerleaders" in Beirut who knew when they were going for an attack, so the Israelis also knew they were coming. When Nasrallah took over, within a year, he cut off the connection between the clergy in Beirut and the Resistance. He wanted a separate Resistance Command with three regions which will report directly to Nasrallah with no middle man.[65]

Goksel said elsewhere that Hezbollah, from 1991 onward, "mainly improved their field security. They had realized that they had allowed themselves in the past to become oversized, and if a guerilla organization is too big then it is easy to track. The military tactics used were of professional caliber. They include intelligence and reconnaissance. Their attacks had all the elements and ingredients of a military operation."[66] Describing their organizational adaptation and professionalization in the 1990s, Goksel observed, "If there was going to be a major operation, they would come to Beirut to talk beforehand with the command, not on the telephone. . . . We eventually stopped getting all those usual signals, with the bearded Hezbollah militants on motorcycles coming in from anywhere preceding an attack against the IDF."[67]

Coupled with efforts to improve Hezbollah's organizational security, to ensure loyalty Nasrallah (originally from southern Lebanon) replaced several military commanders from the Bekaa Valley deemed loyal to hard-line former secretary-general Tufayli, which completed the "formal" separation of Hezbollah's elite military apparatus from the rest of the group, especially pertinent after the assassination of Mussawi.[68] Hezbollah southern Lebanon official Sheikh Nabil Qawook summarized the group's military development throughout the 1990s:

> Hezbollah, on the military level, has taken massive steps forward from when it first started. When the invasion first took place we did not have the experts nor the experience that we do now. The Resistance today can boast of having specialized regiments each with its own particular weaponry. We now have an infantry, an engineering division, an artillery force, a general staff, a signals body, and the financial backing required to carry on. In other words we have all the ingredients of a regular army.[69]

In the period following the assassination of Mussawi, Hezbollah increased its rocket fire into northern Israel, and in response IDF Northern Command changed its targeting policy in a little-known but pivotal decision that set the stage for the establishment of the future deterrence equation between Israel and Hezbollah. According to Col. (Ret.) Ronen Cohen, based in Lebanon as an MI officer at the time, IDF Northern Command under Maj. Gen. Yitzhak Mordechai (1991–94) issued a change in late 1992 to its targeting policy whereby it loosened restrictions on when and where it could strike Hezbollah targets. The policy, code-named Joyous Festivals (Moadim L'Simcha), was a result of the IDF's relatively small target bank on the group. Mordechai had decided "to shoot whenever there was any piece of intelligence that pointed to Hezbollah," even if militants were operating near Lebanese villages.[70]

This change in IDF targeting policy in late 1992 led to a change in Hezbollah's own strategy and resulted in Hezbollah's greater firing of Katyusha rockets at the Israeli home front. Nasrallah reflected on the important lessons learned by Hezbollah after the Mussawi assassination and its use of rockets in a systematic manner: "The first time we concentrated our weapons on Israeli settlements was the day that the former secretary-general, Abbas Mussawi, was killed [February 16, 1992]. . . . After we launched the Katyushas on the [Israeli] settlements, we realized the enemy stopped their attacks on us, and from that day onward we understood the lessons that lay at the heart of the incident."[71]

In response to the flurry of rocket fire in the months after the Mussawi assassination, Maj. Gen. Yitzhak Mordechai, as head of Northern Command in 1992, described his rationale for the change to the IDF's targeting policy: "In the 'Katyusha days' after al-Mussawi, I proposed a certain plan to the chief of staff and the defense minister. The plan was endorsed and launched stage by stage. Following that, it only took a few days to put an end to the Katyushas. . . . Every operation must be examined for its potential to bring about change and for the direct and indirect damages we are liable to suffer."[72]

However, it appears that General Mordechai failed to heed his own warning regarding Hezbollah's response. While Hezbollah had consistently fired volleys of Katyushas since the earliest days of the conflict, they steadily increased such fire after the assassination of Mussawi and even more so after Mordechai's 1992 targeting policy change. This tit-for-tat exchange of firepower marks the origins of the deterrence equation that would evolve throughout the next decade. Colonel Cohen explained: "It was only after our change in policy that Hezbollah started firing rockets into Kiryat Shmona and Nahariya on a wider scale. . . . It was very general, but at this time Hezbollah first created the equation where if we hurt their innocents, they'll start shooting their Katyushas against us."[73]

CONCLUSION

From the early 1980s to 1992, the IDF conceptually viewed Hezbollah as a routine security threat that was easily dealt with in reactive, low-intensity operations. Dysfunctional strategic planning led to the "temporary" establishment of the security zone, as the IDF assumed a relatively static strategic orientation in Lebanon. Toward the end of the 1980s and the early 1990s, the IDF showed a willingness to launch short but higher-tempo operations meant to instill deterrence, but the IDF's overall focus remained on more pressing conventional threats elsewhere. In the wake of the trauma of the 1973 Yom

Kippur War, routine security was not a priority, and the IDF did not focus on it nor prepare for it. The limited threat posed by Hezbollah and the initial IDF tactical successes increased complacency and organizational inertia, which led Israel to downplay its entanglement in Lebanon. This highlights the common tendency of military organizations to avoid change until spurred to adapt by a pronounced rising threat.

Hezbollah underwent significant organizational growth in its first decade based on its bloody battlefield experiences, as its modus operandi evolved from ineffective hill-storming and unsuccessful large frontal assaults toward increased IED attacks, antitank ambushes, and suicide bombings. The IDF's assassination of Abbas Mussawi in 1992 and the subsequent change in IDF targeting policy elicited a strong reciprocal reaction from Hezbollah and accelerated the group's organizational learning processes, as it launched Katyusha rockets into northern Israel on a larger scale for the first time. The pivotal events of this period culminating in the 1992 clashes mark the origins of the mutual-deterrence equation that would emerge subsequently between Israel and Hezbollah in the second decade.

NOTES

Epigraphs: Rabin, speech, February 15, 1985; Nasrallah, interview, February 27, 1992.
1. For example, see Barak, interview, October 16, 1985.
2. Shomron, speech, March 9, 1988.
3. Author interview with Saar Raveh.
4. Author interview with Amos Granit.
5. Author interview with Giora Eiland.
6. Rabin, interview, April 3, 1985.
7. Yaniv, *Dilemmas of Israeli Security*, 279–84.
8. Author interview with Amos Granit.
9. Shomron, speech, March 9, 1988.
10. Nasrallah, speech, February 16, 2014.
11. Cragin, "Hizballah, the Party of God," 43.
12. Ranstorp, *Hizballah in Lebanon*.
13. Geraghty, *Peacekeepers at War*.
14. For background, see Levitt, *Hezbollah*.
15. Author interview with Reuven Erlich.
16. Ghrorayeb, *Hizbullah*, 127–33; Helmer, "Hezbollah's Employment of Suicide Bombing"; Alagha, *Hizbullah's Identity Construction*, 87–112.
17. Fadlallah, interview, December 16–22, 1985.
18. Tufayli, interview, December 4, 1986.
19. Nasrallah, speech, February 22, 2008.
20. Jaber, *Hezbollah*, 49–50, cited an undated interview with *Al-Safir* as the source of this quote. The quotes appear to actually be from Nasrallah, interview, *Nida al-Watan*, August 31, 1993. See Noe, *Voice of Hezbollah*, 127–28.

21. For example, see Tufayli, speech, September 4, 1987; Mussawi, interview, July 10, 1985.

22. Tufayli, interview, December 21–27, 1987.

23. Quoted in Jaber, *Hezbollah*, 150.

24. "Hizballah's Al-Tufayli Urges End to Republic," Radio Free Lebanon (clandestine), July 6, 1988, FBIS. For an example of Hezbollah's so-called rhetorical balancing related to Iran, see Nasrallah, speech, June 4, 2002.

25. Quoted in Jaber, *Hezbollah*, 28, 30.

26. Nasrallah, interview, March 11, 1986, 24.

27. Quoted in Nicolas Tatro, "Israeli Tanks, Helicopter Gunships, Big Guns Repel Guerilla Attack," Associated Press (hereafter AP), February 6, 1987.

28. Author interview with Eitan Azani.

29. For Hezbollah's statement following the raid, see "Islamic Resistance Statement," Voice of the Mountain (clandestine), April 18, 1987, FBIS.

30. For details of the specific assault, see "Hizballah Members Killed in Security Strip," Jerusalem Domestic Service, April 18, 1987, FBIS.

31. Author interview with Timur Goksel.

32. "New Tactic Adopted," Agence France-Press (hereafter AFP), October 19, 1988, FBIS.

33. Rabi and Teitelbaum, "Armed Operations," 127–28.

34. Ibid., 133, table 3.

35. For an overview, see Harris, "Lebanon" (1990), 639.

36. Peled, interview, June 18, 1987.

37. "New Tactic Adopted."

38. Shimon Weiss, "New Fortifications Reducing Terrorist Attacks," *Davar*, August 18, 1988, FBIS.

39. Eshel, "Armored Anti-Guerilla Combat in South Lebanon," 26.

40. For background, see Azani, *Hezbollah*, 76–82, 144–45; Norton, *Hezbollah*, 43–45.

41. Tufayli, interview, April 22, 1991.

42. Quoted in Dan Fisher, "3 Israelis, 40 Guerrillas Die in Lebanon Battle," *Los Angeles Times*, May 5, 1988.

43. Hirsch, "Urban Warfare," 26.

44. Shomron, interview, May 4, 1988.

45. Rabi and Teitelbaum, "Armed Operations," 125–26.

46. Ibid., 124, 128.

47. Lubrani, interview, October 5, 1988.

48. Tufayli, interview, June 15–21, 1987.

49. Mussawi, interview, September 6, 1991.

50. Peter Hirschberg, "Getting Smart," *Jerusalem Report*, December 17, 1992.

51. Author interview with Eitan Azani.

52. Author interview with Giora Segal.

53. Nasrallah, speech, February 22, 2008.

54. Author interview with Roni Amir.

55. Arens, interview, February 16, 1992.

56. Author interview with Moshe Arens.

57. Qassem, interview, February 12, 2010.

58. Nasrallah, speech, February 18, 1992, 54.

59. Nasrallah, interview, February 27, 1992.

60. Author observation on a field trip to the Hezbollah site in Mleeta, southern Lebanon, August 23, 2011.

61. Nasrallah, interview, November 14, 1992.

62. Ibid.

63. Quoted in Blanford, *Warriors of God*, 146.

64. Nasrallah, interview, June 25, 1992.

65. Author interview with Timur Goksel. See also David Rudge, "Hizballah Refines Its Terror Tactics," *Jerusalem Post*, November 13, 1987, FBIS.

66. Quoted in Jaber, *Hezbollah*, 37.

67. Author interview with Timur Goksel.

68. Magnus Ranstorp, "Hezbollah's Future: Part Two," *Jane's Intelligence Review*, February 1, 1995.

69. Quoted in Jaber, *Hezbollah*, 39.

70. Author interview with Ronen Cohen.

71. Nasrallah, interview, May 27, 2003.

72. Mordechai, interview, May 6, 1992.

73. Author interview with Ronen Cohen.

CHAPTER 2

DETERRENCE, GUERRILLA WARFARE, AND THE ESTABLISHMENT OF THE "RULES OF THE GAME" (1993–99)

The rules of the game used to be that we got bombarded, while the [Israeli] settlements remained safe. . . . But the Resistance imposed a new formula through the Katyusha.

—SEC.-GEN. HASSAN NASRALLAH

We must stop treating Hezbollah like a terrorist organization, and start fighting it the way a modern army fights guerillas.

—MAJ. GEN. AMIRAM LEVIN

DESPITE SOCIAL AND political euphoria that emerged in Israel with the launching of the Israeli-Palestinian peace process and the 1993 Oslo Accords, the IDF remained continuously engaged in clashes with Hezbollah in Lebanon in an effort to quell violence and secure quiet for Israel's northern communities. The 1990s can be classified as a period when the IDF operated with "one hand tied behind its back" because of calls for restraint and restrictions imposed by the Israeli political establishment for fear of jeopardizing the sensitive peace process. Political pressure ultimately led the military to limit its responses to Hezbollah's guerrilla activity in scope, size, and severity.[1] This dynamic forced the IDF to confine its responses to the technotactical realm since, barring a peace deal, it was unable to change the fundamental strategic considerations of the Lebanon conflict. The IDF remained overfocused on conventional threats, especially from Syria, deemed by Defense Minister Yitzhak Rabin in 1991 to be "the major threat today."[2] Furthermore, senior IDF generals were involved in the peace negotiations, which obfuscated the military's strategic and operational objectives and hindered IDF initiative, as the IDF attempted to contain Hezbollah's ongoing guerrilla warfare while it concurrently negotiated peace with Hezbollah's patron, Syria.

The IDF adapted its traditional deterrence policy to fit this strategic predicament in Lebanon, as it sought to avoid destabilizing peace negotiations while still intermittently launching operations meant to damage and deter Hezbollah. These "containment operations" had a limited effect and contributed to the IDF's entering into a tacit agreement with Hezbollah by establishing a set of understandings that defined the "rules of the game" between both sides. The origins and establishment of the rules of the game between Israel and Hezbollah were shaped by the senior Israeli political echelon's desire to reach a negotiated solution with Syria. In the mid-1990s, the military eventually pushed back against the restraint imposed by the political echelon and sought to regain the initiative by redefining the military's operational priorities in Lebanon, adapting its classification of Hezbollah from a terrorist group to a guerrilla threat, and creating a new counterguerrilla warfare unit to more effectively fight in Lebanon. In response to the IDF's strategic adaptation toward counterguerrilla warfare, Hezbollah adapted its mode of asymmetrical warfare and underwent a significant period of military refinement throughout the second decade.

1993: OPERATION ACCOUNTABILITY AND THE ESTABLISHMENT OF THE "JULY UNDERSTANDINGS"

Throughout the 1990s, Hezbollah's efforts to increase its organizational security began to bear fruit, which resulted in a slow increase in the number of attacks against the IDF. Following a Hezbollah attack that killed seven IDF soldiers in July 1993, the IDF launched its first large-scale operation of the decade, which lasted from July 25 to July 31 and involved massive air operations against Hezbollah. The IDF operated by intentionally shelling the outskirts of selected villages harboring Hezbollah militants, having issued warnings to residents through radio broadcasts and airdropped leaflets. This caused the temporary emptying of civilians from these villages, with the overall goal of targeting militants hiding in them (for operational aspects, see chapter 6). The head of Northern Command, Maj. Gen. Yitzhak Mordechai, said in a briefing during the operation that the underlying goal of the 1993 operation was to inflict "a heavy price" on Hezbollah by indirectly pressuring the Lebanese population, the Lebanese government ("those from whose territory it operates"), and Syria ("those backing it") to cease support for the group.[3]

Prime Minister Rabin declared Israel's "one and only goal of Operation Accountability: We intend to restore security to our northern citizens by hitting Hezbollah as severely as possible." He continued: "To do that, Israel will provoke an exodus of inhabitants from southern Lebanon toward the north, in order to put pressure on the Lebanese government and to hit those who collaborate with Hezbollah. . . . This affords freedom of action to fight the terrorists without harming civilians and in the wake of the operation gives an opportunity to the Lebanese government and its outside supporters [Syria] to rein in Hezbollah."[4]

However, highlighting the strategic folly of the IDF and the inefficacy of attempts to leverage the Lebanese population against Syria to pressure Hezbollah, Ambassador Dennis Ross, US chief Middle East peace negotiator at the time, reflected, "The [1993] Israeli campaign was based on a flawed assumption. [President Hafez al-]Asad did not care if the Lebanese were suffering; moreover, he was surely pleased by a situation that put the onus on Israel internationally. With 250,000 Lebanese streaming toward Beirut in a human caravan, Asad only saw gains, not losses, in such a situation; and militarily the Israelis could not stop the Katyusha rockets without occupying all of southern Lebanon."[5]

During the operation, Hezbollah fired hundreds of Katyushas into Israeli population centers, with the hope that it would restrain the IDF from carrying out further operations.[6] Amid the context of the secret Israeli-Syrian peace negotiations led by Ambassador Ross for the Golan Heights, an unwritten cease-fire with Hezbollah was agreed in July 1993, known as the July understandings, which was based on a tacit agreement between Israel and Syria. Ross described how "we forged a set of verbal understandings that civilians on each side of the border would not be targeted." While Syria would not commit to stopping Hezbollah attacks against the IDF, "the line was being drawn only on attacks against civilians by each side. . . . If Hizbollah would still be free to attack the IDF in Lebanon, Israeli forces would return fire against any source, even if the fire was coming from within villages. . . . When [Syrian foreign minister] Shara told us that President Asad accepted this point, we had a cease-fire agreement."[7]

During the 1993 operation, Secretary-General Nasrallah defiantly asserted how Hezbollah's use of rocket fire was successfully deterring Israel: "Hezbollah is now even more convinced of the rightfulness of its policies, options, resistance, and methods," and he proclaimed that "we must use a method that can deter a murderous, treacherous enemy."[8] Hezbollah's deputy head of the politburo, Ammar Musawi, elaborated on the group's calculus and outlined the nature of the tacit understandings at the time: "The resistance only fires Katyusha rockets when civilian homes and property in southern Lebanon are exposed to Israeli shelling. In such cases, we find that we have the right to respond against aggression and that our acts are not condemnable."[9]

In a 1993 interview, Nasrallah described the emergence of an equation of mutual deterrence and retaliation, which contributed to the IDF's willingness to agree to the rules of the game: "The Katyusha bombardment has led to a new formula based on mutual forced displacement, mutual destruction, and equal terror. This formula was imposed by the Katyusha. . . . The rules of the game used to be that we got bombarded, while the [Israeli] settlements remained safe. . . . But the resistance imposed a new formula through the Katyusha."[10]

Following the 1993 operation, accusations emerged within the IDF that the army was being restricted from operating effectively against Hezbollah by the political echelon because of the ongoing peace process. In an interview at the time, COS Lt. Gen. Ehud Barak rebuffed these accusations but highlighted the complex underlying strategic and political dynamic: "The army's hands are not tied. It can initiate action as it sees fit, but the reality in southern Lebanon is not simple. . . . There are the understandings resulting from Operation Accountability, although they do not restrict us, that are designed to serve a more far-reaching aim than that of a platoon commander who wants to carry out some operation. There always were, still are, and always will be overall policy considerations."[11]

Aptly summing up the absurd predicament at the time, Rehavam Zeevi, a senior opposition member of Parliament (MP), said in a speech to the Knesset following the 1993 Operation Accountability, "When Hezbollah operatives renewed their terrorist attacks in the security zone, the IDF barely reacted, at the government's request, so as not to kill the joy of the understandings. . . . To a great extent, Syria is responsible for Hezbollah operations. . . . But Syria enjoys the fact that Hezbollah continues to attack Israel, to destroy, and to maim; and the Jews continue to come to peace talks with them."[12]

The rules of the game failed to stop Hezbollah's operational activity, and the IDF's slow-tempo, disjointed operations in Northern Command under General Mordechai were proving inadequate and slowly demoralizing soldiers in the field.[13]

A NEW HEAD OF NORTHERN COMMAND AND A SHIFT TOWARD COUNTERGUERRILLA WARFARE

With the appointment of Maj. Gen. Amiram Levin as the new head of Northern Command (1994–98), the IDF began to push back against the restrictions imposed by the political establishment and sought to turn the tide back in favor of the IDF. General Levin, well known for his earlier service as a bold commander of an elite special forces unit, replaced Mordechai (who became defense minister in 1996). Levin attempted to reinstill a sense of initiative in the IDF and moved it away from slower-tempo, defensive operations that had occurred during the tenure of his predecessors in Lebanon.[14] He declared after his appointment that "we will have to take the initiative in the war against Hezbollah, attack the terrorists and beat them."[15] This new policy of "initiative" was in response to Hezbollah's increasing number of operations over previous years: Hezbollah carried out 19 attacks against the IDF and SLA in 1990, 52 in 1991, 63 in 1992, 158 in 1993 (not including Operation Accountability), and 187 in 1994 and would carry out 344 in 1995, while IDF casualties slowly rose, with 13 Israelis killed in 1992, 12 in 1993, 21 in 1994, and 23 in 1995.[16]

Owing to the rise in IDF casualties, soldiers began to realize that they lacked the tactical knowledge and operational understanding to effectively confront Hezbollah on the treacherous and geographically difficult Lebanese battlefield. A conceptual shift was triggered in Northern Command "from the bottom up" after numerous subordinate officers influenced General Levin, who, according to soldiers on the ground at the time, was deemed more approachable and in touch with events occurring day to day "at the bottom" than his predecessor. General Levin was also seen as more flexible in his command style, while General Mordechai was perceived by soldiers to be overly rule-bound and more rigid in his command style. An IDF major stationed in Lebanon at this time reflected on his impressions: "General Mordechai looked out of touch, even regarding the small stuff. . . . The army pays a lot of attention to how we carried our weapons: to cover the chain so it doesn't shine at night, never go with the Galil [Israeli-made rifle] with the handle closed, always open. But Mordechai had his handle closed on his Galil, and his weapon wasn't well attended. Every time he came to visit our base, he looked out of it."[17]

Soldiers at this time recalled a situation that was "disappointingly routine," with long periods of boredom and an overemphasis on predictable and monotonous security operations with "no serious effects of learning."[18] General Levin's proclamation to shift the IDF's strategic orientation elicited concerns from soldiers in Lebanon related to the limitations of their tactical know-how to confront Hezbollah, which had a transformative effect on his thinking.

A charismatic, visionary officer, General Levin refocused the IDF in Lebanon by relabeling Hezbollah a "guerrilla army," as opposed to a "terrorist group," and opting for a more offensive approach through the use of a specialized commando unit that would master the necessary tactics to bring the rest of the army up to speed regarding counterguerrilla warfare.[19] The IDF's posture in Lebanon until Levin's appointment had ceded the initiative to Hezbollah, forcing the IDF into an attritional paradigm in which it was forced to absorb Hezbollah strikes amid floundering negotiations with Syria.[20] Under Levin's tenure, the IDF gradually understood its mischaracterization of the nature of Hezbollah and reclassified its approach. Levin said in a briefing to Israeli politicians touring southern Lebanon in 1995: "We must realize we are fighting against a political organization with a military arm that conducts guerrilla warfare, not terrorism. We must stop treating Hezbollah like a terrorist organization and start fighting it the way a modern army fights guerrillas. . . . Our goal is to win every battle and inflict as many casualties as possible."[21]

General Levin's statements reflected the IDF's belated understanding that Hezbollah should no longer be characterized as a low-intensity, "Palestinian-type" terrorist threat but rather as a sophisticated enemy utilizing a distinct form of guerrilla warfare, which marked a major conceptual adaptation. However, by Levin promising to "win every battle," it also highlights the fundamentally flawed approach of the IDF by attempting to "accumulate" tactical victories that would hopefully amount to some sort of eventual strategic triumph. Crucially, the framing of the conflict's objectives in this manner predestined the IDF for failure, since tactical achievements were never correlated with broader strategic objectives. It was never clearly outlined how IDF tactical successes could contribute to a resolution of the Lebanon conflict while it was still occupying southern Lebanon, other than to buy time for the politicians engaged in negotiations with Syria. Because of the framing of the conflict in this manner, inevitable tactical losses deeply reverberated on the strategic level.

The increasingly damaging attacks and rising threat of Hezbollah, coupled with growing pressure on General Levin, which emerged in the IDF from the bottom up, triggered the creation of a counterguerrilla warfare unit to train and carry out operations specifically against Hezbollah. The Egoz Reconnaissance Battalion, part of the Golani Brigade, was launched in early 1995 and marked an operational- and tactical-level response to the strategic problem related to the IDF presence in Lebanon. Maj. Gen. Moshe Kaplinsky, commander of the Golani Brigade at the time, later discussed the tactical necessities and speed required when forming the unit: "[COS Lt. Gen. Amnon] Shahak called me and said, 'You've got three months to build a special unit.' We took soldiers from all infantry units with good commanders, people with open minds. We trained them in completely new tactics and in areas that resemble southern Lebanon."[22]

Partially as a result of the IDF's flexible command style, the unit was operationalized within five months and achieved significant results on the battlefield. Brig. Gen. Moshe "Chico" Tamir, a commander of the Egoz unit, credited the COS at this time, Lt. Gen. Amnon Lipkin-Shahak, with "changing the fundamental assumption of the entire army" by empowering General Levin and declaring the conflict in Lebanon "a war and not a routine security deployment."[23] According to Brig. Gen. (Ret.) Shlomo Brom, head of the IDF Strategic Planning Division at the time, the reconceptualization of the threat toward counterguerrilla warfare "hit the margins of the army. The establishment of Egoz was the beginning of the process of change, when we started to understand that we must have specialized specific units who are specialized in this kind of fighting."[24]

The Egoz was designed as a secret reconnaissance unit that mastered sophisticated concealment and camouflage techniques; intelligence-collection and surveillance methods; bush, forest, and mountain warfare; close-range fighting tactics; and the ability to carry out operations deep inside Lebanese territory without the need for resupply. The unit was able to synchronize its operations with attack helicopters and had the ability to rapidly liaise with air support.[25] The Egoz had a significant amount of operational autonomy to rapidly launch operations against Hezbollah and was innovative because of its self-sufficiency and ability to remain embedded in southern Lebanon under deep cover for weeks at a time.[26] The unit's emphasis on initiative and offensive operations marked a major adaptation to the IDF's prior static approach in Lebanon. In a representative operation in October 1995, camouflaged Egoz commandos in southern Lebanon staked out a known guerrilla route for days and eventually ambushed and neutralized Hezbollah cells in the area.[27]

Command of the unit was delegated to free-thinking, battle-hardened maverick officers who were granted broad autonomy to develop new and innovative counterguerrilla tactics, especially related to stealth operations and raiding.[28] The Egoz mastered best practices for operating behind enemy lines in the bushy Lebanese terrain, which eventually affected standard operating procedures of combat units in Lebanon and also influenced doctrine and the IDF's conceptual understanding of Hezbollah. General Levin's command style also fostered a brief period of increased operational risk-taking by the IDF, as it emboldened creative officers with close personal ties to Levin, such as Brig. Gen. Erez Gerstein, a future commander of the Lebanon Liaison Unit, to undertake his own innovative efforts to combat Hezbollah.[29] After several years of a "balancing" of the casualty ratio between the IDF and Hezbollah, the casualty ratio improved in the IDF's favor in the late 1990s, partially because of the tactical innovation of the Egoz unit.[30]

The Egoz's innovations were partially institutionalized since Egoz officers had a significant role in infantry field-craft training at the IDF's counterguerrilla warfare school at Elyakim and also assisted in developing counterguerrilla doctrine.[31] Battle-proven tactics refined by the Egoz were diffused horizontally to units operating in Lebanon, particularly in the fields of tactical reconnaissance, surveillance, and bush warfare. The creation of a specialized commando unit like the Egoz that was granted operational autonomy to develop innovative solutions to solve the IDF's specific battlefield predicaments represents a unique IDF method of learning and adaptation.[32] Notably, the IDF's specialized commando units often act as incubators of military innovation and pivotal mechanisms for driving adaptation and disseminating lessons learned.[33] According to Col. (Ret.) Ronen Cohen, a senior intelligence officer in Lebanon during this time:

> The Egoz was the spotlight leading the ship. General Levin came from the special forces, and he looked at our soldiers and saw how heavy and slow we were; we were clumsy like an elephant.... The spirit was from General Levin, and I think the Egoz was a good example for all the regular battalions how to

act in the field over long periods of time, over far distances, while operating with light equipment, and the Egoz succeeded at that time.[34]

The unit's primary task was initiating "pinpoint operations" against Hezbollah bases outside the security zone, as commandos launched "deep operations" into Lebanon to ambush and pin down Hezbollah fighters who were then targeted with attack helicopters.[35] While these raids were meant to embolden the IDF to regain initiative, they were also meant to limit IDF casualties elsewhere in Lebanon since the raids were carried out predominantly by elite commandos. Owing to the relative success of the pinpoint operations, General Levin asserted at the time that there was a slight drop in Hezbollah attacks over the succeeding months. However, the drop in attacks against the IDF was marked by a rise in attacks against the SLA.[36]

Despite General Levin's bold drive to regain the initiative, there remained an underlying lack of political will for more aggressive operations and a not-so-subtle dispute between the military and civilian echelons. Prime Minister Rabin said, upon Levin's appointment, "There is no clear target for action in south Lebanon, and sometimes the price of such operations is very high. . . . Whoever thinks he has a miracle solution for tackling the situation is mistaken."[37] More hesitancy emerged from Brig. Gen. (Ret.) Benjamin Ben-Eliezer, a senior government minister, who ominously warned, "When it's said that we must go on the offensive, there is another consideration which must be taken into account: What is the price that the residents living here [in northern Israel] will pay?"[38]

While COS Lt. Gen. Ehud Barak asserted at the time that there was no dispute, Rabin openly reprimanded General Levin on numerous occasions, being quoted as demanding that Levin "tone down his reactions and remarks against Hezbollah" amid the Syrian peace process.[39] Rabin's comments came after Levin was quoted on the record declaring that the IDF "will not hold back regarding events in south Lebanon." According to an Israeli government source at the time, Rabin "did not like the general's statements, to say the least, and this is why Rabin talked to him," ordering him to "simply shut up, make no remarks, and not make the situation even worse with his words."[40]

Despite the reluctance of Rabin and the majority of the political leadership to allow more assertive IDF operations because of constraints from the peace process and fears of a lack of public support, a 1994 public opinion poll reported that eight out of ten Israelis supported the IDF's new plan for "military initiative," with 83 percent in favor and only 11 percent against.[41]

Illustrating the dueling dialogue between Israel and Hezbollah, in response to the threats by General Levin and the increased initiative and operational tempo of the IDF, Hezbollah MP Mohammad Raad taunted Israel at the time, saying that since Hezbollah is always on alert for Israeli attacks, the IDF "will not have the initiative, not now, not in the future! The initiative will continue to be in the hands of the Resistance as long as our land is occupied."[42] Hezbollah southern commander Sheikh Nabil Qawook declared that Hezbollah was "mobilized and ready for any eventuality to foil Israeli attempts to change the situation in south Lebanon."[43] Mohammad Hussein Fadlallah, a Hezbollah ideologue, discussed Israel's announcement of the Egoz unit in December 1996: "The talk of the Zionists about a new elite unit is just a new media exercise, following the successful activities of the Islamic Resistance which have shown the Israeli soldier as a miserable coward crying for help, and as one to whom all the military means at his disposal are ineffectual. . . . They are waging psychological warfare against us, while also trying to raise the morale of the Jews."[44]

Hezbollah was not intimidated by General Levin's threats to regain the initiative and was seemingly well aware of Prime Minister Rabin's unsupportive statements for a larger campaign, reflected by Hezbollah deputy secretary-general Naim Qassem's assessment at the time: "Israeli strikes against specific targets are always in the cards. A full-blown attack, however, appears to be less likely in the present circumstances. Furthermore, the confusion Israel is facing in occupied Palestine as it tries to cope with the intifadah and the painful blows dealt by the Palestinian resistance are hardly the kind of conditions under which it would be opportune to take such action. . . . We therefore expect Israeli attacks on a limited scale."[45]

Throughout the 1990s, General Levin sought to establish greater legitimacy for launching immediate reprisal operations in response to Hezbollah provocations, which would theoretically bolster IDF deterrence, with the overall goal to achieve quiet on the border. Levin said in June 1995, "It must be made clear to them in words and in deeds, that attacks on our population will not be tolerated and that if they do not stop them on their own volition, we will have to do it—and we will."[46] Amid these threats, Hajj Hussein al-Khalil, political assistant to Secretary-General Nasrallah, highlighted Hezbollah's own use of deterrence against Israel in a November 1995 interview and the combustible deterrence equation that developed between both sides throughout the second decade: "The Syrians will ask the Americans during the contacts between the two sides to tell the Israelis to comply with the July [1993] understanding and halt the attacks. . . . The Katyusha rockets are a clear signal to the Israelis, namely: Do not forget that there are rules and the July understanding! You are required to return to it!"[47]

1996: OPERATION GRAPES OF WRATH AND THE "APRIL UNDERSTANDINGS"

The IDF's attempt to regain initiative in Lebanon was complemented by the launching of Operation Grapes of Wrath, which erupted on April 11, 1996, in response to ongoing tit-for-tat violence between the IDF and Hezbollah and lasted until April 27. Amid the peace process with Syria, President Hafez al-Assad was excluded from a high-level diplomatic conference in Sharm el-Sheikh that involved Arab and Israeli leaders, and, as Dennis Ross wrote, the Hezbollah escalation "was as if Asad was showing us the consequences of acting without him," highlighting the complex international dynamic that is often overlooked.[48] In 1996, Prime Minister Shimon Peres sought a negotiated solution with Syria, which would have led to implementation of a full cease-fire between Israel and Hezbollah. The deal would have protected IDF troops in Lebanon during a nine-month "trial period," to be proceeded by a complete Israeli withdrawal.[49] According to Israel's chief negotiator with Syria, after Israel came to the conclusion that Syria was "stoking the fire" in southern Lebanon, it sought to punish Syria for this violation of the July 1993 understandings.[50] According to Ambassador Ross, the 1996 operation occurred because "Israeli patience had run out."[51]

Brig. Gen. (Ret.) Shlomo Brom, head of the Strategic Planning Division during this period, reflected on the IDF's strategy and the convoluted application of Israel's deterrence policy in 1996: "We wanted to put a 'lever' on Hezbollah. The lever was the Lebanese government at the time. We didn't think we could deter Hezbollah, but we thought we could deter the Lebanese and Syrian government to stop Hezbollah."[52]

Highlighting the fallacy of the preexisting July 1993 understandings, on the second day of the 1996 operation General Levin scaled back the objectives, stating, "I think all those who tried to promise quiet periods were wrong and misled the people. I will not risk making any forecasts. A lull is our objective, but I cannot promise that we will achieve months or weeks of quiet."[53]

During the 1996 operation, a little-known rift emerged between senior IDF commanders and the political echelon. Army officers bristled at the relative restraint imposed on the IDF, which they believed hindered its ability to adequately respond to Hezbollah's provocations. Brig. Gen. Giora Inbar, commander of the Lebanon Liaison Unit, said in a highly publicized radio interview, "We do not permit a situation in which Peres should suddenly stop us before we have completed our operation. The understandings that will be obtained at the end of the operation must include [quiet in] the security zone as well."[54] Another IDF source said at the time, "What we want, what is desirable is that Hezbollah gives up totally, for at least a long period of time, any activity in the south so peace talks [with Syria] can proceed without being interrupted every two days or two weeks. . . . You can't talk to someone who is killing you."[55] However, illustrating the complex political dynamic and the restraint imposed on the IDF, COS General Lipkin-Shahak openly called General Inbar's remarks "stupid and unnecessary," and Inbar was quickly forced to apologize publicly.[56]

Despite the IDF's high-intensity operation, Hezbollah rocket fire continued. After sixteen days of fighting, a written cease-fire agreement (which formalized the tacit July 1993 understandings) was brokered by Ambassador Ross and agreed on by Israel, Syria, and Hezbollah that appeared as follows:

1. Armed groups in Lebanon will not carry out attacks by Katyusha rockets or by any kind of weapon into Israel.
2. Israel and those cooperating with it will not fire any kind of weapon at civilians or civilian targets in Lebanon.
3. Beyond this, the two parties commit to ensuring that under no circumstances will civilians be the target of attack, and that civilian populated areas and industrial and electrical installations will not be used as launching grounds for attacks.
4. Without violating this understanding, nothing herein shall preclude any party from exercising the right of self-defense.[57]

The agreement was fundamentally lopsided because it legitimated Hezbollah violence against IDF soldiers based in Lebanon while hindering the IDF's response against Hezbollah targets enmeshed among southern Lebanese villages. Regarding the thinking behind the April 1996 understandings, General Brom explained:

We cannot achieve a level of deterrence to lead Hezbollah to accept that part of southern Lebanon will be occupied by Israel. If that's the case, the interest of the IDF is to take the civilian populations of both sides outside the equation. So the fighting would be between the two military forces so that it's something you can live with, it's bearable, but we underestimated the effect it had on Israeli public opinion.[58]

The paradox that the Israeli government was negotiating with Syria while IDF troops were concurrently being killed by Hezbollah with Syrian support slowly eroded Israeli society's support for negotiations and for the IDF's presence in Lebanon. Regarding the notion that this framework could restore deterrence, one retired IDF colonel reflected, "This wasn't deterrence—it was a poor agreement. If we target rocket launchers of Hezbollah in civilian areas, then Hezbollah was free to fire onto Israeli civilian areas. It was an asymmetric situation bound to fail."[59] The April 1996 understandings also established the Israel-Lebanon Monitoring Group under UN auspices, which provided a mechanism for Israel, Lebanon, and Syria to communicate and monitor implementation of the agreement. With US and French mediation, Israeli, Lebanese, and Syrian officials sat at the same table in a UN facility in the southern Lebanese town of Naqoura to discuss violations of the understandings.[60] While the monitoring group was relatively effective in preventing further large-scale outbreaks of violence during the four years it met, it could not contain the grinding day-to-day violence against IDF soldiers in Lebanon.

Despite the failure of the April 1996 understandings to halt Hezbollah guerrilla activity against the IDF in Lebanon, Israel still clung to the rules of the game in some vain hope that abiding by them would cause Hezbollah to limit its attack against the Israeli home front. General Levin said after another deadly Hezbollah attack in 1997, "I hope and advise Hezbollah not to lose its senses and to uphold the agreement of understandings, just as the State of Israel adheres to these understandings. We do everything in our power not to harm civilians, and I hope and advise Hezbollah not to make the mistake of trying to harm Israeli civilians."[61]

From Hezbollah's perspective, Deputy Sec.-Gen. Naim Qassem explained why the group targeted the Israeli home front in violation of the understandings: "The formula of hurting the enemy through direct targeting of Israeli soldiers was proving insufficient to deter Israeli targeting of Lebanese civilian targets. As such, direct bombardment of Israeli civilian areas was a reaction, a reciprocal to what was initiated by the Israeli army. These measures helped achieve the July 1993 Accord and thereafter the April 1996 Accord."[62]

Nawaf Moussawi, Hezbollah's international relations director, explained the mutual deterrence balance and shed light on Hezbollah's perceptions at this time. He said that in the early 1990s, Hezbollah decided that it "needed to harm enemy civilians to achieve a better balance," claiming that Israel agreed to the July 1993 understandings with Hezbollah only "when Israelis sensed we are able to harm their civilians." According to Moussawi, IDF violations of the 1993 understandings forced Hezbollah to "retaliate" against the Israeli home front in 1996, which led to the "excellent" April 1996 understandings.[63] Hassan Nasrallah reflected on this policy: "The April understanding was able to impose an equation of protecting the people especially in southern Lebanon, since attacking southern Lebanon would yield attacks on Israeli settlements."[64]

The strategic folly of IDF policy in the 1990s is evident, as instead of successfully pressuring the Lebanese population to pressure Syria to curtail Hezbollah, the operations actually brought Hezbollah increased popular support.[65] Hezbollah southern commander Nabil Qawook noted, "This has really disturbed the Israelis whose politicians and prime minister have publicly stated on several occasions that no matter how much they have threatened Hezbollah, they have only succeeded in rallying further support for it, even when they have used the policy of purposely attacking civilians in a bid to turn them against the group."[66]

As the conflict progressed, Ambassador Ross reflected on "Syria's real agenda of preserving its control of Lebanon and its ability to use Lebanese-based attacks as a lever on Israel," since "Asad would not let Israel live easily in Lebanon so long as the Golan Heights remained occupied. This was his pressure point on Israel."[67] Despite this apparent dynamic, according to an IDF military intelligence officer active at the time, the IDF carried out only "a small degree of strategic learning" in the 1990s regarding a new way to apply force since "the 1993 and 1996 operations against Hezbollah used the same strategic and operational rationale . . . and showed that the IDF cannot change the basic terms of the conflict if we remain in the security zone."[68] As the second decade of conflict progressed and the IDF remained bogged down in the security zone, Hezbollah refined its own strategy and adapted its modus operandi vis-à-vis Israel.

THE LATE 1990s: A SHIFT IN HEZBOLLAH'S GUERRILLA WARFARE

An oft-cited Hezbollah doctrinal document surfaced in 1996 allegedly belonging Hajj Khalil Harb, Hezbollah's head of military operations in southern Lebanon, which outlined Hezbollah's "13 principles of warfare" for its fighters in the field. The document, purportedly captured by IDF MI, has been used to illustrate Hezbollah's adherence militarily to "classical" guerrilla principles:

1. Avoid the strong, attack the weak—attack and withdraw!
2. Protecting our fighters is more important than causing enemy casualties!
3. Strike only when success is assured!
4. Surprise is essential to success. If you are spotted, you've failed!
5. Don't get into a set-piece battle. Slip away like smoke, before the enemy can drive home his advantage!
6. Attaining the goal demands patience, in order to discover the enemy's weak points!
7. Keep moving, avoid formation of a front line!
8. Keep the enemy on constant alert, at the front and in the rear!
9. The road to the great victory passes through thousands of small victories!
10. Keep up the morale of the fighters, avoid notions of the enemy's superiority!
11. The media has innumerable guns, whose hits are like bullets. Use them in the battle!
12. The population is a treasure—nurture it!
13. Hurt the enemy, and then stop before he abandons restraint![69]

Curiously, the same principles reappeared again in a revised form (and different order) in Hebrew in an IDF doctrinal monograph on asymmetrical warfare in 1999, but the ninth principle above was replaced with "Learning from your mistakes is the drug of life. Without it, you can't fix your ways."[70] This document has been adopted by scholars and journalists as proof of Hezbollah's adherence to guerrilla warfare principles and was even replicated recently in British Army operations doctrine.[71] However, the veracity of this Hezbollah document is highly doubted; in author interviews with senior intelligence officers who served in Lebanon at this time, no intelligence officer recalled any similar Hezbollah doctrinal document. According to an officer formerly of the IDF History Department, the document was actually crafted by IDF MI's Research Department as a representation of how the IDF thought Hezbollah would fight, highlighting the IDF's conceptual understanding of Hezbollah, rather than how Hezbollah viewed itself. In fact, only the first six principles were directly based on Hezbollah's modus operandi, while the remaining principles were copied by IDF intelligence officers from the Hebrew-translation of Mao Tse Tung's *On Guerilla Warfare* because that was how the IDF thought Hezbollah would operate.[72] Rather than definitively proving Hezbollah's subscription to a specific military paradigm, the publication of these guerrilla principles in both open sources (in 1996) and in an internal IDF doctrinal document (in 1999) illustrates that by 1996 the IDF clearly conceptually viewed Hezbollah along the lines of a classical guerrilla adversary.

However, this classification by the IDF of Hezbollah as a guerrilla force was belated, as Hezbollah's military paradigm continued to evolve throughout the decade. By the time the IDF conceptually adapted and reclassified Hezbollah as a guerrilla force in the late 1990s, Hezbollah had already adapted its warfighting concept and enhanced its fighting capability further. An IDF officer with a long career in Northern Command summarized the fundamental misunderstanding in the IDF regarding conceptualizing Hezbollah's military evolution:

> We called Hezbollah a guerrilla organization, but they're not. At this point, by the late 1990s, Hezbollah was already a regular army that specialized in guerrilla tactics. . . . When the IDF called them terrorists, they were guerrillas. And when the IDF called them guerrillas, they were already commandos. . . . Hezbollah used the same techniques the IDF used. Hezbollah understood that if they use their "regular" troops in mass assaults [as they did in the 1980s] in constant wear and tear against the IDF, they'd continue to be massacred. So they built up an elite commando unit. . . . They realized they needed to be a professional army, a regular army, and they built one up.[73]

Hezbollah's evolutionary military advancement from a terrorist militia to a guerrilla army to a commando force can be illustrated over the long term by Hezbollah's dramatically increasing operational activity against Israel since the beginning of the decade. Hezbollah released an end-of-year statement on its television station, Al-Manar, in 1996, accompanied by a host of statistics that laid out its accomplishments over the year, which included launching more than 750 attacks. The statement declared that Hezbollah lost forty-seven fighters, killed twenty-nine IDF soldiers, destroyed four tanks, and carried out seventy-five roadside bomb attacks, 135 assaults on IDF/SLA positions, sixty-five ambushes on convoys, two suicide-bombings, and hundreds of short-range rocket attacks.[74] Notably, as Hezbollah militarily adapted, this upward trend continued as Hezbollah operations rose further from 715 in 1997 to 1,200 in 1998.[75]

After a long period in the 1990s when Hezbollah had been targeting the IDF with direct confrontations, ambushes, and bombing attacks, from 1997 onward Hezbollah generally resorted to operations that were more effective in hitting the IDF from a distance but that were also less dangerous for Hezbollah to carry out. Hezbollah increased the rate of attacks, especially mortar fire and low-signature operations involving small commando units that did not require major face-to-face confrontation. The IDF would generally respond with artillery strikes at Hezbollah areas rather than launch significant ground operations that might incur IDF casualties. Despite the increased operational initiative under General Levin, the IDF's reconceptualization of Hezbollah as a guerrilla threat was late, as Hezbollah had already evolved and was operating as a commando force. In response to Hezbollah's indirect operations, the IDF's operational tempo slowed as troops assumed an increasingly defensive posture in the face of political and domestic pressures.

A Hezbollah militant described the group's modus operandi in the late 1990s:

> We resort mainly to roadside bombs, but also launch attacks in small groups. . . . Most of our casualties come after the operation, when Israel aims artillery barrages at us as we retreat, or sends its airplanes after us. . . . We move in small groups. Sometimes we stay for several days in the occupied zone waiting for the target. They move in big convoys, and are easier to target and hit.[76]

General Levin discussed in 1996 the strategic changes made by Hezbollah, observing that they were seeking to target the IDF indirectly and from longer distances: "Hezbollah has been under pressure. . . . It is now trying again to fire from a distance. We will have to address this problem as well."[77] According to IDF figures in July 1997, Hezbollah carried out 104 operations, mostly rocket and mortar attacks, and only four were close-quarter ambushes.[78] Hezbollah's indirect operations steadily continued at a high tempo, with seventy-five operations in January 1998 alone, and almost all attacks were launched from outside the security zone, involving nondirect, long-range rocket, mortar, or ATM assaults. Despite the increased number of attacks,

Hezbollah's inability to make direct contact with the IDF and its inability to penetrate the security zone to carry out ambushes or plant IEDs actually led to a marked decrease in IDF casualties.[79] Notably, IDF casualties in the last three years of the occupation in Lebanon steadily declined: in 1996, thirty-nine casualties; in 1997, twenty-four (excluding the February 1997 helicopter accident); and in 1998, thirteen. It is noteworthy that Hezbollah casualties over these years also declined (sixty-six in 1997, forty-two in 1998, and forty-two in 1999).[80]

A major contributing factor to the lower casualty count toward the end of the decade was the IDF's slower tempo, defensive mode of operation (a result of lessening societal motivation), dropping army morale, and the increasing difficulty in obtaining political approval for bold military action. This resulted in less IDF kinetic activity against Hezbollah, leading to an overall balancing of the casualty ratio between the IDF and Hezbollah. In 1990, when the IDF was operating frequently and with relative ease against Hezbollah, the ratio was 5:1 in the IDF's favor, but by 1995 the ratio dropped to 3.9:1, in 1996 it was 2.3:1, and in 1997 it dropped further to 1.7:1. Only in 1998 did it rise to 2.5:1, after some notable tactical successes of the Egoz unit.[81]

Timur Goksel, a senior UNIFIL official, recalled the routine, static, defensive posture of the IDF in the late 1990s:

> Every morning at 6:30 a.m., IDF armored patrol leaves the base, and Hezbollah was waiting for them down the road. . . . You're in a guerrilla war, and you're fighting Hezbollah with your set regimens and time schedules, even in the late 1990s! . . . Many IDF casualties were inflicted against their logistical convoys from Metula to Beaufort Castle . . . because they had the same convoy routes at the same day and time, and Hezbollah was waiting for them. . . . The IDF finally realized their mistake and then found a radical solution of using helicopters for logistics and troop rotations instead, to avoid the ground logistical convoys. . . . Then there's that famous [February 1997] helicopter crash. Those were the guys who replaced the road convoys. . . . Why go to that extreme? Just change your daily routine![82]

Providing an ominous assessment of the situation and warning of the dangers of the IDF's static, defensive posture in the late 1990s in the last months of his tenure as head of Northern Command, General Levin said forebodingly (in statements deemed so sensitive that his identity was deleted from initial media reports by military censors):

> The present situation, in which Hizballah is causing us to bleed and we are soaking it up, cannot continue. If you give me the means and the freedom to initiate and implement a large number of offensive activities I would be able to put Amal and Hizballah on the defensive. . . . We would have to hit them with

a blow that they would not forget for a long time (something like Grapes of Wrath, but more painful). Otherwise Hizballah, Amal, and the Palestinians would chase us to the border fence.[83]

Seemingly aware of the IDF's strategic quagmire and noting its defensive posture and apparent fatigue reflected by decreased operational activity, Sec.-Gen. Hassan Nasrallah boasted in an interview:

> The Israelis are exerting all their efforts they can come up with in the border strip. They are using all the technology they can muster to protect their soldiers, but they are not succeeding. The Merkava tank carries three times stronger armor than it used to carry before. The Israeli soldiers carry thick armor. . . . The enemy has used up all its resources and cannot do anything more on top of that. . . . I believe Israel has reached the point where it wants to end everything and come out of this swamp, but at the same time it doesn't want to leave this place without a price or at least with the slightest possible losses.[84]

Describing the slow and ineffectual learning of the IDF throughout the 1990s, Maj. Gen. (Ret.) Giora Eiland, head of the IDF Operations Directorate (1999–2001) at the time, reflected, "It was quite frustrating, because the IDF did allocate more and more resources—more air force assets, more elite units, and more intelligence assets—all to fight Hezbollah, and the best thing that could be achieved was to keep the situation more or less what we had a year before."[85]

Notably, the casualty rate was consistently in Israel's favor. According to a study citing data from Hezbollah's Central Information Office, from 1982 to 1999 Hezbollah suffered 1,248 killed and 1,000 injured; IDF official figures recorded 256 IDF killed and 869 injured in the same period (a 6:1 ratio in favor of Israel). However, the SLA suffered a disproportionate amount, with 1,050 killed and 639 injured.[86] While the casualties inflicted by Hezbollah are extremely modest relative to the IDF's other wars (and other comparable counterguerrilla campaigns in modern history), the small and intimate nature of the IDF and the sacrosanct cultural importance of the IDF in Israeli society as the "guarantors of Jewish survival" ensured that even limited casualties reverberated deeply in Israeli public discourse and civil society and impacted the thinking at the top and bottom of the military. Also, the Lebanon campaign was viewed in some sectors of Israeli society as a military adventure and "war of choice" launched without national consensus, and therefore losses were not justified. General Eiland explained the different impacts of casualties on Israel and Hezbollah: "The casualties of the other side were greater than the casualties on the Israeli side, but because politically, religiously, or because of their mentality, they were much more ready to sacrifice, even if they suffered more casualties, and it did not change the resilience, commitment, or their people's motivation to fight us. So, even if tactically we can say that for every Israeli soldier that they killed, we killed three Hezbollah fighters, strategically it didn't change the situation."[87]

CONCLUSION

The second decade of the conflict is overshadowed by the establishment of rules of the game, which legitimized the IDF as a target for Hezbollah within southern Lebanon while limiting the IDF's ability to respond. In the 1993 and 1996 escalations, the IDF sought to utilize deterrence by targeting Hezbollah within Lebanese villages, thereby pressuring the Lebanese population to pressure the Lebanese government and Syria to curtail Hezbollah. At the same time, Hezbollah used its rocket fire as a means to target the Israeli home front within the context of Israel's ongoing negotiations with Syria, whose role as Hezbollah's patron is pivotal in explaining the IDF's relative restraint throughout the decade. The Israeli political echelon ultimately checked the IDF and inadvertently hindered strategic adaptation because of political sensitivities. In democratic societies, military organizations are inherently limited by the strategic parameters put forth by their political masters, and this period of the conflict illustrates this ongoing tension between the political and military objectives. The Israeli political echelon's desire for "quiet in the north" also highlights the timeless challenge for military organizations of translating elusive political goals, often contingent on a plethora of variables beyond the military's control, into a clear military strategy with achievable military objectives.

Upon his appointment in Northern Command, Maj. Gen. Amiram Levin resisted political restraint and sought to regain IDF initiative and instill deterrence while adapting the classification of Hezbollah from a "terrorist group" to a "guerrilla army" and creating the Egoz counterguerrilla unit to lead the IDF's renewed effort. The Egoz unit became an incubator for military innovation and acted as a beacon for the development and dissemination of new counterguerrilla tactics. Influenced by the rising threat from Hezbollah, General Levin was a major proponent of change, owing to the dynamic interplay of top-down and bottom-up processes: Soldiers on the ground—enabled by the IDF's informal culture—confronted the receptive General Levin about their limited abilities to effectively confront the group. Propagating an open, less hierarchal culture enabled adaptation, as Levin was able to convince the top brass to grant him the leeway to create the Egoz unit. Maverick officers within Egoz then horizontally diffused battlefield lessons learned about counterguerrilla warfare to other units in Lebanon. This highlights the importance of bottom-up learning processes and the "horizontal" dissemination of lessons between units in driving military adaptation.

Meanwhile, Hezbollah's evolution from a guerrilla force to a commando force was a significant challenge for the IDF, which was slow to adapt its conceptualization of the group. Hezbollah increased its rocket firing after the 1993 and 1996 operations, and in the late 1990s it adapted toward "indirect" commando assaults to avoid face-to-face clashes with the IDF. Damningly, Egoz tactical successes did not reverberate on the strategic level because of Israel's inability to influence the strategic environment amid stagnant negotiations with Syria. This limited any adaptation of Israeli strategy, which ultimately contributed to the "tacticalization" of military strategy in Lebanon and led the IDF to assume a defensive, static posture toward the end of the decade. Because of Israeli society's increasing intolerance of IDF casualties in Lebanon, momentum slowly built for an IDF withdrawal, which would have dramatic implications on the strategic equation.

NOTES

Epigraphs: Nasrallah, interview, August 27, 1993, 107; Levin, briefing, February 20, 1995.

1. Author interview with "E."
2. Rabin, speech, June 10, 1991.
3. Mordechai, interview, July 26, 1993.
4. Rabin, speech to the Knesset, July 28, 1993.
5. Ross, *Missing Peace*, 110.
6. Byman, *High Price*, 235.
7. Ross, *Missing Peace*, 110.
8. Nasrallah, speech, July 31, 1993.
9. Musawi, interview, December 1994, 10.
10. Nasrallah, interview, August 27, 1993, 107.
11. Barak, interview, December 15, 1994.
12. Zeevi, speech in the Knesset, August 30, 1993, quoted in Tsur, "Test of Consciousness," 17n19.
13. Author interview with Ehud Eiran.
14. Author interview with IDF officers. See also Zvi Barel, "How Much Will the Initiative in Lebanon Cost?," *Haaretz*, December 18, 1994, FBIS.
15. Quoted in Eytan Rabin, [unknown title], *Haaretz*, December 12, 1994, FBIS.
16. Eisenstadt, "Hizballah Operations."
17. Author interview with Ehud Eiran.
18. Ibid. For another personal account, see Friedman, *Pumpkin Flowers*, 117–19.
19. Author interviews with IDF officers, January–July 2012. For a firsthand account, see Tamir, *Undeclared War*, 141–216.
20. For sharp analysis at the time, see Ehud Yaari, "Worrisome Little War," *Jerusalem Report*, January 12, 1995.
21. Levin, briefing, February 20, 1995.
22. Quoted in Blanford, *Warriors of God*, 148.

23. Quoted in Tamir, *Undeclared War*, 116.

24. Author interview with Shlomo Brom.

25. Amir Rapaport, "The IDF's Secret Weapon against Hezbollah," *Yediot Ahronoth*, December 5, 1996.

26. Author interview with Ronen Cohen.

27. Rapaport, "IDF's Secret Weapon."

28. For a firsthand account of the Egoz commander, see Tamir, *Undeclared War*, 141–216.

29. Eiran, *Essence of Longing*, chap. 9.

30. For military loss ratios, see Kober, "Has Battlefield Decision Become Obsolete?," 112.

31. Libel, "Crossing the Lebanese Swamp," 72–73.

32. This section draws from Marcus, "Military Innovation and Tactical Adaptation," 509–12.

33. Marcus, "Learning 'Under Fire.'"

34. Author interview with Ronen Cohen.

35. Libel, "Crossing the Lebanese Swamp," 73.

36. Levin, speech, January 28, 1996.

37. Quoted in "Rabin Rules Out Major Army Offensive in South Lebanon," AFP, December 12, 1994.

38. Quoted in "Israel Says It Won't Step Up Fighting," United Press International, December 13, 1994.

39. Barak, interview, December 15, 1994.

40. Eytan Rabin, "Rabin Asks Gen. Levin to 'Shut Up' on Hizballah," *Haaretz*, July 16, 1995, FBIS.

41. "Israelis Back Military Adventure in Lebanon," AFP, December 16, 1994.

42. Raad, interview, December 13, 1994.

43. Quoted in "Hezbollah Guerillas on Alert after Israeli Threat," AFP, December 13, 1994.

44. Quoted in Guy Bechor, "Scare Tactics," *Haaretz*, December 15, 1996.

45. Qassem, interview, December 12, 1994.

46. Levin, press statement, June 16, 1995.

47. Al-Khalil, interview, November 30, 1995.

48. Ross, *Missing Peace*, 248.

49. Finaud, "1996 Grapes of Wrath Ceasefire Agreement," 175.

50. For more on this period, see Rabinovich, *Brink of Peace*, 230.

51. Ross, *Missing Peace*, 250.

52. Author interview with Shlomo Brom.

53. Levin, news conference, April 13, 1996.

54. Inbar, press statement, April 16, 1996.

55. Quoted in Majorie Miller, "Israeli General's Comments Reveal Lebanon Rift," *Los Angeles Times*, April 18, 1996.

56. Inbar, press statement, April 17, 1996. See also Arieh O'Sullivan, "Inbar Regrets Remarks, Apologizes," *Jerusalem Post*, April 18, 1996.

57. For the full text, see Israel Ministry of Foreign Affairs, "Ceasefire Understanding in Lebanon."

58. Author interview with Shlomo Brom.

59. Author interview with Gabi Siboni.

60. Finaud, "1996 Grapes of Wrath Ceasefire Agreement."

61. Levin, press statement, August 18, 1997.

62. Qassem, *Hizbullah*, 147.

63. Quoted in Human Rights Watch, *Civilians under Assault*, 105.

64. Nasrallah, speech, August 16, 2013.

65. For background, see Catignani, "Israeli Counterinsurgency Strategy."

66. Quoted in Jaber, *Hezbollah*, 43.

67. Ross, *Missing Peace*, 251–52.

68. Author interview with Amos Granit.

69. Ehud Yaari, "Hizballah: 13 Principles of Warfare," *Jerusalem Report*, March 21, 1996.

70. Nir, "Fighting in the Lebanese Arena," 24.

71. For example, see Blanford, *Warriors of God*, 123; Helmer, *Flipside of the COIN*, 53–54; Matthews, *We Were Caught Unprepared*, 7; Bregman, *Israel's Wars*, 257–58; and Ministry of Defence, *Army Doctrine Publication*, 2A–6.

72. Author interview with Yagil Henkin.

73. Author interview with "E."

74. David Rudge, "Hezbollah Takes a Look Back at 96," *Jerusalem Post*, January 7, 1997.

75. Figures from Murden, "Understanding Israel's Long Conflict in Lebanon," 43.

76. Quoted in Joseph Matar, "A Scent of Victory," *Jerusalem Report*, March 29, 1999.

77. Levin, press statement, August 6, 1996.

78. Ed Blanche, "A Bizarre, Yet Bloody Conflict Drags on in South Lebanon," *Jane's Intelligence Review*, October 1, 1997.

79. "Three IDF Soldiers Killed in Lebanon as Hizbollah Ups 'Attrition War' Pace," *Mideast Mirror*, February 27, 1998.

80. Statistics from Harris, "Lebanon" (2001), 400.

81. Statistics from Kober, "Has Battlefield Decision Become Obsolete?," 112; Eisenstadt, "Hizballah Operations."

82. Author interview with Timur Goksel.

83. *Yediot Ahronoth*, November 26, 1997, quoted in O'Shea, "Israel's Vietnam?," 316. On the backlash to Levin's statement, see "General Calls for Israeli Soldiers to Quit Lebanon," *Evening Standard*, November 27, 1997.

84. Nasrallah, interview, March 30, 1998.

85. Author interview with Giora Eiland.

86. Hezbollah/SLA statistics from Hamzeh, *Path of Hezbollah*, 94, table 5.5; IDF statistics from Kaye, "Israeli Decision to Withdraw," 570 (excludes the 1997 helicopter collision).

87. Author interview with Giora Eiland.

CHAPTER 3

A CHANGE IN THE STRATEGIC EQUATION

The IDF Withdrawal from Lebanon (2000)

Israel, which owns nuclear weapons and has the strongest air force in the region, is weaker than a spider's web—I swear to God!

—Sec.-Gen. Hassan Nasrallah

Those who cannot bear casualties cannot exist in the Middle East.

—Deputy Defense Minister Ephraim Sneh

When there was progress in the Syrian peace process throughout the early 1990s, there were no major calls for withdrawal from Lebanon, but, owing to a perceived lack of progress after the 1996 election of Prime Minister Benjamin Netanyahu, calls for an Israeli unilateral withdrawal slowly emerged in a more significant way.[1] Fierce internal wrangling ensued between the political and military echelons surrounding the decision to withdraw. Despite Israel's strategic adaptation under the direction of new defense minister Moshe Arens, who sought to hit Lebanese government infrastructure in an attempt to deter Hezbollah, the military developments of this period, coupled with domestic pressures and widespread popular protests led by mothers of soldiers serving in the security zone, culminated in an eventual IDF withdrawal from Lebanon in May 2000 and resulted in a dramatic shift in the strategic equation.

THE IDF IN THE RUN-UP TO THE WITHDRAWAL

The Israeli public was able to disregard the folly of the security zone for much of the 1990s mainly because a relatively small number of soldiers (roughly twelve hundred) served there, with an additional nine hundred in the Lebanon Liaison Unit, which separated the conflict from the Israeli public to a limited extent.[2] The IDF brass was vocally opposed to a withdrawal from Lebanon, as demonstrated in 1998 statements by the new COS, Lt. Gen. Shaul Mofaz: "So long as we are in the security zone and fighting against Hezbollah, there will be a price. But any other alternative seems to us to be worse, more dangerous and likely to increase the number of soldiers and civilians in the north who get hurt."[3]

Momentum for an IDF withdrawal began during the tenure of Prime Minister Netanyahu (1996–99). Brig. Gen. (Ret.) Ephraim Sneh, a member of the Knesset at the time, reflected on the transformative process under way, noting that after Rabin's assassination in 1995, "Netanyahu didn't have the clout" that Rabin had regarding his support of the security zone, which contributed to a gradual "erosion of Israeli stamina."[4]

By the late 1990s, increasing societal pressure emerged from Israeli social protest movements, most notably the Four Mothers Movement, a grassroots organization led by mothers of soldiers serving in Lebanon, which called for a withdrawal from Lebanon. This small, committed movement played a key role in rapidly reshaping national security policy, despite objections by most active-duty IDF decision-makers. The movement mobilized public discourse through the Israeli media and questioned underlying assumptions of the need for maintaining the security zone.[5] The movement waged an emotional and vocal campaign in the media and even reached out to prominent American Jewish celebrities such as Barbara Streisand and Goldie Hawn, urging support for their cause.[6] The protest movements capitalized on long-festering sentiment that originated from the IDF's unjustified "war of choice" launched in Lebanon in 1982. Israel's staying power weakened as society grew increasingly intolerant of IDF casualties in the "Lebanese swamp" as the army attempted to achieve elusive and poorly defined strategic objectives.

The Four Mothers Movement primarily sought to dispel several "myths" surrounding the security zone, noting in an official press release that, contrary to IDF assertions, Hezbollah's Katyusha fire was more effectively curtailed by international mediation than Israeli military operations. The organization noted that Hezbollah militants targeted the IDF only within Lebanon and never crossed into Israel proper (at that time), which negated the underlying utility of the security zone. Supported by dovish politicians, the group also highlighted how Syria was using Lebanon as a bargaining chip in its negotiations with Israel, and the IDF's continued presence afforded Syria this advantage.[7]

The protest movements were criticized by active-duty IDF officers, including Brig. Gen. Erez Gerstein, the top IDF general in Lebanon, while another Golani Brigade officer famously disparaged the Four Mothers Movement as "the four dishrags."[8] Illustrating the rivalry that emerged between the domestic social protest movement and the military, General Gerstein said in 1998 that the movement "constitutes a threat for our soldiers" because it pressures the Lebanese in the south to collaborate with Hezbollah and "boosts the morale of the terrorists who feel this is a sign of the IDF's weakness."[9] Gerstein's criticisms of the Four Mothers Movement elicited immediate condemnation from COS Lt. Gen. Amnon Lipkin-Shahak, which reflected the underlying tensions and complexities surrounding the IDF's future in Lebanon. Interestingly, General Lipkin-Shahak castigated Gerstein, declared that "criticizing civilians for exercising their democratic rights is not permissible," and affirmed the "legitimacy" of such demonstrations.[10] In an ironic anecdote, illustrating the increasing clout and broad support of the Four Mothers Movement, an IDF MI official recalled, "One of the main leaders of the Four Mothers Movement was General Amiram Levin's wife! But they still love each other and respect each other's views. He was head of Northern Command leading the fight with the Egoz counterguerrilla unit, and she was fighting and protesting with the Four Mothers in Rabin Square!"[11]

Vocal dissent from retired military officials increasingly emerged in the late 1990s and laid the groundwork for the turning of Israeli public opinion. For example, Brig. Gen. (Ret.) Avigdor Kahalani, a hero of the 1973 Arab-Israeli War who was Israel's internal security minister at the time, said in 1996, "In principle, I believe that Israel should try to find a way to leave south Lebanon. I think that pulling out of south Lebanon would be healthy for the Israeli people." He also noted "most soldiers are being killed on the way to positions and not inside them, which shows that the conception has to be re-examined."[12] Statements emerged from others, such as Maj. Gen. (Ret.) Shlomo Gazit, head of IDF MI (1974–78), who wrote in a high-profile op-ed in 1997 that "today, the security zone is more a liability than an asset. . . . We must get used to the fact that a normal country does not control land beyond its territory solely in order to protect its settlements."[13] By 1999, several brigade commanders serving in Lebanon had also publicly called for a Lebanon withdrawal in meetings with COS Mofaz.[14] High-profile commanders such as Brig. Gen. Giora Inbar, head of the Lebanon Liaison Unit, stated upon his retirement in 1999 that the IDF was in a no-win situation and needed to leave Lebanon.[15] Several reports even emerged that the head of Northern Command, General Levin himself, advocated a withdrawal if the political echelon continued to inhibit and restrain IDF activity.[16]

Highlighting his awareness of a shift in Israeli public opinion, Hassan Nasrallah emphasized in a 1997 interview that "South Lebanon poses a real problem for the Israelis who speak of it as their Vietnam, their quagmire, and it's natural that there should be differences of opinion. . . . If we want to fuel these divergences, we must inflict more heavy losses on them so that they will realize that their logical option is withdrawal."[17]

The grassroots social movements' efforts were bolstered by several high-profile IDF disasters, including the February 1997 accidental collision of two IAF helicopters over northern Israel, which killed seventy-three troops being transported to Lebanon; the botched September 1997 Ansariya operation, in which Hezbollah ambushed and killed twelve IDF naval commandos on a clandestine mission; and the February 1999 assassination by a roadside IED of Brig. Gen. Erez Gerstein, the most senior IDF commander killed in Lebanon.[18] General Gerstein's death, in the words of one Golani Brigade officer, "was a big shock to society" because "he was like a prince. I served with him in Golani Brigade, and he was exceptional, built from the material of great leaders. It had a huge impact on the IDF."[19]

Vividly emphasizing an acute understanding of the IDF's dropping morale, Nasrallah proclaimed in a 1998 interview,

> For years now, the Israeli enemy has felt that it is drowning in a swamp of blood in south Lebanon and the Bekaa. This has sapped its strength and dealt a blow to its political and military ego. . . . Withdrawing . . . implies that the mythical army was defeated at the hands of the Lebanese people's resistance. . . . The Israeli enemy is looking for a way to exit this swamp.[20]

The increasing momentum of Israeli public opposition to the security zone deeply affected the capabilities of the SLA militia, which collaborated with the IDF. Col. Akel Hashem, deputy commander of the SLA (assassinated by Hezbollah in January 2000), described in a 1999 interview the SLA's chief problems regarding efforts to recruit and fight Hezbollah amid Israel's public debate over withdrawal:

> We have two problems nowadays. The first is the Lebanese government, which is assisting Hezbollah and using trials and death sentences to scare anyone who even thinks about cooperating with us. The second problem is the Israeli media. Write this down: Israeli democracy is what killed the IDF and the SLA in Lebanon—much more than Hezbollah and Syria and the Lebanese government combined. Obviously, if your newspapers constantly talk about withdrawal, it will have an adverse effect on our soldiers and on our ability to recruit agents.[21]

STRATEGIC ADAPTATION TO THE DETERRENCE EQUATION

Despite consistent Hezbollah activity and growing public dissent, according to Maj. Gen. Giora Eiland, head of the Operations Directorate at the time, "the IDF was of the opinion that the situation was tolerable, and that it would be possible to continue in the same manner for a long term. In fact, there was no genuine, thorough discussion of what alternatives the state of Israel had at its disposal."[22] One of the only calls for a different approach came from Moshe Arens, a longtime statesman reappointed defense minister in January 1999. Arens, a technocrat from outside the military establishment, recognized that the IDF's ability to confront Hezbollah directly was limited and that directly striking Syria was too high a risk. Instead he proposed placing direct responsibility on the Lebanese government by attacking Lebanese government infrastructure.[23] General Eiland reflected that "Arens was the only one who claimed that Israel should fight Lebanon, and he gave instructions to attack some of the infrastructure in Lebanon, especially electricity facilities, bridges, and other sites, and it was quite effective."[24]

Outlining his thinking on striking Lebanese government infrastructure to force Syria to rein in Hezbollah, Arens said in a 1999 interview:

> We are telling everybody that what we are facing in Lebanon is not the Hezbollah guerrillas and not the Lebanese government—because Lebanon is not an independent country—but the Syrians. Syria is fighting a war against Israel by proxy. . . . President Assad should know he is not going to be able to get away with that. . . . He would like to fight this war of attrition with Israel by proxy until he feels he's weakened Israel enough that Israel will say "uncle" and say "take the Golan Heights, take whatever you want, just call these Hezbollah guerrillas off." That would be a terrible mistake for Israel to do.[25]

Describing the faulty nature of the July 1993 and April 1996 understandings, Arens said elsewhere, "Israel should consider abandoning the truce [the understandings] since it is bad for the Israeli army. We are not free to attack Hezbollah. Our hands are tied and we cannot use our full capability."[26] Arens's statements conveyed the overall futility of the rules of the game and the inhibiting effect of the Syrian negotiations on the IDF. Such sentiment influenced COS General Mofaz, who, after a fatal Hezbollah attack, said in a 1999 interview, "I don't accept that when IDF soldiers are killed it is 'in accordance with the understandings of the Grapes of Wrath agreement.' I demand that we stop using this concept—that soldiers can be killed in accordance with an agreement!"[27]

Arens reflected that his overall policy goal was to "make Syria uncomfortable."[28] After an IDF retaliatory strike against Lebanese government targets in response to a Hezbollah attack, Defense Minister Arens described Israel's strategic adaptation of its deterrence policy and its refocusing on directly targeting Lebanon: "I hope the message we delivered in the form of the IDF operation yesterday was understood by Syria. Everything depends on Syria, not on Hezbollah. If they failed to understand this, it is important that Syria realizes that what the IDF demonstrated yesterday was only the tip of the iceberg in terms of the IDF's power."[29]

This perception of Syrian dominance over the conflict was evident to the international envoys in the region involved in the Israeli-Syrian negotiations at the time. Lord Michael Levy, UK special envoy to the Middle East (1998–2007), explained: "The influence of Syria politically over Lebanon was almost a grip, like a satellite of Syria . . . so I don't think there were too many scenarios where Lebanon was treated entirely on its own without looking at how Syria would react and what do we think Assad Senior would do in this circumstance."[30]

Well aware of Hezbollah's role within the broader Syrian-Israeli conflict, Hezbollah MP Mohammad Raad flatly declared in 1999, "The Syrians will never ask us to stop resisting the occupation of southern Lebanon. The Syrians do not trust Israel because they have failed to honor so many agreements . . . The Syrians will want to keep Hezbollah as a bargaining tool."[31]

Defense Minister Arens's calls for clear reprisal operations against Lebanon and the strengthening of Israeli deterrence deeply affected Prime Minister Netanyahu. Illustrating the creeping understanding of the strategic irrelevance of the security zone, Netanyahu said in 1999, "Rocket attacks cannot be prevented by territorial occupation, because Katyushas can have a longer range. If we extend our presence to 40-km, their Katyushas will have a 45-km range. . . . The only thing we can do to prevent missile attacks on our territory until suitable technology is developed—which will happen in the unforeseeable future—is to deter. This deterrence, this reaction of ours, is a vital factor."[32]

In a farewell interview after his tenure as defense minister was cut short by early elections in May 1999, Arens said bluntly, "If I were remaining in office, I would bring about the abrogation of the Grapes of Wrath Understandings. They created an intolerable situation both for the IDF and the northern towns."[33] Arens also claimed that IDF strikes against Lebanese infrastructure had restored Israel's deterrence equation and changed the underlying rules of the game with Hezbollah. Incoming deputy defense minister Ephraim Sneh disagreed but noted that "it is true, however, that the air action affixed a price tag to violation of that agreement by the other side" and that "perhaps there is something new in the remarks by Hassan Nasrallah about withholding fire against Israeli forces."[34]

THE ELECTION OF PRIME MINISTER EHUD BARAK AND THE IDF WITHDRAWAL

The events of the previous year catalyzed debate in Israeli society, invigorated the social protests movements, and influenced the electoral platforms of Ehud Barak, who ran against Netanyahu for prime minister. Barak laid out his platform in a 1999 interview:

The IDF is operating in Lebanon every day and will continue to do its best. . . . The government must look at the big picture, however, and must assume leadership by bringing about a change rather than remaining stuck, seeing as our sons are being killed in Lebanon. . . . It is necessary to dry up the entire swamp rather than to keep chasing after every Hezbollah mosquito, and I am saying this as someone who has spent most of his life fighting terrorists.[35]

Amid the feverish debate in Israeli society, Hezbollah MP Muhammad Fneish sarcastically described the influence of Hezbollah on Israel's electoral debate:

Whom do you want us to vote for? . . . Whatever happens in South Lebanon has implications in Israel. The election slogans prove that. It is obvious that the number of those demanding a withdrawal is growing. All their speeches focus on Lebanon and Lebanon only, as if Israel has no other concern. Look how the candidates rival each other with promises of who will get out of this quagmire first! We feel that there is the will to get out of Lebanon, but the question is how, in what context and under what circumstances.[36]

It is worth noting that as head of MI fifteen years earlier in 1985, Barak was consulted by Defense Minister Rabin on the fateful decision to set up the security zone. Then Barak was vocally against the policy and adamantly urged Rabin to withdraw all IDF forces south of the border. Barak's dissenting opinion was in opposition to COS Lt. Gen. Moshe Levi, Northern Command head Maj. Gen. Amir Drori, and Brig. Gen. Ephraim Sneh, who was then a commander in the security zone.[37] Barak's election as prime minister afforded him the opportunity to fulfill the goal he originally advocated for in 1985. Describing the importance of Barak's position, an IDF MI official caustically explained in an author interview: "Major strategic learning only occurs with the election of Barak. . . . The IDF and the majority of the intelligence community were against the withdrawal from Lebanon, as they were entrenched in their own stupidity. The IDF had rationalized its stupidity for eighteen years. We were suffering twenty to thirty casualties a year and spending money there, and we needed to justify it."[38]

The persistence of the antiwar movement, several battlefield blunders, and increasingly vocal skepticism about the importance of the security zone from Israeli officials culminated with a change in public opinion and the election of Prime Minister Ehud Barak on the platform of withdrawing from Lebanon. Israeli public opinion was resolute to remain in Lebanon (for example, in 1997 and 1998, 60 percent opposed withdrawing from Lebanon), and it was only when political elites were influenced by Barak's statements to withdraw that a possible withdrawal was legitimated, causing a plummeting of support for remaining in Lebanon.[39] Although there was low morale in the northern periphery of Israel, it did not seem to contribute to a loss of resilience or staying power in the rest of the country: According to a 2000 poll, only 29 percent of the Israeli public attributed the pullout to national weakness, while 61 percent stated that the IDF presence in Lebanon was no longer contributing to Israeli security.[40] Another study indicated that Israeli public opinion favoring withdrawal went from 41 percent in 1997 to 44 percent in 1998 and to 55 percent in 1999 but linked the instability closely to the peace process with Syria.[41] Whatever the case, unusually in Israeli civil-military relations, the political echelon eventually made the radical decision to withdraw from Lebanon, overcoming heated opinions within the IDF from COS General Mofaz and eighteen senior generals who wanted to remain.[42]

With Barak's 1999 electoral victory, a secret dispute occurred between Prime Minister Barak and Deputy Defense Minister Sneh over the future of the IDF in Lebanon, which echoed the same disagreements they had had as young officers advising Defense Minister Rabin in 1985 over the establishment of the security zone. Sneh, a consistently strong proponent of the security zone, devised a plan to keep the IDF in Lebanon. He recommended the IDF withdraw most of its troops from its fortified positions in southern Lebanon and, instead, embed elite IDF troops within the SLA as trainers, advisers, mentors, and air-support officers. In 2015, Sneh described this little-known plan he presented to Barak and COS Mofaz in 1999, which was ultimately rejected:

> I said to Barak, let's change tactics. You are afraid of the casualties. Where are the casualties? They occur in ambushes and attacks against our convoys. So, let's reduce the visibility of our presence. Let's put more SLA out there and evacuate most of the IDF strongholds. . . . Let's keep an Israeli presence in the mode of American Green Berets: liaison officers, instructors, and Arabic-speaking officers. Our officers will be embedded within the SLA. . . . There will be no Star of David flags over the hilltops. It will be SLA.[43]

Serving as Barak's deputy defense minister, Sneh ultimately concluded that Barak was determined to withdraw from Lebanon, regardless of actual military considerations. Sneh cynically believes to this day that Barak made his decision based on "a will to gain popular sympathy and votes" rather than on professional military assessments.[44] Retired defense minister Arens also agreed that Barak's desire to withdraw "came along with politics."[45] Sneh reflected,

> If it was a matter of professional discussion, my 1999 proposal was worth a discussion, but he was politically motivated. It wasn't based on military facts on the ground. Bear in mind Barak was chief of staff [1991–94] while commanding the security zone and did not advocate for a withdrawal at that time.

What he advocated for as head of military intelligence [in 1985], he didn't advocate for as chief of staff. He didn't convince Rabin or Shamir before him to withdraw. What convinced him were the polls that he saw in 1999.[46]

Another little-known dispute between the defense establishment and the prime minister emerged during secret discussions between Barak and General Mofaz in October 1999. Mofaz presented an IDF plan for withdrawal in the event of a negotiated peace deal with Syria (Operation New Horizon), and during these meetings Barak signaled to Mofaz to consider options for an IDF withdrawal *without* a negotiated solution with Syria and the possibility of withdrawing under fire. Barak also told Mofaz not to begin overt preparations and to ensure there was no "paper trail," for fear of leaks to the SLA and the Israeli public and their possible societal effect.[47] According to the transcript of the closed-door meeting, Barak told Mofaz, "You can say that the preference is to withdraw as part of a deal [with Syria] but that in parallel we start preparing ourselves for a withdrawal without a deal. . . . It is necessary that the SLA not know."[48]

On February 21, 2000, General Mofaz circulated an official document that notified the General Staff for the first time of the possibility of a withdrawal (to be known as Operation Morning Dawn) *without* a negotiated deal with Syria.[49] Fierce resistance erupted in the General Staff because Maj. Gen. Gabi Ashkenazi, head of Northern Command, and Maj. Gen. Benny Gantz, head of the Lebanon Liaison Unit, were firmly opposed. Illustrating the IDF's resistance, Maj. Gen. Amos Gilad, head of MI research, distributed an ominous "special intelligence evaluation" to decision-makers on March 3, 2000. In an internal IDF meeting at the time, General Gilad stated,

A withdrawal without an agreement leaves no chance for quiet. . . . It is very possible that at first, a few months after the withdrawal, it will be quiet, as Hezbollah settles down and improves its deterrent capabilities, but then we can expect terror attacks. And the terror attacks wouldn't just be on the Lebanese border, but also abroad and deep inside the borders of the State of Israel.[50]

Such warnings went unheeded by Barak. Illustrating dysfunctional and politicized decision-making, in ensuing deliberations Barak apparently excluded MI head Maj. Gen. Amos Malka from some meetings because it was known that MI was against a withdrawal.[51] Barak also held cabinet meetings in February and March 2000 in which the withdrawal was approved in principle, without including IDF officials.[52] An IDF MI official recently claimed that MI was "constantly blind" to Barak's political intentions and that Barak made the initial decision to withdraw without consulting the army or intelligence assessments.[53] Decision-making surrounding the withdrawal was sequential and improvised because although Barak had already announced his intention to eventually withdraw from Lebanon, he sought to retroactively obtain international consensus for this decision, despite more than 60 percent of border demarcations between Israel and Lebanon being disputed at that time.[54] Interestingly, the idea to withdraw from Lebanon (in accordance with UN Resolution 425) to obtain international "legitimacy" was originally proposed by the two top civilian defense officials in Lebanon, Uri Lubrani, MOD coordinator for Lebanon affairs, and his deputy, Col. (Ret.) Reuven Erlich, while the IDF adamantly opposed the idea.[55]

Highlighting the complex civil-military dynamic and the politicized nature of Barak's decision-making, Deputy Defense Minister Sneh recalled how "Barak had his clout as a former military leader" and his proven expertise on security as a former COS to legitimate his decision and drive through change. Retired defense minister Arens recalled that nearly the entire IDF top brass and all the SLA, especially its head, Gen. Antoine Lahd, were "dead set against the withdrawal."[56]

Sheikh Nabil Qawook, Hezbollah's southern commander, noted at the time, "Without [IDF] losses there used to be no talk of withdrawal but now they are being dragged to accept defeat; they are despairing not merely of victory, but of even the ability to protect their soldiers."[57] In the week before the actual withdrawal, Deputy Defense Minister Sneh lamented, "We are leaving because of the problems with the ability of the Israeli public to stand firm. That is the whole truth. There is no point in pretending. . . . [Hezbollah is] working on Israeli public opinion by means of the dead."[58]

According to UNIFIL official Timur Goksel, Hezbollah was fundamentally surprised by the IDF decision to withdraw:

I spoke with Nasrallah and told him the Israelis were withdrawing in 2000. He said, "How could they leave?" I said, "It's because their mothers want them home." For the Lebanese mind-set, this is unheard of. Then came 2000, it became clear the Israelis were leaving by their moves on the ground. Hezbollah wouldn't believe it. Even after negotiations over the Blue Line started, Hezbollah still didn't believe it. It was unheard of in Israeli military history to give up an occupied area without getting anything in return! . . . Until the very last day, no one believed Israel would leave.[59]

Describing Hezbollah's attritional strategy of targeting the IDF's psyche and Israeli society, Nasrallah said in a 1999 interview,

The cumulative effect of [Hezbollah's] operations on the one hand, and the Israeli losses and the fate of their agents in southern Lebanon on the other, took their toll. Let me say, in this context, that one should not measure the impact of events in southern Lebanon based only on the number of operations or of the Israelis killed or wounded, for there is something more important than that—namely the psychological aspect.

This factor is very important for the Israeli military establishment . . . and what happened has debunked the myth of the army that cannot be defeated, and dealt a severe blow to the high morale that the Israeli military boasts about.[60]

Summing up the IDF experience in the Lebanese security zone, one sharp-tongued IDF MI official said, "1985 to 2000 is a story of strategic stupidity. There were small steps of learning in 1993 and 1996, but Barak understood very well all the absurdity and understood the systemic issues at hand. This represents strategic learning, but this only occurred when the minority opinion of Barak came to power."[61]

Because of increasing social pressure, the deterioration of the SLA, and intelligence assessments that Hezbollah was preparing large-scale attacks to target the IDF during its withdrawal planned for July 2000, the IDF pushed forward the withdrawal date. General Ashkenazi of Northern Command was the most insistent that Barak move the withdrawal date up to gain tactical initiative, as Barak initially sought to remain in Lebanon for at least another month to secure international approval.[62] The withdrawal occurred hastily in one night, on May 24, 2000, which was chaotic and unsystematic, as events on the ground dictated the pace, timing, and order of unit withdrawals.[63] On the eve of withdrawal, Foreign Minister David Levy provided Israel's rationale and justification for a unilateral withdrawal:

The government decision was the result of our recognition that the security zone could not stop the Katyushas that threaten and inflict damage on our northern settlements. Our continued presence there exacted a heavy security and political price:

1. It endangered the lives of our soldiers and citizens.
2. It legitimized attacks against Israel as an occupying force.
3. It severely limited the action of our soldiers by the presence of Hezbollah in the heart of the Lebanese civilian population and our consequent fear of harming innocent civilians.
4. It forced us to accept the rules of the game as dictated by Syria and Iran, implemented by Hezbollah and their like.
5. It resulted in ongoing attrition and the inability to achieve results.

Faced with this reality, the Israeli government has decided to put an end to this absurd situation.[64]

In scenes of chaos, remnants of the SLA fled toward the Israeli border to avoid retribution from Hezbollah, while the IDF destroyed most of its own bases as it withdrew. General Lahd, who had been in Paris for political discussions with the French government about sending French troops to maintain security in southern Lebanon, was forced into exile in Paris.[65] While many SLA officers and soldiers found refuge in Israel, others remained in Lebanon to face the repercussions. The withdrawal from Lebanon marked the end of formal Maronite-Israeli cooperation and was viewed by the SLA as a tragedy and betrayal, highlighting an aspect of the conflict that is often neglected for consideration.[66]

Prime Minister Barak declared Israel's new strategic posture on May 24, 2000: "From now on, the government of Lebanon is accountable for what takes place within its territory, and the Lebanese and Syrian governments are responsible for preventing acts of terror or aggression against Israel, which is from today deployed within its borders."[67] Deputy Defense Minister Sneh dissented with Barak at the time and argued that the abandoning of Israel's SLA ally stained Israel's reputation for future alliances and that the underlying message in Lebanon was that "we run away from places that we bleed." Reflecting on the folly of leaving, Sneh wrote: "What was eroded during those years, particularly in the four years that preceded the withdrawal, was Israeli society's ability to tolerate the constant price of casualties. . . . The political leadership never sent a message of steadfastness to the public and the troops . . . even if there was no blitzkrieg-type victory to be achieved."[68] Summing up, Sneh famously said at the time that "a nation that cannot bear casualties cannot exist in the Middle East."[69] In Nasrallah's best-known speech, mocking Israeli society's low morale, fear of casualties, and lack of resilience, he declared from the Hezbollah stronghold of Bint Jbayl in the aftermath of the withdrawal: "Today we enjoy freedom and security, and enemy aircraft do not dare fly above you. . . . To liberate your land, you don't need tanks, strategic balance, rockets, or cannons; you need to follow the way of the past martyrs who disrupted and horrified the coercive Zionist entity. Israel, which owns nuclear weapons and has the strongest air force in the region, is weaker than a spider's web—I swear to God!"[70]

Hinting at the broader lesson that Hezbollah learned, Nasrallah said in a 2002 interview, "By combining our willpower, our determination, and wisdom with simple strategies carried out at carefully selected times and locations, we succeeded in defeating the strongest army in the Middle East. . . . If you stand strong, if you refuse to give up, if you show you're not afraid of death, then even with the humblest means you can defeat the strongest army."[71]

The head of Israel's proxy SLA militia, General Lahd, lamented how the IDF withdrawal set the stage for future conflict: "In principle I supported a withdrawal with an agreement because I wanted to connect the south with Lebanon. . . . But Barak made a commitment at the time to withdraw unilaterally within a year, he won the elections and carried it out, and look what happened. In truth, I wasn't at all surprised by what happened. I knew that Hezbollah would become an obstacle after the way in which Israel withdrew."[72]

CONCLUSION

The IDF adapted its strategy in the late 1990s under the tenure of Defense Minister Moshe Arens, a determined civilian leader from outside the military establishment who was concerned with impending defeat. Instead of pressuring the Lebanese population, Arens attempted to alter the strategic balance and instill deterrence by using the Lebanese government and its infrastructure as a lever against Syria and Hezbollah. When he was unable to change the underlying strategic equation, societal pressure eventually led newly elected prime minister Ehud Barak, of the minority opinion, to carry out a unilateral IDF withdrawal, which was a rare example of a political leader defying the defense establishment's persistent recommendations to remain in Lebanon until a negotiated deal with Syria could be forged. Both Arens and Barak were determined political leaders who were emboldened by heightened societal discontent with the war in Lebanon to ultimately trigger strategic adaptations. The withdrawal in particular illustrates the overwhelming effect of domestic pressure on the political establishment bogged down in an unpopular protracted war, which acted as the pivotal trigger and key driver of strategic adaptation. Hezbollah's steadfast resilience and persistent attritional warfare against Israel, perceived by Nasrallah to be "as weak as a spider's web," led to the subsequent erosion of Israeli deterrence, which would have dramatic ramifications on the strategic equation and plant the seeds for future war.

NOTES

Epigraphs: Nasrallah, speech given in Bint Jbayl after the IDF withdrawal, May 26, 2000; a well-known quote repeated in an author interview with Ephraim Sneh.

    1. Kaye, "Israeli Decision to Withdraw," 577.

    2. Sela, "Civil Society," 81–82.

    3. Quoted in Deborah Sontag, "Israelis Are Reconsidering South Lebanon Occupation," *New York Times*, November 28, 1998.

    4. Author interview with Ephraim Sneh.

    5. Sela, "Civil Society"; Kaye, "Israeli Decision to Withdraw." For background, see Lieberfeld, "Media Coverage"; Lieberfeld, "Parental Protest."

    6. Linda Ben-Zvi (international coordinator, Four Mothers Movement), letter to Barbara Streisand, October 12, 1997; Linda Ben-Zvi, letter to Goldie Hawn, October 12, 1997.

7. Four Mothers Movement, "Leaving Lebanon in Peace." Available in the electronic archives of Rachel Ben-Dor, chairperson of the Four Mothers Movement, Ohio State University Library.

8. "Israelis Speak Out about War against Hezbollah in Lebanon," AP, February 20, 2000.

9. "Israeli General Says Protests Endanger Soldiers in South Lebanon," AFP, June 8, 1998. A variation of this quote also appeared in Blanford, *Warriors of God*, 201.

10. "Israeli Chief of Staff Says Army Must Not Criticize Peace Protests," AFP, June 9, 1998.

11. Author interview with Ronen Cohen.

12. Quoted in David Rudge, "Kahalani: Israel Should Find a Way to Leave South Lebanon," *Jerusalem Post*, September 2, 1996.

13. Gazit, "Security Zone Has Served Us."

14. "Army Officers Not Happy with Lebanon Deployment," Voice of Israel, May 19, 1999, in *BBC Summary of World Broadcasts*, May 20, 1999.

15. Arieh O'Sullivan, "IDF Hides Dissenting Views on Lebanon," *Jerusalem Post*, May 20, 1999.

16. "Head of IDF Northern Command Denies Proposing Withdrawal from Southern Lebanon," Voice of Israel, November 27, 1997, in *BBC Monitoring Middle East*, November 28, 1997.

17. Hassan Nasrallah, interview, *Monday Morning*, September 22, 1997, quoted in O'Shea, "Israel's Vietnam?," 314.

18. For the best book on this period, see Eiran, *Essence of Longing*. For details on the Ansariya operation, see Alex Fishman, "What Really Went Wrong in Botched 1997 Shayetet 13 Operation?," *Yediot Ahronoth*, June 21, 2017.

19. Author interview with Saar Raveh.

20. Nasrallah, interview, March 29, 1998, 181.

21. Hashem, interview, October 29, 1999.

22. Eiland, "Think before You Act," 75–76.

23. Author interview with Shlomo Brom. See also ibid., 76.

24. Author interview with Giora Eiland.

25. Arens, interview, April 30, 1999.

26. Quoted in Zeina Khodr, "License to Kill Civilians," *Al-Ahram Weekly*, March 11–17, 1999.

27. Mofaz, interview, April 20, 1999.

28. Author interview with Moshe Arens.

29. Arens, interview, June 25, 1999.

30. Author interview with Lord Michael Levy.

31. Quoted in Nicholas Blanford, "Hizbullah: Lebanon's Heir Apparent?," *Jane's Intelligence Review*, November 1, 1999.

32. Netanyahu, interview, January 1, 1999.

33. Arens, interview, July 4, 1999.

34. Quoted in "Barak Will Present His Government to the Knesset Tomorrow," *Mideast Mirror*, July 5, 1999.

35. Barak, interview, Voice of Israel Radio, March 2, 1999.

36. Quoted in Joseph Matar, "A Scent of Victory," *Jerusalem Report*, March 29, 1999.

37. Author interview with Ephraim Sneh. See also Bregman, *Israel's Wars*, 254–55.

38. Author interview with Amos Granit.

39. Henkin, "How Great Nations Can Win Small Wars," 56; Kaye, "Israeli Decision to Withdraw"; Merom, *How Democracies Lose Small Wars*.

40. Kober, "From *Blitzkrieg* to Attrition," 230.

41. Arian, "Public Opinion on Lebanon and Syria, 1999."

42. Peri, *Generals in the Cabinet Room*, 91–96; Freilich, *Zion's Dilemma*, chap. 6. For the secret internal IDF arguments, see Bregman, *Israel's Wars*, 260–73.

43. Author interview with Ephraim Sneh.

44. Ibid.

45. Author interview with Moshe Arens.

46. Author interview with Ephraim Sneh.

47. Bregman, *Israel's Wars*, 262; Gilboa, *Morning Dawn*.

48. Quoted in Bregman, *Israel's Wars*, 264.

49. Ibid.

50. Gilboa, *Morning Dawn*. For many of the revelations, see Ronen Bergman, "Secrets behind Israel's Historic Withdrawal from Lebanon," *Yediot Ahronoth*, March 10, 2016.

51. Bregman, *Israel's Wars*, 266.

52. Freilich, *Zion's Dilemma*, 152.

53. Gilboa, *Morning Dawn*.

54. Freilich, "Israel in Lebanon," 55.

55. Gilboa, *Morning Dawn*.

56. Author interview with Moshe Arens.

57. Quoted in David Hirst, "Withdrawal from Lebanon Begins," *The Guardian*, June 1, 1999.

58. Quoted in Luft, "Israel's Security Zone in Lebanon." See also Laurie Copans, "Israeli Public Wants Lebanon End," AP, May 18, 2000.

59. Author interview with Timur Goksel.

60. Nasrallah, interview, June 21, 1999, 199–200.

61. Author interview with Amos Granit.

62. Gilboa, *Morning Dawn*.

63. For internal IDF deliberations, see Bregman, *Israel's Wars*, 269–73.

64. David Levy, press briefing, May 23, 2000.

65. Lahd, *Midst of a Storm*. See also Lahd, interview, March 5, 2007.

66. Gazit, "Nonstate Actors, Identity, and Change."

67. Barak, speech, May 24, 2000.

68. Sneh, "Why I Opposed Israel's Withdrawal from Lebanon."

69. Quoted in Peter Hirschberg, "Lebanon: Israel's Vietnam?," *Jerusalem Report*, December 11, 1997.

70. Nasrallah, speech, May 26, 2000.

71. Nasrallah, Al-Manar TV, February 17, 2002, quoted in Zisser, "Hizballah and Israel," 88.

72. Lahd, interview, November 26, 2006.

CHAPTER 4

THE EROSION OF DETERRENCE, THE 2006 WAR, AND THE DAHIYA DOCTRINE (2000–2017)

Hezbollah took a significant step toward strategic failure, muffled by tactical successes.

—Lt. Gen. Dan Halutz

The new strategic factor is that the Resistance in Lebanon has found a new deterrence formula.

—Sec.-Gen. Hassan Nasrallah

Israel's deterrent posture was gravely damaged in the eyes of its enemies following the withdrawal from Lebanon. However, it was believed that Israel's strategic position would benefit in the long term because of increased legitimacy gained from its compliance with international demands to withdraw. Israel sought to rebuild its deterrence against Hezbollah in ensuing years as the "rules of the game" were adapted, yet the IDF's failure to seriously respond to Hezbollah's provocations after the withdrawal inadvertently paved the road to war. The erosion of Israeli deterrence, a misreading by Hezbollah of Israel's "red lines," and serious miscalculation by both sides led to the surprise outbreak of war in July 2006. In the war's aftermath, the IDF has promised to inflict a "disproportionate" price against Hezbollah as part of its new "Dahiya doctrine," while Hezbollah has promised to hit Israeli infrastructure in response, resulting in a fragile equation of mutual deterrence.

POST-2000 SHIFTS

Since Israel fulfilled its part of UN Resolution 425 by withdrawing from Lebanon, Israel attempted to pass total responsibility onto Syria for keeping

Hezbollah quiet and made it clear that Syria—which still maintained a military presence and significant influence in Lebanon—would be held responsible for any violence emanating from Lebanon. Partially influenced by the ideas of retired defense minister Moshe Arens, the IDF attempted to adapt its deterrence posture from the "routine security" realm vis-à-vis Hezbollah to the realm of conventional state-on-state deterrence vis-à-vis Syria.[1] With the Syrian loss of Lebanon as a pressure point against Israel in negotiations over the Golan Heights, the IDF believed it would have increased leverage and an improved bargaining position against Syria. The IDF withdrawal also increased the Lebanese population's scrutiny of the Syrian military presence in Lebanon and put newly appointed Syrian president Bashar al-Assad in a difficult strategic predicament.[2]

Prime Minister Ehud Barak explained Israel's new strategic rationale one month after the withdrawal: "I reduced significantly the legitimacy to shoot [at us]. . . . Once we are within Israel, defending ourselves from within our borders, the Lebanese government and the Syrian government are responsible to make sure that no one will dare hit Israeli civilians or armed forces. Any violation of this might become an act of war, and it will be treated accordingly."[3]

Deputy Defense Minister Ephraim Sneh reflected on Barak's stated goal that Hezbollah would no longer have legitimacy to attack the IDF following the withdrawal: "It was full of wishful thinking and misleading because there was the theory that now Hezbollah would turn into a political party, and since we will be out of Lebanon, there will be no reason to attack us. Bullshit! . . . But then Hezbollah created this story about the Shebaa Farms. In the best case, it was naïveté by Barak."[4]

Hezbollah attacks throughout the 2000s, while low in number, were generally confined to the Shebaa Farms / Mount Dov area, an eight-square-mile territory disputed by Israel, Lebanon, and Syria that became Hezbollah's new, central raison d'être.[5] Following the withdrawal, a revised set of rules of the game were tacitly adopted by Israel and Hezbollah, based on mutual acceptance of the Israel-Lebanon border (the "Blue Line"), the acknowledgment of the disputed Shebaa Farms as a legitimate theater of operations, and the establishment of a reciprocal, low-intensity "tit-for-tat" dynamic in response to provocations by either side.[6] The premise of the IDF's post-2000 deterrence posture was reliant on a commitment to diligently retaliate against Syria or Lebanon in response to significant Hezbollah attacks.[7] Notably, Hezbollah carefully calibrated its operations after the withdrawal, forcing the IDF into the difficult predicament of either overresponding to provocations, which would embolden Hezbollah domestically, or underresponding, thereby eroding the IDF's deterrence posture.[8]

Hezbollah attributed the IDF's general inaction and lack of response to provocations to Hezbollah's own formidable deterrent posture. Deputy

Sec.-Gen. Naim Qassem said, following a notable Hezbollah kidnapping operation in October 2000, that "Israel would not have remained inactive after the seizure of its three soldiers in the Shebaa Farms if it had not feared the reaction of the Resistance to any reprisal it might undertake to free them."[9] Clearly, Hezbollah believed its strategic deterrence was strong.

Under newly elected prime minister Ariel Sharon, the IDF responded to Hezbollah violence in Shebaa Farms in 2001 that killed one soldier, not against Hezbollah or Lebanese targets but against Syrian military forces inside Lebanon. Partially influenced by the earlier policies advocated by Defense Minister Arens to shift Israeli deterrence to the state level, Sharon's decision marked a notable adaptation of strategy.[10] Hezbollah, taken aback at the IDF reaction, did not respond to the IDF's strike on April 16, 2001, against a Syrian radar post in Dahr al-Baydar.[11] This illustrates the IDF's attempt to change the rules of the game, as this was the first time the IDF targeted Syria since the 1980s and was also the first time the IDF responded to Hezbollah provocations in any meaningful way since the withdrawal.[12] IDF spokesperson Brig. Gen. Ron Kitri said in a press briefing after the operation,

> The Syrian connection with Hezbollah is well known. . . . I would say the only thing new here is the clear connection established by the IDF through last night's raid between an explicit Syrian target and the message we are seeking to relay to Syria, and through it to Hezbollah, in a clear, distinct and unequivocal language. . . . The operation shows that we have reached the limit of our patience. . . . We are no longer prepared to tolerate the reality imposed on us on the northern border.[13]

After another Hezbollah attack and a second IDF strike, this one on July 1, 2001, against Syrian targets in Rayak in Lebanon's Bekaa Valley, Hezbollah responded with mortar and rocket fire into Shebaa Farms, making clear it would not easily permit the IDF to change the rules of the game.[14] The Syrian army did not directly respond, but, ironically, Hezbollah's response made Hezbollah Syria's defender in Lebanon against the IDF. Nasrallah proclaimed, "Israel is playing with fire. We will not stand idly by and will react in an appropriate manner."[15] Hezbollah MP Mohammad Raad discussed Hezbollah's adherence to the newly revised understandings: "Just as in the past we sought to establish the April equation [1996 understandings] in order to turn the citizens into neutral parties, today we are working at an equation, by our continuous resistance to the enemy, that will deter it from violating Lebanon's sovereign airspace."[16] Notably, the IDF would not overtly strike Syrian targets in Lebanon again for some time.

According to IDF statistics and illustrating Hezbollah's persistent rate of operations, Hezbollah carried out more than 264 attacks of varying nature from 2000 to 2003, including (mostly ineffective) antiaircraft fire and more damaging ATM assaults and cross-border attacks, which resulted in eight soldiers and six civilians killed and forty-six soldiers wounded.[17] Overall, from 2000 to 2006, Hezbollah carried out twenty to thirty attacks that caused casualties, including two successful kidnappings (and several failed attempts).[18] Nasrallah would later describe Hezbollah's actions in Shebaa during this period as "reminder operations": "What was the Resistance's policy and strategy, from 2000 to July 12, 2006? . . . Our responsibility and our job is to thwart any Israeli aggression on our territories. . . . There is the Shebaa Farms, a very small area. We used to carry out an operation once in a while and call it a reminder. . . . We will [continue to] conduct 'reminder operations.'"[19]

The IDF did not generally respond to any of these "reminder operations" or provocations in any meaningful manner, other than carrying out flyovers or launching artillery fire. This was a result of the IDF's intensive involvement in LIC against Palestinian terrorist groups during the Second Intifada, which erupted in September 2000, and reluctance to open a second front in Lebanon while combating the wave of Palestinian suicide bombings. Further eroding the IDF's deterrence in the eyes of Hezbollah was Israel's willingness to engage in a large-scale prisoner swap with Hezbollah in January 2004, trading more than 430 Lebanese and Palestinian prisoners and the remains of sixty Hezbollah militants, for the remains of three IDF soldiers kidnapped in October 2000 and an IDF colonel abducted under suspicious circumstances the same year.

The political echelon and military remained wary of getting reinvolved in the Lebanese quagmire in any significant way. While occasional retaliatory strikes were authorized, troops stationed on the border were withdrawn from frontier bases, given orders to avoid the border fence, and replaced with cameras and electronic sensors, as the IDF attempted to avoid any friction with Hezbollah.[20] Maj. Gen. Udi Adam, head of Northern Command (2005–6), testified to the Winograd Commission that "its practical meaning was relinquishing Israeli sovereignty on the northern border, and giving Hezbollah a free hand on the northern border."[21] Owing to the IDF's fear of becoming embroiled in Lebanon again, it seems that Hezbollah successfully deterred the IDF from hitting Syrian targets and greatly minimized the scope of IDF retaliatory strikes against the group. Maj. Gen. Moshe Kaplinsky, Galilee Division commander during the IDF withdrawal, later described the IDF's mind-set at this time: "Our failure to change the general mindset of the army grew even worse because of the approach . . . at whose center lay the principle of 'sit and wait.' The primary mission was simply to prevent kidnappings and nothing more. The security of the IDF soldiers was defined as of overriding importance."[22]

Critically, the IDF did not generally follow through on its declarations to respond to Hezbollah kidnappings and attacks, which marked the most damning erosion of the IDF's deterrence credibility in the eyes of Hezbollah and emboldened further attacks.[23] Furthermore, any remaining leverage the IDF had over Syria was lost in 2005 amid the Lebanese "Cedar Revolution," during which Lebanese public demonstrations against Syria's military presence in Lebanon forced Assad to withdraw his forces, marking an end to overt Syrian military influence in Lebanon and granting Syria deniability of Hezbollah's actions.[24] From the sidelines, retired defense minister Arens persistently argued for strikes against the Lebanese government since "Lebanon's support for Hezbollah continues only so long as Lebanon remains unscathed. . . . Until this equation is changed, we can expect to be hit by Hezbollah again."[25]

The fundamental problem for the IDF after 2000 was that while its capability for conventional deterrence vis-à-vis Syria was never questioned, its deterrent posture against Hezbollah as an asymmetrical opponent was never strongly enough established. Ominously discussing this phenomenon and the need to strengthen Israel's deterrence, COS Lt. Gen. Moshe Yaalon said in 2002, "If the [Hezbollah] threat materializes, we will have to exact a heavy price from those who are responsible for its development. . . . First of all, Syria, then Lebanon, Hezbollah, and the Iranians in Lebanon. . . . I can say that whereas in the sphere of army versus army, and in the nonconventional sphere, we created effective deterrence. We did not succeed in creating that kind of deterrence in the face of surface-to-surface rockets or terrorism."[26]

It is noteworthy that two months prior to the withdrawal, on March 7, 2000, the head of IDF MI, Maj. Gen. Amos Malka, submitted an intelligence assessment to Prime Minister Barak on the future of Israel's postwithdrawal deterrence, which emphasized the "impracticability of creating a deterrent that would be able to completely overcome the other side's motivation," especially owing to Hezbollah's acquisition of advanced weaponry. It emphasized "the existence of a mutual balance of deterrence in which Hezbollah has a say . . . that would ultimately lead to sustaining a limited conflict confined to accepted rules of the game" but ominously warned that "any deviation from these rules would escalate the conflict into the worst possible scenario for both sides."[27] This foreboding intelligence assessment went unheeded.

THE EROSION OF DETERRENCE AND THE ROAD TO THE 2006 WAR

Ehud Olmert, who became prime minister in January 2006 after Ariel Sharon was incapacitated by a stroke, described the loss of deterrence as the main factor that contributed to the outbreak of war:

The war started the day that Israel promised to shake the ground in Lebanon over the kidnapping of three soldiers in [October] 2000, but then did nothing. . . . The Second Lebanon War began when Israel lost its deterrent capability; when it failed to act, explicitly contradicting its commitment to do so; when it decided to accept a situation in which the other side chose the timing, scope, and manner in which to drag Israel into a situation where it was forced to react rather than dictate.[28]

Uzi Arad, a former official in the Mossad, Israel's foreign intelligence service, and head of the Israeli NSC (2009–11), argued that war broke out because the IDF developed a "cumulative deterrence deficit" since it had failed to react harshly enough to Hezbollah provocations to restore its deterrent image after the withdrawal. He explained that the "pattern of Israel's responses must have instilled with Hezbollah a perception that there is a considerable gap between Israel's threats and its deeds. That deterrence deficit led to Nasrallah's recent miscalculation."[29] The importance to Hezbollah's thinking of the group's earlier kidnapping efforts where the IDF did not respond with "deeds" was echoed during the interrogation of Ali Hassan Saliman, a captured Hezbollah militant who participated in the initial kidnapping operation that sparked the 2006 war. In his interrogation, he explained: "It was during the months November–December 2005. . . . My task was at the Zivanit outpost, to prevent the tanks from firing on Ghajar . . . [by using] ATMs. Our objective was to kidnap soldiers. . . . Our main objective [to kidnap soldiers] was missed. But our secondary objective was to attack the outposts."[30]

The IDF's weak response to such operations bolstered Hezbollah's assumption that Israel would endure these incursions as part of tit-for-tat rules of the game in the postwithdrawal environment. The UK's ambassador to Lebanon during the 2006 war explained in an author interview that "Israeli deterrence failed in 2006 because Hezbollah thought they could get away with an operation like that."[31] Critically, Nasrallah's boldness and overconfidence in Hezbollah's deterrent posture was evident in the months *prior* to the war. Highlighting Hezbollah's reassurance, the group's apparent downplaying of the possibility of future conflict, and the ultimate failure of Israeli deterrence, Nasrallah said in a February 2006 interview, "The presence of the Resistance up until now has been a deterrent, and the Israelis take into account our reactions and retaliations. In these five years [since the IDF withdrawal], we have had feelings of reassurance and confidence. This sentiment of reassurance is because of Hezbollah."[32]

On July 12, 2006, Hezbollah launched an operation that killed three soldiers and kidnapped two others, remarkably similar to five foiled kidnapping attempts in prior years. Because of the severity of the attack and the earlier kidnapping the same month of IDF Cpl. Gilad Shalit on the Gaza border by Hamas, the IDF retaliated dramatically, marking the start of a confrontation that would be known as the 2006 Lebanon War. (For its operational aspects, see chapter 8.) UNIFIL official Timur Goksel explained that largely as a result of the failure of Israeli deterrence, "Hezbollah miscalculated the political reaction of the Israelis. . . . Hezbollah didn't assess what Israel's reaction would be to a breach of a part of the border that is not disputed and usually quiet, instead of in the disputed Shebaa Farms area where attacks were more frequent, so Israel had to respond. The 2006 attack by Hezbollah was outside the 'rules of the game.'"[33]

Brig. Gen. Yossi Kuperwasser, head of research in IDF MI in 2006, offered his own midwar assessment of Nasrallah and the reasons for Hezbollah's surprise:

> [Nasrallah] said to himself, "Israel will not dare do anything from the air because I have a lot of missiles. . . . And you carry the memory of the blows you sustained in Lebanon and therefore you will not enter." . . . He became increasingly convinced that this thesis was correct. . . . He failed to grasp one basic thing. He is not an intelligence officer. He did not evaluate the strategic change. He thought Israel would carry out a local action in the south and that would be that.[34]

Upon the outbreak of war, Hezbollah's strategic surprise was evident. In the words of Mahmoud Komati, deputy chief of Hezbollah's politburo: "The truth is—let me say this clearly—we didn't even expect [this] response." Rather, Hezbollah expected "the usual limited response" since "in the past, Israeli responses to Hezbollah actions included sending in commandos into Lebanon and kidnapping Hezbollah officials or briefly targeting specific Hezbollah strongholds in southern Lebanon," followed by mediation led by the German government to negotiate a prisoner swap.[35] Maj. Gen. (Ret.) Amos Yadlin, head of MI during the war, concluded that "Hezbollah did not plan war but rather kidnapping and bargaining. It was very surprised by Israel's response, especially the attack on the medium-sized rockets that were in the houses of civilians in the villages and the severe damage to the Dahiya [Hezbollah's stronghold in Beirut's southern suburbs]."[36] Such exacerbation was experienced by Hezbollah commanders who operated on the ground. During the interrogation of captured Hezbollah militant Ali Hassan Saliman, he said, "I anticipated a harsh response, but not this harsh. I anticipated that it [the IDF] would destroy all the Hezbollah bases. I expected that it would attack outposts, but I didn't expect it to get all the way to Beirut, the southern suburbs, the central base."[37]

Hezbollah MP Ali Fayyad wrote during the war about the limited objectives of the kidnapping operation, highlighting Hezbollah's lack of preparedness: "From Hezbollah's perspective, the kidnapping of the two Israeli soldiers had a limited objective: it sought to engage in a process of exchange of the two soldiers against Lebanese prisoners held in Israeli jails. There was no intention to escalate or expand the confrontation."[38]

Wafiq Safa, the shadowy head of Hezbollah's internal security, admitted Hezbollah's surprise upon the outbreak of war in a private conversation with the late Lord Michael Williams, UN undersecretary-general for the Middle East and special envoy to Lebanon (2006–11). Lord Williams recounted the conversation: "Wafiq Safa came close to saying to me that they were surprised. . . . He begrudgingly admitted it. . . . I asked him how he could expect a direct attack on an IDF patrol involving some fatalities with no Israeli response, and he said, 'We thought it would be a limited attack,' so that took them by surprise."[39]

Hezbollah's surprise is most evident in an oft-cited interview with Nasrallah following the 2006 war, where he admitted his own intelligence miscalculation, which also illustrates that Israel failed to signal that it wouldn't tolerate such provocations:

> We have a thorough knowledge of the Israelis and how they think about and deal with issues. Based on all past experience, we carried out operations that were much more important than the July 12 capturing operation, and these operations resulted in much bigger losses on the Israeli side, but did not lead to a war of this scale. . . . No state has ever waged war on another state because two soldiers were captured. . . . If there was even a 1% chance that the July 12 capturing operation would have led to a war like the one that happened, would we have done it? I would say no, absolutely not, for humanitarian, moral, social, security, military and political reasons. . . . I believe that even this 1% chance did not occur to any of the 15 political and military individuals [in Hezbollah's decision-making leadership], despite our deep experience.[40]

Hezbollah's kidnapping operation may have been a tactical surprise for the IDF, but according to Maj. Gen. Aharon Zeevi-Farkash, head of MI before the war (2002–6), in late 2005 MI provided decision-makers with "strategic warning" of the threat from Hezbollah, which "prompted the accurate intelligence preparations required for combat, both for the air force and ground forces." Critically, MI warned of "the need to prepare for a possible escalation on the northern border and strengthen the deterrent force against Hezbollah, including the organization's kidnapping attempts."[41]

Contrary to the conventional knowledge, a former MI officer noted that Israeli deterrence from 2000 to 2006 was largely successful in restraining Hezbollah within the revised rules of the game. Owing to the IDF's prior inaction after Hezbollah operations, the IDF was, in effect, tacitly accepting skirmishes and kidnapping attempts in the Shebaa Farms and border areas;

hence, in 2006, Hezbollah acted within what it perceived as Israel's red lines. Notably, Hezbollah had not fired any medium- or long-range rockets prior to 2006, nor did it launch major attacks outside what it perceived to be the rules of the game. Following the 2006 kidnapping, Hezbollah expected the usual IDF artillery strikes targeting the group's border bases but thought the IDF would refrain from a more robust operation, as it had in earlier incidents.[42]

The perceptions of the opponent are critical in determining the actual success or failure of deterrence. Hassan Nasrallah's analysis of Israel's deterrence sheds light on Hezbollah's perceptions and validates the notion of a Hezbollah miscalculation in 2006, largely because of Israel's failure to clearly communicate its red lines. In a 2007 interview, Nasrallah reflected on Israel's containment policy in the years prior to the war:

> Since January 2000, the policies of the successive Israeli governments were based on tolerating and containing Hezbollah in the south and not confronting it. This means that the Barak and Sharon governments, and even the Olmert government, were adopting this behavior. Therefore, we found that since May 25, 2000, until July 12 [2006], some incidents took place on the borders, some sensitive and dangerous, but they did not result in a war because the Israeli policy adopted since May 25 was one of containment.[43]

Maj. Gen. Amos Malka, head of MI during the 2000 withdrawal, concluded that Israeli deterrence failed and Nasrallah ordered the kidnapping in 2006 not because Hezbollah doubted the IDF's capacity or capability to respond, but rather because Israel failed to clearly signal and transmit its deterrence message (red lines) to Hezbollah that would warn of what specific actions would incur a major response. Pivotally, Israel failed to bridge the gap between its "perceived deterrence" and its own "declared deterrence."[44]

IDF STRATEGY IN THE 2006 WAR

Upon the outbreak of war, Israel's leaders failed to set clear strategic goals that could be translated into achievable operational objectives. Five days after the initial kidnapping incident, Prime Minister Olmert outlined Israel's lofty war aims: the return of the kidnapped soldiers, a complete cease-fire, expulsion of Hezbollah from the area in line with UN Resolution 1559 (which calls for Hezbollah's disarmament), and deployment of the Lebanese army in southern Lebanon to maintain security.[45] Olmert later claimed that he launched the operation for the kidnapped soldiers because he did not want to do what his predecessors had done—engage in a large-scale prisoner swap, which would erode Israeli deterrence.[46] Critically, Olmert's goals did not resemble those transmitted by COS Lt. Gen. Dan Halutz to the army. General Halutz claimed that he preferred to exact a disproportionate price against Hezbollah for the kidnapping, impose a sense of security in northern Israel, create conditions to bring about the return of the soldiers, and prevent any escalation that might include Syria.[47] This disparity between Olmert's and Halutz's goals would contribute to strategically muddling the campaign and further complicate objectives the IDF was meant to achieve.

According to Maj. Gen. Giora Eiland, former head of the IDF Planning Directorate, Israel failed to decide clearly on its strategic objectives in 2006. The first option was to target Hezbollah organizationally and significantly damage the group's capabilities, which would have entailed larger-scale ground maneuvers, with at least three reserve divisions over a sustained period of time. The second option was to restore its deterrent image, primarily through a short, decisive, but limited retaliatory aerial campaign against Hezbollah's "quality targets" that would damage the group and impose new rules of the game.[48] According to testimony in the Winograd Commission, immediately following the kidnapping, General Halutz opted for the latter option, telling Defense Minister Amir Peretz that Israel "will have to take a few very aggressive actions in order to establish a new pattern of rules of the game."[49] Halutz reflected in 2016, "I advocated for a pivot to a strategy of response, to build deterrence" and "to make clear that the rules had changed."[50] Prime Minister Olmert stated that he also opted for the latter option: "I took the position that there was no option but to change the rules of the game" in response to the kidnapping since "we had no intention of continuing the policy of containment."[51]

Influenced by its traditional security doctrine that emphasizes rapid and severe retaliation in response to enemy provocations and its cultural proclivity for bold, offensive action, the IDF's underlying goal in the 2006 war was the reflexive instinct to reestablish deterrence vis-à-vis Hezbollah, but this came at the expense of a broader military or political strategy.[52] The IDF's broad strategic goal in 2006 was centered on the notion that its deterrence credibility had to be restored, which required an "offensive booster."[53] This deterrence reflex to inflict a high price is reflected in IDF early combat history since the 1950s and is shaped by IDF strategic culture and ingrained in its security doctrine as a preferred means to ensure Israel's security.[54] General Halutz elaborated in his memoir on the IDF's adherence to "deterrence by punishment": "The way to fight terror is not by employing armored divisions that will capture territory. It is by inflicting continuous, painful blows that will inflict on the other side a much higher price than he ever expects . . . one that produces deterrence."[55]

Continuity from the IDF's past targeting policies in Lebanon during the 1993 and 1996 operations were evident, as General Halutz explained that causing villagers to flee from southern Lebanon in 2006 "served two purposes: to increase our operational freedom to act around the villages, but also to make the price clear to the Lebanese people for its support for Hezbollah."[56] However, in a 2008 interview highlighting the IDF's underestimation of Hezbollah's resilience, Halutz lamented the minimal impact of IDF firepower on Hezbollah's ability to launch rockets: "The idea of using disproportional firepower in order for the other side to realize there is no sense in continuing was definitely there [in 2006]. And the other side definitely received disproportional firepower, but despite this, they continued on."[57] According to General Yadlin, head of MI, "throughout the war, the assessment of Military Intelligence was that once a cease-fire was offered to Hezbollah, it would accept it immediately," partially due to the IDF's effective air strikes and ability to deal "a very serious blow" to Hezbollah.[58]

In a fiery speech during the 2006 war, Nasrallah showed defiance and indicated an astute awareness of Israel's poorly formulated strategy and underlying desire to deter Hezbollah:

> Let each Israeli ask himself a question at present about the performance of his political and military command. . . . Will it bring back the two Israeli soldiers? Never . . . Instead, he [Olmert] could have negotiated like Sharon did in the past. . . .
>
> They must also ask themselves and their leadership a question after they said that the aim of this war was to restore the capacity of deterrence to the Israeli army. Was this capacity enhanced? They said that they wanted to correct the image and reverence of the Israeli army. Was this image corrected, or was it tainted further and further? . . . I say to the Israelis: Ask Olmert, where are his highly aimed great promises that he declared since the first day of the war.[59]

In a postwar interview, despite Israel's limited achievement of its immediate goals of returning the kidnapped soldiers, Defense Minister Peretz explained his rationale for why he approved intensive air operations against Hezbollah in the war's opening days and how it contributed to changing the rules of the game and instilling deterrence:

> What Israel prove[d] to Hezbollah was that the fact that they were capable of firing rockets into Israel does not paralyze us. If we had not succeeded in shattering that psychological thesis, we would still be prisoners of Hezbollah. That was the strategic problem. Hezbollah knew it had Israel by the throat. They believed that no Israeli leadership would dare launch a confrontation that would result in Katyusha rockets being fired at the home front. We had to break that equation.[60]

THE IDF'S STRATEGIC APPROACH AFTER 2006:
THE DAHIYA DOCTRINE

Immediately following the 2006 war, the IDF engaged in rigorous self-criticism over its flawed strategy. The Winograd Commission confirmed some of Nasrallah's allegations about Israel's strategic failures: "We were surprised to notice a significant weakness in the in-depth thinking and multi-dimensional, deep, and sophisticated strategic planning."[61] It added: "Consequently, in making the decision to go to war, the government did not consider the whole range of options, including that of continuing the policy of 'containment,' or combining political and diplomatic moves with military strikes below the 'escalation level,' or military preparations without immediate military action—so as to maintain for Israel the full range of responses to the abduction."[62]

Among strategic lessons learned from the 2006 war, the IDF internalized that in future conflict, because total "victory" over a guerrilla group is not possible in the near term given inherent political and military limitations, containing and deterring Hezbollah is like treating symptoms of a common illness that cannot be cured definitively.[63] The IDF understood that the highly successful opening air operation that destroyed Hezbollah's long-range weapons would have sufficed to instill a short, sharp deterrent effect, but "the continuation of the campaign beyond that point was not necessary for deterrence purposes."[64]

Since the end of the 2006 war, the IDF has reemphasized deterrence as its central tenet, which has even superseded the achievement of military decision in the classical sense. As Maj. Gen. (Ret.) Ilan Biran, former director-general of the MOD (1996–99), said in a recent lecture, "deterrence is the whole objective of the IDF and the military system."[65] According to General Yadlin, even when the IDF carries out preemptive or preventive operations today (illustrated in the numerous strikes against Syrian weapon convoys bound for Hezbollah), it is largely viewed through "its contribution to deterrence."[66] Brig. Gen. Itai Brun, former head of research, IDF MI, succinctly explained the post-2006 adaptation of the IDF's strategic concept: "We used to plan for military decision, and deterrence was the outcome. Now we're planning for deterrence. That's the change."[67]

The overarching strategic goal of the IDF after 2006 (illustrated in the 2008, 2012, and 2014 Gaza operations) is to severely degrade enemy military capabilities—sometimes dubbed "mowing the grass"—through the delivery of a sharp, decisive blow that instills deterrence and buys a period of temporary quiet.[68] Contrary to the IDF's "lever" approach during the 1993 or 1996 operations that indirectly targeted the Lebanese population to pressure Hezbollah, in 2006 there was no assumption that the Lebanese population would ideologically lose support for or actively restrain Hezbollah because of IDF operations. Rather, Israeli strikes in 2006 were primarily designed to illustrate that Hezbollah's hostility toward Israel elicited a high price by the severe degradation of Hezbollah's military capabilities and destruction of its command centers in its Dahiya stronghold. Demonstrating an awareness of the ultimate weakness of Israel's lever strategy in the 1990s, General Halutz conceded three years after the 2006 war that "the expectation that the Lebanese government and army will fight against their own countrymen in order to serve our goals is one that has no chance of being realized, not now and not ever."[69]

The 2006 war demonstrated to IDF decision-makers that hollow, declaratory threats prior to hostilities are ineffective and that a onetime use of force in reaction to Hezbollah aggression did not constitute sufficient deterrence. With the passage of more than a decade, it has been internalized that "the sword itself does not establish credibility: it should be constantly bloodied to maintain deterrence," and periodic execution of threats that are large and dramatic are essential to communicate resolve and credibility in the eyes of Israel's adversaries.[70] The overarching goal for Israel in future conflict with Hezbollah will be the reinstilling of deterrence because the IDF learned that the large-scale destruction of Hezbollah's infrastructure in 2006 consumed the group in a slow and costly rebuilding and rearming process and led to a relatively prolonged period of quiet. Highlighting this adaptation of the IDF's historical "cumulative deterrence" concept, Maj. Gen. (Ret.) Isaac Ben-Israel, former head of IDF research and development (R&D) in the MOD, said in a recent lecture, "When the General Staff meets to discuss a military operation, 80 percent of the discussion revolves around deterrence" since "in Israel's conception of security, wars are actually rounds of violence in one long war" and success in such circumstances is "to see to it that from one round to the next, the enemy's desire to return to the conflict is reduced."[71]

Instead of aiming to decisively "defeat" Hezbollah militarily, counter its ideology, or pressure the Lebanese population to restrain the group, IDF strikes are designed to erode Hezbollah's capabilities as part of a long-term attritional campaign to cumulatively deter Hezbollah.[72] Only as a secondary factor, in light of practical considerations, might the Lebanese population restrain Hezbollah (which acutely monitors domestic support levels) since massive strikes in Lebanon inevitably result in indirect suffering by the local population.[73] Explaining the secondary pressure on the Lebanese population, the current COS and a former head of Northern Command (2006–11), Maj. Gen. Gadi Eizenkot, wrote in 2010, "This is the most significant restraining element for Hizbollah because the meta-goal of the organization is achieving Shiite hegemony in Lebanon, and its main center of gravity in Lebanon is the support of the Shiite population, the very group that experienced significant trauma [in 2006]. . . . Hizbollah leaders would presumably think twice before opening fire from Shiite civilian areas, as they understand the meaning of another confrontation."[74]

In a future war against Hezbollah, the IDF is expected to clearly define its military and political parameters and will likely classify the entire Lebanese state as hostile because of Hezbollah's presence within the Lebanese government's cabinet—a variable not present during the security zone period. While Hezbollah has had members in the Lebanese Parliament since 1992 and representatives in the inner cabinet since 2005, only since 2008 has the group's flagrant domination of the cabinet become most apparent. Wars against non-state groups historically forced Israel to fight in a restrained manner, unlike state-on-state war where Israel's conventional military might is most effective and its deterrent posture is strongest. Because Hezbollah is now deeply entrenched in the Lebanese cabinet, holding the Lebanese government responsible for Hezbollah's actions shifts Israel's deterrence back to the state-on-state level. It strengthens Israel's posture by enlarging the IDF's target bank and applies serious incentive for the Lebanese government to restrain Hezbollah's military activities. This reflects partial reversion to the traditional policies advocated in 1999 by former defense minister Arens, who sought to shift IDF deterrence to the conventional sphere vis-à-vis Lebanon (and Syria). Arens discussed the new equation in a 2012 lecture: "Hezbollah is now in the government, so when the Lebanese delegation sat in the UN in 2006, it was like Hezbollah was sitting in the UN. . . . Because Hezbollah is in the government, maybe this means we have a better opportunity to deter Hezbollah because of the internal Lebanese political situation. . . . This was not possible when they were a small group of terrorists moving around Lebanon."[75]

As former national security adviser Maj. Gen. Giora Eiland advocated in 2008, it is Israel's policy to make it known that "the next war will be between Israel and Lebanon and not between Israel and Hizbollah."[76] This idea to target the Lebanese government reflects a plan advocated by General Halutz during the 2006 war, which was rejected on the first day, after US secretary of state Condoleezza Rice urgently telephoned Prime Minister Olmert and requested that the IDF not target infrastructure of Lebanon's pro-Western government of Prime Minister Fouad Siniora.[77] (For operational implications, see chapter 8.) General Yadlin, head of MI during the 2006 war, lamented the IDF's decision not to strike Lebanese government infrastructure in 2006 and the missed opportunity to strengthen Israel's deterrence: "Attacking infrastructure, while insisting on the principle of 'the state's responsibility,' is at the basis of Israel's security perception. . . . I doubt that sticking to the decision to avoid attacking [Lebanon's] state infrastructures was right. . . . Hezbollah is today a full partner in the Lebanese government, and Israel must go back to the principle it set in the 1950s and 1960s: Casting state responsibility on a country from which the enemy operates against Israel."[78]

In what is most closely associated with current policy and illustrates both a degree of continuity from the IDF's traditional deterrence concept and a major strategic adaptation, General Eizenkot outlined Israel's so-called Dahiya doctrine in an oft-cited 2008 interview. It called for the massive destruction of Hezbollah's infrastructure in Beirut's Dahiya suburb as occurred in 2006, coupled with the destruction of Lebanese state infrastructure linked to Hezbollah. Illustrating a degree of historical continuity from Israel's subscription to "deterrence by punishment," it is believed the threat of large-scale destruction maximizes Israel's deterrence, judging from Hezbollah's near-total quiet since 2006 in regard to Israel: "What happened in the Dahiya quarter of Beirut in 2006 will happen in every village from which Israel is fired on. . . . We will apply disproportionate force on [them] and cause great damage and destruction there. From our standpoint, these are not civilian villages, they are military bases. This is not a recommendation. This is a plan. And it has been approved."[79]

Col. (Res.) Gabi Siboni, a confidante of General Eizenkot, elucidated the doctrine and wrote that to avoid attritional war, the IDF has adopted "the principle of disproportionate strikes against the enemy's weak points as a primary war effort" since "such a response aims at inflicting damage and meting out punishment to an extent that will demand long and expensive reconstruction processes."[80] Eizenkot stressed the new doctrine's contribution to deterrence: "Hezbollah understands very well that firing from villages will lead to their destruction. Before Nasrallah issues an order to fire at Israel, he will have to think 30 times if he wants to destroy his basis of support in the villages. It's not a theoretical thing with him. The possibility of hurting the population is Nasrallah's main restraint and the reason for the calm."[81]

The IDF's top brass maintains a subscription to the Dahiya doctrine since its declaration in 2008. Recently retired COS Lt. Gen. Benny Gantz (2011–15) described the prevailing IDF strategy to instill deterrence by striking "directly against Hezbollah and its state surroundings. Lebanon cannot claim sovereignty but not bear responsibility. If a conflagration erupts, I would rather be an Israeli citizen than a Lebanese citizen."[82]

Statements by Lebanese president Michel Aoun in February 2017 declaring that Hezbollah's weapons "are essential, in that they complement the actions of the Lebanese army and do not contradict them," affirmed for Israel the cooperation between the Lebanese state and Hezbollah. Illustrating continuity of the approach advocated by Defense Minister Arens nearly two decades ago, the IDF has accordingly adapted its deterrence to the state-on-state level and promises to "disproportionately" strike Hezbollah and associated Lebanese infrastructure. COS Gen. Eizenkot affirmed that "the recent declarations from Beirut make it clear that in a future war, the targets will be clear: Lebanon and the organizations operating under its authority and its approval," while government minister Naftali Bennett stressed that "this leads to a simple conclusion: if Hezbollah attacks Israel, it is tantamount to a Lebanese declaration of war against Israel."[83]

The 2015 IDF Strategy: Adaptation for Protracted Conflict

In an unprecedented move, the army released an official *IDF Strategy* document in August 2015, which marks the first time in IDF history that it publicly released a codified document that resembles a national security strategy, which is "a compass for deploying and developing force" for the next five years.[84] The cornerstone of *IDF Strategy* is deterrence and exemplifies the evolutionary adaptation of the foundational principle of Israeli security. The document stresses that Israel's adversaries in the near to medium term will likely be "sub-state military organizations such as Hezbollah," and it is evident the document is fundamentally shaped by hard-earned lessons learned throughout its three decades dealing with Lebanon related to the limitations of its conventional superiority in protracted conflict.

The document outlines three types of situations, each of which requires a different IDF response. First, there are "routine" situations, which resemble ongoing security, LIC, and "campaigns between wars" and entail offensive and defensive actions to maintain security, deter the enemy, and delay the next confrontation, often as part of rules of the game. Second are "emergency" situations, which "use limited military force" to "bring the situation back to a period of calm without striving for an immediate strategic change." Emergency situations are "limited campaigns and operations that do not amount to full scale war" and are designed to restore deterrence. The third type of situation is "war"—traditional, conventional, high-intensity conflict that entails significant mobilization of resources and requires decisive victory.[85] The IDF anticipates that the most likely conflict with Hezbollah will be an emergency situation in which Israel will wage a relatively short campaign using air strikes, firepower, and a modest land component to achieve limited, clearly defined objectives designed to erode Hezbollah's capabilities ("mow the grass") and instill deterrence.[86]

The document *IDF Strategy* designates the COS as the central person to translate political goals into operational tasks, which resembles a clear lesson from the dysfunctional civil-military relations in 2006 and Prime Minister Olmert's wartime Knesset address in which he outlined what proved to be unachievable objectives. The document exemplifies the IDF's strategic learning and will greatly impact and shape its goals, objectives, and use of deterrence in a future conflict with Hezbollah.

HEZBOLLAH'S POST-2006 DETERRENCE

Hezbollah underwent a distinct learning process after the 2006 war and has recalibrated its deterrent position vis-à-vis Israel. Nasrallah noted that before 2006, Hezbollah confronted the IDF with "a guerrilla war of attrition" to liberate land from occupation, but since 2006 Hezbollah's strategic posture has evolved, as it is actively deterring and "preventing" the IDF from initiating any action in Lebanon. He boasted, "I do not think this is paralleled in the world or in history!"[87] Strategic parity between Israel and Hezbollah and the ability of each side to inflict unacceptable damage on the other has led to the maintenance of relative quiet on the border and mutual deterrence.[88] Nasrallah described this equation of mutual deterrence in his first interview after the 2006 war: "We cannot ignore it [the costs of the 2006 war] and say that we will behave and make decisions as if nothing has happened. I would not be human if I behaved in such a manner. We are definitely like this, and so are the Israelis. . . . Anyone who will come in a future Israeli government will think twice and three times before waging a war with Lebanon."[89]

Since 2006, Hezbollah's deterrent posture has matured as it has enhanced its long-range missile capabilities and ability to target the entire Israeli home front. Highlighting the intended deterrent effect of its arsenal, a Hezbollah informational sign observed by the author on a visit to a former military site in southern Lebanon read: "The military unit is commissioned with short, medium and long-range surface-to-surface missiles whose aim is to deter the enemy from targeting Lebanese civilians and civil infrastructure."[90] Similar to the dynamic that originated in 1992 following the IDF's assassination of Abbas Mussawi, Nasrallah has threatened rocket fire in retaliation for any Israeli attack, illustrating the continuation and evolution of the dialectical relationship of deterrence and punishment. Nasrallah outlined Hezbollah's astute awareness of the IDF's Dahiya doctrine: "The word 'dahiya' [suburb] has become part of military lexicons and strategies! What is this 'Dahiya Theory' that the Israelis came up with? They say: We will wreak destruction anywhere in the Dahiya, and therefore in the war you will face destruction. . . . So I tell them today, 'You destroy a building in Dahiya, and we will destroy buildings in Tel Aviv!' That is all we have [to respond to] the 'Dahiya Theory.'"[91]

Nasrallah declared Hezbollah's strategy in response to the IDF's Dahiya doctrine:

What did the Israelis do? They started to threaten the Lebanese government and people. They started to threaten infrastructure with attacks. Thus, today we announce a new position. . . . I would like to tell the Israelis today: We will not only target Tel Aviv if you target the Dahiya. If you bomb Rafiq al-Hariri Airport in Beirut, we will shell Ben-Gurion Airport in Tel Aviv. If you bomb our ports, we will shell your ports. If you bomb our oil refineries, we will shell your oil refineries. If you bomb our factories, we will shell your factories. And if you bomb our power plants, we will shell yours![92]

These provocative statements illustrate Hezbollah's overt efforts to strengthen the equation of mutual deterrence and destruction. In his 2012 "Martyrs Day" speech, Nasrallah described Hezbollah's relative success in deterring Israel: "The enemy is acknowledging the actual status of the deterrence power that was found by the Resistance in Lebanon," and "there is a point of consensus among the Israeli political, military, security leaders, parties, media figures, experts and public opinion. No one in the Israeli entity says today that there is no deterrence in Lebanon. No! There is deterrence!" However, despite Hezbollah's strengthened deterrence posture, Nasrallah also admitted that Israel maintains its long-standing military superiority and ability to deter the group: "There is deterrence by both sides. Israel has deterrence power, and this is not something new. This has been true since 1948. It deters all Arabs and all Muslims. . . . The new strategic factor is that the Resistance in Lebanon has found a new deterrence formula. . . . We have reached a point where the Israeli enemy is acknowledging the deterrence capacity we have created in Lebanon!"[93]

A report on Hezbollah's Al-Manar website summarized its strategic approach for future war, which centered on a number of reciprocal "equations" vis-à-vis Israel and emphasized mutual deterrence, destruction, and retaliation. Hezbollah vowed to target IDF troops if they entered Lebanon and to shell Israel's international airport if the IAF targeted Beirut (reaffirming the "Beirut for Tel Aviv" equation). Hezbollah would target Israel's naval blockade of Lebanon if the Israeli navy imposed one and strike sensitive Israeli industrial facilities in response to any Israeli strikes against Lebanese facilities. Lastly, the most innovative aspect of the equation was Hezbollah's declaration that it would dispatch commandos to attack or capture Israeli villages in the Galilee in response to IDF ground incursions into Lebanon.[94] Nasrallah highlighted this ground component for the first time in 2011:

Twenty years ago, everybody was talking about the Israeli occupation of Lebanon, and nobody even imagined that anyone in Lebanon could possibly take over the north of Palestine or the Galilee. . . . and the greatest achievement of the Resistance was that it made it more difficult for Israel to occupy southern Lebanon. . . . Be prepared for a day when war is forced upon Lebanon and the commanders of the Resistance may ask you to take over the Galilee! In other words, to liberate the Galilee.[95]

As IDF officials have noted, bold, offensive ground incursions into Israeli territory could grant Hezbollah greater initiative in war and increase its overall psychological perception of victory.[96] This threat was given greater prominence since 2012 after Hezbollah published a video depicting its fighters infiltrating northern Israel and attacking critical targets and after Hezbollah's highly publicized, large-scale training exercise that simulated a ground offensive.[97] Hezbollah's vow to retaliate from the air (rockets and missiles) and on the ground (commando incursions) illustrates the strategic parity between both sides and their mutually adaptive military postures. Overall, as Daniel Sobelman has illustrated, Hezbollah's broader strategic posture is designed to instill doubts in the IDF of its ability to achieve decisive victory, which has successfully bolstered the group's deterrence.[98] For example, Nasrallah declared in 2010 that "Israel can no longer go to a war whose result it does not guarantee," and in 2016 he flaunted that "after the First and Second Lebanon Wars, Israel decided it would only wage war if a clear, decisive victory is assured."[99]

General Halutz said in his testimony to the Winograd Commission, "Whatever was or was not achieved [in 2006] must be judged in the perspective of time." From Israel's vantage point, with twelve years' perspective, the 2006 war is generally viewed as a success because it forced Hezbollah to "show its hand" and reveal its most advanced long-range weapon capabilities. It allowed the IDF to reestablish red lines vis-à-vis Hezbollah and reinstall Israeli deterrence and highlighted IDF resolve to fight even while Israeli population centers were targeted with rocket fire. This fundamentally eroded Hezbollah's deterrent posture, which, in the words of General Ben-Israel, "overturned the notion that Israel is not ready to fight with anyone who holds a sword over the heads of its civilians."[100] In a recent lecture, Ehud Olmert noted that "it is safe to conclude we succeeded in creating a strong state of deterrence as a result of the Second Lebanon War" and that "Hezbollah's supposedly highly-resourceful leader, who is still living in his bunker, testified to this when he stated that had he known we would respond in such a way to our soldiers' abduction on the northern border, he would not have acted as he did."[101]

The United Kingdom's ambassador to Lebanon during the 2006 war summed up the mutual deterrence equation: "Israel's doctrine of massive reprisal operations has been successful, in that it has kept Hezbollah quiet, because the stakes are now so high. . . . For the first time since the conflict began with Hezbollah in 1982, there are five-year-olds who go to kindergarten in northern Israel and don't know what the inside of a bomb shelter looks like. This is a remarkable fact."[102]

CONCLUSION

After the erosion of Israel's deterrence in the years before 2006, owing to its failure to respond to Hezbollah provocations and the ineffective crafting of a coherent wartime strategy in 2006, the IDF learned key strategic lessons and adapted its deterrent posture. The Dahiya doctrine represents an adaptation of the traditional principle of "deterrence by punishment" ingrained in IDF strategic culture. It reflects the internalization of the IDF's inherent limitations in protracted, asymmetrical warfare, as the doctrine hopes to simply buy long periods of quiet with the threat of "disproportionate" retaliation. With greater perspective, IDF commanders assess that Hezbollah is "deterred, very deterred but still intent on evil," even though the destructive 2006 campaign greatly degraded Hezbollah's military capabilities and infrastructure, forced Hezbollah to engage in a lengthy rebuilding process, and brought a prolonged period of quiet.[103]

On the other side, Hezbollah's deterrence has been continuously strengthened by its explicit and tacit communication of credible threats, coupled with the group's enhancement of its operational capabilities to strike Israel. Such threats have led Israel to doubt its ability to achieve a rapid, decisive victory against Hezbollah in a future conflict, as each side is increasingly aware of its vulnerability.[104] Hence, the IDF's primary objective outlined in the 2015 document *IDF Strategy* for routine and emergency situations is instilling deterrence with a short, limited operation to defer the next round of fighting. Meanwhile, Hezbollah, emboldened by its so-called divine victory in 2006, has bolstered its own deterrence through enhancement of its long-range missile capabilities and its threats to launch commando squads into the Galilee. Hassan Nasrallah described the ultimate essence of deterrence, which resembles a psychological clash of wills backed up by deeds: "The Israeli enemy recognizes that the Resistance has the ability to wage a balanced psychological war and even a psychological war where we have the upper hand. . . . After thirty-three years of experience of resistance, we have proven this."[105]

NOTES

Epigraphs: Halutz, lecture, July 14, 2016; Nasrallah, speech, November 11, 2012.

1. Feldman, "Israel's Deterrent Power."
2. Brom, "Withdrawal from Southern Lebanon"; Kaye, "Israeli Decision to Withdraw," 580–83.
3. Barak, interview, June 5, 2000.
4. Author interview with Ephraim Sneh.
5. For historical background, see Kauffman, "Who Owns the Shebaa Farms?"
6. Sobelman, *New Rules of the Game*, chap. 5.
7. Brom, "After the Withdrawal."
8. Sobelman, *New Rules of the Game*, 103.
9. Qassem, interview, November 20, 2000.
10. Sobelman, *New Rules of the Game*, chap. 5; Gambill, "Sharon Ends Moratorium."

11. "Lebanese Hezbollah TV Reports Syrian Deaths, Destruction of Radar Sites," Al-Manar TV, April 16, 2001, in *BBC Monitoring Middle East*, April 16, 2001.

12. Feldman, "Deterrence and the Israel-Hezbollah War," 285.

13. Kitri, interview, April 16, 2001.

14. Zisser, "Hizballah and Israel," 97–98.

15. Quoted in Pascal Mallet, "Israeli Warplanes Wound Two Syrian, One Lebanese Soldier in Lebanon," AFP, July 1, 2001.

16. *Al-Sharq al-Awsat*, February 11, 2002, in Sobelman, *New Rules of the Game*, 71.

17. For a complete list, see Israel Ministry of Foreign Affairs, "Main Events on the Israel-Lebanese Border."

18. Israel Ministry of Foreign Affairs, "Hizbollah Attacks along Israel's Northern Border."

19. Nasrallah, interview, May 6, 2007.

20. Shalom and Hendel, "Conceptual Flaws"; Hirsch, *Defensive Shield*, chaps. 12 and 13.

21. Winograd Commission Interim Report, chap. 4, para. 41, quoted in Shalom and Hendel, "Conceptual Flaws," 28.

22. Kaplinsky, "IDF in the Years before the Second Lebanon War," 32.

23. Author interview with senior IDF officials. See also Haloutz, "Second Lebanon War," 62–63.

24. Author interview with Shlomo Brom. See also Feldman, "Deterrence and the Israel-Hezbollah War," 286.

25. Arens, "Hezbollah 2 Israel 0."

26. Yaalon, interview, August 29, 2002.

27. Malka, "Israel and Asymmetrical Deterrence," 14.

28. Olmert, "Second Lebanon War." See also Olmert, "In Retrospect."

29. Arad, "Cumulative Deterrence Deficit."

30. Israel Ministry of Foreign Affairs, "IDF Apprehends Hezbollah Terrorist."

31. Author interview with Frances Guy.

32. Nasrallah, interview, February 2006 (exact date unknown).

33. Author interview with Timur Goksel.

34. Kuperwasser, interview, August 10, 2006.

35. Komati, interview, July 25, 2006.

36. Author interview with Amos Yadlin.

37. Israel Ministry of Foreign Affairs, "IDF Apprehends Hezbollah Terrorist."

38. Fayyad, "Hezbollah and the Lebanese State," 11.

39. Author interview with Michael Williams.

40. Nasrallah, interview, August 27, 2006, 393–94.

41. Farkash, "Intelligence in the War," 80.

42. Bar, "Deterring Nonstate Terrorist Groups," 487–88.

43. Nasrallah, interview, May 6, 2007.

44. Malka, "Israel and Asymmetrical Deterrence."

45. Olmert, speech to the Knesset, July 17, 2006.

46. Olmert, interview, May 5, 2015.

47. Haloutz, *At Eye Level*, 401–4; Lambeth, *Air Operations*, 24–26.

48. Eiland, "Second Lebanon War," 12–13.

49. Quoted in Merom, "Second Lebanon War," 10.

50. Halutz, lecture, July 14, 2016.

51. Olmert, "In Retrospect," 5–6.

52. Henriksen, "Deterrence by Default?"

53. Merom, "Second Lebanon War," 5–11.

54. Vardi, "Pounding Their Feet," 311; Byman, *High Price*; Adamsky, "From Israel with Deterrence."

55. Haloutz, *At Eye Level*, 362.

56. Ibid., 394, quoted in Shamir, "Coping with Nonstate Rivals," 10.

57. Halutz, interview, February 15, 2008.

58. Author interview with Amos Yadlin.

59. Nasrallah, speech, August 3, 2006.

60. Peretz, interview, May 3, 2007.

61. Winograd Commission, final report, chap. 12, para. 7.

62. Israel Ministry of Foreign Affairs, "Winograd Commission Submits Interim Report."

63. Brom, "Political and Military Objectives," 17–18.

64. Evron, "Deterrence and Its Limitations," 39–40.

65. Biran, lecture, February 2, 2012.

66. Yadlin, "Confronting Enemy Force Buildup."

67. Quoted in Rid, "Deterrence beyond the State," 141.

68. Inbar and Shamir, "Mowing the Grass."

69. Haloutz, "Second Lebanon War," 68.

70. Adamsky, "From Israel with Deterrence," 166–69.

71. Ben-Israel, lecture, April 4, 2013.

72. Inbar and Shamir, "Mowing the Grass," 65–75.

73. Shamir, "Coping with Nonstate Rivals."

74. Eizenkot, "Changed Threat?," 31.

75. Arens, lecture, July 12, 2012.

76. Eiland, "Third Lebanon War," 15; Eiland, "Foundations of Israel's Response to Threats." For a counterargument, see Kuperwasser, "Next War with Hizbollah."

77. For context, see Rice, "Secretary Rice Holds a News Conference."

78. Yadlin, "How Israel Created Deterrence."

79. Eizenkot, interview, October 3, 2008.

80. Siboni, "Disproportionate Force."

81. Roee Nehemias, "Hezbollah Says Israel a Cardboard State," *Yediot Ahronot*, October 5, 2008.

82. Gantz, speech, March 11, 2013.

83. Bennet, "Hezbollah Is Lebanon Is Hezbollah"; Gili Cohen and Noa Shpigel, "Israeli Army Chief: If Hezbollah Targets Israel, Israel Will Target Lebanon Itself," *Haaretz*, March 19, 2017.

84. Eizenkot, *IDF Strategy*, 3. An English translation was later published by Harvard's Belfer Center: *Deterring Terror*.

85. Belfer Center, *Deterring Terror*, 12–14.

86. Even, "IDF Strategy and the Responsibility of the Political Leadership."

87. Nasrallah, speech, February 22, 2008.

88. For a basic overview, see Samaan, *From War to Deterrence*.

89. Nasrallah, interview, August 27, 2006, 394.

90. Author observation on a field trip to the Hezbollah site in Mleeta, southern Lebanon, August 23, 2011.

91. Nasrallah, speech, February 16, 2010.

92. Ibid.

93. Nasrallah, speech, November 11, 2012.

94. Sheaito, "Seven Years on July War"; Shapira, "Hizbullah Discusses Its Operational Plan."

95. Nasrallah, speech, February 16, 2011.

96. Brun, lecture, June 9, 2014.

97. "Galilee, Where the Next Confrontation with the Enemy Is!," Al-Ahed News, September 21, 2012; Roi Kais, "Report: Hezbollah Exercise Includes 10,000 Operatives," *Yediot Ahronoth*, August 23, 2012.

98. Sobelman, "Learning to Deter," 189–95.

99. Nasrallah, speech, February 16, 2010; Nasrallah, speech, February 16, 2016.

100. Lambeth, "Israel's Second Lebanon War Reconsidered," 47.

101. Olmert, "In Retrospect," 15.

102. Author interview with Frances Guy.

103. Golan, speech, August 1, 2013.

104. Sobelman, "Learning to Deter," 193–94.

105. Nasrallah, speech, May 9, 2013.

CONCLUSION TO PART I

THE IDF's FUNDAMENTAL strategic mistake throughout its odyssey in Lebanon was the mischaracterization of the nature of the enemy and slow conceptual adaptation. In the early 1980s, the IDF was adept at dealing with the nascent Hezbollah, characterized as a "routine security" threat on a par with Palestinian militias, which could be dealt with by ongoing, low-intensity security operations. The low threat perception from Hezbollah exacerbated organizational inertia and hindered strategic adaptation in the political and military establishment. After Hezbollah's organizational adaptation initiated by Abbas Mussawi and accelerated by Hassan Nasrallah after Mussawi's 1992 assassination, Hezbollah evolved from a militia that carried out kidnappings and suicide bombings into a sophisticated guerrilla force. In response to Hezbollah's increased prowess, the IDF relied more heavily on deterrence to contain the growing threat yet was limited in its response by the Israeli political echelon because of ongoing peace negotiations with Hezbollah's patron, Syria. In the aftermath of the 1993 and 1996 operations, the IDF accepted the lopsided "rules of the game" formulated as part of the "violent bargaining" between both sides throughout the decade.[1]

Despite the political limitations imposed on the military by the "understandings," the IDF sought to regain initiative during the tenure of Maj. Gen. Amiram Levin in Northern Command, who acted as a pivotal enabler of change. Influenced by both the rising threat from Hezbollah and by soldiers in Lebanon enabled by the IDF's informal culture to voice their concerns, Levin pushed the IDF to adapt its conceptualization of Hezbollah from a routine security threat to a "guerrilla army," which illustrates the dynamic interplay between top-down and bottom-up processes of adaptation.

Based on its own lesson-learning following the effectiveness of its rocket fire after the assassination of Mussawi and during the 1993 and 1996 operations, Hezbollah devised a simple but effective two-pronged strategy: wage a guerrilla war of attrition against the IDF and target the Israeli home front with rocket fire to strengthen deterrence. IDF deterrence proved ineffective in the 1980s and 1990s in limiting Hezbollah's operational activity, and, because of Israel's continued presence in the security zone, the IDF was unable to change the fundamental strategic equation that fueled the conflict. The IDF ineffectively adapted its deterrence concept throughout the 1990s by applying indirect "levers" on the Lebanese population in order to pressure Syria to restrain Hezbollah. The 1993 and 1996 operations had little effect on the motivation of Hezbollah or its operational capabilities and illustrated that the Lebanese civilian population is not a suitable target for leveraging pressure against Hezbollah since it lacks the will and capacity to prevent Hezbollah attacks.[2] Only in the late 1990s after the appointment of Moshe Arens as defense minister, a determined civilian leader from outside the military establishment, did the IDF briefly attempt to adapt its approach to the conventional state-on-state sphere by directly targeting Lebanese government infrastructure and, later, Syrian installations in Lebanon. Maj. Gen. Giora Eiland explained the IDF's underlying folly in the 1990s in Lebanon:

> Israel found itself in a catch-22, where the real political powers in Lebanon, namely Hezbollah and Syria, were officially or practically "out of the game" and the government of Lebanon used its weakness in order not to be accountable for many things, and we, in a quite stupid way, did accept these rules of the game. So, we were left to fight Hezbollah only on the tactical level, something that did not give us any of the advantages of those a state like Israel can enjoy.[3]

Israel's dysfunctional civil-military relations contributed to this dynamic, in which IDF tactical considerations on the ground did not correlate with broader strategic considerations and resulted in the "tacticalization of strategy" in Lebanon. This astute insight was noted in a 1999 IDF asymmetrical warfare doctrinal publication prior to the Lebanon withdrawal: "The uniqueness of [Hezbollah's] strategy is the ability [of the guerrilla organization] to reverse the success of the fighting on the tactical level, into achievements on the strategic level."[4] Devastatingly, Brig. Gen. Chico Tamir, a commander of the Egoz Reconnaissance Battalion, described the entire security zone period in his memoir as an "undeclared war" in which the IDF was involved in constant tactical adaptation and counteradaptation with Hezbollah while lacking greater strategic planning or direction.[5] The IDF performed adequately militarily, suffering only twenty to twenty-five combat deaths per year over the eighteen-year period while seriously damaging Hezbollah through air operations and innovative tactics developed by the Egoz unit. Nevertheless, Hezbollah's ongoing guerrilla war of attrition exacerbated intense domestic pressure on newly elected Prime Minister Barak and acted as a major trigger for change. Barak sought to change the fundamental strategic consideration underlying the conflict in Lebanon. Illustrating the conceptual rigidity present in the defense establishment, some, such as former deputy defense minister Ephraim Sneh, still maintain to this day that the security zone was "the right policy" and that the IDF should have remained in Lebanon indefinitely until Israel's northern residents were secure.[6] Barak's decision to withdraw marked a rare instance of the political echelon's carrying out a major strategic adaptation contrary to the recommendations of the military establishment.

Following the withdrawal, according to General Eiland, who later led the Israeli NSC during this time (2004–6), the Israeli political echelon did not hold a single discussion regarding refining policy in Lebanon. Hezbollah launched persistent "reminder operations" (as Nasrallah called them) in the Shebaa Farms area, while the IDF responded with a policy of restraint and "containment" in order to maintain calm for Israel's northern residents, avoid opening a second front during the Second Intifada, and prevent international political fallout from any escalation.[7] Lt. Gen. Dan Halutz lamented in his postwar testimony to the Winograd Commission that he "thought this [containment] policy was wrong. . . . I believed that a retaliation policy, even surrounding the abduction of soldiers in [October] 2000, should have been different, but a different decision was made."[8]

The strategic equation changed dramatically when the IDF withdrew in 2000, but Israel's deterrent posture, reliant on deftly responding to Hezbollah provocations, never materialized. Israeli deterrence was heavily eroded in the years following the withdrawal, and, from 2000 to 2006, Hezbollah's leadership maintained reassurance in the group's ability to deter any major IDF escalatory response as part the revised rules of the game. Israel's failure to clearly communicate its declared "red lines" after the withdrawal led to miscalculation by Hezbollah, which sparked the 2006 Israel-Hezbollah War. The Winograd Commission noted that this spiral was not a process that can be blamed solely on Prime Minister Olmert, as blame lies with the muddled policies for Lebanon shaped under his predecessors, Ehud Barak and Ariel Sharon.[9]

In strange agreement, Nasrallah concurred with the conclusions of the Winograd Commission:

> The published [Winograd] Report . . . has laid a great deal of responsibility on former premiers, chiefs of staff, defense ministers, and governments. The responsibility of the current government *lies in the continuation and preservation*

of the former approach. . . . . It says that subsequent governments since May 25, 2000, until July 12 [2006]—taking note that those governments included the best and the elite of Israeli political and military leaderships from Ehud Barak to Sharon and this current government—it describes them all in terms of failure, impotence, lack of strategic outlook and planning, and being distracted by local issues.[10]

Upon the outbreak of war, the IDF's wartime strategy was ill defined and poorly formulated, and Israel later castigated itself for not achieving its overly lofty military objectives. With the passage of time, initial perceptions of failure have shifted after more than twelve years of postwar quiet, as the IDF assesses that quiet ensues because of the strong deterrent effect caused by the massive destruction of Hezbollah's infrastructure during the war. This led to the formulation of Israel's Dahiya doctrine, which represents an adaptation of its traditional principle of "deterrence by punishment" that is ingrained in IDF strategic culture. Since 2006, Hezbollah has undergone massive rearmament and rebuilding in order to bolster its own strategic posture and has declared its own "Beirut for Tel Aviv" deterrence equation while it has successfully instilled doubts in the IDF in its ability to achieve decisive victory at an acceptable cost. As both sides continuously adapt, they each have reestablished strong mutual deterrence against one another, and a tense quiet exists on the border, for now.

The preceding four chapters have discussed the historical evolution of the Israel-Hezbollah conflict from a strategic perspective, focusing on the IDF's conceptualization of the nature of threat, how it chose to confront Hezbollah, and how it adapted its deterrence concept. It has examined Hezbollah's evolution and organizational adaptation from its origins to its present formidable strategic posture and discussed the origins and development of the mutual deterrence relationship that has emerged. With a strategic understanding of the conflict, this book next turns to assessing operational aspects of the IDF's response to Hezbollah over the preceding decades and the development of Hezbollah's unique warfighting concept.

NOTES

1. Sobelman, "Learning to Deter," 162.
2. Maoz, "Evaluating Israel's Strategy of Low-Intensity Warfare," 331–32.
3. Author interview with Giora Eiland.
4. Nir, "Fighting in the Lebanese Arena," 7.
5. Tamir, *Undeclared War.*
6. Author interview with Ephraim Sneh.

7. Eiland, "Think before You Act," 80.

8. Lt. Gen. Dan Halutz, Testimony to the Winograd Commission, January 28, 2007.

9. Martin Van Creveld, "Ehud Olmert Is Not Solely to Blame," *The Forward*, May 4, 2007.

10. Nasrallah, interview, May 6, 2007 (emphasis added).

PART II

OPERATIONAL ADAPTATION

INTRODUCTION TO PART II

THE WINOGRAD COMMISSION discussed the IDF's organizational and operational successes and failures during the 2006 Israel-Hezbollah War but only briefly outlined the prevalent trends buzzing around the IDF that influenced the development of a new operational conception for warfighting in the years before the war. The commission stressed the importance of "clarifying the principles of the operational concept that were supposed to be the IDF's guidelines in the war," especially because "some people believed that the 'new' operational concept was the cause of some of the flaws exhibited in the war." Highlighting a gap in our understanding of the 2006 war, the commission's report stated that "the IDF's operational concept—along with their derivative operational concepts for specific sectors or forces and along with the principles of combat theories and plans—is therefore a central instrument in the thinking, planning, build-up, and force activation. *Our job did not necessitate a systematic discussion of this important issue.*"[1] The commission highlighted an important omission beyond the scope of its task: "We do not deal here [in the report] with the fascinating processes of the development of an operational concept and the stages of assimilating it in the IDF. This is an important topic that is worthy of an in-depth examination."[2]

Part II of this book primarily seeks to fill this gap left by the Winograd Commission and attempts to understand the conceptual sources, organizational diffusion, and assimilation of the IDF's new operational concept for warfighting. It chiefly examines the evolution of this new "Israeli way of war" and how it affected the IDF's operational decisions and its performance in Lebanon in the 1980s and 1990s, pivotal decades of learning and adaptation vis-à-vis Hezbollah. The IDF's operational approach to war in 2006 reflects the culmination of the IDF's innovative experiences in developing and adapting operational concepts, force structure plans, and new weaponry in the decades leading up to the war. While part I of this book focused on the IDF's strategic adaptation, part II tells a different aspect of the complex story and focuses on operational adaptation during the three-decades-long Lebanon conflict.

The Winograd Commission highlighted three dominant trends that influenced an incremental reexamination by the IDF of its traditional warfighting concept and triggered a number of processes of operational innovation and adaptation in the decades preceding the 2006 war.[3] First, the prevalence of asymmetrical opponents with increased access to sophisticated technology and weaponry, embedded in dense urban environments and focused on waging attritional warfare, brought new operational challenges that made the achievement of traditional "battlefield decision" more difficult, as the conquering of enemy territory increasingly became more of a burden than a sign of victory.

Second, deep societal shifts were affecting the IDF's role in Israeli society as a "people's army" largely made up of conscripts and reservists. Sociological shifts in Israeli society led to greater individual self-realization compared to national collective responsibility. Increased societal risk aversion and a lower tolerance for large-scale military operations due to fear of incurring casualties had a subtle but significant effect on the military's operational preferences, fighting spirit, and willingness to utilize reserve units.

Third, there was the influence of and perceived benefits from the so-called Revolution in Military Affairs (RMA), the American-formulated military concept that formally emerged in the 1990s espousing the benefits of advances in military technology, intelligence, and precision targeting for military operations. Proponents of this "revolution" believed that these advances would enable the rapid destruction of enemy forces by highly accurate long-range firepower. This concept was viewed as having unique benefits that correlated with the IDF's distinct operational and social circumstances and that would improve its overall warfighting capabilities.

The impact of the RMA and associated military transformation programs was the most tangible of these three trends that influenced the development of the IDF's operational conception and preferred "way of war" in the years leading up to 2006. Without downplaying the importance of the two other trends, the RMA was viewed as uniquely suitable to the IDF as a way to cope with the sociological shifts in Israeli society and the evolving nature of Israel's enemies. Hence, the RMA became the vehicle that would shape much of the large-scale military innovation and organizational adaptation in the decades leading up to the 2006 war.

These processes of military innovation and adaptation in Israel were not uniformly implemented and are more accurately a variety of concepts that partially emerged from a local context following the 1973 Arab-Israeli War and were adopted and adapted by the IDF in a piecemeal fashion. The story of the RMA in Israel centrally incorporates three related processes of organizational change related to force structure, precision firepower, and operational design.

First, in the 1980s and 1990s, the IDF chose to adapt its force structure in an attempt to design a "slimmer and smarter" military in the spirit of the RMA, which would result in a smaller but more capable and technologically advanced force. Second, in conjunction with force structure changes, the IDF's emphasis on precision firepower, standoff capabilities, and airpower was viewed as being the appropriate mechanism by which to improve its innovative capacity and fighting edge in an era of immense operational challenges, societal shifts, and budgetary constraints. Third, a deep interest in "operational design" accelerated in the mid-1990s in the form of the IDF-developed concept of Systemic Operational Design (SOD), which attempted to give Israeli commanders the methodological tools to cope with increased complexity on the battlefield and is perhaps one of the best examples of the turmoil associated with integrating a groundbreaking operational-level innovation.

The Winograd Commission defined "operational concept" as

> a generic term for the principles of activating the military system; generally speaking, the operational concept reflects and integrates the principles for the use of force and provides a common infrastructure for the commanders and the fighters, which is mandatory for the proper functioning of a complex military system.
>
> It would similarly be correct to view an "operational concept" as the interim level between the defense theory and global strategic principles on the one hand, and the combat theory and detailed operative plans on the other hand.[4]

Highlighting the conceptual and methodological difficulties in outlining and analyzing the IDF's operational concept, the commission explained that "it is difficult to characterize the main principles of the 'new' conception, since it was based on characteristics on many levels that were not necessarily logically connected and that were also not always consistent," largely because the concept was an unsystematic "combination" of oral and written ideas from diverse sectors of the IDF.[5] Additionally, the principles underlying the operational concept, battle plans, and force activation were "usually more general" and "were not anchored clearly or unequivocally in one central document."[6] In line with the Winograd Commission, the IDF's evolving operational concept is broadly understood in this book as embodying the IDF's preferred "way of war," rather than as a set of formal principles in a specific doctrinal document.

The following chapters also delve into the development of Hezbollah's way of war and the evolution and adaptation of the group's military concept. Describing its own innovative operational evolution, an official Hezbollah informational sign observed by the author on a field trip to a Hezbollah site in south Lebanon explained, "The Resistance developed its military structure since 1982, hence inventing a *unique military concept* blending classical and nonclassical guerrilla tactics. It also obtained a system of different weapons, constituting modern with ancient military techniques and specializations, which it professionally utilized on both tactical and in maneuvering fields."[7]

The development of Hezbollah's "unique military concept" was influenced by its frictional learning experiences vis-à-vis Israel and was tailored to its specific operational context against the conventionally superior, tech-savvy IDF. This led Hezbollah to emphasize organizational survivability and resilience, enhance its camouflage and concealment techniques, enmesh itself among the people, and develop its rocket capabilities and other simple but effective counteradaptations. In line with Clausewitz's conceptualization of a war between two rivals as "a duel on a larger scale," the evolution of the operational concepts of Israel and Hezbollah illustrate the mutual dialectic of learning and adaptation by both sides.

Part II begins with chapter 5, which examines the sources of the innovative processes of change associated with the RMA and details its slow and arduous implementation within the IDF throughout the 1980s and 1990s. It delves into the theoretical and operational origins of the RMA in Israel, which influenced the IDF's attempts to transform into a "slimmer and smarter" military, and discusses the IDF's RMA-inspired adaptations throughout the 1990s. Chapter 6 analyzes the RMA in action and focuses on the IDF's increased use of precision airpower, standoff firepower, and other RMA-inspired concepts in Lebanon throughout the 1990s. This chapter illustrates Hezbollah's military learning, operational development, and counteradaptations during this period. It also discusses the impact of a short-lived operational concept for "Limited Conflict," which emerged in the late 1990s as the IDF searched for an alternative approach to Hezbollah's asymmetrical warfare. Chapter 7 centrally discusses the origins and implementation of the innovative concepts associated with "operational design" in the IDF. The main concept, SOD, was developed in the IDF's Operational Theory Research Institute and greatly impacted the IDF's way of thinking about war in the 1990s and 2000s. It also examines the wider diffusion of related concepts within the military and analyzes the important effects such concepts had on IDF war-planning for Lebanon in the run-up to 2006. Chapter 8 analyzes the IDF's decision-making and operational performance during the air and ground campaigns of the 2006 Lebanon War and explains why the IDF operated the way it did. It also discusses Hezbollah's innovative counteradaptations during the war, which circumvented the IDF's conventional superiority. Chapter 9 evaluates the IDF's various operational concepts in action on the battlefield in 2006. In light of the blame game that erupted in Israel in response to the IDF's shortcomings, this chapter offers a nuanced and balanced reappraisal of these operational concepts and analyzes what went wrong with greater perspective since the war.

WHAT IS THE REVOLUTION IN MILITARY AFFAIRS?

The RMA is a conceptual term only *formally* coined in the early 1990s but is utilized to describe certain related military concepts that originated before this period. Before the story of the development of the IDF's operational conception for warfighting continues, a brief explanation follows of what the RMA is in a definitional sense.

With the end of the Cold War and the dawn of the information-technology age, the American strategic agenda emphasized its overwhelming conventional military dominance as the only remaining superpower. The ease of the victory by US-led coalition forces in Iraq in the 1991 Gulf War was evident, as Saddam Hussein's army was disoriented and defeated by meticulously sequenced, highly mobile American precision firepower. This dazzling defeat was made possible by technological superiority, skillful utilization of forces, and impressive demonstrations of precision cruise missiles (coupled with Iraqi military ineptitude), which deftly eliminated Iraqi air defenses and other strategic targets.[8] After this overwhelmingly decisive victory, greater emphasis was placed on standoff precision firepower, networked information systems, and technological weapon platforms as the advantages seemed evident, and a Revolution in Military Affairs was proclaimed.

The RMA became a formal concept firmly rooted in the notion that surveillance, networked communications, and information technology would deliver dominant battlespace awareness and allow the United States to continue to achieve overwhelming and rapid victory in brief, intense, one-sided wars largely utilizing precision-strike capabilities.[9] One of the main precepts of the RMA was that due to this rapid fusion and dissemination of intelligence to networked units, the "fog of war" could be lifted, enabling the US military to alter, define, and shape the initial conditions of conflict, thereby narrowing an adversary's strategic options and avoiding the need for extended ground conflict or protracted warfare.[10]

Elements of this concept originated from the Soviet notion of a "Military Technical Revolution" in the 1970s and US "AirLand Battle" doctrine of the 1980s developed by US Army generals William DePuy and Donn Starry, which envisioned deep air and precision strikes on the Soviet Union's full depth, enabled by advances in weapon technology, that would affect the enemy physically and cognitively.[11] The strategic philosophy of the RMA transformation sought to replace heavier forces historically utilized for prolonged, conventional ground combat with lighter, agile forces with greater situational and battlespace awareness that could be more easily supported by precision strikes.[12] The RMA would be enabled by network-centric technology and space assets that would provide information and intelligence superiority, and the number of ground forces would be cut, supposedly balanced with a qualitative increase of technology, satellites, and precision munitions.[13]

The RMA is best viewed as the culmination of a series of technological and conceptual processes in the military and should be considered an important milestone in the continuous evolutionary process of military change and transformation. Therefore, while the formal notion of RMA in this context only emerged after the Gulf War, the origins of the concepts are evident, particularly in the Israeli case, in the innovative trends of the preceding two decades.[14] As the following chapters illustrate, the RMA in Israel has had its own independent trajectory but was partially influenced at various stages by the American military, as well as by IDF battlefield experiences with Hezbollah.

NOTES

1. Winograd Commission, final report, chap. 7, para. 6 (emphasis added).
2. Ibid., 271n7.
3. Ibid., paras. 9–10.
4. Ibid., para. 5.
5. Ibid., paras. 7 and 12.
6. Ibid., paras. 5–7.
7. Author observation on a field trip to the Hezbollah site in Mleeta, southern Lebanon.
8. Biddle, "Victory Misunderstood"; Freedman, *Transformation of Strategic Affairs*, 13.
9. McMaster, "On War," 21.
10. Department of Defense, *Military Transformation*, 2–30; Freedman, *Transformation of Strategic Affairs*, 14.
11. Metz and Kievet, *Strategy and the Revolution in Military Affairs*, 2–3; Romjue, "Evolution of the AirLand Battle Concept." For historical background, see Freedman, *Revolution in Strategic Affairs*, chap. 2; Freedman, *Strategy*, 214–20.
12. Rumsfeld, "Transforming the Military," 27.
13. Hoffman, "Complex Irregular Warfare," 396.
14. Freedman, *Revolution in Strategic Affairs*, 7–9.

CHAPTER 5

THE ORIGINS OF THE RMA IN ISRAEL

We must prevent a situation in which goals of war and strategy are subject to the whims of technocrats and armchair strategists who view technical solutions as the whole picture and as miracle drugs for the most complex matters.

—Maj. Gen. Israel Tal

[Not even the] strongest air force in the world . . . [can destroy a] popular resistance. . . . All cases prove this: Iraq, Yugoslavia, and all the rest.

—Sec.-Gen. Hassan Nasrallah

The theoretical and operational origins of the RMA in Israel are centrally linked to the IDF's experiences in Lebanon in the early 1980s. These experiences contributed to the IDF's attempts to transform into a "slimmer and smarter" military in a process guided from the top down by COS Lt. Gen. Dan Shomron. The innovative processes of change associated with the RMA were slowly and arduously implemented within the IDF throughout the 1980s and 1990s and gained further traction after the US military's impressive victory during the 1991 Gulf War, which "validated" the RMA in the eyes of the IDF. The IDF would implement several large-scale RMA-inspired programs throughout the 1990s and carried out massive organizational streamlining and budgetary cuts to subsidize the army's "revolutionary" adaptation, which would have a significant impact on the IDF's future preparedness in 2006.[1]

SOURCES AND ORIGINS OF THE RMA IN ISRAEL

Since the surprise and failure of the IAF to cope with Egyptian surface-to-air missiles (SAMs) and Sagger antitank weapons during the 1973 Yom Kippur War, Israel was acutely aware of the importance of precision-guided missiles and associated technology.[2] In 1973, implementation of the main pillars of Israel's security concept—deterrence, intelligence warning, and rapid decision—had failed them. When learning postwar lessons, instead of a strategic rethinking of doctrine, the IDF learned the wrong lessons and focused on technical issues that arose during the war, especially related to the temporary shortage of manpower and hardware.[3] Following the trauma of the 1973 war, Israel undertook massive military spending, expanded its force size, acquired new technologies, and developed and upgraded its weapon capabilities, which severely strained the economy.[4] These programs were partially influenced by visits of IAF delegations to the United States in the 1970s to learn applicable lessons following the Vietnam War, especially those that pertained to dealing with highly mobile, smaller forces, mobile missile launchers, and electronic warfare.[5] The technological upgrades carried out by the IDF at this time were facilitated by the microelectronics revolution, the rapid evolution of missile technology, and the invention in 1971 of the microprocessor (enabling precision-fire capabilities).[6]

According to Brig. Gen. (Ret.) Shlomo Brom, one of the IAF delegates to the United States who was involved in doctrine development at this time, the IDF formulated a three-tiered system following the 1973 war that greatly resembled RMA-style technology that would emerge in ensuing decades. First, the IDF battle system involved tracing and tracking an enemy; second, being able to simultaneously protect its own force using electronic warfare while launching long-range precision-guided munitions; and, third, developing advanced command-and-control mechanisms to feed a real-time picture of the situation to commanders—"and that is RMA, although we didn't give it this name." General Brom elaborated: "The pioneers for using this were the IAF. . . . We developed the concept of the RMA before the name RMA was coined. We didn't know it was called RMA. We developed these concepts after the 1973 war as a lesson of the war, and a lesson we learned was that we needed to deal with the enemy air-defense systems. . . . By the 1982 Lebanon War, we had quite a perfect system."[7]

In the opening phase of the 1982 Lebanon War, the IDF (specifically the IAF) masterfully overcame Syrian SAMs and other air-defense systems by using precision-guided weaponry and cutting-edge technology, gaining air supremacy with astounding success. This marked the successful utilization of next-generation technology that would be a major enabler of the RMA in Israel.[8] The IDF's Bekaa Valley air operation on June 9, 1982, which downed at least eighty-two Syrian MiGs (with no IAF losses) and destroyed at least seventeen Syrian SAM sites, was called by Defense Minister Ariel Sharon at the time "one of the most brilliant, complicated, and intricate operations" ever launched by the IDF.[9] The IAF utilized precision and laser-guided bombs, electronic warfare, real-time intelligence dissemination, unmanned aerial vehicles (UAVs), and radar and communications jamming, synced with standoff firepower, while sensor-to-shooter and command-and-control systems operated in a networked feedback loop.[10] To some in the IDF, this overwhelming success signified the benefit of the IDF's technological acquisitions and force modernization and that they had learned the right lessons from the 1973 war experience. However, the familiar nature of the operational environment, IAF numerical and qualitative superiority, and the poor tactics and quality of the Soviet-supplied Syrian air force should put into perspective the sense of a "revolutionary" Israeli success in this specific case.[11]

Basking in glory following the IAF's impressive victory against the Syrians in the Bekaa Valley, Israel further invested in qualitative technological improvements to military hardware because of its perceived utility but without formulating new doctrine or organizational structures.[12] The investment in RMA-style technology was spearheaded by the IAF, even though most of the IDF continued to prepare for traditional, large-scale ground or armored maneuver in case of an Iraqi or Syrian invasion on the eastern front.[13] Despite massive investments made after 1973, the IDF's ground offensive in the 1982 Lebanon War was disappointing, as it was disjointed, slow, and riddled with tactical mistakes.[14] The growing disparity between the IAF and other services continued, exacerbated by the allocation of US military aid, with the head of IDF Ground Forces Command claiming in 1986 that the IAF received 82 percent of total US funding.[15]

The IDF witnessed the rise of guerrilla warfare in Lebanon from Hezbollah between 1982 and 1985. General Brom, active in Lebanon during this time, said in a 2012 interview, "In 1982, we already used RMA technology and concepts. It was examined if RMA can help in low-intensity conflict, and the conclusion was that it cannot help." His opinion represented the IDF's conceptual focus then, despite the technological leaps that were occurring: "During these years, I don't think the IDF considered Hezbollah a real fighting force," hence the Lebanon campaign did not benefit operationally from the advent of RMA technology.[16] Brom reflected, "When it concerns Hezbollah, as long as we were in the security zone facing those kinds of Hezbollah operations, the RMA didn't seem to be so relevant to this kind of fighting." In the 1980s, the RMA "hit the margins of the army" and did not significantly affect IDF ground operations in Lebanon.[17]

As the IDF slowly became entrenched in Lebanon throughout the late 1980s, a debate emerged between "traditionalists" and "reformists" regarding the future of IDF force structure and doctrine and the role of technology.[18] The traditionalists, epitomized by legendary tank commander Maj. Gen. Israel

Tal, viewed a large, offensive, armor-centric force to be the solution to avoid fighting defensive, protracted, attritional war. General Tal was one of the most innovative military minds of the century, and his opinions held great sway in the IDF. While Tal did not downplay the importance of technology, he wrote prophetically in 1989, "We must prevent a situation in which goals of war and strategy are subject to the whims of technocrats and armchair strategists who view technical solutions as the whole picture and as miracle drugs for the most complex matters. . . . When tactics are subjugated to technique . . . often battles are won, but wars are lost."[19]

The reformists argued for a major conceptual rethinking of IDF doctrine since they assessed that new precision-guided technology and standoff firepower would greatly benefit the IDF and was preferable to the IDF's traditional principle of rapidly seizing enemy terrain with a large offensive ground force.[20] The traditionalists were criticized by the reformists for their overly reflexive preference for offensive action (dubbed the "cult of the offensive") and overadherence to the IDF's "classic" security doctrine.[21] These reformists emphasized the need for an initial defensive concept of operations whereby the enemy could be weakened with precision firepower and deep strikes before traditional ground maneuvers would be launched.[22] One outspoken reformist, Brig. Gen. Shimon Naveh, who would be a key figure in IDF innovation in the ensuing decade, noted the "total detachment of the Israeli doctrine of offensive preemption from the strategic reality" and encouraged air mechanization and flexible synchronization of combined arms using RMA-style "advanced technologies."[23] Ultimately, Defense Minister Yitzhak Rabin took the middle road between the two schools, choosing to develop and adopt weaponry and technology advocated by the reformers but incorporate it into the IDF's traditional force structure and concept of operations.[24]

The sources of the RMA in Israel emerged both from changes to the external strategic environment regarding the proliferation of long-range and unconventional threats and as a result of internal shock following the 1973 war. The seedlings of the RMA were planted in Israel by the validation of the technology during the 1982 Bekaa Valley air battle in Lebanon. Encouraged by reformist circles in the IDF, it is at this point that these budding concepts began to be more widely implemented, although they still lacked a clear theoretical formulation.

SHOMRON'S PUSH FOR A SLIMMER AND SMARTER IDF

The realization that despite Israel's clear conventional superiority the proliferation of modern military technology enabled its adversaries to strike the home front utilizing long-range or unconventional weapons without having to overwhelm its military was a critical driver behind the IDF's transformation. To maintain its qualitative and technological edge and to compensate for its force expansion and unsustainable military budget, COS Lt. Gen. Dan Shomron developed a plan to make the IDF slimmer and smarter during his tenure (1987–91). The concept implied that by downsizing and streamlining command and organizational structures, this would "slim down" the IDF, improve efficiency, and facilitate its historical preference for quality over quantity. The IDF would become "smarter" by increasing its intelligence capabilities and incorporating new precision technology, which would enable the slimming process and facilitate a qualitative professionalization of the force.[25] These principles were in sync with the nascent RMA, meant to enable IDF superiority in wars of short duration to be fought with long-range firepower.

General Shomron acted as a key visionary and enabler of change, laying the foundations of the formally undeclared RMA. Upon becoming COS and being motivated by a confluence of internal budgetary, societal, and operational factors, Shomron sought to develop a slimmer and smarter force by enhancing IDF precision-guided capabilities, improving early-warning systems, and emphasizing combined-arms operations.[26] Profound societal changes regarding decreased enlistment rates and troop motivation, coupled with increased casualty sensitivity amid ongoing operations in Lebanon, led to a gradual shift toward professionalization of the IDF, as the economic environment could not sustain a bloated army filled with expensive-to-maintain reservists who increasingly favored personal realization and self-fulfillment over military service, sacrifice, and collectivism.[27] This was coupled with major changes in Israel's operational environment, including the rising threat from Hezbollah's asymmetrical warfare and the possibility of an Arab-Israeli peace deal that could result in concessions of Israeli territory and loss of strategic depth. The increasingly tight budget associated with maintaining expensive technology and the increased manpower put in place after 1973 also necessitated a downsizing of the IDF force structure.[28]

The newly acquired sophisticated weapon systems (and associated prohibitive costs) required specialized training best carried out by professionals and contributed to a slide toward professionalization and a smaller, more specialized fighting force.[29] Modernization made the reserves less useful and gradually exacerbated a dichotomy in the IDF between highly trained, well-funded professionals and undertrained, bloated reserve units—which would have key implications in the 2006 war.[30] The poor readiness and lessening utility of the reserves also had profound sociological implications regarding the IDF's role as the "people's army."[31]

General Shomron subscribed to the budding yet unformulated RMA as the ideal remedy to help the IDF cope with these profound social issues, operational challenges, and budgetary constraints.[32] He described the logic for the cuts in a 1987 interview:

We must develop weapons that allow us to come out of a war with fewer casualties, and in order to have this we are forced to cut the army. . . . Obviously I am in favor of a large, top-quality, and inexpensive army . . . only unfortunately, these things do not go together. . . . This is why I say quality is the first thing. A large army for us is like Swiss cheese, more holes than cheese.[33]

The RMA in Israel maintained a technocentric emphasis throughout the late 1980s, as technology was thought to be able to partially replace manpower, reduce IDF casualties and the likelihood of attritional war, enhance the ability to inflict precise damage from a distance, and bolster the IDF's extensive intelligence capabilities. However, Israeli weapon and technology experts cautioned in the 1980s against the overzealous procurement of expensive technology that had not been thoroughly battle-tested and also urged for the fitting of technology into a revised security paradigm, which never occurred.[34]

THE GULF WAR: THE "VALIDATED" RMA PICKS UP STEAM

In the Gulf War, Israel witnessed the decisive crushing of the massive but ineffective Iraqi army by the US-led coalition during Operation Desert Storm, which strongly reaffirmed Israel's need to maintain its qualitative military edge in the Middle East regarding its weaponry and intelligence capabilities.[35] Defense Minister Rabin described the impact of the decisive defeat of Iraq in a 1991 speech:

The Gulf War is a prime example. We would never have believed, one year ago, that the scenario for the next Middle East war would involve the military force of one of the two countries most hostile to Israel being crippled by a foreign power; advance warning of five months; and Israel suffering only negligible damage, without a spilt drop of IDF blood. I assume that if someone had predicted this he would have been told to "go sleep it off" or sent to a sanitarium. . . . The American army conducted a remarkable war in the Gulf. The air force was utilized to the utmost, resulting in the decisive defeat of the enormous Iraqi force with minimum casualties—something we never managed to achieve in any of our wars.[36]

The success of the US military led to the proclamation of a "Revolution in Military Affairs," epitomizing the ideal "Western way of war" regarding the use of precision technology, low tolerance for casualties, and low collateral damage, as the concepts and terminology of the RMA began to formally influence Western militaries globally.[37] General Brom, deputy head of the IDF Strategic Planning Division at the time (1990–94), explained: "The First Gulf War verified our basic concept, which was already in place before that."[38]

It marks the period in which the IDF began to formally adopt and implement newly validated RMA concepts on a larger scale.

While COS General Shomron was the first to call for a slimmer and smarter force in the late 1980s, the RMA concept gained traction after the Gulf War and was heavily supported by his successor, Lt. Gen. Ehud Barak (1991–95). While Shomron planted the seedlings, Barak acted as the driving force for change within the military from the top down and advocated for force modernization, professionalization, reducing the economic burden of reserve duty, and increasing organizational efficiency.[39]

The IDF intensely studied the Gulf War and gleaned several important lessons. In an IDF report on the subject, the IDF was impressed with the decisive military leadership of Gen. H. Norman Schwarzkopf and the benefits of AirLand Battle, based on expanding the width and depth of the battlefield, cooperation between air and ground forces, heavy use of intelligence, and use of the "indirect approach," believed to ideally suit the IDF. The report noted that the conditions of war that the United States and Israel face are dramatically different, as Israel does not enjoy the "luxury" of a long pre-war buildup period or phased operations, owing to its economic limitations, insufficient staying power, and an assumed lack of international support. The operational benefits of the RMA exhibited during the Gulf War reaffirmed the IDF's emphasis on its qualitative military edge, precision firepower, combined-arms warfare, intelligence capabilities, attack helicopters, and close air support.[40] The dire need for Israeli-developed missile-defense technology was driven home when Saddam Hussein launched at least forty Scud missiles at Tel Aviv during the war, which led to the creation of IDF Home Front Command in February 1992 to deal with civilian defense and unconventional threats.

RMA-inspired capabilities were initially advocated by IDF technology engineers and specialists within the defense industry throughout the 1970s and 1980s, and only after the Gulf War was a more focused program formulated regarding harvesting these "revolutionary" technological developments. A key figure who spearheaded the process after the Gulf War and drove the innovation forward from the top down was Maj. Gen. Isaac Ben-Israel, a senior air force officer with a PhD in physics and chief of military R&D.[41] General Ben-Israel reflected on the initial lukewarm sentiment toward the RMA and the importance of the Gulf War on his thinking: "At the time, I thought it wouldn't justify the investment. Two things changed my mind: The Gulf War and the fact that the Iraqis fired missiles at us. Even though the damage was marginal, it was a blow to the consciousness. The second point is that most of the money was given by the U.S. [Moshe] Dayan once said that only a donkey doesn't change his opinion."[42]

While the RMA gained traction in the IDF after the Gulf War, Israeli troops in Lebanon—still continuously bogged down in protracted security operations—failed to see how the RMA would change or improve their operational circumstances.[43] The focus on the RMA and making the IDF slimmer and smarter were not in line with its changing military commitments throughout the 1980s and 1990s, as the IDF was increasingly involved in LIC and "routine security" in Lebanon and the Palestinian territories.[44] In a little-known 1993 interview, General Naveh reflected, "To tell you the truth, and this may be close to being a military secret, but we have wanted to reduce our military forces even more but have been prevented from doing so because we needed battalions of soldiers to serve as policemen," illustrating how the slimmer and smarter force transformation was not in line with the IDF's day-to-day operational needs.[45]

The IDF was arguably the first military to develop, master, and integrate RMA-style technology—on the Lebanese battlefield in the 1980s—during a time period Dima Adamsky calls "the unconscious RMA" in Israel. However, Israel was slow to develop a theoretical or conceptual framework regarding the role of technology and RMA concepts in IDF doctrine. After the Gulf War, the RMA gained further traction in Israel because it provided an elegant and "revolutionary" theoretical framework that fit with the IDF's existing military technology.[46] According to General Brom, head of the IDF Strategic Planning Division (1994–98):

> During these years, the discussions started in the US, and we understood that this RMA they're talking about is what the IDF has been doing for a number of years already, and so a process of mutual feedback started between the IDF and the US. We started to have discussions about the theoretical framework of the RMA because, in what is typical of the IDF, we are developing concepts but without discussing them or writing the theoretical framework. We need someone external, like the US, to put it on paper, and then we also start putting it on paper.[47]

THE IMPLEMENTATION OF THE RMA IN ISRAEL: ORGANIZATIONAL STREAMLINING AND BUDGET CUTS

The IDF's transformation, originally encouraged by Generals Shomron and Barak, was encouraged further by COS successors who sought to base Israel's military supremacy on advanced technology. Barak's immediate successor, Lt. Gen. Amnon Lipkin-Shahak (1995–98), was more subdued in his support of RMA-inspired changes but did support various other avenues of reform related to the IDF's slide toward professionalization and significantly increased the IDF's use of civilian contractors.[48] Most notably, in 1995, he approved the creation of the Operational Theory Research Institute (OTRI; Hebrew: Maltam), an innovative group that would strive to improve the

IDF's understanding of the operational level of war by developing new theoretical methodologies (see chapter 7). General Lipkin-Shahak's tepid approach to RMA reforms were encapsulated in his 1998 farewell interview as COS: "Revolutions are necessary in extreme circumstances. It's very populist to say, 'I'll transform, I'll make the army into this, that or the other.' But an army is like a ship at sea. It needs stability as long as it's moving ahead. Storms interfere with its movement and frequent changes of direction slow down its progress. I don't believe in unnecessary revolutions for populist needs."[49]

During the tenure of his successor, Lt. Gen. Shaul Mofaz (1998–2002), the IDF rolled out a broad program of reform aspiring to improve its quality and efficiency called Aviv Neurim ("Spring of Youth"), which was inspired by the RMA but ultimately shaped by budgetary conditions. General Mofaz wrote that the reforms were "aimed at changing the corporate culture in order to achieve optimal use of resources," which is "a process centered on decentralization."[50] The plan was designed to make the IDF "flatter" and more efficient by giving brigade commanders budgetary and administrative authority.[51] However, the reforms were criticized for being overly managerial, as some of the plan's advisers were organizational consultants without serious military backgrounds, resulting in an intellectual facade being placed over these reforms.[52]

During General Mofaz's tenure, the IDF unveiled several (classified) multiyear plans, which detailed the general strategic trajectory of the military and its main priorities over the next five to ten years.[53] The longer-range Idan 2010 plan,[54] inspired by the American RMA, was a modernization plan that bolstered the armored corps, air force, missile defense, and UAVs and also technologically enhanced the IDF's special forces in Lebanon, while concurrently decreasing force size and increasing professionalization.[55] The shorter-term Tzahal 2000 plan was another formulation of various RMA concepts, as it emphasized the enduring importance of the IAF and the need for continuous, high-quality intelligence synced with standoff firepower, as well as the need to invest in space assets, smart weapons, and information systems.[56] To pay for the new technology, Mofaz reduced career military posts, noncombat personnel, and the number of reserve forces, which marked a radical change in IDF force structure, as now regular units were expected to be capable of blocking a surprise attack without the reserves.[57] This signaled another dramatic shift from the Israeli "citizen army" to a smaller, smarter, more professional standing army.

The main changes in these plans were related to force structure and slimming the IDF, as Mofaz reformed the Ground Forces Command (GFC, Hebrew: Mazi), which streamlined all force structure, training, logistics, technology, and supply issues and acted as an umbrella for support services required by the ground forces.[58] Under these reforms, many training bases were closed and logistics organizations were downsized, which would deeply affect IDF preparedness in ensuing years. Highlighting the disconnect between the senior command and the messy situation on the ground in Lebanon in the late 1990s, an Operations Directorate was created in the General Staff to oversee all operational issues and "routine defense missions," which freed the COS from managing day-to-day low-intensity operations.[59]

The IDF acquired expensive new weapon systems (mostly through US subsidies), which qualitatively improved its capabilities and filled the gap left by manpower reductions and the shrinking force size.[60] Defense budget increases were approved in 1999, and greater funds were allocated for military technology, which led to the development of homemade Israeli RMA technology, including Arrow-2 ballistic missile defense systems, Ofeq surveillance satellite systems providing continuous real-time intelligence, UAVs capable of firing air-to-air missiles, and huge amounts of other air, ballistic-missile, and network-centric technologies.[61] The Israeli navy also acquired *Dolphin*-class submarines and various missile boats. As shown by this massive military spending, the IDF clearly subscribed to the American-inspired military transformation, believing that missile and space technology, a superior air force, and networked troops could counter future threats.

Further RMA-related organizational changes and budgetary cuts were carried out into the mid-2000s during the tenure of COS Lt. Gen. Moshe "Bogie" Yaalon (2002–5), outlined in another five-year strategic review called Kela 2008,[62] which emphasized professionalization of the force, reservist-training cuts, and army digitalization.[63] Kela 2008 upgraded various weapon systems but contained a 10 percent cut in the senior officer establishment, with the highest cuts directed against ground forces training. More importantly, the plan undertook huge training cuts specifically of reserve units, citing the lack of utility of reservists for LIC operations, as some reservist training exercises were postponed for up to three years.[64] These training cuts and budgetary diversions would have a major impact on IDF preparedness in 2006.

During the tenures of Mofaz and Yaalon, both strong supporters of the RMA, it is not surprising that the head of the IAF at the time, Maj. Gen. Dan Halutz (2000–2004), also supported such reforms. General Halutz, the future COS during the 2006 war, publicly proclaimed that the IAF needed a "great imagination" to push Israel's warfighting capabilities into space and harness the operational benefits of space assets in the air force.[65] From the IDF's perspective, successful US military operations in the opening phases of the 2001 Afghanistan War and the 2003 Iraq War further validated the utility of the RMA and associated precision technologies. Perfectly exemplifying the influence of the US military's air operations in Kosovo, Afghanistan, and Iraq on the IDF's "way of war," Halutz said in a speech upon becoming COS in 2004,

The American coalition forces operating in Iraq in the First and Second Gulf Wars demonstrated the advantage of high technology and air power. Kosovo proved to be the first military victory achieved by air power alone. The U.S. defeat of the Taliban in Afghanistan was an example of a joint operation by air power and Special Forces. Recent U.S. operations in Iraq offer an excellent demonstration of a new doctrine that combines ground movement and the use of air power—day and night, in all kinds of weather—in a very sophisticated way.[66]

Halutz then outlined the capabilities that the IAF would need for a future war: precision strike and long-range capabilities, air supremacy, information supremacy, network-centric systems, and unmanned vehicles. These statements clearly demonstrate Halutz's deep affinity for the RMA, which would have ramifications on many of Halutz's command decisions as COS during the 2006 war.

CONCLUSION

The RMA in Israel emerged from a local context as a result of rising threats in the external strategic environment and efforts by military officers shocked by the IDF's performance during the 1973 war. The process, spearheaded from the top down by General Shomron without major involvement from the political echelon, was validated internally during the 1982 Bekaa Valley air battle and accelerated further by successors after validation during the 1991 Gulf War. The Gulf War episode contributed to the IDF's emulation of the US military and adoption of concepts and programs that were externally legitimated by an "authoritative" source, the Pentagon. This process led to the zealous implementation of elements of the American RMA into the IDF (as well as other military forces around the world).[67] Successive IDF chiefs of staff, along with several well-placed proponents, all enthusiastically embraced the RMA, which led to increased investments in air assets, standoff firepower, and military technology. This effort to professionalize the force and make it "smarter" enhanced the IDF's precision-firepower and intelligence capabilities but also led to the slow erosion of the ground forces and less focus on reservist training, owing to budgetary cuts throughout the 2000s.

Given the IDF's experiences in Lebanon since the late 1980s and specifically the 1993 and 1996 operations against Hezbollah, the head of Israel's Weapons Development Authority, Zeev Bonen, prophetically noted that Hezbollah was "blunting and perhaps even overturning the advantages of the [RMA]. Unless these [guerrilla] areas can be bypassed, they must be attacked primarily by infantry forces." He proclaimed that the RMA is "largely irrelevant to this kind of warfare," as Israel's enemies will resort to asymmetrical means because of the IDF's superior RMA capabilities.[68] The next chapter examines the implementation of RMA concepts and weaponry on the Lebanese battlefield in the 1990s and how Hezbollah adapted and "overturned" the advantages of this new Israeli way of war.

NOTES

Epigraphs: Quoted in Tal, "Offensive and Defensive in Israel's Campaigns," 46; Al-Mayadeen, August 14, 2013, quoted in Sobelman "Learning to Deter," 172.

1. A very abridged version of this chapter appears in Marcus, "Israeli Revolution in Military Affairs," 92–96.

2. On these surprises, see Finkel, *On Flexibility*, chaps. 8 and 9.

3. Bar-Joseph, "RMA," 2.

4. Van Creveld, *Sword and the Olive*, 253–58.

5. Author interview with Shlomo Brom.

6. Bonen, "Sophisticated Conventional War."

7. Author interview with Shlomo Brom.

8. Ben-Israel, "Revolution in Military Affairs," 63–70.

9. Quoted in Henry Kamm, "Israel Reports Its Aircraft Have Wrecked Syria's Antiaircraft Missiles," *New York Times*, June 10, 1982.

10. David Ottoway, "Wars and Missiles: Israel Said to Master New Technology to Trick and Destroy Soviet-Made Rockets," *Washington Post*, June 14, 1982; Adamsky, *Culture of Military Innovation*, 95; Grant, "Bekaa Valley War."

11. Hurley, "Bekaa Valley Air Battle."

12. Adamsky, *Culture of Military Innovation*, 96.

13. Bar-Joseph, "RMA," 4.

14. For such criticism, Wald, *Wald Report*, 29–74; Naveh, "Cult of the Offensive," 177; Schiff and Yaari, *Israel's Lebanon War*, 109–80.

15. Drori, interview, May 16, 1986.

16. Author interview with Shlomo Brom.

17. Ibid.

18. Adamsky, *Culture of Military Innovation*, 96–98.

19. Tal, "Offensive and Defensive in Israel's Campaigns," 46.

20. Levite, *Offense and Defense*, especially chap. 3.

21. Naveh, "Cult of the Offensive"; Levite, *Offense and Defense*, 84–85.

22. Bar-Joseph, "RMA," 4; Adamsky, *Culture of Military Innovation*, 96–97.

23. Naveh, "Cult of the Offensive," 176.

24. Adamsky, *Culture of Military Innovation*, 97.

25. Cohen, *Israel and Its Army*, 85.

26. Levite, "Changes of the Guard in Israel"; Cohen, "Small States and Their Armies."

27. Cohen, Eisenstadt, and Bacevich, "Israel's Revolution in Security Affairs," 53–62; Cohen, *Israel and Its Army*, 93.

28. For example, see Shomron, interview, June 4, 1986; Shomron, statement, August 30, 1987; and Shomron, interview, October 28, 1988.

29. Cohen, "Small States and Their Armies," 90.

30. Demchak, "Coping, Copying, and Concentrating," 363; Cohen, *Israel and Its Army*, 50–51.

31. Horowitz, "Strategic Limitations of 'a Nation in Arms.'"

32. Cohen, "Peace Process and Its Impact."

33. Shomron, interview, September 23, 1987.

34. Bonen, "Technological Arms Race."

35. Cohen, Eisenstadt, and Bacevich, "Israel's Revolution in Security Affairs," 50.

36. Rabin, speech, June 10, 1991.

37. Freedman, *Revolution in Strategic Affairs*, 14–17.

38. Author interview with Shlomo Brom.

39. Cohen, *Israel and Its Army*, 83–84; Cohen, "Peace Process and Its Impact," 5–6.

40. Inbar, *Decisive Factors in the Gulf War*, 33–35.

41. Cohen, *Israel and Its Army*, 42–43.

42. Ben-Israel, interview, December 18, 2001.

43. Bar-Joseph, "RMA," 5–6.

44. Cohen, "Changing Emphases on Israel's Military Commitments."

45. Naveh, interview, November 20, 1993.

46. Adamsky, *Culture of Military Innovation*, chaps. 4–5.

47. Author interview with Shlomo Brom.

48. Cohen, "Small States and Their Armies," 83.

49. Excerpts appeared in Amos Harel, "Amnon Lipkin-Shahak: The Last of the Army's Princes," *Haaretz*, December 20, 2012.

50. Mofaz, "Spring of Youth," 1. The entire issue of *Maarachot* (no. 358, 1998) was devoted to these reforms.

51. Cohen, *Israel and Its Army*, 92.

52. Kober, "Israeli Military Thought," 717; Kober, *Practical Soldiers*, 53.

53. Col. (Ret.) David Eshel, "Israel's Future Forces," *Jane's Defence Weekly*, August 25, 1999; Cordesman, *Peace and War*, 208.

54. *Idan* translates as "era" or "epoch."

55. Eshel, "Israel's Future Forces."

56. Mofaz, "IDF toward the Year 2000," 9–11.

57. Ed Blanche, "Israel Addresses the Threats of the New Millennium: Part Two," *Jane's Intelligence Review*, March 1, 1999.

58. Cohen, *Israel and Its Army*, 87–88; Cordesman, *Peace and War*, 209; Cohen, "Israel's Three Strategic Challenges."

59. Mofaz, "IDF toward the Year 2000."

60. "Israeli Defence Budget in Crisis," *Jane's International Defence Review*, September 1, 1997.

61. Blanche, "Israel Addresses." For more details, see Col. (Ret.) David Eshel, "Looking into the Future . . . What Are Israel's Options?," *Jane's Defence Weekly*, August 16, 2000.

62. *Kela* translates as "catapult" or "slingshot."

63. Catignani, "Organizational Changes"; Cordesman, *Arab-Israeli Military Forces*, 99–100.

64. Alon Ben-David, "All Quiet on the Eastern Front so Israel Will Revise Organization and Doctrine," *Jane's International Defence Review*, March 1, 2004.

65. Haloutz, "Air and Space Strategy for Small Powers."

66. Haloutz, "21st Century Threats Facing Israel."

67. See various chapters in Collins and Futter, *Reassessing the Revolution in Military Affairs*.

68. Bonen, "Sophisticated Conventional War," uses the term "SCW" for RMA. For consistency, the term "RMA" is utilized.

CHAPTER 6

THE RMA IN ACTION

IDF Operations in Lebanon and Hezbollah's Adaptation in the 1990s

There's a limit to what you can get out of a barrel [of a gun] in terms of accuracy.

—MAJ. GEN. MATAN VILNAI, IDF DEPUTY CHIEF OF STAFF

I am not underestimating the Israeli soldier's abilities; I am just saying that he hides behind his technology, his artillery, his helicopters, and his heavy gunfire.

—SEC.-GEN. HASSAN NASRALLAH

THROUGHOUT THE 1980S, the influence of the RMA was minimal on the IDF's "routine security" operations against Hezbollah. It was not until the targeted assassination of Sec.-Gen. Abbas Mussawi in 1992 that Hezbollah witnessed "firsthand" the IDF's new technological capabilities. Mussawi, while travelling in his motorcade in southern Lebanon was located by optical surveillance technology and tracked by the IAF as a "time-sensitive mobile target," and Northern Command made the improvised decision in real time to assassinate him using the "find-fix-kill chain," which is a process reliant on technological assets to rapidly locate and engage targets on the battlefield. The helicopter strike was the first notable occurrence in which RMA capabilities were utilized directly against Hezbollah.[1] The assassination of Mussawi was a painful wake-up call for Hezbollah regarding the IDF's precision-guided capabilities. Hezbollah was also likely influenced by the experiences of its patron Syria, which received an eye-opener after witnessing US precision-guided firepower capabilities as a member of the international coalition in the 1991 Gulf War.[2] In an interview following the IDF's aforementioned change in targeting policy in 1992 (see chapter 2), Sec.-Gen. Hassan Nasrallah perceptively acknowledged the IDF's increasing preference for airpower and its growing hesitancy to launch large-scale ground operations in light of "human, material, and political" calculations and casualty aversion: "It is possible and most probable that [Israel] will continue their air attacks. . . . This kind of policy has become part of the enemy's firm policy in dealing with the Resistance. There are people in Israel who advocate the constant use of such a method because it greatly reduces the possibilities of human and material losses by the Israeli army."[3]

Nasrallah's 1992 assessment of the increasing IDF preference for airpower proved accurate, as the major offensives against Hezbollah in the 1990s—the 1993 Operation Accountability and the 1996 Operation Grapes of Wrath—were both large-scale air operations that used massive standoff firepower capabilities. The IDF's operational preference for RMA-inspired warfare and precision firepower triggered significant processes of innovation and operational adaptation in Hezbollah, which evolved, counteradapted, and incrementally developed its own operational paradigm to circumvent the IDF's conventional superiority and technological advantage. In response to Hezbollah's successes and the limited efficacy of the RMA on the Lebanese battlefield, the IDF searched for an alternative approach to asymmetrical warfare in the late 1990s. This led to the creation of the short-lived "Limited Conflict" doctrine by officers in Lebanon, which impacted the IDF's modus operandi and preparedness for future war.

1993 OPERATION ACCOUNTABILITY: OPERATIONAL ASPECTS

Amid the continuous cycle of attritional tit-for-tat violence, the IDF launched the seven-day Operation Accountability on July 25, 1993, after seven Israeli soldiers were killed in a roadside bomb attack in southern Lebanon, which was coupled with short-range rocket fire by Hezbollah into northern Israel. As a means of preventing Lebanese civilian casualties in the area and as a punitive measure to apply pressure and "accountability" against the Lebanese population for enabling Hezbollah's militant activity in the south, the IDF's large-scale air and artillery campaign caused the relocation of thousands of civilians from southern Lebanese villages. (The strategic aspects of the 1993 operation were discussed in chapter 2).

The precision strikes, artillery shelling, drones, and airpower that utilized elements of the RMA became the means of choice for the IDF, largely owing to the low probability of suffering casualties. The increasing affinity toward "postheroic" warfare related to the societal expectation and preference for minimal casualties in wars of short duration was evident.[4] A senior IDF officer in Northern Command said at a press conference during the 1993 operation, "The less casualties we suffer on our side, the more successful we consider the operation to be. . . . We have methods by which we can inflict intolerable damage on the other side, while minimizing the casualties on our side."[5]

The IDF's preference for air operations was evident, as it launched a thousand air-to-surface rockets and twenty-two thousand artillery shells throughout the operation, including fifty-seven air raids and ten thousand artillery shells in less than ten hours on July 27, the third day of the operation.[6] However, Hezbollah's fluid and flexible operations network was not significantly affected by the aerial assault or displacement of civilians, and, within three weeks of the operation's end, IDF troops were again targeted by deadly ambushes and rocket fire as part of Hezbollah's sustained guerrilla campaign.[7]

Hezbollah's leadership maintained an acute awareness of the IDF's increasing reliance on airpower and standoff fire, as Deputy Sec.-Gen. Naim Qassem noted that the UN counted 1,224 Israeli air raids and more than twenty-eight thousand shells launched at Lebanon in 1993.[8] While the IDF incorporated various RMA technologies in the 1993 operation, including precision fire, advanced information technology, UAVs, and sensor-to-shooter and command-and-control systems, they were of limited effectiveness in curtailing Hezbollah's militant activities. Brig. Gen. (Ret.) Shlomo Brom, deputy head of the IDF Strategic Planning Division during the operation, reflected on the shortcomings of the RMA in Lebanon:

> The IDF incorporated the RMA but on the margins. It wasn't really necessary because of the nature of the operations. . . . The RMA was not so relevant to three Hezbollah fighters who laid an IED in the middle of the night along a route that the IDF used. RMA wasn't relevant to the rockets that were launched at our cities because these rockets were short-range and very small and launched from improvised launchers. It wasn't something we could engage with our very sophisticated systems.[9]

Despite the diffusion of sophisticated RMA technology throughout the previous decade, in 1993 the RMA had still only caught on in the air force, as the IDF as a whole was not fully harnessing its technical abilities and, more importantly, had no coherent operational framework for how to apply advanced technology against Hezbollah. Even though the IDF used precision firepower to hit Hezbollah targets to avoid unnecessary casualties, the IDF was harshly criticized in the global forum for its operational decisions to shell near civilian areas, which caused the flight of the local population and, inevitably, Lebanese civilian casualties.[10] Driving home the radicalizing effect the operation had on the local population, one Hezbollah rank-and-file member said after the 1993 operation: "The Israeli government has helped the Islamic Resistance by this operation because it has brought Hezbollah closer to the people. . . . They have done us a great service."[11]

Col. (Ret.) Ronen Cohen, a senior intelligence officer in Lebanon at the time, explained the IDF's operational goals and how the 1993 operation reflected the IDF's new preferred "way of war":

> Hezbollah thought that the IDF would enter Lebanon with infantry and tanks like in 1982. They didn't believe we'd carry out an operation like Operation Accountability, but many of the IDF generals were fascinated with the 1991 Gulf War. It's part of the story of the RMA. . . . [The] 1993 [operation] was our first operation in which we didn't enter with infantry. . . . Hezbollah started to understand that we prefer the kinds of wars which are in the style of the 1993 operation and the Gulf War.[12]

Hezbollah had prepared for an IDF ground offensive in 1993 and was surprised at the destructive potential and effective use of the IDF's heavy air and artillery firepower, which impacted the group's preparations for future conflict, as would be evident in 1996.[13] It motivated Hezbollah to learn and operationally adapt regarding the development of its fortified defensive positions and enhancement of its firepower-projection capabilities (see below). Despite the damage inflicted by the IAF, in a postoperation interview in 1993, Secretary-General Nasrallah praised Hezbollah's ability to endure bombardment, which provides an ominous window into Hezbollah's future building of fortifications:

> The [Israeli] air force and artillery were bombarding all the valleys and points from which Katyushas were being fired; but despite our lack of fortification and bunkers, the missile barrage never stopped until the seventh [final] day of the operation. This means that the Israelis who possess the strongest military force in the region were not able to stop the Katyusha bombardment of the settlements militarily. This is not so much a military defeat as a military scandal, given Israel's military capabilities.[14]

Colonel Cohen, later deputy head of research in IDF MI, explained Hezbollah's perceptions and learning processes that occurred during this period:

> I think the 1993 operation was the operation that made Hezbollah understand that they need to change their entire system. . . . This was the first war for Nasrallah [as secretary-general], and at that time Hezbollah understood that they should use guerrilla warfare in "routine security" but that they must also build their strengths for a future war that will look like the 1993 operation, and by 1996 they were a completely different organization. In three years, they did amazing work.[15]

1996 OPERATION GRAPES OF WRATH:
OPERATIONAL ASPECTS

Less than three years later, in response to another cyclical round of violence, which resulted in the death of IDF soldiers in the security zone, the IDF launched Operation Grapes of Wrath (April 11–27, 1996). It was the IDF's second large-scale air force operation of the decade. During the sixteen-day operation, the IDF heavily relied on precision capabilities and flew over a thousand sorties, carried out over six hundred air raids, and fired twenty-five thousand artillery shells.[16] The IAF utilized UAVs, sensor-to-shooter technology, network-centric capabilities, and sophisticated precision munitions to ensure accurate and lethal strikes against Hezbollah targets. Maj. Gen. Herzl Bodinger, head of the IAF (1992–96), discussed the military's conceptual framing of the conflict and stated at the time that "as this was not a real war but a limited operation, we used all types of aircraft to give the younger pilots the chance to get some combat experience." He discussed the IDF's preference for airpower and associated operational challenges:

> Wherever we could employ fighter aircraft we did. The idea was to go after the infrastructure of Hezbollah, so there was a lot of emphasis to destroy buildings and bunkers. . . . Extreme precision was required, because the apartment buildings [housing Hezbollah operations centers] also housed the families of Hezbollah fighters. We did not want CNN to broadcast scenes of dead women and children.[17]

Despite Hezbollah's increasing prowess, General Bodinger noted that "as it turned out, we didn't even have a single aircraft scratched," which reflected the IDF's immense technological superiority.[18] In a midoperation briefing, the head of Northern Command, Maj. Gen. Amiram Levin, declared, "I think Hezbollah is in what could be called great difficulty, because of its inability to repel the IDF's accurate hits."[19] Gal Hirsch, a brigadier general in the 2006 war who was a young commander of the IAF's elite Shaldag aerial commando unit at this time, described how the unit provided vital forward air and targeting support in Lebanon to ensure that the IAF's precision strikes accurately struck their targets during the 1993 and 1996 operations. He described how the IDF adapted its modus operandi in 1996 in an effort to deal with Hezbollah's concealment in civilian areas: "The objective [in 1996] was to remove the population out of those areas so that we could successfully deploy our precise weapons, especially during aerial bombardments, and conduct special operations aimed at hitting the enemy without harming the uninvolved population."[20]

Despite the IDF's advanced efforts during the 1996 operation to avoid civilian casualties while it targeted Hezbollah within Lebanese villages, IDF artillery inadvertently struck an encampment near a UN facility on April 18 in the Lebanese village of Qana, killing dozens of civilians, which was a tactical error that had major strategic impact. In response to calls for help from a Maglan special forces battalion that was pinned down near Qana by Hezbollah mortar teams, IDF artillery units launched several salvos of "rescue fire" at Hezbollah fighters in the area, which unintentionally struck the village.[21] Despite the internationally recognized understanding that Hezbollah was blatantly fighting enmeshed among the civilian population, because of a simple mapping error by the IDF (which used an outdated map that was inaccurate by seventy meters), the inherent limitations of precision technology were disastrously revealed. Defending the inadvertent IDF strike, Deputy COS Maj. Gen. Matan Vilnai described Hezbollah's tactics at the time:

> [Hezbollah's] position was very close to the UN base. . . . We used . . . Firefinder mortar-locating radar to pinpoint the firing position. That works well. But in southern Lebanon the conditions are very difficult, with the hilly terrain and the presence of civilians. That means we have had to adopt very strange and unusual procedures, which involve reacting with very short warning times. On the other side, Hezbollah are doing their utmost to get civilians killed by sheltering among them and by firing their Katyushas and mortars from positions very close to UN or civilian positions. We know from UNIFIL that the terrorists who fired the mortar fled into the UN camp.

After describing the various sophisticated laser-guided systems and networked technologies utilized by the IDF in 1996, Vilnai admitted, "There's a limit to what you can get out of a barrel in terms of accuracy."[22]

RMA precision weapons were the preferred way of war for both the political and military echelons during this period, resulting from perceptions of the RMA as a surgical, low-risk mode of warfare. In a Knesset address during the 1996 operation, Prime Minister Shimon Peres discussed "the use of sophisticated and accurate weapons, which reflect the IDF's advantage in human and technological abilities, mobility, intelligence collection, and accurate, pinpointed hits." He clearly stated that "in the guidelines for the operation, the government determined that civilians or civilian targets should not be hit and the operation should concentrate solely on Hezbollah installations and the terrorists themselves" but lamented that, "nonetheless, however much one tries to observe an ethical use of arms, military operations involve accidents and innocent civilian casualties."[23]

Despite its best efforts, Israel suffered condemnation in the international arena because of inadvertent civilian deaths caused by the Qana strike.[24] Following the 1996 operation, the longtime head of the Israel Weapons Development Authority warned that war "will remain bloody and destructive. The dream that [the RMA] based on precision firepower will lead to clean, surgical war with little collateral damage and minimal casualties will remain, in most cases, only a dream." The botched precision strike at Qana vividly demonstrated that advanced weapons are often of little use without a readiness to accept casualties on both sides and a certain margin of error.[25]

Throughout this period, the IDF overutilized standoff firepower capabilities in Lebanon to achieve inadequately defined operational goals. Lt. Col. (Ret.) Roni Amir, former head of the IAF Doctrine Branch, noted the operational similarities between the 1993 and 1996 operations and highlighted the IDF's fundamental lack of clarity for how air strikes and precision firepower would contribute to the achievement of strategic or operational goals in its Lebanon campaign: "The main element in airpower is targeting and destroying targets. . . . So, the context in which we viewed things was of destroying targets—if you destroy more targets, then we thought we could be more successful—but it doesn't work that way because a target bank is not a strategy, but this is the Israeli approach."[26]

HEZBOLLAH'S OPERATIONAL ADAPTATION FOLLOWING OPERATIONS ACCOUNTABILITY AND GRAPES OF WRATH

Hezbollah's primary achievements in the 1993 and 1996 operations were its ability to endure IAF bombardments, sustain rocket fire into Israel, establish favorable "rules of the game," prevent Israel from leveraging the Lebanese population against Hezbollah, and prevent the group's political or social isolation.[27] Secretary-General Nasrallah attributed Hezbollah's relative success to its organizational learning between the 1993 and 1996 operations in an interview immediately after Grapes of Wrath: "July 1993 was a very good lesson for us as far as confronting this kind of aggression is concerned, because we pinpointed our strengths and weaknesses at the beginning of the war, and were therefore ready when the [1996] confrontation came."[28]

After Hezbollah's painful learning experiences in the early 1990s coping with IAF firepower, a senior IAF officer reflected that "the 1993 operation was a turning point for Hezbollah's learning," as they began a slow process of organizational adaptation to enhance the central pillars of its military concept: persistent rocket fire, endurance, and organizational survivability.[29] Hezbollah's primary adaptation was the expansion of its rocket and missile capability, a lesson it initially learned after witnessing the effects of its Katyushas launched in response to the 1992 assassination of Abbas Mussawi and further internalized after absorbing the IDF's painful precision strikes in 1993. UNIFIL official Timur Goksel, in Lebanon at this time, described Hezbollah's central motive to adapt: "Hezbollah maintained a healthy respect for Israeli intelligence, especially their signal and air intelligence assets. They also learned they can't cope with Israeli air superiority on the same terms. They learned this in 1996, that they couldn't do anything with the air force."[30]

Based on lessons learned in 1993 and 1996, Hezbollah developed its ability to maintain persistent rocket fire against the Israeli home front and effectively forced the IDF to engage in an attritional rocket and firepower competition. Hezbollah's ability to sustain rocket fire into Israel despite IDF bombardment enhanced the group's ability to project a victory narrative in 1996. As part of the rules of the game, Hezbollah's firepower projection also became central to its deterrent posture against Israel. Colonel Amir explained the advancement of Hezbollah's "rocket doctrine":

> In 1993 Operation Accountability, Hezbollah found that they were not ready for something that was different than daily "routine security." . . . They just fired a few [rockets] every day, and they found themselves without enough rockets, without enough launching squads. . . . I think they started to realize that if their number of rockets is decreasing, then we are successful. They started to realize that this "rocket doctrine" works well only if they have the stamina to do it for a long time. . . . They realized that this rocket activity is more than just firing rockets, it's more than just targeting—it's not just a target bank, it is a strategy. And in this sense, they are more advanced than the regular Israeli strategy of deterrence.[31]

Hezbollah's gradual realization of the importance of *persistent* rocket fire as a central pillar of its military system is illustrated by the rate of rockets launched throughout the conflict. While figures vary slightly, over the seven days of the 1993 operation Hezbollah fired 151 Katyusha rockets into Israel (and an additional 122 into the security zone), killing two Israeli civilians in the border town of Kiryat Shmona.[32] After the operation, the number of Katyushas launched by Hezbollah increased gradually from 93 in 1994 to 121 in 1995 and 68 in the first three months of 1996 (prior to Operation Grapes of Wrath), ending with about 275 for the year.[33] In the 1996 operation, Hezbollah increased the number of rockets it fired—launching 639 Katyushas into Israel—but was unable to sustain consistent rocket salvos each day, with rocket fire ranging from eleven and eighty-one launched on the second and third day to thirty-nine and nine, respectively, on the last two days of the operation. Demonstrating Hezbollah's still limited ability to sustain consistent firepower projection, nearly a third (28 percent) of all rockets fired by Hezbollah during the sixteen-day 1996 operation were fired on the third and eighth days.[34] There were no fatalities during the 1996 operation in Israel, but twenty civilians were wounded. Moderate damage was caused to about three hundred buildings in Kiryat Shmona, which received the brunt (15 percent) of total rocket fire.[35] In the future, Hezbollah would continue to adapt and enhance its rocket capability, as seen during the 2006 war when close to four thousand rockets were fired into Israel (see chapter 8).

During Grapes of Wrath, Deputy Sec.-Gen. Naim Qassem noted that it was the first time since 1982 that Hezbollah's Dahiya stronghold was directly shelled. He described Hezbollah's learning in 1993, which impacted preparedness in 1996:

> It [Grapes of Wrath] was viewed as tougher than the July 1993 aggression, for it covered a wider geographic scope and lasted for 16 days. . . . But the Resistance put up a show of resilience that stunned the enemy. Katyusha rockets were fired on a daily basis, and benefitting from previous experience, the mujahedeen planned well for a new aerial invasion. Israel was incapable of directly targeting and hitting any jihad combatant, or of preventing one rocket pad from launching attacks. The dynamics of military resource distribution proved durable when back provision lines were cut off or during coverage of the skies by enemy raids. . . . Contrary to Zionist expectation, the intensity and scope of shelling did not deter the thrust of retaliation with Katyusha rockets until such time as a ceasefire was declared.[36]

Throughout the 1990s, Hezbollah developed an increased capacity to organizationally absorb and withstand strikes by the IDF, which was another major adaptation of its military system. Qassem's statements reflect the difficulty the IDF had curtailing Hezbollah's rocket fire and the group's preparations from 1993 to 1996 to improve its resilience against IAF firepower. By structurally operating in loosely networked, low-signature tactical units, making use of sophisticated defensive fortifications, and operating within the civilian population, Hezbollah maintained the ability to fire short-range rockets despite being under heavy assault, while preserving its relative strength and resources.

Reflecting the fundamental pillar of Hezbollah's military paradigm, informational signs observed by the author in 2011 at a Hezbollah site in Mleeta in southern Lebanon stated, "The Main Commandment: *Preserving the Resistance* by means of endurance, steadfastness, and sacrifice." Hezbollah's commitment to its "Main Commandment" led the group to emphasize survivability and maintenance of its fighting capabilities, exemplified by its early development of sophisticated bunkers and concealed tunnels seen during the IDF's 1988 Maydun operation (see chapter 1).[37] The author also entered a cave formerly occupied by Hezbollah fighters in the 1990s and observed an informational sign that highlights the importance of such fortifications for the group:

> Initially the cave was a 1-meter gap used as a refuge against the Israeli enemy bombardment and harsh weather elements. It was later transformed into a

200m tunnel. Over the course of 3 years, in excess of 1,000 men dug and prepared it in rotation . . . in a camouflaged manner that made it difficult for the enemy air observation to discover. After completion, the cave was transformed into an integral military base. . . . It was equipped with electricity, safety devices, and ventilation, allowing more than 7,000 resistance militants to use it as a barracks and main base to resist the enemy in that area.

Sec.-Gen. Hassan Nasrallah described the benefits of such concealment and low-signature techniques three years after the 1996 operation: "Sometimes, in a guerrilla war, the party that cannot defend itself when confronting the enemy can detract from the air force's significance by camouflaging targets and refraining from overt appearances. These are some of the advantages of the Islamic Resistance."[38] Deputy Secretary-General Qassem described Hezbollah's low-signature modus operandi in the 1996 operation as "not many resistance fighters were allowed on the front lines in south Lebanon and the western Bekaa, as the nature of the conflict required a mode of performance that did not call for direct participation except by a limited number of individuals."[39] Based on a keen awareness of the lethality of Israel's precision weapons experienced in 1993 and 1996, Hezbollah mastered the ability to sustain its military activities despite the IDF's advanced surveillance, intelligence, and sensor-to-shooter capabilities. By bolstering its resilience and organizational survivability, Hezbollah was developing its ability to counter firepower-centered warfare and perfected the timeless principle of "victory by not losing" used by technologically inferior forces throughout history.[40]

Despite the adaptation of its rocket capabilities and organizational resilience, Hezbollah still incurred difficulties from IDF aerial bombardments during the 1996 operation. Hezbollah's ultimate preference at this time remained on waging "traditional" guerrilla warfare, which dampened IDF conventional military superiority and muted its technological prowess. Hezbollah's awareness of its own limitations would contribute to its concerted organizational effort to further develop its central military pillars. Nasrallah admitted after the 1996 operation, "The war we are keen to fight is the guerilla war. . . . In our opinion, the guerilla war is far more important and effective and has more impact on the enemy and its plans and morale than this recent despicable tit-for-tat war [1996 operation]. The war we want is the kind that makes the enemy bleed slowly, puts it under pressure, and forces it to leave our country."[41]

In summary, after enduring damaging aerial strikes in the 1993 operation for which it was relatively unprepared, Hezbollah made a concerted organizational effort to enhance its rocket-fire projection, organizational survivability, resilience, and absorptive capacity, the gains of which were illustrated to an extent in the 1996 operation. However, the fruits of Hezbollah's continuing efforts would become most evident in future conflict in 2006. Addressing Hezbollah's practical achievements of the 1990s, Qassem described the group's masterful ability to "compensate for military imbalance and infliction of losses on enemy ranks: This was realized through simple and humble technologies, that on the one hand, shook the Israeli army's ability to defend itself, and on the other, unsettled its ability to retaliate."[42]

THE RMA IN LEBANON IN THE LATE 1990s

The RMA had its most evident impact on the IAF, which acted as the chief incubator for innovation, a process accelerated by the massive amount of technology and combat aircraft received from the United States, which hastened the diffusion of the RMA further into the IDF.[43] Exemplifying the RMA's influence on the IAF's mode of thinking, a prominent paper written by an IAF colonel after the 1996 operation that was circulated around the military explored alternative ways to combat Hezbollah. An oversubscription to airpower and RMA-style precision weaponry is evident as the author, Col. (Res.) Shmuel Gordon, head of the IAF Command-and-Control Center, recommended the IDF utilize "counter-guerrilla air warfare" in Lebanon.[44] This unconventional approach is opposed to more traditional counterguerrilla strategies that involve "boots on the ground." The study advocated utilizing aerial platforms requiring real-time intelligence, unity of command, space assets, networked sensor-to-shooter technology, and UAVs, under the control of a proposed IAF task force. This task force would exploit the advantageous characteristics of airpower and standoff firepower to suppress Hezbollah's guerrilla activities, which would be enhanced by the flexible use of counterguerrilla airborne forces synced with enhanced command-and-control systems.[45]

Two major themes are evident from this influential report: While not explicitly mentioning the RMA by name, the proposal relied heavily on the precepts of the RMA and its associated technology while advocating a greater role for the air force and helicopters in counterguerrilla warfare. Illustrating the social effects and sensitivity of Israeli society during the Lebanon campaign, this airpower-centric proposal would be uniquely suitable for the IDF as it would avoid ground-force casualties by relying on standoff firepower to combat Hezbollah.

Colonel Amir noted that this document was especially influential because it partially conceptualized a framework for the effective integration of helicopters in Lebanon, which would force guerrillas out into the open where they could be targeted by the IAF. He explained, "He didn't invent the idea, but Colonel Gordon tried to find a way to conceptualize it. By doing this, he moved everything forward. *We did not have a concept*, we had techniques, tools, and we were experimenting."[46] Evidently, even in the late 1990s, the IAF still lacked a systematic conceptual framework for harnessing the benefits of the RMA toward its operational requirements related to Hezbollah.

As ground forces assumed an increasingly defensive posture in Lebanon throughout the late 1990s because of domestic pressures (see chapter 3), the IDF relied more heavily on airpower and RMA capabilities and drastically increased the number of air operations in Lebanon. Despite the limited efficacy of Operation Grapes of Wrath, the IAF carried out more than ninety air raids against Hezbollah in 1997, compared to twenty-four in 1994, twenty-nine in 1995, and twenty in 1996.[47] Throughout the late 1990s, COS Lt. Gen. Shaul Mofaz increasingly used the air force to counter Hezbollah activity in southern Lebanon. Reflecting a continued adherence to RMA-inspired concepts and intense casualty aversion, the IAF carried out 231 offensive sorties in Lebanon in 1998, 669 in 1999, and 602 in the first five months of 2000, as ground operations were severely curtailed.[48] This was in line with Mofaz's subscription to the RMA and the IDF's transformation, while showing that postheroic sentiment was present throughout all command levels.[49] It seems the IDF replaced its historical doctrinal principle of rapidly transferring the war to the enemy's territory to instead transferring fire to the enemy's territory.[50]

An April 1999 broadcast on Hezbollah's Al-Manar TV taunted Israeli leaders for their ineffective air strikes, which rather than harming Hezbollah's formidable guerrilla capabilities only boosted recruitment and popular support for the group. In response to Hezbollah's claims, General Mofaz denied Hezbollah's assertions but acknowledged difficulties caused by Hezbollah's unwillingness to confront the IDF directly: "There is no doubt [Hezbollah has the upper hand in this kind of conflict]. There is no Western military that can achieve significant gains against Hezbollah . . . when the rules of conventional warfare no longer apply."[51] Mofaz insisted the IDF was instead attempting to destroy Hezbollah's artillery and antitank weapons, counter the IED threat, and continuously develop new technology "to replace soldiers in the field." Reflecting the dialectical nature of the conflict, Mofaz's comments were noted publicly by Nasrallah two months later:

> We read in the newspapers that Shaul Mofaz, commander of the Israeli army, had said that there was not a single army in the world capable of defeating Hezbollah. But when his soldiers and officers, hunkering down on the front-lines, hear this admission, their morale will undoubtedly sink. . . . What is important, in the final analysis, is that the Israeli army has humiliated itself and lost its strongman image, and you know as well as I do that this army's strength resides mostly in its aura, well before its size and lethality of its weapons. . . . This is why I say that the Israelis have endured a lot in Lebanon.[52]

Statements by Deputy Defense Minister Ephraim Sneh, a major opponent of the IDF withdrawal, encapsulated the IDF's static modus operandi in Lebanon and its reliance on technology in 1999: "What we are really doing is introducing technologies that partially substitute for the physical presence of soldiers. . . . The bottom line is that it has improved the efficiency of our presence in southern Lebanon. We can stave off the guerrillas from our border with a lower price."[53]

Maj. Gen. Isaac Ben-Israel, head of weapon development in the MOD and a chief advocate of the RMA in Israel, explained in his farewell interview in 2001 that he considered his primary accomplishment to be the perceptual transformation of the role of weapon systems and technology for use in LIC in Lebanon:

> There was a time that people said that technology is needed for big wars. With ongoing ["routine"] security, the soldier faces off against another soldier, and they fight with their hands, teeth, rifle or a knife. Four or five years ago [1996–97] we changed that perception. We decided to introduce technology into the war in Lebanon. We worked on a project that aimed to create a situation in which instead of soldiers lying in ambush and waiting for Hezbollah men to walk past them in the wadi, they would be able to take advantage of the technologies of sensors for search and discovery. . . . [The IDF developed] eavesdropping techniques, remote photography, pilotless drones and balloons. . . . We have developed sensors to detect personnel and armaments in order to reveal their activity. . . . We developed technologies to zero in on sources of gunfire.[54]

However, despite the IDF's technological capabilities and some notable achievements against Hezbollah, Brig. Gen. Shlomo Brom said in 1999, "I'm afraid it's not the end of the story. Hezbollah will now look for tactics that will make it less vulnerable to airborne attacks, and then we're back to the drawing board. There is no silver bullet that will allow us to withdraw to the international border and have everything be OK."[55]

Competitive operational adaptability between both sides was explicitly demonstrated in 1999, when Israeli sources affirmed that Hezbollah had drafted strategies directly based on IDF planning and training manuals, as well as elements of RMA concepts, in order to counter IDF technological superiority.[56] One year before the withdrawal, Nasrallah provided a damning analysis of the IDF and its way of war during the era of the security zone:

> I am not underestimating the Israeli soldier's abilities; I am just saying that he hides behind his technology, his artillery, his helicopters, and his heavy gunfire, and the human element comes last in the Israeli military estimates. This

is why I know it is possible to defeat Israeli soldiers if we know how to use the elements of the battle on the ground to our advantage.[57]

Overall, the technological revolution being carried out under the banner of the RMA still had limited utility on the Lebanese battlefield. It had little effect on Israel's ability to curtail Hezbollah's short-range rocket fire or prevent low-signature guerrilla operations. This realization spurred a small number of frustrated intelligence officers from the IDF's Lebanon Division to seek an alternative approach for dealing with Hezbollah, which led to the development of a new, innovative doctrine for asymmetrical conflict.

THE RISE AND FALL OF THE LIMITED CONFLICT DOCTRINE

Amid intractable conflict with Hezbollah, the IDF slowly adopted a new operational paradigm for dealing with asymmetrical conflict in the late 1990s.[58] Developed in the years leading up to the 2000 withdrawal from Lebanon, these ideas marked a dramatic transformation of the IDF's traditional way of war. This new doctrine represented the IDF's reconceptualization of asymmetrical conflict and reframed the way the IDF viewed military engagement, attritional warfare, and the achievement of "battlefield decision" in LIC. The doctrine was codified by a handful of intelligence officers who spent a significant portion of their careers in Lebanon. Leading this adaptive process was Col. Shmuel "Samo" Nir, who wrote a series of articles published in IDF journals and classified army publications about how the IDF should conceptualize asymmetrical warfare. Based on his analysis of Hezbollah's operations throughout the 1990s and motivated by the apparent lack of utility of the IDF's operational methods, intelligence-gathering capabilities, and technologies, Colonel Nir outlined a common system of theoretical ideas and new terminology, coining the concept of "Limited Conflict."[59] In a classified IDF monograph series established by Nir in 1999, he described a lack of theoretical knowledge of the nature of nonstate opponents such as Hezbollah and made significant efforts to institutionalize lessons learned from the Lebanese battlefield. He also provided a broad but innovative construct that outlined the strategic and operational paradigm by which such nonstate organizations operate.[60]

Colonel Nir elucidated Hezbollah's operational concept, which was based on a "strategy of fatigue" and aimed at exhausting Israel militarily and socially. This strategy allowed Hezbollah to preserve its strength, enable protracted fighting, and maintain battlefield initiative, thus preventing the IDF from bringing its conventional military strength to bear.[61] In his writings, Nir proposed a fundamental change to how Israel should achieve battlefield decision, historically enabled by rapid offensive action, physical destruction of enemy capabilities, and capture of enemy territory: "The definition of decision between unbalanced forces is changing the consciousness of society: changing the belief of society in the necessity of the cause, its ability to persist in fighting, and its ability to pay the price of the conflict. . . . In conflict between unbalanced forces, each side is to decisively reach a decision by achieving 'a consciousness of decision.'"[62]

By targeting the "consciousness" of the opponent, this would affect the determination of the enemy to continue fighting, as Colonel Nir believed that a gradual, sustained attack would have a deep psychological impact on the enemy. Unlike the RMA's notion of rapid, decisive culmination of victory, the Limited Conflict doctrine emphasized planning a "gradual attack" to "fatigue" the opponent over the long term to erode enemy determination. Nir outlined a "strategy of fatigue" that "gradually exhausts the resolve of society and its fighters by cumulative physical and emotional attacks."[63] He continued:

In order to reach high effectiveness in attacking the determination of the enemy, there is a need to plan the process of fighting for the long run as much as possible (and not for twenty-four to thirty-six hours like in a regular war). . . . We must focus on the accumulative influence and not on physical attacks. The results of the fighting are tested by the measure of time because the loss of determination is not a result of a onetime move but a result of a *gradual fatigue*.[64]

The notion of Limited Conflict was influential on the IDF's operational concept for dealing with asymmetrical threats throughout the late 1990s, and Colonel Nir's writings were eventually formally codified in published doctrine in 2001. One IDF insider noted that Nir's ideas gave "theoretical justification for what was already happening in Lebanon after the 1996 operation": The IDF was engaged in attritional slow-tempo, counterguerrilla warfare in which its RMA technology was of limited efficacy, while restrained by the political echelon wary of eliciting Hezbollah's rocket fire.[65]

Quoting from the doctrine itself, Colonel Nir summed up the differences between the achievement of battlefield decision in conventional war and Limited Conflict: "Israel's past wars were existential wars, and the way to deal with them was through deterrence and decision. Limited Conflict is, by contrast, a battle over consciousness, and the side that can exhaust its adversary will win by wearing down the adversary's resolve to pay the heavy price of a prolonged confrontation."[66]

In ironic use of language, Colonel Nir wrote that in order to exhaust the adversary and break its resolve to fight, the IDF must militarily cause "a *revolution* in the consciousness of the society."[67] This conceptual framework for battlefield decision and military engagement marked a major shift away from the IDF's traditional approach of minimizing the possibility of attrition. Notably, the central reason that the RMA and associated weapon systems and technologies were enthusiastically adopted into the IDF in the 1980s and 1990s was because it was believed the RMA would enhance the IDF's very ability to achieve a rapid, decisive victory. RMA-inspired technology improved situational awareness and intelligence gathering that was meant to prevent attritional warfare and facilitate short wars with minimal casualties that would have a limited effect on the Israeli home front. Sustained operations in protracted conflict to psychologically "fatigue" Hezbollah over the long term were therefore diametrically opposed to the swift and one-sided victory sought by Israel's adoption of the RMA.

Despite the massive technological investments made and the force structure designed for high-intensity war under the banner of the RMA, by the early 2000s and less than five years since the ideas first emerged, "anybody considered an up-and-coming somebody in the IDF hierarchy seemed to be chanting the mantra of the Limited Conflict."[68] This shift to LIC was accelerated out of operational necessity, triggered by the eruption of suicide bombing and terrorism during the Second Palestinian Intifada in September 2000, less than four months after Israel's Lebanon withdrawal. Exemplifying the IDF's shift in conceptual focus, the proportion of all articles dealing with LIC in the IDF's official journal from 2000 to 2006 rose 20 percent.[69] The IDF hosted its first international conference on the Limited Conflict doctrine in March 2004 and also published an edited volume covering numerous aspects of Limited Conflict and asymmetrical warfare.[70]

Despite its popularity and influence in some circles, the Limited Conflict doctrine was criticized by a small number of senior officers for being unsuitable for the Israeli context. Critics argued that it was inappropriate that the IDF be expected to "fatigue" and "outlast" its opponent using defensive means and superior determination. The most vociferous critic was Col. (Res.) Yehuda Wegman, a longtime lecturer at the IDF Staff College, who contended that a fundamental erroneous assumption is that the IDF is unable to "win" or achieve a clear battlefield decision against asymmetrical opponents. He argued that this false "pessimism" adversely affects society's ability to endure hardship and maintain resilience in conflict and augments societal risk aversion. Most critically, the Limited Conflict doctrine "does not derive its logic from the security doctrine of which it is part," since a protracted "war of fatigue" totally "contradicts the basic assumption of the IDF's traditional doctrine," which calls for decisive, rapid culmination of victory.[71] Criticism also emerged from Maj. Gen. Yaakov Amidror, head of the IDF National Defense College, who concluded that a "mistaken assumption" of Limited Conflict is the false belief that "victory is always a matter of cognizance rather than the outcome of physical or coercive measures."[72]

Despite criticism from segments of the IDF, the Limited Conflict doctrine enjoyed significant support in the early 2000s. Jargon related to gradually "fatiguing" the enemy's "consciousness" and the notion that IDF territorial conquest actually benefits Hezbollah's attritional strategy subtly influenced senior commanders.[73] For example, in a 2002 interview, COS Lt. Gen. Moshe Yaalon, a proponent of Limited Conflict, famously declared that in order for Israel to be victorious in attritional conflict, its superior resilience and military might must be "burned into the Palestinian and Arab consciousness."[74] Notably, the head of the IAF at the time and a future COS during the 2006 war, Maj. Gen. Dan Halutz, tellingly proclaimed in a 2001 lecture, "Is war over territory relevant at all in the future? In my opinion, no! . . . Decision is an issue of consciousness. Airpower influences, in a meaningful fashion, the consciousness of the enemy," while also downplaying the significance of ground maneuver to achieve "operational decision," preferring a "decision of the consciousness."[75]

The use of Limited Conflict terminology by the top brass represented the creeping belief that clear-cut battlefield decision was increasingly difficult to achieve against asymmetrical opponents, that territorial conquest was more of a burden than a sign of victory, and that LIC was mostly won on the psychological front.[76] This adherence to "gradual fatigue" was despite Israel's force structure and acquisition programs over the preceding two decades for short, decisive, RMA-inspired warfare. The mismatch between the IDF's daily operational focus on attritional warfare and Limited Conflict on the one hand and its RMA-inspired force structure, order of battle, and technological focus on the other would significantly affect the IDF's performance in 2006.

Despite the influence it enjoyed, Limited Conflict faded out of fashion in the mid-2000s amid its relative ineffectiveness in dealing with widespread Palestinian militancy and suicide terrorism. This became most evident when, contrary to the principles of Limited Conflict that advocated for a gradual, slow-tempo approach, the IDF launched a large, high-tempo, offensive urban warfare campaign in the West Bank in 2002 (Operation Defensive Shield), which decimated Palestinian militant groups.[77] Nevertheless, as discussed in chapters 8 and 9, conceptual remnants of Limited Conflict lingered in the IDF and would subtly influence the IDF's operational thinking and conduct in 2006. Significantly, the IDF also remained operationally focused on Palestinian counterterrorism throughout the 2000s, which impacted operational readiness of the ground forces for Hezbollah's advanced mode of warfare.

CONCLUSION

Despite the brief but influential impact of Limited Conflict, the RMA was the central institutional vehicle for change in the 1990s, driven largely by the military's operational leanings toward technocentrism, as well as by domestic societal pressures related to casualty aversion. The IDF utilized the RMA to justify its greater reliance on technology and standoff firepower in Lebanon, exemplified in 1993 and 1996, which was coupled with the increasingly static modus operandi of the majority of troops in Lebanon throughout the late 1990s. Hezbollah's hard-earned lessons following the 1993 and 1996 operations and its awareness of Israel's aversion to casualties and collateral damage led it to enhance the central pillars of its military system: persistent rocket fire against Israel's civilian areas, organizational survivability, low-signature operations, and construction of bunkers and fortifications to endure Israeli air strikes. These innovations were all designed to circumvent the IDF's conventional military superiority.

After witnessing the IDF's relative ineffectiveness in restraining Hezbollah, the head of the Israel Weapons Development Authority, Zeev Bonen, warned in 1996 that the RMA "may serve as a basis for a revolution of some sort . . . but in order to be indeed revolutionary, the mere utilization of [RMA] capabilities, the grafting of new technologies onto existing force components and doctrine does not create an RMA. Radical changes are essential in strategy and tactics, in warfare style, and in force structure."[78]

The air force was leading the Israeli RMA process, which brought it increased prestige, funding, and resources—central drivers of change in military organizations. However, illustrating the risks and pitfalls of such "uneven" diffusion, interservice competition was exacerbated. It augmented the disparity between the capabilities of the air force, which enjoyed the full benefits of the RMA, and the ground forces, especially infantry and the armored corps, which suffered budgetary and training cuts amid the diversion of resources to RMA-inspired programs. This competition and resource inequality would have a damaging effect on the performance of ground forces in 2006.

Without systematically assimilating the technology into doctrine or a conceptual framework, the innovation process remained insufficient, although Bonen added, "When this finally occurs, it will lead to a veritable RMA." Using digital technology or advanced air and space weaponry does not necessarily imply embracing the RMA, as "to be revolutionary, what is required is a true metamorphosis to a new framework which utilizes effectively [RMA] capabilities."[79] In order to guide the army's "metamorphosis," the IDF would establish the OTRI in 1995, tasked to develop a new methodology for thinking about the operational level of war that would enhance the army's RMA-inspired transformation.

NOTES

Epigraphs: Quoted in Joris Janssen Lok, "Israel Defends Record on Grapes of Wrath," *Jane's Defence Weekly*, June 5, 1996; Nasrallah, interview, June 21, 1999, 206.

1. Author interview with Roni Amir.

2. Brun, "While You're Busy," 539–41. See also Tamir Eshel, "Evolving into Hybrid Forces: Challenging IDF Precision-Fire Domination," *Defense Update*, September 13, 2011.

3. Nasrallah, interview, November 14, 1992.

4. Luttwak, "Towards Post-Heroic Warfare."

5. *Haaretz*, June 29, 1993, quoted in Kober, "Israeli War Objectives," 191.

6. Human Rights Watch, *Civilian Pawns*, 102; "Hizballah Vows to Resists," AFP, July 28, 1993, FBIS.

7. "Massive Israeli Assault Ravages South Again," *Lebanon Report* 4, no. 8 (July/August 1993): 2–3; Reuters, "Hizbullah: We Didn't Agree to Stop Rocket Attacks," *Jerusalem Post*, August 2, 1993; "7 Israeli Troops Die in Attack in Southern Lebanon," *New York Times*, August 19, 1993.

8. Qassem, *Hizbullah*, 200–201.

9. Author interview with Shlomo Brom.

10. For an example of such criticism, see Human Rights Watch, *Civilian Pawns*, especially chaps. 3–5.

11. Quoted in Julie Flint, "Hizbullah Thrives on Israeli Blitz," *The Guardian*, August 2, 1993.

12. Author interview with Ronen Cohen.

13. Kulick, "Hizbollah vs. the IDF."

14. Nasrallah, interview, August 27, 1993, 104.

15. Author interview with Ronen Cohen.

16. Human Rights Watch, *Operation Grapes of Wrath*, 12.

17. Quoted in Joris Janssen Lok, "Israel Defends Record."

18. Ibid.

19. Levin, news conference, April 13, 1996.

20. Hirsch, "Urban Warfare," 28–29.

21. Details of this incident recently reemerged due to political mudslinging, as the Maglan company commander on the ground in 1996, Naftali Bennett, has since become a government minister. Ben Caspit, "Israeli Left's Attack on Bennet Boomerangs," Al-Monitor, January 6, 2015.

22. Quoted in Lok, "Israel Defends Record."

23. Peres, speech, April 22, 1996.

24. For example, see United Nations, "Security Council Calls"; Human Rights Watch, *Operations Grapes of Wrath*; Amnesty International, *Unlawful Killings*.

25. Bonen, "Sophisticated Conventional War."

26. Author interview with Roni Amir.

27. Sobelman, "Lebanon 2007."

28. Nasrallah, interview, April 30, 1996, 150.

29. Author interview with Roni Amir.

30. Author interview with Timur Goksel.

31. Author interview with Roni Amir.

32. Human Rights Watch, *Civilian Pawns*, 102.

33. Eisenstadt, "Hizballah Operations."

34. For the total number of rockets fired by date, see Human Rights Watch, *Operation Grapes of Wrath*, n. 156.

35. Ibid., 41, as well as n. 157 in the report.

36. Qassem, *Hizbullah*, 207.

37. Valensi and Brun, "Revolution in Military Affairs of the Radical Axis."

38. Nasrallah, interview, March 19, 1999.

39. Qassem, *Hizbullah*, 138.

40. For a prescient assessment, see Scales, "Adaptive Enemies."

41. Nasrallah, interview, April 30, 1996, 148.

42. Qassem, *Hizbullah*, 125.

43. Joris Janssen Lok, "Surplus US Fighters Swell Israel's Air Fleet," *Jane's Defence Weekly*, June 19, 1996.

44. Gordon, *Vulture and the Snake*.

45. Ibid., chaps. 3–4.

46. Author interview with Roni Amir.

47. Statistics appeared in Arieh O'Sullivan, "The Great Gamble: Leaving Lebanon," *Jerusalem Post*, January 8, 1998.

48. Brun and Rabinovich, *Israel Facing a New Middle East*, 45.

49. Nina Gilbert, "Mofaz: Unilateral Withdrawal Dangerous," *Jerusalem Post*, November 10, 1999.

50. Catignani, *Israeli Counter-Insurgency*, 71.

51. Quoted in Barbara Opall-Rome, "Hizballah Applies Israel, US Military Strategies to Guerilla War in Lebanon," *Defense News* 14, June 21, 1999, 4.

52. Nasrallah, interview, June 21, 1999, 200.

53. Quoted in Deborah Sontag, "Israel Changes Its Style in South Lebanon," *New York Times*, October 7, 1999.

54. Isaac Ben-Israel, interview, December 18, 2001.

55. Quoted in Sontag, "Israel Changes Its Style."

56. Opall-Rome, "Hizballah Applies Israel," 4.

57. Nasrallah, interview, June 21, 1999, 206.

58. A related version of this section on Limited Conflict appeared in Marcus, "Israeli Revolution in Military Affairs," 99–102.

59. Cohen, *Israel and Its Army*, 48–49; Libel, "David's Shield," 66–67.

60. Nir, "Fighting in the Lebanese Arena"; Nir, "Intelligence in Limited Conflict between Asymmetric Rivals."

61. Nir, "Fighting in the Lebanese Arena," 5.

62. Ibid., 9.

63. Ibid., 7.

64. Ibid., 11 (emphasis added).

65. Author interview with Yagil Henkin.

66. Col. Shmuel Nir, *The Limited Conflict* (IDF, 2001), quoted in Peri, *Generals in the Cabinet Room*, 125.

67. Nir, "Attrition and the Test of Adaptation," 166 (emphasis added). Thanks to Dr. Yagil Henkin for sharing this insight with me.

68. Cohen, *Israel and Its Army*, 48.

69. Ibid.

70. Hecht, "Low-Intensity Wars"; Nir, "Nature of the Limited Conflict."

71. Wegman, "Israel's Security Doctrine and the Trap of 'Limited Conflict'" (2004).

72. Amidror, *Winning Counterinsurgency War*, 14.

73. For examples, see Wegman, "Distorted Self-Image," 25–26; and Berman, "Capturing Contemporary Innovation," 129–30.

74. Yaalon, interview, August 29, 2002; Yaalon, "Preparing the Forces for the Limited Conflict." Such ideas were repeated in Yaalon, "Lessons from the Palestinian 'War,'" 11.

75. Maj. Gen. Dan Halutz, "Airpower as a Variable of Decision," in *Between Decision and Victory*, IDF National Defense College Seminar Proceedings, Haifa University, January 28, 2001, 96–98, quoted in Berman, "Capturing Contemporary Innovation," 129.

76. Author interview with IDF officers. See also Kober, *Israel's Wars of Attrition*, 43–47.

77. Wegman, "Israel's Security Doctrine and the Trap of 'Limited Conflict'" (2005).

78. Bonen, "Sophisticated Conventional War."

79. Ibid.

CHAPTER 7

THE RISE OF THE IDF'S OPERATIONAL THEORY RESEARCH INSTITUTE AND SYSTEMIC OPERATIONAL DESIGN

Learning is a liberating experience. But most people don't like to be free. Most people are slaves and have a slave mentality. The real free guys are those who have the courage to step out of their zone of convenience of what they know and walk into the dark and illuminate it.

—Brig. Gen. (Ret.) Shimon Naveh

An internal process was eventually launched within the IDF to formally reassess its operational concept as a response to intractable conflict with Hezbollah, the technological benefits of the RMA, the proliferation of unconventional weapons, and the subtle sociological shifts affecting the IDF as "the people's army." According to the Winograd Commission, "due to the acknowledgment of the great importance of these changes, since the 1990s, the IDF had begun the process of systematically consolidating, adopting, and assimilating a new operational concept that was intended to adjust the activation of the army to the new circumstances. . . . This reassessment was concentrated mainly in the hands of a special team."[1] This "special team" sought to revamp and enhance the IDF's abilities to think systematically about the operational level of war and, through the development of a methodology for campaign planning, would assist the IDF in adapting to the complex operational environment. The maverick who led this team that was instrumental in triggering dramatic internal change was Brig. Gen. Shimon Naveh, who was given the authority to establish a military think-tank in 1995 called the Operational Theory Research Institute (OTRI). The evolution of the ideas developed at OTRI that emerged parallel to the RMA would deeply affect the IDF in the ensuing decade.

The most significant contribution associated with OTRI was its development in the mid-1990s of the innovative concept of systemic operational design (SOD), whose conceptual origins and diffusion throughout the IDF are examined in detail in this chapter. OTRI acted as an incubator for innovation in the IDF, and various original and creative ideas emerged from its disciples. An intricate relationship existed between OTRI and American proponents of the RMA in the US Department of Defense (DOD), which impacted the diffusion of various RMA-related concepts in the IDF. From its creation in 1995 to its formal shutdown in 2005, OTRI's decade-long role teaching IDF officers and propagating innovative concepts and methodologies has been the subject of much controversy and has often been unfairly blamed for causing many of the IDF's shortcomings in the 2006 Israel-Hezbollah War. Based on discussions with IDF personnel involved, the rise, diffusion, and influence of OTRI's ideas on the IDF is next critically assessed, as is the actual impact of SOD on the IDF's various war plans in the run-up to 2006.

THE ORIGINS OF OTRI

A group of untraditionally minded military officers emerged from the reformist school of the 1980s (see chapter 5) and were motivated to internally develop a new conceptual agenda for the IDF. Officers such as Maj. Gen. Doron Rubin, head of the IDF Doctrine and Training Department, had come to the "bitter realization" that the enormous force-modernization and expansion programs of the 1980s had yielded mediocre results in the 1982 Lebanon War, on the battlefield against Hezbollah, during the First Palestinian Intifada, and regarding preparedness for the 1991 Gulf War when Saddam Hussein's Scud missiles hit Tel Aviv.[2] With the perception that the IDF was "institutionally sick," an ideological circle of like-minded mavericks formed around General Rubin, who sought new ways to improve IDF generalship and professional education.

Rubin, a charismatic and well-respected visionary officer, was able to rally support from within the IDF from lower- and midranking officers to implement desired reforms because of his close relationship with COS Lt. Gen. Dan Shomron.[3] Maj. Gen. Rubin and his supporting officers, which included the outspoken and charismatic Brig. Gen. Shimon Naveh, were inspired partially by US AirLand Battle doctrine and the US performance in the 1991 Gulf War, which they attributed to the promotion of operational art in the US military throughout the 1980s.[4] Rubin planned to institutionally develop a theoretical framework for operational art that would improve IDF education, generalship, and command and sought to formulate a new operational vocabulary to reintroduce critical discourse and institutional learning in the IDF.[5] Rubin's charisma, intellectual support, and foresight were crucial in providing fertile soil for the development of innovative concepts by his disciples.

General Naveh, who emerged from this reformist circle, personified the quintessential military maverick and had also been developing innovative concepts for the IDF because of its "perceptual vanity" and dearth of operational-level knowledge and systemic thinking.[6] The idea for the development of a new operational concept started as a project between IDF Training and Doctrine Command and Tel Aviv University, which cosponsored Naveh, who had retired from the IDF in 1991 after a distinguished military career, to complete his PhD on the subject of operational art in the Department of War Studies at King's College London.[7] While in London and during an earlier term of study at the Royal College of Defence Studies, Naveh briefly interacted with leading British military operational theorists, including Gen. Sir Nigel Bagnall and Brig. Richard Simpkin, an expert on Russian military theory. In fact, Simpkin personally encouraged Naveh during his studies to develop a "tailor-made" Israeli version of operational art.[8]

As General Naveh explained upon his return to Israel in 1994, the ideas he developed in the United Kingdom "fell on fertile soil" as he strengthened General Rubin's budding "intellectual insurgency."[9] Naveh joined in 1994 with two other esteemed soldier-scholars, both with PhDs and long careers in the IDF: Col. (Ret.) Dr. Zvi Lanir, a philosopher and cognitive scientist who had founded the Praxis Institute in 1994, an organizational consultancy working closely with the IDF, and Brig. Gen. (Ret.) Dr. Dov Tamari, a hero of the 1973 Arab-Israeli War and former deputy head of IDF MI. Together they planted the seeds of the think tank that would formulate and develop the concept of SOD, which would have a significant impact on IDF (and Western) military thought.[10] A younger, like-minded officer from the Intelligence Corps, Lt. Col. Amos Granit, later joined them in 1996. Notably, Maj. Gen. Rubin of Training and Doctrine Command, as well as Naveh and Tamari, were all from the paratroopers, friends, and part of the military elite. According to OTRI staffer Dr. Ofra Graicer, an "intimate milieu" developed among these men since "they were all friends and all knew each other, and each had lots of experiences in the field, so it all started as an intimate think tank," which enabled cooperation and rapid development of innovative concepts.[11] Lanir reflected, "We were all versatile, in infantry and different units. This was one of the reasons we could move quickly between different things and see the relationship between them."[12]

Amid the IDF's force modernization, the Praxis Institute, the organizational consultancy headed by Lanir, had numerous contracts with the IDF, especially in Central Command, and was solicited to develop computer software that would enable systemic planning and enhance cognitive thinking and organizational effectiveness. The small team of systems analysts, cognitive scientists, and philosophers at Praxis successfully developed innovative, sophisticated software for cognitive graphic mapping on the individual, group, and organizational levels.[13]

The sources of Lanir's ideas on systemic thinking and military cognition drew from an earlier study based on his experiences as an intelligence officer during the surprise of the 1973 Yom Kippur War. Lanir attributed the "fundamental surprise" of the IDF not to intelligence-collection failure or situational factors, but to a shocking "cognitive failure" to connect the dots, as well as a personal, group, and national mind-set that was "irrelevant and misleading in interpreting the occurrence."[14] Lanir proceeded to develop a new concept for how to cognitively adapt to surprise and disruptive change, developing a process called "Systemic Reframing Thinking."[15] This concept, grounded in systems theory, Aristotelian philosophy, and postmodern thought, was meant to enable knowledge creation based on analyzing patterns of human interaction that needed to be continuously revised and reinterpreted using a systemic learning mechanism.[16] Based on this mode of thinking, the software that was developed (called "Reframer") was meant to harness the benefits of new technology to improve systematic human thinking and cognitive adaptation in rapidly changing environments. More importantly, it was meant to facilitate a change in organizational culture by "creating and developing knowledge" and facilitating the active "molding and transforming" of the operational environment by the commander, rather than passively "information-absorbing."[17]

After Lanir joined with Naveh and Tamari, the innovative work that emerged from this small group of soldier-scholars gained significant traction (at this stage, referred to alternatively as the "Advanced Operational Group" and the "Think-Tank for Operational Studies"). At this time, the group acted, in Naveh's words, as a "wandering circus," providing seminars to colonels and brigadier generals on a "soft version of operational art," which alerted participants to the need for institutional change.[18]

The group's initial ideas were crystallized in a December 1994 report submitted to Brig. Gen. Yaakov Orr, General Rubin's successor, which laid out the IDF's limitations related to operational art. Owing to a lack of IDF generalship and an obsession with "the goddess of action," the group advocated for a formal research institute within the IDF to focus on enhancing operational art. As Naveh wrote, General Orr supported the group's efforts, but, forebodingly, "he also warned us to keep a low profile" and likely foresaw organizational hurdles related to the unique and unconventional nature of the group's work.[19]

Momentum increased for the group's efforts after the success of the various seminars and lectures given in 1994 and 1995 to select midlevel and upper echelons. The group was bolstered by official recognition from the top brass, including COS Lt. Gen. Amnon Lipkin-Shahak and deputy COS Maj. Gen. Matan Vilnai (who, like General Naveh and the others, were both former paratrooper commanders), who agreed in 1995 to create OTRI.[20] From

1995 onward, OTRI began formally teaching the "Advanced Operational Command Course."[21] OTRI also worked in collaboration with the two heads of the defense colleges at the time, who both expressed their support for Naveh's endeavor, as both had been associated with General Rubin's reformist circle. Naveh sought this collaboration with the IDF colleges to avoid organizational or bureaucratic friction in spreading the innovation.[22]

The Advanced Operational Command Course would emphasize the learning and practice of the newly developed concept of SOD as the "principal learning method and command practice to be utilized in operational experiments."[23] The course would teach generalship and critical cognitive methodologies that would enable continuous learning, which would eventually lead to a reframing of operational art in the IDF.[24] General Naveh noted that "OTRI performed the functions of a cultural *agent provocateur*, cognitive enabler, and conceptual promoter" to encourage innovation.[25]

According to Ofra Graicer, who joined OTRI as a researcher in 1999, the responsibility of OTRI was threefold:

> First, it was a school, [running] a course once a year and other teaching events to teach systemic thinking and operational art. Second, it was a research unit, developing a methodology, concepts, and ideas, all originating in operational thinking in different contexts. Third, most importantly, it was a laboratory for experimentation. . . . We brought [commanders] together, and we had a methodology and software that supported it, and we ran experimentations on scenarios. . . . That's how SOD developed. We were meeting with practitioners. . . . They were our lab rats.[26]

WHAT IS SOD?

Systemic Operational Design is a methodology for designing operational campaigns. It is a holistic process meant to rationalize complexity by utilizing a systemic logic, which translates strategic direction and policy into operational-level designs.[27] SOD is "the application of systems theory to operational art," which enables adaptive planning and is reliant on the generalship, creativity, and cognitive abilities of commanders. Following a deep, systematic assessment of the opponent's physical and cognitive traits, SOD enables the mapping of "the relationships between entities in the system to develop rationale for systemic behaviors," which is then scrutinized in a continuous cycle of postaction learning and operational reframing. Putting it simply, one American SOD developer who collaborated with OTRI wrote, "In one sense, this is an adaptation of John Boyd's OODA (observe, orient, decide, act) loop. . . . Adaptive campaigning is the art of continually making sense of dynamic situations and evolving designs, plans, modes of learning, and actions to keep pace."[28]

SOD facilitates the "designing" of campaigns that allows commanders to map and reframe their understanding of their continuously evolving opponent using systems theory, while facilitating the sharing of opponents' "mental constructs" within the command system from the top down and the bottom up. In technical terminology, design is carried out by constructing a broad conceptual frame of reference regarding the strategic context (the "systems frame"), followed by constructing a narrower conceptual frame (the "operating frame") that facilitates an understanding of trends and weaknesses of the enemy. Then a campaign is designed using a mental model of a desired end state, while the plan is continuously reassessed and challenged as the operation proceeds.[29] The differences between the military's "logic" (read "disposition," "raison d'être," "cultural background") and the opponent's "logic" require different conceptual understandings. For example, in asymmetrical warfare with Hezbollah, the military must outline a "systematic contextual logic" that lays out unique strategic, cultural, and institutional challenges imposed by the asymmetry of the group, as well as its perceptions of time and space.[30] This brief description is not intended to be an authoritative account of the extremely complex SOD methodology but will suffice for the purposes of this book.

THE CONCEPTUAL SOURCES OF SOD

General Naveh drew his inspiration for SOD from diverse areas, including general systems theory (as developed by Austrian theorist Ludwig von Bertalanffy), AirLand Battle doctrine, the Soviet theory of deep operations, and the notion of "operational shock" as mastered by the Soviet generals, especially Mikhail N. Tukhachevsky.[31] Naveh was heavily influenced by British theorist Brig. Richard Simpkin (to whom Naveh dedicated his book), various architectural theories, French postmodern philosophy (especially Gilles Deleuze, Félix Guattari, and Paul Virilio), complexity and chaos theories, and biological and evolutionary theories, as well as a host of other diverse social-scientific theories.[32] Zvi Lanir contributed his foundational ideas related to cognitive thinking and adaptation ("reframing"), philosophy, and the sophisticated enabling software developed by the Praxis Institute.[33] Brig. Gen. Dov Tamari, as a war hero, brought the needed prestige, legitimacy, and clout, which, according to one OTRI staffer, "enabled the subversive ideas to take an organizational form," facilitating the institutionalization of OTRI within the IDF.[34] As Naveh wrote, Tamari was a "mythological figure in the IDF due to his feats as a special forces unit commander, his exceptional mind, and his unmatched intellectual integrity."[35]

Naveh deeply admired the Soviet general Tukhachevsky, a senior officer in the Red Army during the 1920s and 1930s, whom he praised for his innovative use of offensive and defensive maneuver that culminated in deliverance of an "operational shock" (*udar*) to the enemy.[36] According to Naveh, the Russian theory of operational shock implies deliberately thinking about the rival as a system to design a "systemic maneuver that dismantles the rival system's ability to exploit its operational potential."[37] Naveh seems to have viewed himself as a Tukhachevsky-esque character, as both operated in the face of intellectual inertia and organizational opposition (in Tukhachevsky's case, Stalin's opposition!), seeking to enhance a greater understanding of the operational level of war. Like Tukhachevsky, Naveh advocated establishing an academy that would teach operational art and promote creative, operational-level thinking among officers.[38]

OTRI was also influenced by the notion of "strategic raiding" and conceptually drew from the experiences of the great British colonial officer Capt. Orde Wingate. Naveh and senior OTRI personnel were enamored of Captain Wingate's campaign with the Chindit commandos deep in the jungles of British India and Burma in the 1940s during World War II, where they operated as autonomous guerrilla units that carried out "strategic raiding" and "long-range penetration" behind enemy lines to disorient, "disrupt," and "shock" the Japanese opponent.[39] General Naveh was also impressed with Wingate's influence as a colonial officer in prestate Israel, which he believed fostered a culture of operational learning, adaptation, and critical reflection in the IDF.[40]

The influence of Brigadier Simpkin led Naveh to attempt to find concepts that synergized scientific concept development, command practice, and generalship.[41] Simpkin's criticism of Western military incompetence (because of an organizational culture that idealizes tactics, lacks intellectualism or generalship, and ignores operational art) would often be repeated by Naveh as applying to the IDF.[42] OTRI believed that SOD was, in Naveh's words, "a pragmatic vehicle possessing the potential for healing, at least partially, the institutional disease" of the IDF.[43]

THE INFLUENCE OF EFFECTS-BASED OPERATIONS ON THE IDF

When designing campaigns, SOD was meant to facilitate the projecting of "effects" onto the "logic" of the opponent. Drawing partially from ancient Chinese theory and postmodern philosophy, SOD sought to positively influence and shape the battlefield based on the potential in the situation ("potentiation"). Owing to an inherent level of battlefield uncertainty, effects would be "potentiated" through questioning and design, in order to capitalize on emerging human behavior and systemic contextual factors to shape a desired outcome (which, according to SOD enthusiasts, is in line with Sun Tzu's holistic war theory).[44] Illustratively, General Naveh said in 1998, "In the past in order to create that basic strategic resource that we lacked we had to project troops into enemy territory. . . . Today we can compensate for this lack by projecting . . . not troops but by projecting effects."[45]

As they are subject to much confusion, it is important to note that effects in SOD were understood differently than in the American-developed concept of Effects-Based Operations (EBO), despite often being grouped together inaccurately.[46] EBO emerged in the United States in its contemporary, refined form after the successes of US airpower and campaign planning during the Gulf War. EBO, a concept for force application, was heavily reliant on advanced command-and-control technology and precision-firepower capabilities, which would facilitate the military hitting critical enemy targets ("nodes"), which would have a physical and cognitive effect and render the enemy incapable of responding. EBO regarded the enemy as a system held together by vital strategic "centers of gravity" that should be given priority in any targeting campaign.[47] Defined by US Joint Forces Command, EBO is "a set of actions planned, executed, and assessed with a systems perspective that considers the effects needed to achieve policy aims via the integrated application of various instruments of power."[48]

SOD enthusiasts criticized EBO for its flawed simplicity in identifying cause and effect as well as ends and means, due to the inherent complexity of the opponent and OTRI's philosophical issues with the notion of "causation." EBO assumes the ability to "cause" an effect by destruction of a critical node, while SOD encourages the military to "potentiate" an effect within the constantly changing environment by disrupting the opponent's relationships both cognitively and physically. Dr. Graicer explained how OTRI conceptualized EBO and its influence on the IDF:

> OTRI perceived EBO, which was adapted into the IDF, to emphasize precision strikes, as ontological or physically driven. . . . We knew original EBO language was close to the notions of SOD: to treat the rival as a system, that effects weren't just physical but also cognitive, and to use effects abstractly. But the ways EBO was adopted in certain parts of the IDF were not abstract but rather just as precision strikes and more physical.[49]

Put simply, compared to EBO the emphasis in SOD was on "moving from destruction to disruption."[50] This distinction between SOD and American EBO would be blurred in the IDF's 2006 operational concept and would cause considerable confusion in the IDF and academic community (see chapter 9).[51]

THE DIFFUSION OF SOD

Midlevel officers learned OTRI's innovative concepts at the Advanced Operational Command Course throughout the mid-1990s as part of their military education. While the source of the innovation was the mavericks at OTRI and the initial push came from them, the diffusion of SOD throughout the IDF largely came from rising midlevel officers who brought the concepts back to their units and exposed their superiors to SOD methodology. The concepts then gained traction among open-minded commanders in the military elite, who started to push the innovation back down to lower command levels. A major turning point occurred in 1996, when, after being exposed to SOD by subordinate officers who had attended OTRI's course, Maj. Gen. Uzi Dayan, head of Central Command, specifically requested SOD be taught since "when he heard about it . . . he said that he wanted it."[52] According to General Naveh, "By accident, a certain guy [General Dayan] was at a certain time in the right place, and bang! A breakthrough occurred."[53]

OTRI purposely chose to focus its operational design training in Central Command and targeted those considered highly competent, most likely to be promoted to higher positions, and with the greatest cognitive skills and intellectual potential. Once candidates grasped SOD, "their ability to bring about institutional change, in an intimate organization such as the IDF, would be immediate."[54] As the innovation gained traction in Central Command, subscription to SOD and OTRI's thinking became a means for gaining intellectual prestige and, often, a promotion, which is a key facilitator in the diffusion of a military innovation.

The innovation was primarily diffused at midlevels of the IDF as a result of the achievements of several officers considered "rising stars," most of whom went on to senior positions and brought their knowledge of SOD with them. Notable officers, most of whom emerged out of Central Command, included Aviv Kochavi, Gal Hirsch, Itzik Eitan, Nitzan Alon, Gershon HaCohen, and Yossi Kuperwasser.[55] Clearly, SOD conceptually affected some of the best and brightest of the IDF.

OTRI staffer Dr. Orit Gal discussed the diffusion of SOD, and highlighted the inherent dangers of misinterpretation of the methodology because of its "unmanaged" implementation by the "rising stars" (which would have a future effect on the uniformity of SOD's application in 2006):

> Overall, the diffusion of ideas came by finding key people who took on the mode of thinking and who acted as "early adopters." It was about finding entrepreneurs within the system that would take that on rather than managing the implementation process. When you have those kind of people, they take on the ideas, then they run with it, so they might change it, give it their own inter-

pretation, and may not understand it the way it was intended. There is an evolutionary process throughout the diffusion process. But you have mutations.[56]

SOD's success can be attributed to the fact that Naveh "championed his product" and protected his disciples; however, this was coupled with the claim that "those who did not buy into the Naveh intellectual revolution were challenged and sometimes marginalized."[57] As SOD spread throughout the IDF, a subtle division emerged between SOD "insiders" and "outsiders," and the outsiders felt marginalized and left out.[58] According to a former researcher at the Dado Center for Interdisciplinary Military Studies, OTRI's successor organization, "OTRI were accused of being totalitarian, that if you don't agree with their approach regarding the operational level and their whole organizational structure they created, you were criticized as stupid and not part of the system."[59]

Supporting OTRI's concepts became a means for promotion and an accepted way to think, whether or not officers understood or devoted any of the required intellectual attention to actually learning SOD. For example, despite receiving support from COS Lt. Gen. Shaul Mofaz, Naveh lambasted him: "[Mofaz] realized that this thing, which he never bothered to learn about, provides him with an intellectual façade . . . so in the end he became our strongest supporter. We reached the peak of our strength thanks to him. I know him. He stinks, he is an idiot but a terrifying bastard, a paratrooper but absolutely from the garbage."[60]

Central Command is often viewed as the turf of the Paratrooper Brigade, and the associated prestige made it a model for imitation by other IDF commands.[61] The paratroopers acted as the main proponents of the innovation, as the most supportive chiefs of staff as identified by Naveh—Lipkin-Shahak, who established OTRI; Mofaz, who institutionalized OTRI; and Yaalon, a "patron of OTRI"—were all products of the Paratrooper Brigade. Two of the respective deputy chiefs of staff during the same time period, Matan Vilnai and Uzi Dayan, also "supported the operational transformation trend and protected OTRI," and both were paratroopers.[62]

After General Dayan's success with SOD, his successor as head of Central Command, Maj. Gen. Moshe "Bogie" Yaalon, studied SOD and nurtured the innovative process. In Naveh's words, Yaalon would act as "the advocate of OTRI but also as the command agent who led the process of operational learning throughout the entire IDF" through his career, as head of Central Command (1998–2000), deputy COS (2000–2002), and eventually as COS (2002–5).[63] Central Command would act as the main incubator for the innovation and where SOD matured. When Yaalon became COS, he brought SOD to the very pinnacle of the IDF. Highlighting the need for SOD, General Yaalon said in an interview that, in the 1990s, "I felt that the discourses in Central Command as well as in other places were not deep enough. They dealt with foam on water. . . . As I began my duty as Central Command commander, I understood we had to build a different process."[64]

To improve the IDF's situational assessment capabilities, Yaalon became one of the strongest proponents of SOD, establishing and running brainstorming and "reframing" sessions, often multiple times per week, while he himself grappled with SOD's mode of thinking. Yaalon developed new methods for operational planning and design that utilized SOD, its unique command language, and the software developed by Praxis to create "knowledge maps."[65]

The organizational investment made dominantly by Central Command led to the fragmented diffusion of SOD and its command language to other sectors of the IDF. The unequal diffusion of SOD would have key implications for the IDF during the 2006 war. Lt. Col. (Ret.) Saar Raveh of the IDF Behavioral Science Unit, who was involved with implementing some of these reforms in Central Command, judged the success of the innovation: "There's a debate. Some people said our project was a failure because the army actually had two languages: the language which was spoken in Central Command which was more fluid and more heuristic, not dedicated to military terms, and was more interdisciplinary, and the other side, which was the rest of the army and the reserves who were still using the old language."[66]

Upon the outbreak of the Second Intifada, General Yaalon's support enabled various operations in Central Command to be designed by OTRI insiders utilizing SOD.[67] Notably, the highly successful 2002 Operation Defensive Shield, an urban warfare campaign in the West Bank against Palestinian militants, was designed using SOD and its postmodern architectural components.[68] The commanders in the field included several OTRI graduates, among them Aviv Kochavi and Gal Hirsch, who implemented SOD in the operation. Hirsch wrote that rather than confront Palestinian militant groups head-on in asymmetrical urban combat, the IDF assumed a "subversive logic" and "abandoned linear patterns of action," which included the IDF breaking through walls to avoid traversing booby-trapped alleyways, thereby delivering an operational "shock" to militants operating there. Utilizing OTRI jargon, Hirsch described how the IDF reduced its vulnerability to asymmetrical attack by attacking from multiple directions like a "swarm of hornets," "fracturing" the battlespace through simultaneous, multidimensional assaults, "stinging" the enemy through low-signature operations, and psychologically overwhelming the enemy by carrying out continuous "noisy" maneuver ("humming").[69]

The dramatic success of the 2002 operation in stymieing Palestinian terrorism brought increased credibility to OTRI's ideas and jargon, boosted the organizational prestige of the operation's commanders, and led to the IDF's renunciation of the ideas of the Limited Conflict doctrine related to the "gradual fatiguing" of Israel's adversaries (see chapter 6). OTRI staffers argued that SOD "peaked" in 2002 partially owing to the success of Operation Defensive Shield. At this time, OTRI was running training sessions based on SOD methodology for diverse sectors of the IDF, ranging from the Spokesperson's Unit to the special forces. For example, SOD was diffused throughout the navy mainly by its head, Vice Adm. Yedidia Yaari, an experienced commander who was considered a critical thinker and was also a close friend of Naveh.[70] IDF MI made various reforms to its intelligence-collection apparatus and structure based on systemic analysis and SOD-inspired methodologies, led by OTRI confidantes Brig. Gen. Yossi Kuperwasser and Lt. Col. Amos Granit.[71] Ofra Graicer described the reasons for the successful diffusion of SOD throughout the IDF: "It has to do with organizational culture and intimacy of all the players. . . . The OTRI founders were considered experienced veterans and elders with the knowledge. . . . Everyone had to support it during this time, some actually supported it, and some say they supported it but actually didn't, and some tried behind the scenes to destroy it. The period from 1995 to 2005 was the 'bon temps' for SOD."[72]

Since, in Orit Gal's words, "OTRI's idea was to help generals redefine the system," the diffusion of SOD fostered an environment of intellectual creativity and independent experimentation among the IDF's most creative commanders.[73] Admiral Yaari, together with IDF systems analyst Haim Assa, developed their own operational concept of "Diffused Warfare" using methodologies drawn from brainstorming sessions carried out in 2003 while Yaalon was COS, in consultation with OTRI graduates including Aviv Kochavi and Nitzan Alon. The concept was based on the precepts of the RMA, SOD, network-centric warfare, effects-based concepts, and biological theories and proposed carrying out "linear," "horizontal," and "diffused" operations simultaneously on the enemy's multiple physical and cognitive "pressure points."

The fundamental feature of Diffused Warfare is that each unit (termed a "molecule") contains "independent, multidimensional, sensor and shooter components, capable at all times of tying into other molecular systems operating in proximity" while networking ground, sea, and air components.[74] It highlighted a new mode of diffused warfare reliant on light land components operating with a low signature "that takes place, simultaneously, on the entire battle space, distributing the force mass to a multitude of separate pressure points, rather than concentrating it on assumed Clausewitzian centers of gravity."[75] It advocates the use of massed network-enabled precision firepower, which creates a "virtual mass" on the battlefield and replaces the "outdated notion" of linear, massed columns and control of territory, especially in LIC. This diffused "virtual mass" of standoff firepower in turn produces a systemic shock on the asymmetrical rival.

Diffused Warfare was criticized for its overreliance on technology and standoff firepower, deemphasizing the importance of ground forces, maneuver, and the control of territory, underestimating the enemy's ability to adapt, and deemphasizing the human element of war.[76] Nevertheless, these concepts did permeate segments of the IDF and did have a subtle but significant effect on commanders who were exposed to it, particularly the preference for light, low-signature forces and standoff precision firepower over large land formations. This illustrates the innovative potential that SOD held, often triggering independent inquiry, experimentation, and complex concept development by its proponents.

REVOLUTIONS CONVERGE: THE MEETING POINT OF OTRI AND THE RMA

The RMA was permeating the IDF at full steam at this time as a result of perceptions by the senior command of the utility of precision technology and its unique social and budgetary benefits (see chapters 5 and 6). By the late 1990s, the RMA was viewed as a savvy concept validated by US military experiences in the Gulf and Kosovo and became a means of prestige for the IDF and for opening doors to the US defense community. OTRI's ongoing discussion with the DOD's Office of Net Assessment and its legendary long-time director, Andrew Marshall, partially shaped the IDF's perceptions of the RMA throughout the decades. According to Naveh, Marshall and OTRI "developed a special relationship over the years and fantastic dynamics, during which Andy taught us how to organize to think strategically and behave strategically, while exposing us to his own sources of inspiration . . . all in his 'Yoda' talk."[77]

The IDF emulated the US military and imported aspects of the theoretical framework of the RMA from US professional networks and common sources of military education. Deep technological cooperation between the IDF and the US military also facilitated the diffusion into the IDF of RMA-related ideas "validated" and legitimated by the Americans.[78] In a 2001 meeting headed by OTRI confidante Brig. Gen. Gershon HaCohen, head of the IDF Training and Doctrine Department, Generals Naveh and Tamari met with Marshall to discuss OTRI's studies on SOD and operational art.[79] In the same meeting, proponents of the IDF's Limited Conflict doctrine shared with the Pentagon their expertise related to Hezbollah's guerrilla warfare and Palestinian LIC during the US counterinsurgency in Afghanistan, while other officers discussed with the DOD technological developments related to the RMA, illustrating the convergence of several parallel conceptual streams in the IDF.[80]

These in-depth knowledge exchanges in the late 1990s and early 2000s led elements of the IDF to enthusiastically adopt many of the structural and doctrinal components of the US RMA and associated US defense transformation. Many IDF planners were intrigued by Secretary of Defense Donald Rumsfeld's new way of war and accepted many of the conceptual and operational principles without critical scrutiny. The most important result of these exchanges with the Office of Net Assessment was that it led the IDF to partially import aspects of the generic US framework for the RMA because of the professional and intellectual prestige it offered, despite the organic development of RMA weaponry and technology in Israel in decades prior.[81]

During the ongoing debate in the late 1990s regarding the various aforementioned RMA-inspired force plans (see chapter 5), General Naveh presented a little-known reform plan in 1999 for adapting the IDF to the new operational environment.[82] He proposed expanding the air force and reducing the size of the ground forces, while modernizing armored units and artillery that would carry out combined-arms and synchronized operations.[83] He supported the shift toward professionalization within the IDF by cutting the length of military service on par with earlier "slimmer and smarter" proposals and privatizing and outsourcing various logistics functions to civilian contractors. Naveh also called for increasing the long-range missile capabilities of the navy, making it a "strategic arm" of the IDF. It is evident that even unconventional, free-thinking sectors within the IDF were influenced by and advocated RMA-related ideas.

Describing the complex and nuanced correlation between OTRI and the RMA, Ofra Graicer explained:

> Everything that goes on in the US military is read and circulated here. . . . From 1999 onwards, there was a lot of cooperation and collaboration with OTRI and the US military, especially with SAMS, Andrew Marshall, and TRADOC [US Army Training and Doctrine Command], and there was a lot of going in between. We knew it all, we were reading it all, we met the people who developed RMA. . . . If you're asking me if some of the concepts at certain times had a certain overlap, we felt that it allowed us to talk to Americans, and we were sold by Rumsfeld's ideas and the way he was doing it. . . . SOD predated the RMA [in Israel]. We were doing our own revolution here since 1995. We were aware of the RMA, but it would be a different story if you looked at the air force and the rest of military.[84]

While there was an overlap between these two conceptual revolutions under way in the United States and Israel, OTRI fiercely maintained its intellectual autonomy but was still undoubtedly influenced by RMA-related concepts. Notably, OTRI was involved in US military officer education at

SAMS at Fort Leavenworth, Kansas, and took part in several of the US Army's "Unified Quest" war-game exercises from 2003 to 2007, where SOD was utilized and received high marks from the US defense community.[85] The warm reception given to OTRI and the apparent validation of SOD by the US military and the Office of Net Assessment caused an acceleration of the diffusion process of SOD within the IDF. Naveh explained, "Andy [Marshall] was not our sponsor in the formal manner but gave us the confidence to continue pursuing our unique approach. . . . As long as he showed interest and was enthusiastic with what we were doing, we knew we were on the right path."[86] With this boost of momentum, SOD moved from its conceptual "incubator" in Central Command to Northern Command, where it would have profound influence on IDF operational planning for Lebanon.

SOD AND PRE-2006 WAR PLANNING FOR LEBANON

SOD diffused into other sectors of the IDF when several officers from Central Command were transferred to senior positions in Northern Command. Maj. Gen. Benny Gantz, a division commander in Central Command, who previously commanded the Lebanon Liaison Unit, became the new head of Northern Command in 2002 and was a key proponent of SOD. Owing to his prior familiarity with SOD in Central Command in 2001 and 2002, according to Ofra Graicer, upon assuming command "it took Gantz two years to develop a new concept with OTRI. . . . He used strategic raiding, Diffused Warfare. He had a different concept for how to deal strategically with Hezbollah."[87]

During Gantz's tenure as head of Northern Command (2002–5), the IDF developed a large-scale operational contingency plan for possible war with Hezbollah code-named "Northern Storm," designed using SOD with methodological support from OTRI.[88] In the little-known plan, rarely discussed in open sources, the IDF would carry out multidirectional and simultaneous assaults to isolate and home in on Hezbollah's militant component. General Naveh described the planning process:

> For about four years, we were initiating and experimenting; we developed some very interesting ideas of a joint campaign, which was basically conducted and driven by light infantry, Special Forces, Air Force and intelligence, to assault them and then infest the area. Not just attack from the east and from the south, which were the expected directions of advance, but assault from all over and isolate the Shi'a militant component—listen to what I tell you now— from the political. Our idea was not to kill Nasrallah or destroy his organization. This was stupid. Our idea was basically to create conditions which will force him to give up the militant [component], to stop this duality.[89]

The plan drew partially from IDF experiences in 2002 Operation Defensive Shield in the West Bank and, indirectly, from the Diffused Warfare concept and Capt. Orde Wingate's "strategic raiding" concept. It sought to "shock" Hezbollah and trigger a change of "the logic of Hezbollah's system." According to General Naveh, the campaign would involve an assault of "90 company-sized columns from all directions. Some elements airborne, some coming from the sea and others infiltrating almost without armor. The idea was to move in small teams and identify, feed the intelligence circles, exploit our advantage in the air."[90]

OTRI personnel explained that small, "autarkic" units would operate autonomously "in a distributed fashion using maneuver with tiny IDF molecules" to seek and destroy Hezbollah "nodes," which "works like a special operations raid" but represents "a different form of maneuver." OTRI personnel described their conceptualization of Hezbollah's three main components in 2002 when Northern Storm was designed:

> The first was the strategic assets, like the long-range rockets in the Bekaa, which we hit in 2006; the second was the command-and-control mechanism in the Dahiya and Nasrallah; and the third was the southern Lebanon Katyusha threat. . . . The first, from the air, with concrete intelligence, you can do it in thirty minutes. The second phase, you need a few weeks, boots on the ground. Casualties will be inflicted on us, but we'll get it done. The third phase, we'll need special operations with special units. In Northern Storm, we weren't talking about special operations—we were talking about regular units being trained specially. . . . They would be trained in raiding and urban operations, especially "swarming" and "infestation." . . . But this plan wasn't accepted.[91]

Despite his support for OTRI, COS Yaalon said it was "premature," and the highly innovative campaign designed with SOD was ultimately rejected. The organizational investment and potential disruption of training regular combat troops to operate autonomously in low-signature cells of ten to thirteen soldiers, while linked to intelligence and fire assets on par with capabilities usually reserved for special forces, was deemed too severe. Additionally, Yaalon preferred the IDF's "strategic lever" approach that aimed to pressure Hezbollah by using standoff firepower and air strikes (see chapters 2 and 6), which was deemed less costly casualty-wise for the IDF and less disruptive to Israeli society.[92]

When the 2006 war erupted, several officers in the General Staff who knew about Northern Storm, including OTRI confidante Brig. Gen. Gal Hirsch, wanted to explore the available options for the IDF's response.[93] However, without the necessary training and preparation in the years leading up to the war, the IDF was not ready to implement Northern Storm. Yaalon's rejection of the specialized training required for the plan in 2005 made the plan unusable in the 2006 war.[94]

Northern Storm, the only operation designed for Lebanon *formally* using SOD, was one of several battle plans for Lebanon. During the tenures of Northern Command head Maj. Gen. Benny Gantz and his predecessor, Maj. Gen. Gabi Ashkenazi, several detailed operations were drawn up. In 2002, Northern Command came up with a plan code-named "Defense of the Land" (Hebrew: Magen Haaretz), which involved heavy air strikes on Hezbollah and Syrian targets in Lebanon. Ground forces would cross into Lebanon while elite units would be helicoptered in to carry out vertical flanking, thereby surrounding Hezbollah.[95] The IDF would seize key positions and focus on targeting rocket-launcher sites, hence "controlling" (rather than "capturing") the territory. The next stage would involve a six-week operation whereby IDF forces would raid specific Hezbollah targets and, together with close air support, gradually reduce Hezbollah rocket fire before withdrawing into Israel. The Winograd Commission noted that "'Defense of the Land' was adequate as long as the Syrian Army occupied Lebanon and prior to the great build-up of Hezbollah's defense alignment in southern Lebanon."[96] However, when Syrian forces pulled out of Lebanon during the April 2005 Lebanese "Cedar Revolution," the original rationale for pressure directed against Syria was nullified.

In 2005, Northern Command drafted an operational plan code-named "Elevated Waters" (Hebrew: Mai Marom), which resembled Defense of the Land but without the pressure on Syria. The basic tenets remained the same: Katyusha rockets could not be stopped by airpower alone, any operation would involve ground and reserve forces, and political pressure had to be maintained against Hezbollah and the Lebanese state.[97] OTRI senior staffer Lt. Col. (Ret.) Amos Granit described his role in developing Elevated Waters with Gen. Gantz:

> We advocated forgetting about Syria and instead planned to target Hezbollah with the large-scale use of force, intensive firepower, but primarily based on infantry. We deemphasized mechanized armor columns and emphasized simultaneous raids, in order to create friction and kill Hezbollah. . . .
>
> The rationale in Elevated Waters was to articulate the strategic logic of Hezbollah post-2000, which was basically "winning by not losing." This was the basis of the asymmetry between us and them. . . . They project firepower against the Israeli home front, while protecting and ensuring the continuity of their firing units (ATM and rocket squads). . . . The IDF understood Hezbollah's rationale, and Elevated Waters was specifically designed to deal with these two logics.[98]

Another smaller, alternative plan, code-named "Ice Breaker" (Hebrew: Shoveret Kerach), was designed as a seventy-two-hour precision-standoff-fire operation, which had an option built into it to concurrently prepare for a limited counteroffensive by a large reservist mobilization.[99] Ice Breaker would incidentally activate the three reserve divisions needed if the IDF chose to launch Elevated Waters, but, more importantly, "the plan aimed to use external political pressure against Hezbollah [triggered by the reservist mobilization] which would enable the IDF to 'win by points.'"[100] This would signal the sincerity of the IDF to fight and pressure Hezbollah while enhancing IDF preparation for future escalation. Contrary to the conventional wisdom, Colonel Granit explained,

> it was a more limited operation that would allow the situation to cool down and become resolved by external international political pressures after a limited, successful engagement by the IDF. We were not willing to occupy Lebanon, but rather we would use airpower in a limited engagement to avoid casualties. . . .
>
> However, Maj. Gen. Udi Adam, head of Northern Command, didn't understand Ice Breaker and thought that Ice Breaker was a preparation for Elevated Waters. When we designed it, it was not designed to precede Elevated Waters. . . . The main problem in 2006 was the IDF tried to achieve Elevated Waters using the more limited tools of Ice Breaker.[101]

General Naveh and Dr. Graicer asserted that Elevated Waters and Ice Breaker were planned using traditional planning and did not *formally* involve SOD methodology.[102] However, despite having formally left OTRI in 2004 after a dispute with Naveh, Colonel Granit claimed he and General Gantz used OTRI's "discourse and thinking," which was "very instrumental in designing both plans" in 2004 and 2005 and shaped the planning process.[103] This shows the deep influence of SOD on its proponents even after formally severing ties with OTRI.

THE DOWNFALL OF OTRI

In the mid-2000s, SOD was at its conceptual peak, having gone from its humble beginnings being taught to midlevel officers as a course in OTRI, to finding its way into operational battle planning a mere decade later. COS Yaalon was fully supportive until the end of his term in 2005, and his deputy COS, Maj. Gen. Dan Halutz, paid lip service to supporting OTRI, despite assuming command in OTRI's final months and never truly developing an understanding of its concepts. Amid the departure of General Yaalon and the ascension of General Halutz to COS, OTRI was formally shut down after an investigation by the state comptroller in mid-2005, ostensibly accused of mismanagement and financial irregularities.

After Yaalon was squeezed out in 2005, General Halutz, in the words of one OTRI staffer, "purged" the IDF of OTRI supporters, having "deliberately decided to remove both the personalities and institutions that served the interests of the preceding regime."[104] The end of OTRI led many of the commanders who had subscribed to SOD because it was "fashionable" or had brought them prestige to flip-flop and drop what they now viewed as the "irrelevant habits, abstract deliberations, and time-consuming sessions" of the former COS.[105] This period marks the abrupt end of OTRI's ten-year intellectual odyssey. Supportive officers were purged, including Yaalon's deputy COS and the chiefs of the Intelligence, Operations, and Planning Directorates (Generals Gabi Ashkenazi, Aharon Zeevi-Farkash, Israel Ziv, and Yitzhak Harel, respectively). Halutz replaced them with his own supporters over ensuing months: respectively, Moshe Kaplinsky (a longtime opponent of Naveh), Amos Yadlin (an air force general), Gadi Eizenkot (a disciple of Kaplinsky), and Ido Nehushtan (also from the air force). Naveh claims Halutz succeeded in "obliterating, within a period of 18 months, every remaining trace of institutional knowledge that had been developed and assimilated in more than a decade."[106]

CONCLUSION

SOD spread in the IDF through the rising stars recruited by the maverick general Naveh, who were the early adopters that facilitated its diffusion throughout the IDF. OTRI created new theories of war whose adoption became a means of promotion and professional prestige for officers, key enablers of innovation. OTRI eventually secured institutional support and protection from supportive paratroopers in the top brass, which illustrates the dynamic interplay of top-down and bottom-up processes of innovation. While SOD emerged from a local context, the US military transformation had significant theoretical influence on OTRI, whose embrace of RMA concepts brought prestige and opened doors to the wider American defense community. The associated institutional prestige contributed to a wider process of uncritical adoption of American RMA concepts by the IDF.

In the years before the war, SOD was validated in Central Command and diffused to Northern Command, where it was utilized to design battle plans for Lebanon. After General Halutz purged SOD in 2005 and nullified its associated professional prestige, many in the IDF dropped their support of OTRI and SOD. This should act as a cautionary tale for other military organizations that are implementing innovative but highly controversial programs without a critical mass of support to ensure continuity of the innovation. It is also essential to protect early adopters from retaliation by resistant successors.

Following the purge and just three months before the surprise outbreak of war, COS Lt. Gen. Halutz signed into effect a new (classified) operational doctrine in April 2006. Ironically, this doctrine was largely influenced by the work carried out by officers active during the tenure of his predecessor, General Yaalon—the same officers Halutz marginalized upon his appointment in 2005.[107] As illustrated in the next two chapters, the actual content of this document and its effects on IDF conduct during the 2006 war would cause much confusion and debate within the IDF and broader academic community.

NOTES

Epigraph: Author interview with Shimon Naveh.

1. Winograd Commission, final report, chap. 7, paras. 10–11.
2. Naveh, *Operational Art and the IDF*, 78.
3. Ibid.
4. For his analysis on AirLand Battle, see Naveh, *In Pursuit of Military Excellence*, chap. 8.
5. Naveh, *Operational Art and the IDF*, 79.
6. Naveh, "Cult of the Offensive," 177.
7. Naveh, "From *Vernichtungsschlacht* to AirLand Battle."
8. For the origins of his ideas from his own perspective, see Naveh, *Operational Art and the IDF*, 12–14.
9. Ibid., 16–18.
10. Based on author interviews with OTRI personnel.
11. Author interview with Ofra Graicer.
12. Author interview with Zvi Lanir.
13. Ibid.
14. Lanir, *Fundamental Surprises*.
15. Lanir, *Reframing Strategy*, 9–11.
16. For the complex philosophical origins of these ideas, see Lanir and Sneh, *Beyond Post-Modern Deconstruction*.
17. For details of the software, see Lanir, *Reframer*, 10.
18. Naveh, *Operational Art and the IDF*, 81.
19. Ibid.
20. Ibid., 97; author interview with Ofra Graicer. The think tank was signed into formal existence on April 27, 1995.
21. Author interview with OTRI personnel; Adamsky, *Culture of Military Innovation*, 99–100.
22. For details, see Naveh, *Operational Art and the IDF*, 90–91n181.
23. Ibid., 92–96.
24. Ibid., 93–95. For the course syllabus, see ibid., 93.
25. Ibid., 1–2.
26. Author interview with Ofra Graicer.

27. For the most accessible explanation of SOD, see Sorrells et al., *Systemic Operational Design*; Wass de Czege, "Systemic Operational Design."

28. Wass de Czege, "Systemic Operational Design," 4.

29. Ibid., 7–9.

30. Naveh, "Asymmetric Conflict," 20–21. An English translation of this chapter was kindly provided by Ofra Graicer.

31. Naveh, *In Pursuit of Military Excellence*; Naveh, "Mikhail Nikolayevich Tukhachevsky."

32. For SOD's controversial use of architectural theories in the 2002 IDF Operation Defensive Shield, see Weizman, "Art of War"; and Weizman, "Walking through Walls." For more on the conceptual sources of SOD, see Naveh, interview, July–October 2017.

33. Author interview with Zvi Lanir.

34. Author interview with Orit Gal.

35. Naveh, *Operational Art and the IDF*, 80.

36. Naveh, *In Pursuit of Military Excellence*, 164–236.

37. Naveh, *Operational Art and the IDF*, 14, 40n73.

38. Naveh, "Mikhail Nikolayevich Tukhachevsky," 272.

39. OTRI researcher Ofra Graicer wrote her PhD dissertation on Wingate: Graicer, *Two Steps Ahead*. See also Graicer, "Between Teaching and Learning" (2008).

40. Naveh, *Operational Art and the IDF*, 43–55.

41. Ibid., 14.

42. Ibid., 15.

43. Ibid., 82.

44. Challans, "Tipping Sacred Cows," 23, 28; Wass de Czege, "Systemic Operational Design," 5. Brig. Gen. Huba Wass de Czege and Lt. Col. Tim Challans worked together with Naveh to further develop SOD at Fort Leavenworth, KS.

45. Quoted in Jonathan Marcus, "Israel Sharpens Its Military Strategy," BBC News, April 29, 1998.

46. Earlier studies on the 2006 war propagated this inaccuracy. For example, see Matthews, *We Were Caught Unprepared*, 62–63; and Tira, *Limitations of Standoff*, 33–36.

47. Meilinger, "Origins of Effects-Based Operations"; Matthews, *We Were Caught Unprepared*, 23–25. For a quintessential US assessment of EBO at the time, see Deptula, *Effects-Based Operations*. For a different perspective, see Correll, "Assault on EBO."

48. Meilinger, "Origins of Effects-Based Operations," 116.

49. Author interview with Ofra Graicer.

50. Ibid.

51. For one explanation of EBO, see Johnson, *Hard Fighting*, 32–33.

52. Author interview with Ofra Graicer.

53. Naveh, interview, November 1, 2007, 3.

54. Naveh, *Operational Art and the IDF*, 5; Watts, *US Combat Training*, 50–51.

55. Naveh, interview, October 25, 2007.

56. Author interview with Orit Gal.

57. Berman, "Capturing Contemporary Innovation," 130–31.

58. Cited in Johnson, *Hard Fighting*, 28n53.

59. Author interview with Eitan Shamir.

60. Naveh, interview, October 25, 2007.

61. Naveh, *Operational Art and the IDF*, 6.

62. Ibid., 2–3, 4n4.

63. Ibid., 32–33.

64. Quoted in Michael, "Israel Defense Forces as an Epistemic Authority," 431.

65. Ibid., 431–34.

66. Author interview with Saar Raveh.

67. For an overview, see Bilmyer, *IDF*, 59–71.

68. For a dramatized account of the 2002 operation, see Naveh, "Between the Striated and the Smooth." See also Weizman, "Lethal Theory."

69. Hirsch, "Development of the Campaign"; Hirsch, "On Dinosaurs and Hornet"; Hirsch, *Defensive Shield*, 163.

70. Author interview with Ofra Graicer.

71. Kuperwasser, *Lessons from Israel's Intelligence Reforms*, 13–21.

72. Author interview with Ofra Graicer.

73. Author interview with Orit Gal.

74. Yaari and Assa, *Diffused Warfare*, 25–30.

75. Ibid. For a related version, see Yaari and Assa, "Dynamic Molecules."

76. For critiques, see Caroline Glick, "The Imperatives of War," *Jerusalem Post*, September 6, 2007; and Henkin, "Confused Warfare."

77. Naveh, interview, July–October 2017, 37.

78. For theoretical literature, see Farrell, "Culture and Military Power," 412; and Goldman, "New Threats," 63–64. See also, Tira, *Nature of War*, 125–28; Finkel and Shamir, "From Whom Does the IDF Need to Learn?"

79. Author interview with Ofra Graicer.

80. Amir Oren, "IDF to Share Anti-Terror Expertise with Pentagon," *Haaretz*, October 14, 2001; Amos Harel, "Disquiet on the Eastern Front," *Haaretz*, August 20, 2004.

81. Adamsky, *Culture of Military Innovation*, 103–4; Marcus, "Israeli Revolution in Military Affairs," 102.

82. "Reform Plan for Israel's Army," *Jane's Foreign Report*, April 22, 1999.

83. Naveh, "Cult of the Offensive," 180–83.

84. Author interview with Ofra Graicer.

85. Naveh, "Operational Art"; Department of the Army, *Full-Spectrum Operations*, 39–44; Schmitt, *Systemic Concept for Operational Design*, 48n3.

86. Naveh, interview, July–October 2017, 37.

87. Author interview with Ofra Graicer.

88. Ryan, "Applications of Complex Systems to Operational Design," 1258–59.

89. Naveh, interview, November 1, 2007, 7.

90. Ibid.

91. Author interview with OTRI personnel.

92. Author interview with Ofra Graicer.

93. Author interview with Shimon Naveh.

94. Author interview with Ofra Graicer.

95. Harel and Issacharoff, *34 Days*, 61.

96. Winograd Commission, final report, chap. 7, n. 17.

97. Harel and Issacharoff, *34 Days*, 62.

98. Author interview with Amos Granit.

99. Lambeth, *Air Operations*, 28.

100. Author interview with Amos Granit.

101. Ibid.

102. Author interviews with Shimon Naveh and Ofra Graicer.

103. Author interview with Amos Granit.

104. Caroline Glick, "Halutz's Stalinist Moment," *Jerusalem Post*, June 8, 2006; Naveh, *Operational Art in the IDF*, 6n8.

105. Naveh, *Operational Art and the IDF*, 7.

106. Ibid., 9.

107. Ibid., 10n14.

CHAPTER 8

THE 2006 LEBANON WAR

Military Adaptation and Counteradaptation

We planned for a bullet train, but what we got was an urban bus with many stops.

—Maj. Gen. Benny Gantz

If you have an army with marvelous capacities—air force, tanks, cannons, rockets—but which lacks information about the enemy, it would be as a blind elephant which slaps right and left.

—Sec.-Gen. Hassan Nasrallah

On July 12, 2006, an IDF reserve unit patrolling the border with Lebanon was sent to investigate border-intrusion alerts reported the night before near the Israeli village of Zarit. At 9:05 a.m., an IED exploded near the IDF vehicles, killing three soldiers and wounding four. Hezbollah fighters previously spotted across the border crossed into Israel and pulled two of the wounded soldiers, Ehud Goldwasser and Eldad Regev, back into Lebanon. Hezbollah released footage of the kidnapping incident in 2012, which showed well-prepared Hezbollah fighters in camouflage ambushing the patrol from concealed positions within dense woodlands overlooking the road, shooting down at the patrolling convoy with suppressing fire while other units moved toward the damaged IDF jeep. In an effort to cause chaos, Hezbollah also fired rockets and mortars across the border. Over an hour later and amid much confusion, armored IDF units and a Merkava tank crossed into Lebanon in a rescue operation, as another IED exploded under the Merkava, killing four crew members. In the ensuing recovery operation, another infantry soldier was killed. Hezbollah later released further footage of its training and preparations for the ambush and its surveillance of the border location under the direction of senior Hezbollah commander Khaled Bazzi, indicating its awareness that the patrolling IDF units would be briefly out of radio range of the IDF border command center.[1] The IDF's bloody, slow, and disorganized response to the kidnapping, despite several existing plans for this kind of scenario, would come to symbolize the IDF's haphazard war effort against Hezbollah.

The IDF's preference for airpower, cautious use of limited ground forces, belabored decision to launch a larger ground offensive, and sloppy tactical performance in 2006 were influenced by the concepts and trends evolving throughout Israel's two decades of fighting in Lebanon. Hezbollah developed simple but innovative counteradaptations to the IDF based on its own lessons learned throughout the 1990s and ultimately circumvented the IDF's conventional and technological superiority during the war.

THE AIR CAMPAIGN

The IDF had several battle plans for a variety of contingencies to respond to Hezbollah. According to Brig. Gen. Itai Brun, head of research, IDF MI (2011–15), because of a lack of urgency on the Lebanon front in the years prior to the war, neither operational plans Elevated Waters nor Ice Breaker were thoroughly synthesized by the time war broke out, and the Winograd Commission also concluded that neither was ever formally implemented.[2] Nevertheless, these plans did significantly shape the conceptual framework in which the IDF operated during the war.[3]

Upon the outbreak of war, COS Lt. Gen. Dan Halutz opted for a limited standoff counteroffensive, at least for the campaign's initial phase, which resembled Ice Breaker in a sense, as it was heavily reliant on airpower but, crucially, contained no reservist mobilization component. Halutz ordered the IAF to carry out a planned operation (Operation Specific Weight) to destroy Hezbollah's "strategic weaponry" on the first night of the war. In less than thirty-four minutes, the IAF destroyed hundreds of Hezbollah's high-value targets and midrange and long-range weapons (including fifty-nine Iranian-made Fajr and Zelzal rocket launchers), described by General Brun as "a case study in operational perfection."[4] The stunning operation, enabled by the IDF's RMA sensor-to-shooter and precision technology, hit launchers concealed within the densely populated Lebanese operating environment and caused fewer than twenty civilian casualties, far less collateral damage than IAF estimations.[5] This opening overnight air operation (dubbed the "Night of the Fajrs") represented the culmination of years of painstaking intelligence and target collection and emptied the IAF's target bank. MI and the IAF were later praised for this impressive operation by the postwar commission.[6]

The IAF's initial success led some top officers, including Deputy COS Maj. Gen. Moshe Kaplinsky and head of Operations Directorate Maj. Gen. Gadi Eizenkot, to urge Halutz that if he was unwilling to mobilize reserves to expand the campaign, then the IDF should push for a cessation of hostilities since Israel had already demonstrated its resolve and superior operational capabilities. This view was shared by Israel's NSC and senior figures within the Foreign Ministry.[7] Some claim that this reflects the belief that Israel achieved the pinnacle of its success and the "culmination of victory" on the first day of the war.[8]

However, the IDF failed to convey the ramifications to the government of continuing the conflict, as government ministers were not privy to critical internal army debates related to Hezbollah's inevitable escalation, the mobilization of reserves, the effects of delaying a ground operation, and the lack of preparation of IDF ground forces. According to Maj. Gen. (Ret.) Amos Yadlin, head of MI during the 2006 war, "from the point of view of the political and military echelon in Israel, a cease-fire was not relevant in the first two weeks [as] they believed in the ability to achieve a very serious blow to Hezbollah with massive air-only activity." It was assessed that Nasrallah could not escalate further since Hezbollah's long-range missiles had been neutralized and that "he was in a bunker—rather scared."[9] Poor communication at the highest political and military levels prevented Israel from pursuing a cease-fire at this point, as a retaliation operation slid into full-blown war.[10]

The IDF's aforementioned battle plans were not implemented decisively since both the IDF command and political echelon were wary of an extended ground campaign, largely influenced by domestic considerations, including popular pressure and the trauma of previous experiences in Lebanon.[11] In remarks to the Knesset in the early days of the 2006 war, Halutz said, "In this day and age, with all the technology we have, there is no reason to start sending ground troops in."[12] In an interview during the war, Maj. Gen. Benny Gantz, who had become head of GFC in 2005, lamented that the operational plan he had developed (with Lt. Col. Amos Granit) in Northern Command was not decisively implemented. He described the rolling, sequential plan: a week of standoff air-land battle, a three-to-four-day intensive ground assault, and a four-week "cleansing" phase, followed by a two-to-three week withdrawal into Israel. Instead, ground forces were not utilized decisively during the war because of political considerations, and a different, haphazard plan was implemented:

> We planned for a bullet train, but what we got was an urban bus with many stops. . . . When we started this planning [2002–5], I said I didn't want to deploy a single soldier there. My force was the last to leave [Lebanon in 2000] and I couldn't stomach the thought of going back. . . . But after months of

careful study, I understood that if we didn't put in three divisions, we wouldn't get out of the situation with any meaningful advantage.[13]

IDF opening strikes elicited a meticulously planned "rocket war" from Hezbollah and resulted in massive Katyusha fire directed at Israel's home front. Contrary to the inaccurate notion propagated in some of the scholarship, neither the IAF nor MI ever believed they had the ability to cease Hezbollah's rocket fire with airpower alone and had discussed "the need for a ground strike if the need to remove the threat from the border arose" in earlier planning meetings.[14] The Winograd Commission highlighted January 2006 prewar army intelligence estimates: "Recognition of the limitations of intelligence was one of the important reasons, alongside others, for the assessment according to which the aerial strike would not, by itself, be able to create decisive and equation-changing results vis-à-vis [Hezbollah], and would not be able to halt or significantly reduce a massive attack by surface-to-surface rockets on the Israeli home front."[15]

According to Maj. Gen. Aharon Zeevi-Farkash, former head of IDF MI (2002–6), an assessment prepared in late 2005 highlighted the risk from the IDF's lack of preparedness for Hezbollah's standoff firepower capabilities and "took pains in all discussions to point out that it was unable to provide the combat forces with accurate intelligence regarding the exact location of Hezbollah's short-range rockets."[16] The head of the IAF, Maj. Gen. Eliezer Shkedy, warned COS Halutz during the 2006 war that the IAF would be unable to stop short-range rocket fire and that the success rate in destroying these launchers would be between 1 percent and 3 percent. Maj. Gen. Amos Yadlin, of MI, and the head of Mossad, Meir Dagan, also warned that the IDF's actions in the opening stage of the war would elicit Katyusha fire against the Israeli home front.[17] General Yadlin later asserted in an author interview that "it is important to know that military intelligence constantly claimed that at least one of two legs be added to the air strikes—either a ground operation or damage to Lebanese state infrastructure."[18] Simply put, the Winograd Commission noted: "The Air Force stated from the outset that it would not have great effectiveness in hitting the short-range rocket alignment."[19] In a balanced assessment that was drowned out immediately after the war, General Gantz firmly refuted those who faulted COS Halutz for a misplaced reliance on airpower to cease rocket fire and highlighted the political and domestic factors that were more influential on decision-making: "There was absolutely no one in any military leadership position who claimed airpower alone could deliver the goods. But the political level wanted to maximize the stand-off firepower and the air campaign and, if there wasn't any other choice, to implement the ground war."[20]

While General Halutz's experience as an air force general undoubtedly did influence his mind-set, his airpower-centric focus, and his de-emphasis on the ground component to an extent, a greater issue was his systemic resistance to calling up reservists because of fear of casualties and "postheroism" in the IDF. Demonstrating such sentiment, once the reserves were finally mobilized, despite the IDF having a hundred thousand troops ready for battle, only nine thousand were ever used at a time.[21] The IDF had become organizationally conditioned to short, low-risk operations reliant on standoff firepower and airpower, largely a result of the influence of the RMA over previous decades. In a 2010 interview, General Halutz maintained his doubts of the utility of ground forces to stop Hezbollah rocket fire at an acceptable cost: "I'm not saying there isn't a need for massive ground-maneuvering forces. Future scenarios may demand ground action and control of the ground. But then you have to be prepared for these operations to take much more time—months or even years—and you need to be ready to pay the penalties."[22]

This airpower-centric mode of conduct also jibed with the IDF's adopted strategic paradigm for dealing with Hezbollah in the 1990s (see chapters 2 and 6). Lt. Col. (Ret.) Roni Amir, former head of IAF Doctrine Branch, explained, "If you look at Gen. Dan Halutz specifically, the 1993 and 1996 operations were the concepts which he was trying to adopt, and later on this was leading his line of thought in the 2006 war."[23] Halutz's ultimate failure, more so than his casualty aversion or preference for RMA-inspired airpower, was his subscription to the IDF's static "lever" policy of the 1990s that sought to use standoff firepower to coerce the powerless Lebanese state to rein in Hezbollah, although it had been unwilling and unable to do so over the previous two decades owing to its own weak sovereignty. Colonel Amir explained, "When Halutz went to the government, his idea was something you can call a 'strategic attack and coercion campaign,' to attack 'the state of Lebanon' and Hezbollah. By the way, he didn't use the planning that was already done before; he invented his own, even though we had many different plans."[24]

There were divergent opinions between the military and politicians about who the IAF should target upon the outbreak of war. Contrary to the position of the politicians who advocated for a campaign that focused solely on Hezbollah, Halutz and other generals viewed the state of Lebanon to be the best target for constraining the group.[25] For example, Maj. Gen. Yitzhak Harel, head of the Planning Directorate, urged Halutz during the war's opening hours to strike Lebanese state targets, stating at the time: "For the past year we've been saying that the Lebanese government is responsible for what happens on its side of the border. Now we'll show them we mean business!"[26] Strikes against Lebanon's infrastructure were intended to show Lebanon's population that Hezbollah, which had presented itself as "the defender of Lebanon," actually brought great destruction to the country.[27]

Deluded into a false sense of triumph after the successes of the IAF's opening Operation Specific Gravity, Halutz believed that political barriers imposed by the international community regarding striking the Lebanese government would be eased after the world witnessed Hezbollah's Katyusha onslaught against Israel. This would enable the IDF to carry out its traditional lever strategy, which illustrates how the IDF's flawed strategic approach used in Lebanon in the 1990s deeply affected operational decisions made in 2006.[28] Colonel Amir criticized Halutz's subscription to this static strategic approach reliant on standoff firepower: "I don't think it has to do with the fact he's a pilot. It's much deeper, more systemic. . . . I think his failure was in this misunderstanding of the situation, that Lebanon isn't a state and doesn't have the power to coerce Hezbollah, and that Syria was out of the game. . . . It's too simplistic to say he's just a pilot—it misses the point."[29]

General Yadlin described the actual internal deliberations: "The General Staff convened to prepare operative suggestions for the political echelon, focusing on the suggestion to massively damage state infrastructures in Lebanon, including power stations in Beirut. A second alternative was to attack the Fajr arsenal—the long-range rockets located inside homes in southern Lebanon villages."[30]

The IAF had planned for a rapid, decisive operation to send a clear signal to both the Lebanese government and Hezbollah that would enable the establishment of favorable terms in a cease-fire. However, political pressure from the United States constrained the IDF's targeting of infrastructure of the government of Lebanon—a US ally—that could not be linked to Hezbollah's military efforts (see chapter 4).[31] The pivotal decision of the political echelon to reject General Halutz's plan to strike infrastructure of the "pro-Western" Lebanese government represents a misreading of the damaging effect a drawn-out war waged solely against Hezbollah would have on Israel.[32]

General Halutz maintained his subscription to the approach that the Lebanese state would have been an effective lever against Hezbollah. In his memoir, he clarified his central mistake of the 2006 war: "In meetings of the Security Cabinet, I wasn't convincing enough about implementing the plan to attack the national infrastructure of Lebanon. It was a plan I believed in, and in my opinion, its implementation would have lent itself to a clear and sharp response that would have exceeded expectations of the enemy and helped shorten the war-fighting."[33]

Despite the preference of Halutz and the IDF, Defense Minister Amir Peretz, a former head of Israel's national trade union with no significant military experience, chose to focus on the Fajr arsenal. He later reflected on his decision to avoid targeting Lebanese infrastructure: "I tell the Chief of Staff that we have to use logic and not fall into Hezbollah's trap. . . . I said attacking the power stations would make the whole population of Lebanon rally around Hezbollah. . . . I rejected the army's proposal and preferred an attack on the Fajrs. That is what I urged and that is what was authorized."[34]

While the operation to destroy Hezbollah's Fajrs was highly successful, the decision to avoid targeting Lebanese infrastructure forced the IDF to find alternative means to pressure Hezbollah and indirectly led to prolonging the conflict.[35] After the Fajr operation, the IAF continued to bombard Hezbollah's areas of support throughout the first week of the war. In response, Hezbollah escalated its rocket campaign by firing dozens of rockets toward Israel's third-largest city, Haifa. In a live televised broadcast on July 14, Hassan Nasrallah famously urged viewers to look toward the ocean as Hezbollah fired a C-802 ground-launched antiship missile, hitting the Israeli navy corvette *Hanit*, which was imposing a naval blockade against Lebanon. The warship's defenses were not switched on because of a tactical mishap and resulted in four sailors killed. While the ship did not sink, the event had a significant psychological effect on Israeli society, as Nasrallah proclaimed, "The surprises I've promised you shall now begin. Right now, out at sea facing Beirut, you can see the Israeli military corvette that assailed our civilians and our infrastructure. Watch it burn and sink, with dozens of Zionist soldiers. This is only the beginning. There will be a lot more said before the end!"[36]

"RAIDS" AND "SWARMS": THE IDF'S LIMITED GROUND OPERATIONS

More than a week after the outbreak of war, a painfully slow decision by the political echelon authorized the IDF to begin carrying out limited ground operations against Hezbollah strongholds in southern Lebanon. Defense Minister Peretz reflected on the slow decision to launch ground operations and the IDF's preference for air operations:

> I felt we were treading water. I understood that we had to decide either to stop and announce a unilateral ceasefire, or go to a broad ground operation. . . . There were disagreements in the army, but the IDF position, as presented by the Chief of Staff, was to go all the way with the air campaign. He said there was no need to mobilize the reserves. It was only two weeks later that I persuaded everyone to call up the three divisions.[37]

Peretz asserted that General Halutz and Prime Minister Olmert were both against expanding the operation and that he was the first of the three to push for a ground campaign. Halutz had rejected a proposed operation to airdrop special forces by the Litani River that would move southward to surround Hezbollah, as he still preferred to avoid a large ground invasion or reserves call-up. As a compromise, Halutz reluctantly authorized limited battalion- and brigade-sized "raids" into villages in southern Lebanon, intended to target key Hezbollah members and symbolically significant targets.[38] Halutz admitted his mistake in his first postwar interview in 2008 regarding the late activation of the reserves: "I made a mistake in the timing of calling up the reserves. Even if there wasn't a need to activate them in the beginning, they should have been called up. It is true that I thought [the war] could have ended before [calling them up]."[39]

There were four divisions active in Lebanon: the Ninety-First Galilee Division, led by Brig. Gen. Gal Hirsch; the 162nd Division, led by Brig. Gen. Guy Tzur; the Ninety-Eighth Division, led by Brig. Gen. Eyal Eisenberg; and the 366th "Pillar of Fire" Division, led by Brig. Gen. Erez Zuckerman. All four divisions operating in Northern Command primarily conducted battalion- and brigade-sized operations against Hezbollah, as there was no coordinated Northern Command campaign to accomplish collective objectives linked to strategic goals, despite numerous battle plans designed prior to the war (see chapter 7).[40]

The Winograd Commission noted "very grave" training deficiencies in all four divisions that contributed to their poor tactical performances and had "significant implications on the war in Lebanon." For example, the "storming echelon" of the 366th Division had not trained for four or five years before the war. Owing to cuts in the budget that resulted in the reallocation of resources from ground forces training toward RMA programs or ongoing counterterrorism missions in the Palestinian territories, ground divisions were poorly supplied and had barely trained for high-intensity warfare or combined-arms operations. Many units in the divisions trained only on simulators or in computer war games, and "here and there, a skeleton exercise was held with very limited participants."[41] Critically, the operative plan that several divisions had prepared for prior to the war was "Defense of the Land," even though its operational rationale was outdated and irrelevant due to Syria's 2005 withdrawal from Lebanon. The IDF had several updated plans (e.g., Elevated Waters), but as a result of training cuts they had not been synthesized by the divisions. The damaging effects of the cuts were demonstrated in the sloppy performance of ground troops throughout the war.

Limited ground operations were launched in southern Lebanese villages, best epitomized by those in the villages of Maroun al-Ras and Bint Jbayl. These operations should be viewed as exemplifying the IDF launching ground offensives hesitantly, without clear operational objectives, and with an insufficient number of troops, who also sometimes lacked adequate training. For example, a two-day battle in Maroun al-Ras was ordered on July 20 with a small number of elite Egoz counterguerrilla commandos who were deployed to reinforce a paratrooper battalion holding the village that was being led by a commander who had never conducted a battalion training exercise due to budgetary cuts in prior years.[42] The IDF faced uniformed and nonuniformed Hezbollah fighters in the village, which was saturated with booby traps, including IEDs. Hezbollah fighters targeted the IDF from fortified defensive positions within the village, while others carried out offensive assaults and engaged in fierce close-quarter fighting.[43] The Egoz commandos waged a bloody extended firefight with minimal reinforcements, even while a large number of IDF troops were massed on the border restlessly awaiting orders to cross into Lebanon.[44] Overall, the IDF seized key positions in Maroun al-Ras despite sustaining casualties, and MI picked up chatter at the time that Hezbollah was "showing signs of panic" since the group had incorrectly assessed that the IDF would continue air strikes rather than enter the village.[45]

IDF casualties sustained by the Egoz unit caused concern in other infantry soldiers in the field, who remarked that if the commandos—specially trained to deal with Hezbollah—were taking casualties, then how would nonspecialist units fare in the complex operational environment?[46] In response to the IDF losses in Maroun al-Ras, increasingly frenetic criticism from the media, and the heightened sensitivity of the Israeli public, the head of Northern Command, Maj. Gen. Udi Adam, ordered a partial retreat from the village and temporarily forbade attacks on Hezbollah's bunkers in the bushy Lebanese terrain (dubbed "nature reserves" in IDF jargon) because of the large number of ground troops required for the task and inevitable casualties.[47] Ninety-First Division commander Gal Hirsch clashed with Adam about this decision, as Hirsch sought to hold Maroun al-Ras (Hezbollah's main operations center in the sector) and pushed to carry out a novel "swarming" operation. Inspired by OTRI's teachings, Hirsch sought to "swarm" and "shock" Hezbollah, thereby "casting a blanket over the fire and suffocating it by creating multiple friction points with as many enemy fighters as possible leading to suppression of its operating capabilities" to fire rockets. General Adam ultimately rejected this plan because of concerns about casualties.[48]

Limited raids against the Hezbollah stronghold of Bint Jbayl were planned because of its symbolic importance as the site of Hassan Nasrallah's famous "spider web" victory speech after Israel's 2000 withdrawal (see chapter 3). The IDF sought to demonstrate resolve and symbolically rebut Nasrallah's assertion that Israel was militarily and societally "weaker than a spider's web" and—keeping with the spider theme—bombastically named its Bint Jbayl operation "Web of Steel." General Adam stated on July 23 that IDF forces "were not to conquer Bint Jbayl, but seize it" by conducting a "raid," killing as many terrorists as possible, and withdrawing. According to Brig. Gen. Gal Hirsch, the goal of the operation, initially meant to be limited to forty-eight-hours, was motivated by a desire by the senior echelon for a "symbolic" or "perceptional" victory to impact the "consciousness" of Hezbollah to continue fighting.[49] The misguided nature of this approach, never synchronized with the realities on the battleground, was displayed when the 890th Paratrooper Battalion—after several significant engagements in the village—was ordered by General Halutz to battle back into the village from a forward position to plant an Israeli flag in front of the Bint Jbayl municipal building, despite Hezbollah still actively firing Katyushas from the area.[50] There was even a plan for Defense Minister Peretz to deliver a "victory speech" on the site of a former IDF position from the security zone period in the village, which was to be photographed and videotaped for symbolic propaganda purposes.[51]

In Bint Jbayl, different units were given contradictory tasks, and the objectives of units involved were not coordinated with one another or with the realities on the ground. The units disjointedly advanced with poor communication through the village's narrow alleys, where IDF technological superiority had limited utility. Soldiers involved in Operation Web of Steel later reflected that they felt they were going into the "unknown" and lacked adequate training and equipment for the rigorous battlefield challenges they faced. A soldier who received aerial intelligence on the village from MI that was dated from 2002 remarked with concern that he had felt like a "small cog in a machine in need of oiling."[52] Damningly, some troops that made contact with Hezbollah were unprepared for the scope and high intensity of combat with dug-in Hezbollah fighters who engaged the IDF in lengthy gun battles from fortified positions and used offensive and defensive tactics, indirect mortar fire, and mobile assault squads that carried out bold offensive operations.[53] Hezbollah squads also launched several deadly ATM assaults against IDF troops who had clustered together while seeking cover in buildings in the village.

While the IDF's preference for limited symbolic ground operations was largely influenced by casualty aversion and the top brass's desire to avoid a large-scale ground campaign, the Ninety-First Division's Brig. Gen. Hirsch, tasked with carrying out the Bint Jbayl operations, has often been scapegoated for the IDF's poor performance in the village.[54] Hirsch, a disciple of Brig. Gen. Shimon Naveh and OTRI, utilized SOD's distinct command language in Bint Jbayl, which he had learned from his experiences with SOD as a commander in the 2002 Operation Defense Shield in the West Bank. According to the Winograd Commission, Hirsch used "creative" and "poetic" jargon in Bint Jbayl that was unfamiliar to some of his subordinates when he ordered units to conduct a "systemic demonstration" by launching "simultaneous, multi-dimensional swarms" and a "wide-spread low-signature infiltration (wasp cloud)" to cause "shock and awe."[55]

Hirsch was influenced by his exposure to the never-implemented "Northern Storm" plan designed using SOD in Northern Command and the OTRI-related concepts of Diffused Warfare and "strategic raiding" that espoused unconventional types of maneuver warfare (see chapter 7).[56] In his memoir, Hirsch described his plan in Bint Jbayl, which was designed to "swarm" Hezbollah villages by "diffusion tactics" and "maneuvering without distinct vector patterns in a chaotic and unpredictable manner" that "would collapse the rival system." He believed such multidirectional operations would be better suited to combat Hezbollah's low-signature asymmetrical guerrilla tactics.[57] Hirsch later admitted that his plan in Bint Jbayl, developed independently during the war and without direct consultation with OTRI, had been for a limited ground raid that resembled some sort of SOD-inspired variation of "operational swarming" but conceded that brigade-level units were not meant to execute such a maneuver. Hirsch acknowledged that each brigade in the village should have performed a conventional maneuver that, together, would have formed a division-level, multidirectional attack.[58] This seems to reflect his belated realization that such SOD-related concepts were inappropriate for implementation in brigades in combat in Bint Jbayl.

Some brigade commanders under Hirsch were understandably confused by such unfamiliar concepts and terminology. Since brigades had not trained together in many months as a result of aforementioned budget cuts, they had not been exposed to these innovative ideas, had not prepared for such maneuvers, and found the mission objectives ill defined and imprecise. The Winograd Commission conceded that "some subordinates were very familiar with [Hirsch's command language] and had no difficulty understanding it. However, not all of the commanders who fought under the command of the division commander were his subordinates before the war. It is no surprise that they and their troops had difficulty in understanding these terms and translating them into operational military language."[59] The commission noted elsewhere that exposure to the innovative operational concepts consolidated in Northern Command and especially in Hirsch's Ninety-First Division were "neither tested nor properly drilled in actual fact in the units or in exercises" because of training budget cuts.[60] While it is true that OTRI propagated ideas related to "strategic raiding," Diffused Warfare, and "swarming," such concepts were meant for an entirely different operational context and involved rigorous training, planning, and preparations that had not occurred prior to the war.[61]

General Halutz's decision not to mobilize reserve forces or launch a larger ground offensive and the damaging effects of the limited training ground units received for such grueling, high-intensity warfare were, however, far more damaging to the IDF's war effort than General Hirsch's "poetic" command language. General Naveh explained, "Gal Hirsch was dictating the pace in the whole northern arena. Gal told Halutz immediately that this is war, so mobilize! Mobilize and do whatever you like with the air force, but we need to go to all-out war, a big maneuver, but Halutz didn't want to."[62] Hirsch recalled that his persistent demands to activate the reserves were only fulfilled seventeen days into the war, on July 29.[63] The directives in Bint Jbayl issued by General Adam and General Halutz were shaped by fears of incurring casualties and changed confusingly numerous times, with orders to occupy the village, withdraw some troops, and then advance deeper into the village.[64] The change of mission directives was illogical, as some units were withdrawn while others were still advancing under fire. It was noted that Hirsch's Ninety-First Division fought bravely and bore the brunt of the fighting in the area with limited reinforcements but, overall, suffered serious casualties in the village and made limited gains that did not translate into operational success.[65]

The Winograd Commission criticized the illogical "raiding" maneuvers in Bint Jbayl waged for symbolic purposes to impact Hezbollah's "consciousness" and noted that the pace of the operation took place "in the shadow of indecision, between avoidance of ground operations or a broad ground maneuver," largely because of casualty aversion. The commission noted that the decision to attack Bint Jbayl was made "specifically on the basis of symbolic status," and, owing to numerous tactical mistakes, IDF operations "did not achieve any of the aforementioned results" on either "the amorphous-consciousness or tangible" levels.[66] The commission also noted that Web of Steel did not correlate to the IDF's preexisting Ice Breaker battle plan, which did contain a limited raid component but was "originally intended for a short transitional period before a phased delay and a decision to either return to containment or [to launch] a broad ground maneuver."[67]

The battle in Bint Jbayl, which lasted from July 23 to July 29 and cost eight IDF soldiers killed and twenty-seven wounded, for unclear military objectives and unclear gains, depressed Israeli society. The Winograd Commission noted, "In retrospect, Operation 'Web of Steel' did not create a sense of victory for Israel, but rather to Hezbollah."[68] The commission damningly continued:

> It seems that the failures of Bint Jbayl are the result of the inappropriate planning and setting of goals that do not fit, blurred operational goals and purposes, a mismatch between operational objectives and the order of battle to reach them, the search for intangible "effects" on the consciousness with a doubtful basis, indecisive operations of the forces, frequent changes of orders, fear of casualties among our forces, poor communication between officers at senior levels, poor tactical operations of the forces, and malfunctions in battle procedures and battle management.[69]

A July 30 press conference during the war by Brig. Gen. Gadi Eizenkot, head of the Operations Directorate, exemplified the hesitant modus operandi and pace of ground operations: "We have decided that ground operations will be limited in time and space. We do not intend to occupy parts of Lebanon, or even southern Lebanon. . . . The operation is progressing and this pattern of activity will be maintained." He also noted that even on the eighteenth day of war, "the number of reserve army personnel recruited is relatively low."[70] Throughout the war, more directives were issued to raid the psychologically symbolic village of Bint Jbayl with limited ground troops, each time with unclear objectives, as bloody losses ensued during the battles (August 1–3 and August 6–9) and Hezbollah continued to fire rockets from the area throughout the war's duration.

IDF special forces launched several additional raids inside Lebanon to achieve psychological effects on Hezbollah, including a bold overnight operation on August 1 in which commandos were helicoptered deep behind enemy lines to capture Hezbollah fighters hiding in a hospital in Hezbollah's stronghold of Baalbek. The IAF released footage of the daring raid, which ended up only capturing several lower-level Hezbollah members and was later criticized for being launched at a very high risk, primarily for symbolic purposes.[71] General Halutz stated at the time that this operation was meant to "make noise" and show Hezbollah "that we can operate deep inside Lebanon and wherever else we want to."[72] Interestingly, following the raid, Hezbollah carried out an in-depth review and lesson-learning process and ultimately released the Hezbollah regional defense commander in the Bekaa Valley from duty. It also replaced in 2008 the head of its antiaircraft unit, who was deemed responsible for the failure to spot the incoming IDF commandos.[73] While autonomy and flexibility are virtues of Hezbollah's military structure, mistakes are scrutinized and learning is paramount, as mistakes are corrected and rectified in a timely manner.

Throughout the weeks of raiding operations, the IAF pummeled critical targets throughout Lebanon and mastered the ability to locate Hezbollah's medium-range launchers within an astounding two to three seconds of a launch and then track and destroy them. This was largely because of the advanced benefits of the IDF's RMA network-centric programs and investment in sophisticated sensor-to-shooter technology.[74] However, no effective solution existed at this time to deal with the short-range Katyusha rockets. (This realization led to Israel's accelerated development of the Iron Dome short-range missile defense system after the war.)

The IAF continued to target Hezbollah's rocket-launching sites within villages, and, in grim resemblance of the 1996 debacle, a precision strike aimed at a launch site in the village of Qana on July 30 inadvertently struck a compound, killing twenty-eight civilians. Despite the IDF issuing warnings and dropping leaflets on the village and the release of drone surveillance footage of Hezbollah fighters firing more than 150 rockets from inhabited areas of Qana in the days preceding the strike, the inadvertent deaths marked a turning point in global public opinion.[75] The public relations damage for Israel was severe, and the clear limitations of airpower and precision weaponry against enemies embedded among the civilian population were catastrophically demonstrated once again in Qana. Hezbollah's short-range rocket fire continued as Israeli public opinion plummeted, especially after a fatal rocket attack on August 6 in which twelve reserve soldiers resting in a field outside a kibbutz near the border were killed.

Bint Jbayl and Maroun al-Ras were viewed as unnecessary missions that wore out troops in search of symbols and led to a growing discontent and squabbling between Northern Command and General Halutz over the decision to launch further ground raids.[76] While General Adam had sought to initially implement larger ground maneuvers, Halutz's pressure led to the initial ordering of the raids, but, by July 28, Adam concluded that a larger ground offensive was necessary because of a realization that "this is a war."[77] In his testimony to the Winograd Commission, Adam explained the internal deliberations over the limited raiding operations:

> Halutz decided on his own without me being present, without asking my opinion about cancelling everything that had been learned studied, planned, and practiced in "Defense of the Land" or "Elevated Waters." Instead he drafted a completely new plan of action, based on what he considered to be the success of the air campaign . . . a combination of attacking short-range missiles from the air and enough pressure to cause the [Lebanese] inhabitants to escape to the north, using only the regular army, not resorting to reserves, small and short raids, limited in time and scope.[78]

The Winograd Commission criticized the raids and the IDF's avoidance of rigorous ground operations to clear and hold territory: "The structure of the activity was not one of progress and fighting toward conquest and delivering a serious blow to the enemy, but of 'raids' that were very limited in time and range. . . . The fighters and commanders did not always understand why it was crucial for them to place their lives in jeopardy and take risks to launch a raid on a location that would be evacuated immediately after the encounter."[79]

The effectiveness of Northern Command was partially impacted because of bitter rivalry and egotistic competition between top brass, including General Adam and the Ninety-First Division's General Hirsch. Each complained of the other disrespecting his authority, and Hirsch, a disciple of OTRI and an adherent of SOD, complained of a lack of common language with Adam, who subscribed to the old paradigm. Adam criticized the raiding operations as "Gal's tricks," even though Hirsch had been one of the first to argue for a broader ground campaign, while Hirsch criticized Adam in a midwar meeting for "driving me crazy" over his intense risk aversion and fear of casualties.[80]

COS General Halutz also bickered with General Adam, who had voiced his opposition to Halutz's extended air campaign. Halutz allegedly excluded Adam from briefings and muted his microphone during IDF conference calls.[81] In an unprecedented move, Adam was eventually replaced in the middle of the war by Halutz's confidante, deputy COS Maj. Gen. Moshe Kaplinsky. Halutz even claimed in a 2015 television interview that General Eizenkot told him during the war that other members of the General Staff from the ground forces were subverting Halutz, owing to competition and interservice rivalries related to his air force background.[82] Interpersonal rivalries and egoistic competition between military leaders, commanders, and politicians polluted the IDF's planning and critical thinking, which is a deeply complex and troubling issue.

THE GROUND OFFENSIVE THAT CAME TOO LATE

After weeks of air strikes and limited ground raids in southern Lebanon, the IDF finally made the decision to launch an extensive ground operation after the belated realization that it was necessary to halt Hezbollah's rocket fire.[83] Operation Change of Direction-11, the IDF's ground campaign plan, which began too late to achieve any kind of practical outcome, was deliberated throughout the second week of August and represented the eleventh update to the ground plan since the war's start.[84] As the politicians and military hesitantly and indecisively deliberated the ground offensive, the United States announced that an internationally brokered cease-fire could be implemented in the coming days. The US ambassador to the UN, John Bolton, who was involved in brokering the cease-fire, recalled in his memoir that on August 5, Israel's diplomatic corps "publicly announced it could accept the resolution" even as the IDF indicated that it deemed a ground invasion necessary to improve the overall outcome of the war, illustrating an egregious lack of communication between Israel's political, diplomatic, and military echelons. Ambassador Bolton noted that four days later "the Israelis finally decided to expand their Lebanon operation north to the Litani River, leaving me wondering what had taken them so long."[85]

According to Maj. Gen. Benny Gantz, head of GFC during the war, the slow launching of the ground offensive was a major failure: "From the aspect of building and fortifying [domestic] legitimacy, I recognize this kind of introspection and debate [leading up to the August 9 cabinet decision for a large-scale ground offensive] had to be done, despite my professional military opinion that it should have been done three weeks ago."[86]

General Adam of Northern Command reflected that "ground forces should have entered earlier and should have been called up earlier" and blamed the delay of the "late" ground offensive on "mainly the political echelon." Displaying sensitivity to casualties at all levels of leadership, he also admitted, "I can also understand them, but they did not reach decisions fast enough," and he concluded that "the wise thing to do would have been to begin the operation earlier, just as we had planned."[87] General Halutz also eventually admitted in 2015 that his reluctance to use ground troops or activate the reserves was deeply impacted by political considerations surrounding ground forces casualties.[88] In his testimony to the Winograd Commission, Halutz candidly explained his error in delaying a larger ground campaign: "I believe that with the information we had, and the means we had at our disposal, we could have achieved a lot more—had we been more decisive. . . . I have already said that with regards to preparation I erred in not preparing more fully, widely, and earlier."[89]

In the very short, final phase of the war, a major ground operation was finally approved in the fifth week of fighting to achieve Halutz's newly stated goal of "reducing the launching of short-range rockets"—thirty-one days after the war's start and sixty hours before the US-brokered cease-fire was to go into effect.[90] The operational plan resembled a ground campaign put forth by the IDF Operations Directorate in the early days of the war, which was originally predicted to last four to eight weeks. The plan envisioned the Ninety-First Division entering from the east to "clean and sweep" areas, minimize Hezbollah's rocket-firing abilities, and capture Bint Jbayl and Aita al-Shaab. The 162nd Division was to traverse Wadi Saluki (a dry riverbed valley) and take up positions in the west; the Ninety-Eighth Division was to hold key villages, secure logistical routes, cross the Litani River, link up with the Ninety-First Division, and move toward Tyre; and the 366th Division was meant to take the Marjayoun area north of the Israeli town of Metula.[91] None of the divisions fully achieved their missions successfully, and all suffered significant casualties in several high-profile blunders.

On the eve of the cease-fire, units that had been stationed on the Lebanese border for weeks were finally given orders to advance. In a fateful operation, ground troops from the 162nd Division were ordered to advance northwestward to meet up with another unit in the village of Ghandouriya before advancing toward Tyre. While crossing Wadi Saluki, Brigade 401, a reserve column of armored units, was ambushed by dozens of Hezbollah fighters hidden in the valley's bushy terrain who launched advanced laser-guided Kornet antitank missiles. Hezbollah damaged eleven out of twenty-four Merkava tanks and inflicted serious casualties. Miscommunication between IDF reconnaissance and tank units was inevitable because of a lack of joint training exercises in the decade prior to war, and, owing to the rushed nature of the ground campaign, units raced against time to carry out hasty and exhausting battle procedures that were continuously altered.[92] The IDF suffered twelve fatalities, with over fifty wounded during the Wadi Saluki crossing (nearly 10 percent of total IDF casualties). Numerous tactical mistakes were made, such as a failure of tank operators to deploy smoke screens and critically poor communication between units meant to provide cover fire for each other. Sheikh Nabil Qawook, Hezbollah's chief official in southern Lebanon, described the importance of the incident: "Israel developed the Merkava and turned it into a symbol of Israeli military technology. It showed it off to all the armies of the world. It became a legend. And so, in response to this, Hezbollah acquired weapons with the aim of destroying the Merkava. They developed, and we developed too. And we surprised them!"[93]

The battle at Wadi Saluki, acerbically described by UNIFIL official Timur Goksel as a "a turkey shoot," characterizes all the IDF's problems during the 2006 war: the political echelon's isolation from battlefield events, the General Staff's detachment from political developments, decision-makers overly influenced by the media and public opinion, and the damaging effects of training cutbacks in prior years, which materialized in the poor performance in combat.[94] The IDF's divisional investigation concluded that failures at Wadi Saluki resulted from poor operational planning and poor tactical coordination as a result of insufficient reservist training.[95] Failures should also be attributed to the damaging effects of Intifada-style fighting on the IDF's competency and earlier training budget cuts, which diverted resources away from ground forces to fund the IDF's transformation into a "slimmer and smarter" professional force.[96]

With thirty-three soldiers killed in the last forty-eight hours of the war, the symbolic perception of victory that Halutz and Peretz had sought was unattainable. After the Wadi Saluki debacle, as troops were still being airlifted into southern Lebanon, an IAF transport helicopter was downed by Hezbollah near the village of Yatar on August 12 moments after unloading thirty paratroopers from the Ninety-Eighth Division. The belated ground operation was cut short by the cease-fire implemented on August 13. The cease-fire was brought about by UN Resolution 1701, which outlined the redeployment of the UNIFIL international force to maintain security in southern Lebanon. The IDF would withdraw from Lebanon, and the Lebanese Armed Forces would deploy to maintain security, while Hezbollah was ordered to disarm as outlined in previous cease-fire agreements. The IDF's ground operation had failed to meet its objectives: Hezbollah defiantly launched a record high number of rockets (253) on the last day of war, ground troops did not reach sectors marked for them, and the kidnapped soldiers were not returned.[97] Despite some significant achievements by the IDF credited to its RMA capabilities, the fact of 118 soldiers killed in action coupled with thirty-four days of rocket fire on the Israeli home front, resulting in forty-four civilians killed, made it impossible to proclaim any sort of decisive victory in the immediate aftermath of the war.

In summary, the ineffectual decision-making processes in 2006 reflect the confluence of four evolving trends that influenced the IDF in previous decades. First, the resistance to launch a large-scale ground operation reflects domestic considerations—namely, increased postheroism in Israeli society, casualty aversion, and an unwillingness to reengage in the Lebanese quagmire. The desire by the senior brass to avoid a large-scale, messy ground campaign manifested itself on the battlefield with the IDF's preference for limited raiding operations and the desire to achieve symbolic objectives with inadequate troop numbers. Second, the strong emphasis on the air force and standoff firepower reflects Israel's preferred "way of war" largely because of the influence of the RMA over the previous decades and its perceived technological advantages, but it is also inextricably linked to the Israeli societal shifts related to casualty aversion. Third, the desire to target Hezbollah and Lebanese government infrastructure reflects General Halutz's misreading of the ability of the Lebanese government to curtail Hezbollah and reflects a continued adherence to the IDF's ineffective lever strategy used in the 1993 and 1996 operations. Fourth, the mediocre performance of ground forces was a result of the concerted focus on Palestinian counterterrorism in the years prior to the war that weakened the IDF's operational capabilities for high-intensity warfare. Resources diverted away from the ground forces toward the air force and other RMA-inspired programs elsewhere in prior years left ground units undertrained and underequipped to deal with Hezbollah. The haphazard decision-making and ineffective IDF performance in 2006 represents the grand manifestation of these four trends.

HEZBOLLAH'S MILITARY ADAPTATION IN THE 2006 WAR

Compounding the IDF's muddled decision-making, Hezbollah challenged the IDF's way of war in 2006 based on its own frictional learning and organizational adaptation throughout the previous decade. Nasrallah proclaimed in a speech during the war, "During the Grapes of Wrath in 1996, or Operation Accountability in 1993, in the beginning they had the upper hand and our situation was much worse. But today [2006], the situation is now different!"[98] Despite the IDF's technological and conceptual revolution, Hezbollah managed to compensate for its qualitative and quantitative weakness by adapting its operational paradigm to emphasize organizational survivability, military and societal resilience, attritional warfare, and deterrence that was achieved by persistent firepower projection against the Israeli home front.[99] Since the 2000 IDF withdrawal, Nasrallah explained that Hezbollah had intensely focused on enhancing its military capabilities: "This new stage concentrated on developing the work of the Resistance on the qualitative level by opening new horizons and on the quantitative level by enlarging and intensifying available capabilities, escalating operations, and changing the strategy of the Resistance from adopting traditional guerrilla warfare to setting up an unparalleled new school that functions as a combination of a regular army and guerrilla fighters."[100]

The central pillar of Hezbollah's enhanced military paradigm was its rocket-fire capability, whose importance was first seen in the 1990s (see chapter 6). Nasrallah affirmed the significance of this improved capability for Hezbollah in a foreboding interview in the months *before* the 2006 war:

I said it publicly, we have a very important rocket-fire capability in Lebanon, and we can precisely hit a large number of targets, and the Israelis can do nothing. *We are not a classical army. This is the point of our strength.* They do not know where our missiles are or where they are being stored, or their platforms, or their sizes or types, or what targets we can hit. This secrecy is a major element of our strength.[101]

Hezbollah's enhancement of its rocket-firing capability since the 1993 and 1996 operations was made apparent when it fired more than 3,917 rockets into Israel over the thirty-three days of the 2006 war, which killed forty-four Israeli civilians and twelve soldiers.[102] Upon the outbreak of war, Hezbollah averaged about 100 rockets fired into Israel each day from July 13 to August 1 and sustained between 160 and 240 per day from August 1 to August 13, with a notable 253 on the last day (the second-highest amount fired in a single day during the war).[103] In 2006, 23 percent of Hezbollah rockets landed in developed areas, with many reaching as far south as Haifa and beyond. Compared to the fluctuating and inconsistent rate of rocket fire in the 1990s, at one point during the war Hezbollah sustained a rate of 150 rockets fired per hour, and overall Hezbollah averaged 130 rockets per day during the thirty-three-day 2006 war, compared to roughly 55 per day during the sixteen-day 1996 Operation Grapes of Wrath (see chapter 6).[104]

The IDF suffered a conceptual failure to learn the right lessons from the 1993 and 1996 operations and did not internalize Hezbollah's evolving reliance on rocket fire. According to Colonel Amir,

Hezbollah developed this [capability] into a more sophisticated concept because they realized they don't need to destroy more targets in Israel—they just need to be able to keep on firing rockets. This is clever. We didn't realize this in 2006.

No matter what anyone tells you today, I can tell you clearly, this concept that Hezbollah calls "persistent firepower"—I didn't hear about it before 2006, and I was in a place that I should have heard it, as I was already in the IAF Campaign Planning Department.[105]

Hezbollah's acquisition of longer-range rockets, the increased rate of firing, and the increased damage caused in 2006 illustrate qualitative and quantitative improvements to its firepower-projection capabilities. The statistics illuminate Hezbollah's military adaptation and the bolstering of the central pillar of its military paradigm. Nasrallah described the importance of sustaining attritional rocket fire into northern Israel in a 2007 interview: "Our capacity for this capability until the very last day of the war was a very significant element of our strength on our part. The entire Israeli Air Force, on which they rely, was unable to prevent the firing of missiles to the very last day."[106]

While the IDF had moderate success in destroying Hezbollah's long-range weaponry and preventing resupply, its success in eroding the short-range rocket capability is still disputed because most evidence remains classified.[107] While IDF counterattacks had no significant effect on Hezbollah's rate of firing short-range rockets, it did affect the accuracy and geographical range of short-range rocket launching to an extent.[108] Short-range rockets (90 percent of Hezbollah's arsenal) were fired in multiple salvos from both stationary and mobile launchers, which increased accuracy and lethality, partially based on lessons learned about shortcomings of their rocket campaign during the 1996 operation. While the IAF destroyed between 60 percent and 90 percent of Hezbollah's total long-range missiles, Hezbollah's short- and medium-range rocket fire persisted, as its arsenals and auxiliary launchers were concealed in underground bunkers and within residential areas. Hezbollah maintained the ability to rapidly replace its destroyed launchers, exemplifying the depth and massive redundancy of its rocket arsenal. Despite IAF strikes, Hezbollah maintained persistent rocket fire, as it had innovatively built a system of expendable decoy launchers and bunker positions with fake heat signatures, which it assumed would be spotted and targeted by IAF surveillance.[109] This was a simple but effective innovation by Hezbollah that combined concealment and stealth with effective concentration of firepower.[110]

Despite the IDF's significant achievements in curtailing Hezbollah's long-range weaponry with its own RMA sensor-to-shooter systems (for example, during the Night of the Fajrs), Brig. Gen. (Ret.) Uzi Rubin, former head of the Israel Missile Defense Organization, assessed Hezbollah's adaptability and ability to circumvent the IDF's conventional strength thus:

> Hizbullah seemed to have been preparing for exactly such an eventuality and countered it, not with any sophisticated technologies of its own, but by the simple expedient of treating its own launchers as expendable. The IAF's carefully prepared technologies for launcher-hunting proved irrelevant and futile. . . . Whether sidetracked by decoys or frustrated by abundant replacements, the carefully contrived and undoubtedly expensive technologies nurtured by the IAF for destroying launchers proved technically sound yet operationally irrelevant. Simply put, Hizbullah succeeded in outsmarting the IAF.[111]

Hezbollah rocket fire penetrated deep into Israeli territory, demoralizing the IDF while generating perceptual "effects" of insecurity on the consciousness of Israel's civilian population. Hezbollah's persistent rocket fire targeted the Israeli population, which then pressured the political echelon to restrain the IDF in a phenomenon that resembles Hezbollah's own version of "reverse" Effects-Based Operations. Observed by Timur Goksel, senior UNIFIL official,

Hezbollah countered Israeli "Effects Doctrine" by firing rockets. The IDF's Effects Doctrine was supposed to demoralize Hezbollah and hit their communications and command centers. . . . This was ineffective because the IDF totally underestimated the resiliency and tolerance of Hezbollah and the Lebanese people.

Instead, Hezbollah fired rockets to counter the Israeli strikes, and Hezbollah's rockets had massive effects on the Israeli people, so who exactly was carrying out Effects Doctrine against who?! . . . Effects Doctrine for the IDF means standoff fire and not wanting to take casualties, but, *habibi*, it doesn't work that way![112]

In a 2014 author interview, a Hezbollah official spokesperson highlighted how the resilience of Hezbollah's popular base in the Lebanese population is an integral part of its organizational strength. It raises doubts about the efficacy of the IDF's long-adhered-to policy of leveraging the Lebanese population against Hezbollah. The Hezbollah official emphasized the relationship between the steadfastness of Hezbollah's supporters and their contribution to enhancing Hezbollah's military endurance:

Steadfastness is of chief importance. . . . It is always this golden equation that [our leaders] adhere to and which they repeat always, and want it to be deeply entrenched. . . . It is the goal of "the people, the army, and the Resistance."

There are two sides of the equation when you talk about steadfastness. . . . Hezbollah has always acknowledged the very important role of the people in the Resistance's actions because when you talk about the Resistance fighters, they are part of the villages, members of the society, and from every walk of life. They are supported by their families, villages, towns, and cities, so really when we talk about steadfastness, it directly leads you to the people, and the people are a very important part of the equation against occupation or against any aggression.[113]

The second major pillar of Hezbollah's military system is organizational survivability, which it enhanced after the lessons learned from the damaging IAF strikes in 1993 and 1996.[114] Timur Goksel explained: "Because they studied their enemy, Hezbollah decided that they cannot challenge the Israelis in open field warfare; it is too asymmetrical, especially with the strength of the Israeli air force. Hezbollah wouldn't be able to cope with that."[115] Hezbollah addressed the IDF's precision-weapons capability by reducing its own weapons signature and target-appearance time and operating in decentralized, tactically autonomous cells without support from commanders.[116] For example, according to a Hezbollah fighter who fought in 2006, to thwart the IDF's surveillance and targeting technology and RMA-inspired precision weaponry that operates in tightly networked sensor-to-shooter loops, he and his comrades adapted by riding bicycles to concealed rocket-launching sites to avoid detection.[117]

Hassan Nasrallah confirmed adherence to the command approach that grants operational autonomy to field units, which posed a constant challenge for the IDF over the years:

> [Hezbollah's strength comes from] constant improvement and creativity. Fighters in south Lebanon and the western Bekaa Valley do not see themselves as mere receivers of orders; even local resistance commanders consider it part of their responsibilities to sit and think together, study various options, and figure out what the best courses of action are, and how to improve the resistance's operations. There is no single group charged with figuring out how to improve our operations—it is everybody's responsibility to do so.[118]

Hezbollah enhanced its survivability and resilience by constructing a sophisticated network of bunkers and tunnels after the 2000 IDF withdrawal, when it was no longer consumed by day-to-day security engagements with the IDF. While Hezbollah utilized bunkers in the 1990s to an extent (see chapter 6), it elaborately developed and enhanced its network of bunkers with astonishing sophistication, using thick concrete and steel reinforcement, plumbing, ventilation and air-conditioning, medical facilities, weapon stockpiles, and large dormitories, which could keep a large group of fighters underground for many weeks without the need to resupply.[119] With Iranian assistance, rocket-firing positions were concealed in heavily fortified positions camouflaged in Hezbollah's "nature reserves" within the dense vegetation in southern Lebanon. Bunkers were also built within civilian areas in villages, some of which were only accessible by entering residences or mosques.[120] Colonel Amir explained the targeting challenges posed by the concealed positions:

> Hezbollah realized airpower is about targeting, so in order to make Israeli airpower an ineffective tool, they needed to prevent themselves from supplying targets for us. . . . We called it "disappearance.". . .
> One of Hezbollah's goals was to make sure that terrorists will survive air attacks, so they started using timers to launch the rockets. They realized that if there is a rocket launch, then they knew the IDF would hit the launch area. So they said, why should we be there? So they got a kitchen timer, and they connected it to the launcher. This was new in 2006.[121]

The UN's humanitarian-aid chief, Jan Egeland, was quoted during the 2006 war admitting that Hezbollah "cowardly blended" into the Lebanese civilian population, fought and launched rockets while embedded among the people in urban areas, and utilized human shields.[122] Hezbollah fired rockets from windows of civilian dwellings in Lebanese villages, from within covered apartment parking garages, and from residential areas near mosques, shops, and schools. Hezbollah documents captured by the IDF provide evidence that Hezbollah rented civilian houses in villages for use during combat as part of a comprehensive military system embedded within the fabric of the civilian population. Another captured Hezbollah document revealed a planned rocket campaign with coordinates and required trajectories to strike Israeli towns from stationary launchers embedded in civilian areas.[123] Clear photographic evidence released by the IDF showed Hezbollah's military positions and rocket fire positions based within residential areas.[124] Hezbollah's propensity to operate while embedded "among the people" highlights the challenge and lessening utility of military technology against well-prepared, asymmetrical opponents.[125] By utilizing unconventional methods tailored to its specific operational context, Hezbollah maintained the capability to operate and fire rockets despite being under intense pressure from the IDF, thereby countering the IDF's RMA-inspired way of war.

Hezbollah's relatively simple operational innovations and overall military paradigm were designed to circumvent the IDF's technological superiority in other sectors as well. In a vivid example, Nasrallah described Hezbollah's adaptation to the IDF's advanced surveillance capabilities:

> I was speaking about how simplicity can defeat complexity. For example, the IDF used very sophisticated technology with their weapons and communications. Hezbollah is a popular resistance, and most of the young men are just ordinary village boys from farms, small towns, and agricultural communities, and they speak on ordinary walkie-talkies, no complications about it. They are very simple devices, but when they use code, they simply use the kind of language and slang that is used in their villages and among their family, so anyone listening, behind the surveillance devices and having computers trying to decode their kinds of language, they will not easily be able to find out what this means unless they've lived for years among these villagers.
>
> So, for example, they use certain words—village terms—you know, the cooking pot, the donkey, even village sayings like "the father of the chicken" or something like this. You know no Israeli intelligence agent or computer will be able to figure it out.[126]

Concealment, camouflage, fighting among the people, and maintenance of its rocket-firing capability were emphasized by Hezbollah as part of its concerted effort to militarily adapt. Each one of these elements contributed to increasing its organizational endurance, survivability, and ability to attain "victory by not losing," whose importance was elucidated by Nasrallah in a fiery wartime speech:

The general headlines we can speak about clearly on the military level are steadfastness—and secondly, full absorption of Israeli strikes. . . . *The victory we are talking about is when the Resistance survives.* When its will is not broken, then this is victory. . . . As long as there is a missile that is fired from Lebanon and targets the Zionists, as long as there is one fighter who fires his rifle, and as long as there is someone who plants a bomb against the Israelis, then this means that resistance still exists.[127]

Nasrallah further emphasized Hezbollah's asymmetrical perception of victory:

The fact that we remain standing today—this is victory! We are talking about Israel! I have always claimed that Israel was no laughing matter. We are not fighting a militia, a party, or the army of a poor, weak state. We are fighting against an army, which defeated several Arab armies simultaneously. . . . Consequently, our survival and steadfastness until now means victory. Our absorbance of the strike is victory, and our continuation of the confrontation is victory![128]

As predicted by IDF MI in the early 2000s, the IDF was unable to significantly mitigate the rate of Hezbollah's short-range rocket fire, which had a deterrent effect on Israel and granted Hezbollah a victory narrative because it "survived." Brig. Gen. Yossi Kuperwasser, head of research, IDF MI, in 2006, lamented in a midwar interview, "Rockets are falling in Israel, and until they stop, from our point of view, we have not won. Here people thought the air force would wrap up things in three minutes, so there is a feeling of helplessness that is creating the frustration."[129] As if to illustrate General Kuperwasser's point, Nasrallah discussed Hezbollah's limited operational objectives, highlighting the inherently asymmetrical situation Israel faces regarding the achievement of war aims:

What did we say when the July [2006] war erupted? We did not say through the July war that we were seeking to eliminate Israel. Never. We did not say that through the July war, we would recover the Shebaa Farms and Qafr Shuba Heights. *All we said was that our aim during the July war was to delay the realization of the enemy's aims.* The Resistance's aim was achieved. And none of Israel's aims was achieved. *This is what we called victory!*[130]

CONCLUSION

The latter half of chapter 7 discussed the IDF's operational planning in the run-up to 2006, and this chapter compared the IDF's planning to its actual operational performance and decision-making during the air and ground campaigns of the 2006 war. A toxic combination of factors—the influence of the RMA, budgetary diversions away from the ground forces toward the air force, reservist training cuts, casualty aversion stemming from the IDF's past Lebanon experiences, an operational focus on LIC in years prior to the war, and Halutz's misguided subscription to the IDF's lever strategy of the 1990s—all contributed to disappointing results on the battlefield.

The IDF's effectiveness in 2006 was partially dampened by Hezbollah's innovative military adaptation, based on lessons it learned about the importance of persistent rocket fire throughout the duration of the conflict, survivability, concealment, low-signature operations, and organizational resilience that circumvented the IDF's way of war and technological supremacy. All Hezbollah had to do by the setting of limited, minimalist war objectives was "survive," as it was able to achieve a fundamental victory by avoiding defeat. In the next chapter, the various components of the IDF's operational concept are appraised in relation to the IDF's overall performance during the 2006 war.

NOTES

Epigraphs: Gantz, interview, August 15, 2006; Nasrallah, speech, November 11, 2012.

1. Video footage of the kidnapping was aired as "Exclusive: Hezbollah 2006 Capture of Israeli Soldiers," Al-Mayadeen TV, July 27, 2012 (Arabic). Video footage of Hezbollah's preparations for the operation was aired as "Truthful Pledge: Preparations to Capture the Israeli Soldiers 2006," Al-Manar TV, July 21, 2013 (Arabic). See also "Enemy Stunned with Video on Hezbollah's July 2006 Capturing Operation," Al-Ahed News, July 30, 2012. For more on Bazzi, see Al-Manar Group, *Hajj Khaled Bazzi*.

2. Winograd Commission, final report, chap. 10, para. 47; Matthews, *We Were Caught Unprepared*, 36–37, imprecisely described the two war plans.

3. Brun, "Second Lebanon War," 301.

4. Lambeth, *Air Operations*, 29–30.

5. Harel and Issacharoff, *34 Days*, 91.

6. Winograd Commission, final report, chap. 6, para. 27, and chap. 9, paras. 8 and 20–21.

7. Harel and Issacharoff, *34 Days*, 95–96.

8. Bar-Joseph, "Hubris of Initial Victory," 151.

9. Author interview with Amos Yadlin.

10. Kober, "Israel Defense Forces in the Second Lebanon War," 4.

11. Merom, "Second Lebanon War," 17–24.

12. Sheera Frenkel, "Halutz: No Need to Send Ground Troops," *Jerusalem Post*, July 18, 2006.

13. Gantz, interview, August 15, 2006.

14. Winograd Commission, final report, chap. 6, para. 25.

15. Ibid., para. 6.

16. Farkash, "Intelligence in the War," 80–81.

17. Bar-Joseph, "Hubris of Initial Victory," 150, 153; Harel and Issacharoff, *34 Days*, 62.

18. Author interview with Amos Yadlin.

19. Winograd Commission, final report, chap. 9, para. 31.

20. Gantz, interview, August 15, 2006.

21. Merom, "Second Lebanon War," 21.

22. Halutz, interview, February 22, 2010.

23. Author interview with Roni Amir.

24. Ibid.

25. Brun, "Second Lebanon War," 304.

26. Quoted in Rapaport, *Friendly Fire*, chap. 1.

27. Brun and Rabinovich, *Israel Facing a New Middle East*, 74–75.

28. Bar-Joseph, "Hubris of Initial Victory," 153–54.

29. Author interview with Roni Amir.

30. Yadlin, "How Israel Created Deterrence."

31. Siboni, "Military Campaign in Lebanon," 64; Brom, "Political and Military Objectives," 22.

32. Author interview with Roni Amir.

33. Haloutz, *At Eye Level*, quoted in *Defense News*, February 22, 2010.

34. Peretz, interview, May 3, 2007.

35. Yadlin, "How Israel Created Deterrence."

36. Nasrallah, speech, July 14, 2006.

37. Peretz, interview, May 3, 2007.

38. Matthews, *We Were Caught Unprepared*, 43; Bar-Joseph, "Hubris of Initial Victory," 156.

39. Halutz, interview, February 15, 2008.

40. Johnson, *Hard Fighting*, 69–70.

41. Winograd Commission, final report, chap. 7, paras. 40–59.

42. Hirsch, *Defensive Shield*, 257–58.

43. Biddle and Friedman, *2006 Lebanon Campaign*, 35–45, 57–58.

44. Harel and Issacharoff, *34 Days*, 135–36.

45. Hirsch, *Defensive Shield*, 260–62.

46. Lubotzky, *From the Wilderness*, 36–37.

47. Ibid., 260; Harel and Issacharoff, *34 Days*, 137.

48. Hirsch, *Defensive Shield*, 274.

49. Ibid., 277–78, 331–32; Harel and Issacharoff, *34 Days*, 139.

50. Opall-Rome, "Hoisted by Its Own PR"; Harel and Issacharoff, *34 Days*, 176.

51. Hirsch, *Defensive Shield*, 331–32; Rapaport, *Friendly Fire*, chap. 23.

52. For a Golani Brigade soldier's recollection from the operation, see Lubotzky, *From the Wilderness*, 39–43.

53. Biddle and Friedman, *2006 Lebanon Campaign*, 35–39.

54. For example, Matthews, *We Were Caught Unprepared*, 52–54, unduly shaped future analyses of the war. See also Amos Harel, "Lebanon Officer Gal Hirsch Takes Off the Gloves," *Haaretz*, December 11, 2007. For his defense, see Hirsch, *War Story*.

55. Winograd Commission, final report, chap. 10, para. 65, 372–73; English translation from Johnson, *Hard Fighting*, 88–89. (Page numbers correspond to the original

Hebrew document. Johnson cited the incorrect page numbers of the Winograd Commission's report in his study.)

56. Author interviews with OTRI personnel, January 2012–July 2015.

57. Hirsch, *Defensive Shield*, 318–19.

58. Henkin, "On Swarming," 323.

59. Winograd Commission, final report, chap. 10, para. 66.

60. Ibid., chap. 7, para. 45.

61. Author interviews with OTRI personnel, January 2012–July 2015.

62. Author interview with Shimon Naveh.

63. Hirsch, *Defensive Shield*, 284.

64. Harel and Issacharoff, *34 Days*, 139.

65. For example, see Rapaport, *Friendly Fire*, chap. 11; and Hirsch, *Defensive Shield*, 276–84.

66. Winograd Commission, final report, chap. 10, paras. 52 and 58.

67. Ibid., paras. 43–47.

68. Ibid., para. 43.

69. Ibid., para. 45.

70. Eizenkot, press conference, July 30, 2006.

71. IDF Spokesperson, "IDF Special Ops Raid on Hezbollah Hospital HQ Deep inside Lebanon."

72. On the specific raid, see Yaakov Katz and Anshel Pfeffer, "Raid Sends Message to Hezbollah," *Jerusalem Post*, August 2, 2006; Amos Harel and Yoav Stern, "IDF Commandos Nab Five Low-Level Hezbollah Men in Baalbek Raid," *Haaretz*, August 2, 2006.

73. Zeev Schiff, "Hezbollah Officers Going Home Too," *Haaretz*, November 29, 2006; Amos Harel, "Hezbollah Sacks Commander for Wartime Failures," *Haaretz*, January 3, 2008.

74. Yaari, lecture, June 20, 2008.

75. Eizenkot, press conference, July 30, 2006; Israel Ministry of Foreign Affairs, "Completion of Inquiry into the July 30 Incident in Qana." See also Brun, "Second Lebanon War," 312.

76. Rapaport, *Friendly Fire*, chap. 15.

77. Hirsch, *Defensive Shield*, 282; Avi Issacharoff and Amos Harel, "Halutz Objected to Ground Offensive Almost until End of War," *Haaretz*, January 23, 2007.

78. Quoted in Harel and Issacharoff, *34 Days*, 126.

79. Winograd Commission, final report, chap. 11, para. 28.

80. Hirsch, *Defensive Shield*, 267–70; Harel and Issacharoff, *34 Days*, 125–28.

81. Harel and Issacharoff, *34 Days*, 127–28.

82. Halutz, interview, May 5, 2015.

83. Harel and Issacharoff, *34 Days*, 119.

84. Yaakov Katz, "Security and Defense: The Story of Changing Direction-11," *Jerusalem Post*, October 1, 2008.

85. For details on the diplomatic initiative, see Bolton, *Surrender Is Not an Option*, 405–8.

86. Gantz, interview, August 15, 2006.

87. Adam, interview, August 16, 2006.

88. Halutz, interview, May 5, 2015.

89. Halutz, testimony, January 28, 2007.

90. For the internal deliberations, see Winograd Commission, final report, chap. 4, paras. 515–27; Johnson, *Hard Fighting*, 72.

91. Johnson, *Hard Fighting*, 73–78.

92. Harel and Issacharoff, *34 Days*, 221–26.

93. Quoted in part 1 of the two-part documentary *God's Chariot*, Al-Jazeera English, May 7, 2007.

94. Author interview with Timur Goksel. See also Harel and Issacharoff, *34 Days*, 229.

95. Harel and Issacharoff, *34 Days*, 225–26; Shelah and Limor, *Captives of Lebanon*, chap. 30.

96. On the impact of the Intifada, see Winograd Commission, final report, chap. 7, para. 4.

97. Rubin, *Rocket Campaign*, 13; Makovsky and White, "Lessons and Implications," 8–9, 14–15.

98. Nasrallah, speech, July 17, 2006.

99. Brun, "While You're Busy," 546–47. For a related version, see Valensi and Brun, "Revolution in Military Affairs of the Radical Axis."

100. Nasrallah, speech, February 22, 2008.

101. Nasrallah, interview, February 2006.

102. Human Rights Watch, *Civilians under Assault*, 10. Official estimates differ slightly, but the general range is consistent. Some Israeli sources claim forty-two hundred rockets were launched. Hezbollah's claim of eight thousand launched is exaggerated.

103. Israel Ministry of Foreign Affairs, *Preserving Humanitarian Principles while Combating Terrorism*, appendix A.

104. Rubin, *Rocket Campaign*, 10–11; Rubin, "Hizballah's Rocket Campaign against Northern Israel."

105. Author interview with Roni Amir.

106. Nasrallah, interview, July 23, 2007.

107. For the nuanced debate, see Cordesman, *Lessons of the 2006 Israeli-Hezbollah War*, 10–16.

108. For an early assessment, see Rubin, "Hizballah's Rocket Campaign against Northern Israel."

109. Alastair Crooke and Mark Perry, "How Hezbollah Defeated Israel: Winning the Intelligence War," *Asia Times*, October 12, 2006; Rubin, *Rocket Campaign*, 25–26; Nicholas Blanford, "Deconstructing Hezbollah's Military Prowess," *Jane's Intelligence Review*, November 1, 2006.

110. Rubin, *Rocket Campaign*, 20–21, 25–28; Biddle and Friedman, *2006 Lebanon Campaign*, 65.

111. Rubin, *Rocket Campaign*, 26–27.

112. Author interview with Timur Goksel.

113. Author interview with "I.," a Hezbollah official spokesperson.

114. For an overview, see Brun, "While You're Busy," 549–59.

115. Author interview with Timur Goksel.

116. Author interviews with IDF officers, July 2012–January 2014; Exum, "Hizballah at War," 5, 10.

117. Mitchell Prothero, "Paintballing with Hezbollah," *Vice Magazine*, March 26, 2012.

118. Nasrallah, interview, June 21, 1999, 202.

119. Nicholas Blanford, "Deconstructing Hezbollah's Military Prowess," *Jane's Intelligence Review*, November 1, 2006; Nicholas Blanford, "Inside Hizballah's Hidden Bunkers," *Time*, March 27, 2007.

120. Erlich, *Hezbollah's Use of Lebanese Civilians*, 86.

121. Author interview with Roni Amir.

122. AP, "UN Chief Accuses Hezbollah of 'Cowardly Blending' among Refugees," Fox News, July 24, 2006. For specifics, see Human Rights Watch, *Why They Died*, 54–61; Whitson, "Hezbollah Needs to Answer."

123. Erlich, *Hezbollah's Use of Lebanese Civilians*, part II; see also appendixes 1–4.

124. Israel Ministry of Foreign Affairs, "Hizbollah's Exploitation of Lebanese Population Centers and Civilians."

125. Smith, *Utility of Force*.

126. Nasrallah, interview, April 17, 2012.

127. Nasrallah, interview, July 20, 2006 (emphasis added).

128. Ibid (emphasis added).

129. Kuperwasser, interview, August 10, 2006.

130. Nasrallah, interview, May 6, 2007 (emphasis added).

CHAPTER 9

THE BLAME GAME

A Reappraisal of the IDF's 2006 Operational Concept

One of the distressing problems of this war is that it fits dramatically the notion that victory has many fathers but failure is an orphan.

—Defense Minister Amir Peretz

When this enemy [Israel] achieves victory, we must learn a lesson. When this enemy is defeated, we must learn a lesson. When this enemy deals with its defeat with respect, we must also learn a lesson.

—Sec.-Gen. Hassan Nasrallah

Following its disappointing performance in the 2006 Israel-Hezbollah War, the IDF launched no fewer than forty inquiry subcommittees led by senior generals to investigate different aspects of the war. A "blame game" erupted in Israel in which all the major personalities involved in the war, including active and retired generals, former chiefs of staff, politicians, and a plethora of officers who served in Lebanon over the last three decades, rallied in warring camps that each developed its own narrative for what went wrong in 2006 and who was at fault for the IDF's performance. The blame game was further muddied when academics, the media, and international observers entered the debate and took sides in the still unresolved disputes. In the aftermath of the war, much of the initial blame was laid on the IDF's elusive "operational concept," which was embodied in a formal doctrinal document bearing the same name signed into effect by COS Lt. Gen. Dan Halutz in April 2006, even though this document, which remains classified, was inadequately synthesized and poorly understood.[1] The Winograd Commission noted it is "misleading and deceptive" to label this document as wholly representational of the IDF's operational concept, which was "not anchored clearly and unequivocally in one binding document."[2] However, in the tumultuous aftermath of the war, many claimed the April 2006 concept was unduly influenced by SOD, and OTRI was controversially scapegoated in many of these military committees for the IDF's failures in 2006. One IDF postwar committee, led by Maj. Gen. Gadi Eizenkot, head of the Operations Directorate at the time, declared that "a virus has infiltrated the IDF's basic doctrine" and directed culpability at OTRI's complex concepts. Another committee, led by former head of Northern Command Maj. Gen. Amiram Levin, blamed the April 2006 concept, which "had a crucial contribution to the flaws exposed during the war against Hezbollah. The doctrine is fundamentally wrong. It could not have succeeded and shouldn't have been implemented."[3]

OTRI was unduly faulted for dominating the April 2006 concept, despite OTRI's having been shut down in 2005 and claims by OTRI personnel that SOD was not formally utilized in 2006 because the document was signed into effect only three months earlier and had not been integrated adequately. OTRI's proponents consistently maintained that SOD was simply a methodology for thinking about complex problems and not an operational battle plan or doctrine.[4] There is little consensus on what elements were explicitly or implicitly included in the IDF's broader operational concept, and there is even less agreement as to what degree these various elements impacted Israel's "way of war" in 2006. The contents and utility of the IDF's operational concept and its impact on the IDF's performance in 2006 is reappraised in this chapter.

THE IDF'S 2006 OPERATIONAL CONCEPT

In April 2006, Brig. Gen. Shimon Naveh described the dangerous situation that had occurred after COS Halutz signed into effect an operational concept that was based on staff work of officers purged by Halutz because of their association with his predecessor, Lt. Gen. Moshe Yaalon. This led to a situation in which Halutz endorsed the savvy concepts embedded within the document without internalizing them. Naveh explained the associated pitfalls: "This document, which has some good rules, is full of paradoxes and full of holes, but it was still a first attempt, and it could have been [a success] if the IDF would have possessed this culture of reframing, of going to the base and learning. . . . The core of this document is the theory of SOD, but it was never really linked to the other elements. . . . It was never synthesized both socially, conceptually."[5] OTRI staffer Ofra Graicer reflected that the final product was filled with "many contradictions and logical gaps" and "was a mismatch of old and new" because the last IDF exercise at the operational–strategic command level was two years before the document was released, which left the IDF with "a novel paradigm but obsolete modes of action."[6]

General Naveh blamed the IDF's "addiction" to tactics, its anti-intellectual culture, and Halutz's own lack of intellectual interest as an air force general since General Halutz "looked at the world through the cockpit" and disregarded "jointness" because "he was a victim of his prejudices or his biases."[7] Naveh ranted:

> Halutz is a victim of subculture. He might have been a good fighter pilot . . . but he's totally innocent of any education that could have prepared him for the challenges that awaited him as a general. Being both arrogant and ignorant, he never bothered, like so many generals, to really study. . . . He's the kind of man that if you can't really comprise your words into two lines, he'll never go through with it. . . . He is an idiot. . . . He's really a fool. He's a clown. He signed something he never bothered to learn and I was trying to tell him to wait a minute. . . .
>
> As being the mentor or force behind all this . . . what really worried me were the blind followers, and the IDF was full of them. They were just mumbling the words without really appreciating what lay in the base of these words—and Halutz was such a guy. He was using the right words, but never really bothered to understand. Understanding implies learning, and learning is painful.[8]

Confusingly, many academic studies that emerged shortly after the war imprecisely described the contents of this April 2006 operational concept in several different manners, with various studies claiming that it centrally incorporated RMA concepts, SOD, EBO, and standoff firepower. In the most-cited study on the war, it ambiguously conflates the two concepts, describing an "EBO/SOD doctrine" propagated by OTRI.[9] On the surface, SOD drew from many of the concepts related to EBO but in fact remained conceptually distinct. Compounding the confusion, General Naveh said in an interview with the author that "nobody will be able to give you the logical explanation (especially our Israeli colleagues) of SOD" since "this somewhat magical praxis" is misunderstood and underappreciated.[10]

According to Lt. Col. (Ret.) Roni Amir, former head of the IAF Doctrine Branch, the oft-cited notion of EBO came to the IDF in a piecemeal fashion, not from OTRI or SOD but as part of the influence of the RMA and lessons learned from the successful American standoff firepower operations in Kosovo, Afghanistan, and Iraq. These ideas were viewed beneficially to avoid incurring casualties, and the IDF, not the IAF, adopted a version of EBO as part of the April 2006 doctrine. Despite inconsistent scholarship asserting otherwise, General Halutz maintained that EBO was not a product of the IAF and never fit into any General Staff meeting as a guide to strategies pursued in 2006.[11] Colonel Amir asserted that "when Halutz was head of the

IAF [2000–2004], he said that no one under the rank of colonel can use the term EBO, and during the 2006 war we in the IAF never used the term EBO—not even once."[12]

Qualifying the impact of EBO, according to a former fighter pilot in the IAF Campaign Planning Department, the partial influence of EBO in 2006 led the IDF to focus on "cognitive-strategic" effects, which would be carried out by standoff and precision firepower. Rather than hitting a target, which would have a direct causal effect on linking tactical action to direct military achievement, precision strikes were utilized in 2006 in an attempt to allow the IDF to bypass expending significant operational resources and time and skip straight to achieving a "cognitive collapse" as a shortcut to military achievement. Remnants of the Limited Conflict doctrine related to "burning the consciousness" of the opponent were indirectly conflated with these concepts as well. The ultimately ineffective RMA-inspired "effects-based precision strikes" were intended to generate a complex chain of causal connections: destroying a symbolic target, which creates a functional effect on the enemy, and yielding a cognitive effect on its leadership, which would generate the desired behavioral change of removing Hezbollah's rockets.[13] This reflects the confluence of the IDF's historically ineffective approach that sought to leverage the Lebanese government and population against Hezbollah with the IDF's preference for minimal casualties and standoff firepower, under the obtuse and poorly synthesized moniker of EBO.

The Winograd Commission noted the convoluted application of concepts related to the "consciousness element" of Hezbollah, which is "especially important in a conflict where there is no clear unequivocal military decision" and "requires deep awareness on our part of the components and thinking processes of the enemy whose consciousness we wish to 'burn.' We did not find systematic deliberations that dealt with the basic assumptions of this complex and important subject."[14]

The immense confusion that led to the conflation of SOD and EBO is a reflection of the lack of clarity of the 2006 operational document itself. The document was poorly written, complex, and inadvertently distorted SOD methodology while confusingly attempting to do a number of things beyond the scope of the operational concept. Contrary to arguments put forth in earlier academic studies, according to Brig. Gen. Itai Brun, former head of research in IDF MI, this document had little influence on how the IDF actually operated during the war owing to its formal implementation less than three months before, but it is important because it reflects the understanding of the senior defense establishment about the changes inherent in Israel's strategic and social environment.[15]

Some of OTRI's most vociferous critics have recently moderated or recanted their initial criticisms of SOD and qualified their assessments of the actual contents of the April 2006 concept. One of the main critics of SOD and a key source in the most often cited study on the 2006 war, Lt. Col. (Res.) Ron Tira, an IAF campaign planner, explained: "The written formal implementation of SOD, EBO, and other timely RMA concepts was via a document dated April 2006, which was a horrible document, impossible to read . . . which meant many people including people like myself, attributed to it things that it didn't say. . . . I don't know who they expected would read it, because I think I'd be the natural reader of the document as a campaign planner."[16]

The April 2006 operational document blended four different elements into a single document. First, there was a timely net assessment, which discussed the local and international challenges facing Israel leading up to 2006, including the critical regional implications of the US war in Iraq. Second, the document outlined a methodology for facilitating and transmitting operational directives in the Senior Headquarters. It was meant to outline a methodology for "how the Senior Headquarters should work, once they receive a directive from the government, and how they would give an order to the relevant force application headquarters."[17] The methodological aspect of this component of the doctrine incorporated core elements of campaign design and SOD.

Third, an assessment of "what is the timely, trendy way to fight wars, which emphasized stand-off fire, UAVs and related concepts" was included.[18] This section outlined the preferred RMA-inspired Israeli way of war, reliant on standoff firepower, airpower, and precision targeting capabilities. Based on LIC experiences in Lebanon and the Palestinian territories and the subtle influence of the Limited Conflict era, this section de-emphasized the utility of the IDF's traditional doctrinal principle of territorial conquest, which it argued promoted protracted, attritional warfare, and instead emphasized the shift in the role of airpower from a supporting element to the central factor in achieving military decision. General Brun noted that the document did *not* advocate the possibility of winning wars by airpower alone—without ground operations—but did highlight the need for "a different form of ground maneuver than had been executed in the 1973 War" (the epitome of IDF traditional maneuver).[19] This "different form" of maneuver remained imprecise and ill defined but is thought to be partially influenced by the US military's joint operation of standoff fire synchronized with light ground forces during the opening phases of the 2003 Iraq War. Elements of EBO influenced aspects of this section, though not explicitly by name, which led some to imprecisely compare the IAF's opening air campaign in 2006 to the US "Shock and Awe" concept used in Iraq.[20] The fourth aspect of the document included a dictionary and glossary to help explain the new command language and complex methodological terminology for designing campaigns with SOD.

The Winograd Commission confirmed the unclear nature of the operational concept signed by General Halutz that blurred numerous elements "not necessarily linked to each other" but noted that, "at the same time, the influence of the operational concept was based on the combination of elements from all these strata put together."[21] It highlighted the second element of the doctrine for causing considerable confusion related to command authority between higher and lower echelons in the General Staff and Northern Command. Also, "there was talk about the need for that element to create 'a campaign design,'" but "on the eve of war . . . this preference was not complemented by the proper organization of the force-activation mechanism or the command-and-control apparatus."[22]

Describing the element of the doctrine that incorporated SOD-related methodologies for campaign planning in the Senior Headquarters, Colonel Tira explained:

> That component is important, you need that methodology, but it didn't really exist then. . . . It wasn't stupid, which is what I wrote previously. It was inaccessible, but it wasn't dumb. The blame that it [SOD] took from many people including myself was exaggerated because it was incomprehensible, impossible to read it, and because it mixed four different contents, which should not converge in the same document. . . .
>
> Had they [OTRI] published only a methodology on how Senior Headquarters should work, the message would have been much clearer. . . . But that's not what happened.[23]

Exacerbating the confusion, the Winograd Commission noted, "OTRI did not publish any written code for the IDF."[24] In a 2006 report by the Israeli state comptroller, who had ordered the shutdown of OTRI because of financial irregularities, OTRI was scathingly criticized for its lack of written documentation, especially regarding codifying an understandable command language. The report claimed OTRI did not publish a single report on large-scale military tactics in over twelve years, which damaged the IDF's ability to adapt: "This severe situation runs the risk of preventing the creation of a common professional military language, needed to manage and command large IDF frameworks in routine [operations] and during states of emergency."[25]

The chief problem, according to Colonel Tira, was that "OTRI tried to entice others to write their own documents, and a lot was lost in translation between their original intent [and the final document]. . . . The document which was eventually published was not written by them, because they wrote it via proxy [the Doctrine Division in the IDF Operations Directorate] and that proxy was out of control." In Tira's apt musical analogy, "the 2006 doctrine was written by the conductor rather than the composer" and led to OTRI's already complex concepts to be further "lost in translation."[26]

A GAME OF "BROKEN TELEPHONE"

While the April 2006 document represents one manifestation of the IDF's operational concept, other nebulous concepts impacted the IDF's war efforts that were not explicitly discussed in the document. Some early scholarship has suggested, only partially accurately, that the IDF's goal to "burn the consciousness" of Hezbollah by carrying out "symbolic" operations in Bint Jbayl and elsewhere was conceptually inspired by EBO and SOD.[27] In an extremely difficult issue to resolve, IDF officers asserted that the conceptual origins of the IDF's operations to burn the consciousness of Hezbollah actually emanated from the Limited Conflict doctrine of the late 1990s as a way to fatigue Israel's opponents psychologically.[28] While the formal Limited Conflict doctrine was discarded in the mid-2000s (see chapter 6), remnants of the jargon related to burning the consciousness of Israel's opponents diffused throughout the army and found its way into various IDF doctrinal publications in a piecemeal fashion, often without the original contextual analysis related to attritional conflict.[29] The terminology partially endured in pockets of the IDF and was *indirectly* conflated by outsiders with the poorly synthesized concepts of EBO and SOD, though this conflation was *not* propagated by OTRI. OTRI personnel asserted that SOD had no conceptual relation to "consciousness burning" or any ideas related to the Limited Conflict and that the only superficial similarity is that both these concepts took into account nonphysical, cognitive aspects of warfare.[30] (One IDF insider even recalled that General Naveh was "contemptuous" of Limited Conflict concepts.)

A senior IDF officer noted that the various ideas diffused throughout the army in a manner resembling the children's game "Broken Telephone," in which "people read or listen to ideas, often second-, third-, or even fourth-hand. Often they do not know the origin, but it sounds good. They might not even get the accurate original version but an 'evolved' version."[31] Illustrating the lack of clarity surrounding the origins and impact of such concepts whizzing around the IDF, Col. Meir Finkel, former head of the Concept Development and Doctrine Department, noted that "Col. Samo Nir's writings are almost unknown today" but that "parts of his ideas were embedded in ground forces doctrine [prior to 2006], but nine out of ten commanders today won't know his paper."[32] Similar to the organizational diffusion of SOD, the terminology and concepts of the Limited Conflict diffused in a haphazard fashion as "short slogans stuck easier than the long explanations. Ideas evolved, fused with other ideas and got passed on, and soon no one remembered the origins. . . . Not everybody read the actual manuscripts Colonel Nir wrote—many just heard of them verbally in various second- or thirdhand lectures in courses or planning discussions."[33]

Rather than illustrating subscription to any specific effects-based concept floating around the IDF, the desire to achieve a symbolic victory by burning the consciousness of Hezbollah more profoundly represents the "postheroic" preference of the IDF to avoid messy ground operations and achieve wartime objectives with limited ground troops and minimal casualties. The Winograd Commission astutely confirmed this assertion: "The purpose of the response to a Limited Conflict (implying that it referred, by and large, to the Palestinian issue) was defined as a concept designed 'to bring about a "consciousness" change among the adversary's decision-makers' *in order to shorten the duration of the war, maintain a long-term calm, and achieve goals with minimum resources.*"[34]

The ideas represented a misunderstanding of the idea that LIC can be won mostly on the psychological front and by avoiding heavy ground combat. As one senior IDF officer concluded, "one problem with the Second Lebanon War was that the IDF didn't realize it was not fighting a low-intensity war against an enemy trying to avoid combat but, rather, a medium-intensity war against an enemy determined to fight."[35]

The impact of allusive concepts such as EBO that sought to have a cognitive or symbolic effect on Hezbollah in 2006 caused much confusion in the wider defense community. In a debate that has still not been fully resolved, despite IAF assertions that EBO was *not* utilized in 2006, the US military (the creators of EBO) formally discarded EBO as a result of its *perceived* shortcomings during the 2006 war. In a damning 2008 assessment, the highly respected head of the US Joint Forces Command, Gen. James Mattis (currently secretary of defense), wrote:

> Although there are several reasons why the IDF performed poorly during the [2006] war, various postconflict assessments have concluded that overreliance on EBO concepts was one of the primary contributing factors for their defeat. . . .
>
> Other critical warfighting functions, such as campaign design [SOD] and planning, combined arms training, command and control (C2) relationships, and so forth, were overlooked or neglected in favor of EBO operating principles designed to create a "consciousness of victory" for friendly forces and a "cognitive perception of defeat" for enemy forces.[36]

As previous chapters illustrate, the IDF's failings go far beyond its use of EBO, and scholars have criticized General Mattis's narrow assessment of EBO in 2006 as a "misapplied and overextended example."[37] Compounding the confusion, OTRI personnel, who briefly adopted terminology related to "operational effects" in the mid-2000s before discarding it, argued that the IDF overrelied on American EBO and standoff firepower in 2006 to its detriment and did not implement or utilize SOD in Lebanon in any consistent manner.[38]

A CRITICAL ASSESSMENT OF SOD

SOD has been harshly criticized by soldiers and scholars in Israel and abroad for being overly complex and "essentially unintelligible," inconsistently defined by its advocates, and riddled with inaccurate comparative interpretation (particularly regarding Soviet and ancient Chinese military theory).[39] Within academic circles, SOD was criticized for its obtuse blurring with American-developed EBO and for overemphasizing the "cognitive" aspects of war.[40] Others pointed out that systems theory as a discipline was erroneously applied to military thought in the development of SOD.[41] SOD was criticized by academics for neglecting classical military theory in favor of a "pretentious postmodern approach" that uncritically emulated American doctrine, blurred the distinction between operations and grand strategy, and too broadly interpreted operational art to include "consciousness-shaping operations," which left troops stuck attempting to translate battlefield achievements into elusive operational and strategic gains.[42] OTRI was accused of encouraging a facade of pseudo-intellectualism, largely through its "arrogant, meaningless and even irrelevant" language.[43] Even the eminent scholar Martin van Creveld harshly criticized General Naveh's original theoretical framework (while reviewing Naveh's 1997 book) as being historically inaccurate, "difficult to read and not always convincing," and "as a guidebook for the future, it is almost completely lacking in relevancy."[44]

In the years before the 2006 war, OTRI was accused by a small group of senior officers of creating "practical and intellectual anarchy" by obfuscating the main principles of war. IDF officers bemoaned the difficulty of creating meaningful situational assessments using SOD, because of SOD's "faulty" intellectual basis. Col. (Res.) Yehuda Wegman, a longtime traditionalist in the IDF Staff College and the most outspoken critic of SOD, cuttingly wrote in several publications that instead of creating clarity on the battlefield, SOD's vague language "compounded the obscurity" as it arrogantly drew from "transient, fashionable ideas borrowed from realms and disciplines that share no common ground with the IDF" to enhance its producer's status in the IDF.[45] Another fierce critic was Maj. Gen. Yaakov Amidror, a former MI official and head of the IDF National Defense College, who wrote an article in the IDF journal a year before the 2006 war that sarcastically mocked the use of SOD's complex language to describe basic war principles.[46] He elaborated elsewhere that these "mellifluous words and pseudoscientific arguments" are "frequently put forward in unprofessional language which creates a new terminology, which is unintelligible to everybody. This, in turn, facilitates the avoidance of a genuine clarification of what is being discussed and of the actual situation."[47]

Maj. Gen. Moshe Kaplinsky, deputy COS to General Halutz, who relieved the ineffective head of Northern Command Maj. Gen. Udi Adam during the 2006 war, reflected on the IDF's operational approach in 2006:

> [The concept] touched on strengthening firepower at the expense of maneuver. . . . That was the direction the army was taking at the time; that was its intention. At the same time, a new language with unique terminology developed in order to describe this new approach. Unfortunately, this field was not developed professionally or well enough. The language stayed within a small cadre in the army and did not succeed, because of our internal failures, to reach the rank and file or to become the language common to all the echelons.[48]

The Winograd Commission gave a more balanced view, describing OTRI's positive contribution to improving the IDF's capacity for innovation: "[OTRI] developed ideas and concepts concerning operational theory, held seminars for senior officers, and pushed for change in the operational concept. [OTRI's] performance and accomplishments are controversial, but one cannot overlook the fact that it had operated for 10 years and that it has made a significant contribution to motivating senior IDF officers to develop a new concept."[49]

Despite OTRI's positive contribution, the commission crucially notes that the IDF failed to synthesize OTRI's complex methodology. This partially vindicates OTRI and validates OTRI's defense that its concepts were not fully integrated or utilized in the 2006 war itself: "On the eve of the Second Lebanon War, these organizational aspects of the new operational concept were incomplete; they had not been drilled and were not assimilated. Moreover, there were in effect considerable gaps that literally precluded reliance on the operational concept from the organizational aspect."[50]

Furthermore, an IAF lieutenant colonel who was one of the authors of the doctrine in the Operations Directorate noted that while the document was dated April 2006, it was actually only released in May, giving the IDF even less time to internalize and assimilate the new concepts before the outbreak of war.[51]

THE IDF'S SHORTCOMINGS AND THE SCAPEGOATING OF GENERAL HIRSCH

The inability of the IDF to synthesize SOD was attributed by the Winograd Commission to the "flowery" operational jargon developed by OTRI, "which many people thought was fuzzy, unclear, confusing, and empty of any real content" but was not actually a necessary part of the systemic approach.[52] The commission highlighted the operations of OTRI confidante Brig. Gen. Gal Hirsch's Ninety-First Division in Bint Jbayl for special scrutiny.[53] In 2006, General Hirsch utilized SOD in his command and had several notable successes, including identifying the pattern and deployment of Katyusha rockets in his area and launching small reconnaissance units to intercept Hezbollah rocket teams using rapid sensor-to-shooter feedback loops.[54] An interim IDF postwar investigative committee led by Maj. Gen. (Ret.) Yoram Yair found that all engagements with Hezbollah by battalions and companies within Hirsch's division were in favor of the IDF. However, a long list of systemic deficiencies were cited by the Yair Committee: The missions were not clearly articulated to soldiers, especially regarding time frame and mission purpose; there were frequent changes to the mission and order of battle, often using unfamiliar command language and terminology; and there were illogical "raiding" operations, which involved capturing, withdrawing from, and then recapturing Lebanese villages, as well as other logistical and planning issues.[55] General Yair caustically stated that he required a dictionary to decipher the tactical military language issued by General Hirsch.[56]

In a more nuanced assessment, the Winograd Commission concluded that beyond difficulties with Hirsch's command language, the goal in Bint Jbayl to carry out limited ground "raids" or "swarming" operations generated confusion owing to a far more critical shift in the IDF's operational concept that had not been internalized, which once again vindicated OTRI's assertions that their ideas were never fully integrated:

> We would like to emphasize once again that the problem lay not only in the actual ambiguity of the language or the fact that it was not commonly shared, as in the use of terms like "brigade attack" or "swarm-like attack," but that this unclear language complemented a principal and substantial change in the operational concept itself in terms of the types of targets goals of activating the military force. The way it looks, this combination, which was not properly assimilated, contributed to the flaws that were exposed during the fighting in the Lebanon war.[57]

Notably, General Hirsch was not personally faulted for any of these more far-reaching general deficiencies, though he was controversially faulted in a separate investigative committee led by Maj. Gen. (Res.) Doron Almog for his responses to the initial kidnapping incident that sparked the war.[58] General Almog stated that reservists in Hirsch's division were "victims of an ambiguous culture of authority," and despite having a plan in place for kidnapping, Hirsch "neglected to make sure this plan was also implemented by those under his command."[59] Hirsch would counter that the government's strategic policy of "containment" adopted to deal with Hezbollah in the years prior to the war was the key factor inviting the kidnapping (see chapter 4). He also asserted that steady budgetary cuts against his division, partially because of RMA force structure changes, had eroded the IDF and invited Hezbollah's attack.[60] He rightly asserted that his division had rebuffed five previous kidnapping attempts in prior years and claimed that IDF MI did not share all available intelligence with his division. The Almog Committee noted that *prior* to the war, Hirsch asked MI to install surveillance positions overlooking the border area, including at the site of the future abduction, and also asked for a better-trained, better-equipped battalion to replace the patrolling reservist battalion that was later ambushed. Both requests were rebuffed because of budgetary constraints, illustrating the unintended consequences of the RMA's budgetary allocations.[61]

General Naveh remarked that General Hirsch was "the most creative thinker, the most subversive thinker and the victim of this entire affair."[62] Israel's most respected military pundit quipped that "Hirsch is a devoted and skilled officer who was kicked around like a soccer ball by forces larger than him—the chief of staff, the politicians, the intense and sometimes hysterical media, and an Israeli society that wants one-sided victories."[63] Hirsch was barred from command positions and resigned in protest at the Almog Committee's findings.

In the postwar media frenzy, SOD's jargon, and Brig. Gen. Hirsch in particular, became the focal points of much criticism and continued to be blamed for many of the IDF's failings. In a balanced reappraisal, Brig. Gen. (Ret.) Meir Elran, senior consultant to the Winograd Commission and former deputy head of IDF MI, explained that, overall, OTRI "affected the IDF on a relatively thin basis. . . . The phenomenon had an effect, but to those who say that this was a major disruption which caused a less than successful operation in 2006, this is somewhat an exaggeration."[64] Former head of the IDF Strategic Planning Division, Brig. Gen. (Ret.) Shlomo Brom, who was on an official government committee established by the MOD to reexamine Israel's security doctrine prior to the 2006 war, noted that OTRI's culpability was "overplayed" and remarked that OTRI and Hirsch became "convenient scapegoats":

I think there is a lot of exaggeration. . . . There is a kind of suggestion that one of the results of the relatively poor performance of the ground forces was a problem of command language. I doubt this very much. I don't think it played such an important role. I think, as usual, "A fish stinks from its head." The problem of the [2006] war was the strategic decisions we were taking, not what happened at lower levels, and the failures of lower levels were mostly results of lack of training, not of language.[65]

General Hirsch waged a bitter legal appeal that eventually led to the nullification of the Almog Committee's findings and the decision to bar him from command. In what can be viewed as a vindication, after more than five years in forced retirement, Hirsch was appointed deputy head of the newly formed IDF Depth Corps (2012–15), which deals with complex long-range operations and specialized missions deep in enemy territory.[66] Interestingly, his reappointment was noted openly by Hezbollah.[67] Hirsch was further vindicated when the late Judge Eliyahu Winograd, chief of the commission bearing his name, wrote a public letter to COS Lt. Gen. Benny Gantz in 2014 imploring that Hirsch be allowed to return to full active service as "my conscience has tormented me" because of Hirsch's treatment in postwar inquiries.[68] Hirsch was later floated to become the next head of Israel's national police, but his name was ultimately withdrawn because of political considerations and, to a lesser extent, domestic pressure from families of fallen soldiers from the Ninety-First Division.

General Hirsch is still nevertheless criticized by IDF insiders and fellow OTRI members for his overzealous application of SOD and his independent utilization of its complex language on lower command levels. Hirsch's chief error was the application of SOD below the regional command level, as from the major-general echelon downward the methodology and command language should have been "plain vanilla."[69] OTRI researcher Ofra Graicer explained that OTRI staff were "coaches rather than advisers, since our philosophy stated that only the commander in charge could design the operation he was to implement."[70] OTRI cofounder Zvi Lanir reflected: "I was Gal Hirsch's teacher in one of the military courses, but he went on and he developed a lot of these concepts himself," highlighting the atmosphere of intellectual experimentation fostered by OTRI.[71] Partially because of this atmosphere, Hirsch's battle plans were part of his own independent intellectual efforts. Graicer continued:

> OTRI trained Gal Hirsch to think SOD, but we didn't even write the plans for Gal—he did it himself. That was part of the confusion. . . . Gal Hirsch was the only person who [formally] wrote about SOD. He put it on paper, so they went for him [in postwar inquiries]. He was in the spotlight because he wrote about it, and they used it against him. . . .
>
> As a division commander, if he talks with his seniors, he can talk in operational jargon, there is merit in using systemic methodology. . . . But when he talks down to his soldiers, he's not supposed to use systemic jargon. . . . He was always a wizard of words, and maybe he took it too far.[72]

General Naveh remarked that General Hirsch "failed due to a combination of factors: jargon was only one. He totally misunderstood how he should communicate with the lower levels in such a situation. . . . Another factor was that no one above provided him the space so Gal could be creative." While in Central Command, Hirsch was previously under the tutelage of OTRI to prevent him "overstepping" his conceptual bounds, and Naveh joked, "Hirsch is brilliant. I love him. I encouraged him, but sometimes I would have slapped him in the face and told him, you don't know what you're doing!" After the purge of OTRI, Hirsch was left in Northern Command without a "community of practice" of intellectually minded soldiers and without institutional support from above. Naveh lamented that since COS General Halutz had no coherent operational plans, Hirsch was "alone in space" in Northern Command and there was no one to work with him to engage in detailed systemic operational planning, nor could those under his command fully understand his OTRI-inspired ideas. The result was that "his creativity reinforced his isolation."[73]

Critically, the process of translating SOD for use by commanders on the ground was a point of contention within the OTRI leadership. In a profound insider's opinion, Zvi Lanir, who stopped working with OTRI in 2001 when the contract between his Praxis consultancy and the IDF terminated, explained his reasons for leaving:

> One of the reasons we at Praxis left OTRI is because we thought OTRI wasn't implementing systems thinking in a professional way; they were moving too fast. The ideas were too theoretical, and OTRI should be careful using these ideas on the tactical level—maybe they should leave it for the operational level. . . .
>
> We thought from our experiences that the theories weren't precise enough, translated, and transformed to the tactical level. . . . Naveh and Tamari were a little naive in how long it might take to make these kinds of transformations. They must be much more patient. . . . Now everyone understands that the process was a little rushed, because to change an army is not a simple thing.[74]

Lanir preferred working with smaller, more manageable operational-level units in Central Command, where he continued working throughout the 2000s. The operational-level insights of OTRI were not yet refined enough to be transferred to commanders in the field, which would explain why division commanders such as Gal Hirsch had mixed results in translating and implementing SOD in battle in Lebanon. In an author interview in 2015, General Naveh later admitted that "Lanir is right in a sense. He's right that it was premature on the tactical level, and maybe we were moving too quickly because we didn't appreciate the IDF's inherent limitations."[75]

General Naveh reflected, "The introduction of a theory of operational art happened, almost naturally, to possess a potential for rousing, especially among higher ranking officers, suspicions, if not animosity."[76] Established senior officers were against investing in OTRI's "not-locally-made" theories because of its "subversive" nature, which is why SOD diffused mostly through mid-level "rising stars" seeking promotion. High-ranking generals who did not want their own organizational standing compromised were wary of Naveh, whom they viewed as "a 'wild guy' both intellectually and operationally." Naveh openly admitted he had a "deep contempt" for some colleagues and superiors as a result of their lack of operational-level insight.[77] Illustrating this contempt in an expletive-laden postwar interview published in an Israeli newspaper, Naveh pointed to his dog and said, "See him? He is smarter than most of the people on the General Staff!"[78] Evidently, there was significant tension against the OTRI-driven reforms because of cultural factors and intraorganizational rivalry between OTRI "insiders" and "outsiders," as well as Naveh's crass and problematic style.

Pondering the ultimate failure of the innovation to diffuse more permanently, Naveh considered it a "grave miscalculation of institutional demographics," as despite the "operational alliance" with the paratroopers who temporarily preserved the innovation, OTRI supporters lacked the "critical mass" to protect the continuity of their innovation. (By mid-2005 only fourteen OTRI graduates were still active.)[79] Naveh's final verdict was "Despite the impressive renaissance in Israeli operational art during 1995–2005, potential centers of opposition and regression within the IDF were never mollified. ... As a result, when the opponents of ... [OTRI] finally had the opportunity under Gen. Dan Halutz to undo what had been done, they seized it."[80]

In a thoughtful and reflective assessment, and ultimately highlighting the shortcomings of both SOD and the IDF's action-oriented, anti-intellectual organizational culture, Ofra Graicer explained:

> To learn design [SOD] and understand that there is no end, that you can always be in the process of designing or reframing ... no one wants to live like this. So there are many reasons why SOD is the "way to do business," but maybe it's also the reason why it will never be fully implemented. What makes it so strong also makes so many people resist it, for the same reasons. It's very powerful, but very demanding.
>
> It needs intellectuals and an intellectual effort, but not all generals are intellectual. They come from combat, from tactics, from the field of action, which they are very good at, but when we tell them that whatever they've done until now doesn't serve them as generals, that they need to start something new, they're resistant.[81]

THE NEGLECT OF THE GROUND FORCES: BETWEEN THE INTIFADA AND THE RMA

In addition to the poor performance of IDF ground forces resulting from the misapplication of SOD and the confusion generated related to the April 2006 doctrinal document, the IDF was criticized for its overreliance on airpower and precision firepower. Israel's new preferred way of war, which emphasized RMA-inspired standoff firepower over large-scale maneuver, was evident in 2006. The Winograd Commission somewhat prosaically noted that "the Second Lebanon War demonstrated both the Air Force's impressive capabilities and the results of its low acknowledgment of its own limitations. . . . It should not be regarded as a 'miracle solution' for every wartime need. One should particularly be wary of entertaining excessive expectations with respect to stand-off fire capabilities in a confrontation with a well-prepared guerrilla enemy such as Hezbollah."[82]

With palpable frustration, Lt. Col. (Ret.) Amos Granit, the senior OTRI staffer who designed the unimplemented battle plans in Northern Command, criticized the IDF's inappropriate focus on precision firepower and the simplistic and banal postwar criticisms that ensued:

> Damn all the people who needed this war to realize we shouldn't use precision firepower to deal with Hezbollah! Naveh and I were some of the only people in the entire IDF who realized this would be inadequate, so we developed plans accordingly. . . . The Winograd Commission and all those morons who criticized the command language of the IDF are focusing on a microproblem that detracts from the main issues, which were strategic in nature—specifically the weakness of Halutz and the incompetence of Prime Minister Olmert and Defense Minister Peretz.
>
> Naveh has his edges, but OTRI was scapegoated despite having the right plans and right ideas for the Hezbollah threat. Damn those people who write these stupid reports after the war, saying that after the fact, we shouldn't have used firepower. It was our job in the IDF to know this before the war, not after the fact! And we did know this before the war, and we even had a perfect plan to deal with it![83]

While both SOD and the IDF's preference for airpower were narrowly criticized in 2006, criticism of previous IDF policies associated with the RMA were less prevalent. The RMA should be faulted for diverting necessary funds and training programs over the preceding decades away from the ground units (especially reserve units) toward acquisition of expensive standoff weaponry and technology that was less relevant for the fight against Hezbollah. Interservice competition emerged between the air force and ground forces, as the IAF became the recipient of the influx of funding and resources as part of the RMA, while the army suffered large-scale training and supply cuts throughout the 1990s and 2000s owing to diversion of funds toward expensive RMA acquisition programs. The air force and the special forces and other elite units benefited from Israel's military transformation and indeed enjoyed qualitative and technological improvements as they became "slimmer and smarter." Meanwhile, reserve units called up to fight in the 2006 war were neglected as part of this transformative process toward increased professionalization and remained underfunded, undertrained, organizationally bloated, and ill prepared logistically or operationally to confront Hezbollah.[84] Defense Minister Amir Peretz reflected: "There were [reserve] units that had not conducted exercises in years. Commanders who had not physically seen their soldiers for long periods of time. A drop in the competence and fitness of the reserve soldiers. We had to devote time to training exercises in the midst of the war."[85]

This was also a result of the operational focus by a large number of ground units on LIC during the IDF's campaign to quell Palestinian terrorism during the Second Intifada.[86] Given the scale of fighting with Palestinian militant groups in the 2000s, ground units were operationally consumed with LIC and had little time and few resources to focus on conventional ground combat and high-intensity war training. Owing to the residual effect of the Limited Conflict era, soldiers who had been engaged in policing and counterterrorism prior to 2006 were not operationally ready to fight Hezbollah, which utilized a high-intensity mode of warfare that was more challenging for the IDF. The Winograd Commission noted that training of ground forces and reservists for major combat operations "or even those elements that addressed a confrontation with Hezbollah, which was significantly different than the conflict on the Palestinian front, were neglected" in favor of LIC.[87] Out of operational necessity, the IDF focused on LIC and Palestinian counterterrorism from 2000 to 2006 and inadvertently neglected its traditional warfighting skills that it needed for Hezbollah. Maj. Gen. Benny Gantz lamented in 2007 as the outgoing head of IDF GFC, "We might have shifted too sharply from one paradigm to another."[88]

Exacerbated by training budget cuts, some units were poorly prepared for the high-intensity fighting and made operational and tactical mistakes that had damaging strategic ramifications.[89] For example, the sloppy tactical performance of sailors aboard the Israeli naval ship who failed to activate the ship's defenses, the tankers in Wadi Saluki who did not activate smoke screens, and the soldiers who clustered together in buildings in a village west of Bint Jbayl who were targeted by Hezbollah's ATM onslaught all had a particularly detrimental effect on the morale of the Israeli public.[90]

The Winograd Commission concluded that the IDF's flawed operational concept during the 2006 war reflected the confluence of both its prior focus on LIC and an overemphasis on the air force because of the impact of the RMA:

> It is true that the new operational concept's emphasis on the characteristics of a low-intensity Limited Conflict, and on the use of counter-fire mainly from the air based on precise intelligence information, was not unambiguous. But it contributed to the feeling that there is a correct theoretical basis to expect a

battlefield decision following an aerial move alone and consequently, to avoid a ground operation even under the conditions which, according to the IDF's plans, made such a move mandatory.[91]

SOD REDUX

When the postwar dust settled, General Halutz was replaced as COS by Lt. Gen. Gabi Ashkenazi (2007–11), who brought the IDF "back to basics" regarding its operational and tactical focus, illustrated by the improved IDF performance in the 2008 Gaza War.[92] General Ashkenazi drafted a new IDF plan (Teffen 2012) that emphasized the importance of decisive ground maneuver, bolstered ground forces training, and increased armored corps exercises, largely in response to the sloppy performances in 2006. In response to the budgetary cuts that impacted IDF readiness prior to the war, Ashkenazi improved reservist training, remedied logistical and supply issues, and reemphasized live-fire training exercises, which had become scant in prior years.[93] He returned the IDF to its "traditional" doctrine, shedding the "pseudo-intellectualism" and command jargon that OTRI had propagated. Ashkenazi purged the IDF of remaining remnants of SOD and "burned the doctrine" that inspired SOD.[94]

Despite this "burning," the innovation appears to survive through OTRI graduate Maj. Gen. Aviv Kochavi, who rose to head of IDF MI (2010–14), head of Northern Command (2014–16), and, since 2016, to IDF deputy COS. Lt. Col. (Ret.) Amos Granit remained active in MI, where he headed the Institute for Systemic Intelligence Analysis, which was staffed by several former OTRI members who worked closely with General Kochavi when he was head of MI. Hence, the innovative benefit of SOD partially endured through the successes of IDF MI. Whether Deputy COS Kochavi's experiences with OTRI and SOD might influence the IDF's future plans remains to be seen.

In what can arguably be viewed as ultimate validation of the value and benefit of SOD, General Naveh was brought in as an organizational consultant to the US Army and US Marine Corps following OTRI's shutdown, where SOD was further developed and notably simplified, adapted, and implemented.[95] Following the US Army's exposure to SOD after the large-scale "Unified Quest" exercises from 2003 to 2007, which involved OTRI staff, TRADOC noted that the unique IDF command culture that encourages institutionalized questioning of superiors as part of the design/reframing process and SOD's "arcane and complex" language posed challenges for SOD's adoption into the US military. A 2008 TRADOC publication stated that "while these may be obstacles to understanding, they do not detract from the value of the ideas themselves; but they do require translation into terms and language that will speak more clearly to U.S. officers."[96] Significant intellectual attention has been devoted to SOD in the US defense community in an effort to integrate it into the military, where it continues to be refined.[97] Naveh was praised by senior US officers, including US Army brigadier general Huba Wass de Czege, US Marine Corps lieutenant general Paul Van Riper, and others in SAMS, while he worked for close to a decade at Fort Leavenworth and Special Operations Command (SOCOM). Elements of SOD and "operational design methodology" have been modified and implemented into the SAMS curriculum and also subtly influenced numerous doctrinal publications and several US Army field manuals.[98] SOD has also received significant intellectual attention from the Canadian and Australian militaries.[99] In a report for the US defense community that sums up American perceptions, one retired US Army colonel wrote that "Naveh is a charismatic genius" and his theories represent "the parent of all operational design theories."[100]

General Naveh had significant success in SOCOM refining design methodology and developing a new leadership course. In a surprising turn of events, after word spread of Naveh's relative success in SOCOM, Naveh was approached in 2014 by Maj. Gen. Yossi Baidatz, head of the IDF Defense College, and urged to return to Israel with the approval of COS Lt. Gen. Benny Gantz (both are former OTRI confidantes). With the growing understanding in the IDF that "the discarding of operational art amounted to throwing out the baby with the bathwater,"[101] Naveh returned to Israel from self-imposed "exile" in the United States. Together with former OTRI staffer Ofra Graicer, he was instructed to develop an Israeli version of the US military's leadership course that he had developed in SOCOM, which includes instruction on a new concept related to generalship, systemic design, and operational art.

General Naveh explained that he "licked his wounds" while working with the US military in the decade following 2006, reflected on his mistakes and shortcomings, and adapted and improved SOD. He admitted that SOD "was too advanced and too revolutionary" for the IDF and that working with SOCOM provided him "with a real learning community and the opportunity to test ideas at all levels: new methodologies, new approaches to learning, new languages, new modes of research, and some new concepts." Naveh and Graicer are currently teaching select IDF officers a new theory related to operational art that they have dubbed "Operational Mediation," which involves developing critical thinking skills to "mediate" between strategy and operational art.[102] A major component of the Operational Mediation course is to teach senior generals the necessary skills to tightly synergize the strategic and operational levels of war, which Naveh believes represented a shortcoming of SOD and "a critical failure" of the IDF more broadly in 2006. The new concept was created as a "methodology for learning," seeks to "link strategy and operational art conceptually and philosophically," and was designed to avoid the institutional, organizational, and cultural mistakes that OTRI made related to the diffusion of SOD.

Naveh and Graicer have developed an innovative "Teach the Teacher" program, in which senior generals are instructed how to teach the new concept and methodology to their comrades, which facilitates its diffusion.[103] Naveh and Graicer oversee the process and operate "in the shadows," while they "let the guys [officers] deal with the contents and the patterns, and we focus more on helping them to reset their thinking."[104] Naveh noted, "The ideas of the new course are that we are trying to institutionalize a project that will provide those relevant agents with the experience to educate themselves, to become creators of knowledge, designers, and strategists."[105] Several of the IDF's current top brass attended the course in 2016, including Maj. Gen. Herzi Halevy, head of MI; Maj. Gen. Roni Numa, head of Central Command; Maj. Gen. Nitzan Alon, head of the Operations Branch; and Maj. Gen. Aviv Kochavi (the latter two were former OTRI disciples). Naveh noted wryly, "I was the devil, and the IDF brought the devil back. . . . At the end of the day, for me, this was redemption."[106] The SOD saga is not over, and it is worth watching if Naveh and his disciples can get it right this time around.

CONCLUSION

In the aftermath of the 2006 war, much of the blame for the IDF's shortcomings was attributed to the poorly synthesized, incoherent doctrinal document signed by General Halutz three months before the war, which outlined the utility of the RMA, the role of SOD in the Senior Headquarters, and other timely topics. This document inaccurately came to represent for many inside and outside Israel the focal point of what went wrong in 2006. SOD and its proponents who used the associated command jargon became convenient scapegoats for much wider, systemic problems. The IDF's operational focus on LIC and counterterrorism had a damaging impact on ground forces' readiness at a time when the army's force structure was still largely focused on RMA-inspired warfare. Hezbollah's mode of warfare in 2006 fit somewhere between these two ends of the spectrum of combat, which meant the IDF was ill equipped and unprepared for the battlefield challenges it faced during the war. The IDF's obsessive criticism of SOD's command language in the war's aftermath prevented a more pertinent, critical assessment of the war's wider failings, and only with the passage of time has SOD and its proponents been redeemed and slowly brought back into the IDF.

NOTES

Epigraphs: Peretz, interview, May 3, 2007; Nasrallah, speech, May 2, 2007.

1. The document was officially titled *The IDF General Staff's Operational Concept*, April 2006, and contained a preface by COS Lt. Gen. Dan Halutz. See Winograd Commission, final report, chap. 7, n. 4 and n. 7.

2. Winograd Commission, final report, chap. 7, para. 7.

3. Alon Ben-David, "Debriefing Teams Brand IDF Doctrine 'Completely Wrong,'" *Jane's Defence Weekly*, January 3, 2007.

4. Author interviews with OTRI personnel, January–July 2012.

5. Naveh, interview, November 1, 2007, 3–4.

6. Graicer, "Between Teaching and Learning" (2017), 27–28.

7. Naveh, interview, November 1, 2007, 5.

8. Ibid., 3–4.

9. Matthews, *We Were Caught Unprepared*, 62–63.

10. Author interview with Shimon Naveh.

11. Lambeth, *Air Operations*, 279–81, 336.

12. Author interview with Roni Amir.

13. Tira, *Limitations of Standoff*, 22–27.

14. Winograd Commission, final report, chap. 7, para. 22.

15. Brun, "Second Lebanon War," 308.

16. Author interview with Ron Tira. Tira was the primary source for the study by Matthews, *We Were Caught Unprepared*. See also Tira, "Breaking the Amoeba's Bones"; Tira, *Limitations of Standoff*.

17. Author interview with Ron Tira.

18. Ibid.

19. Brun, "Second Lebanon War," 308; Brun and Rabinovich, *Israel Facing a New Middle East*, 60–61.

20. Lambeth, *Air Operations*, 36; Matthews, *We Were Caught Unprepared*, 62; Tira, "Breaking the Amoeba's Bones," 8; Arkin, *Divine Victory*, 128.

21. Winograd Commission, final report, chap. 7, para. 14.

22. Ibid., paras. 14–17.

23. Author interview with Ron Tira.

24. Winograd Commission, final report, chap. 7, n. 6.

25. Quoted in Yaakov Katz, "IDF Think-Tank Chief: Better Tactical Language Needed," *Jerusalem Post*, December 20, 2006.

26. Author interview with Ron Tira.

27. Matthews, *We Were Caught Unprepared*, 28; Tira, *Limits of Standoff*.

28. Author interview with "E."

29. Author interviews with IDF officers, February 2015.

30. Author interviews with OTRI personnel, January–July 2012.

31. Author interview with "E."

32. Author interview with Meir Finkel.

33. Author interview with "E."

34. Winograd Commission, final report, chap. 7, para. 21 (emphasis added).

35. Author interview with "E."

36. Mattis, "USJFCOM Commander's Guidance."

37. Henriksen, "Misapplied and Overextended Example."

38. Author interview with Ofra Graicer.

39. Vego, "Case against Systemic Operational Design."

40. Matthews, *We Were Caught Unprepared*, 22–28, 60–65.

41. Vego, "Systems versus Classical Approach to Warfare."

42. Kober, "Israel Defense Forces in the Second Lebanon War," 31–32; Kober, "Rise and Fall of Israeli Operational Art," 181–90.

43. Michael, "Israel Defense Forces as an Epistemic Authority," 435; Kober, "Israeli Military Thought," 717–18.

44. Martin van Creveld, "Diffusion Strikes," *Haaretz*, September 28, 2001.

45. Wegman, "Distorted Self-Image."

46. Amidror, "Military Strike as a Cognitive Paradigm of Effects."

47. Amidror, "Can a Conventional Army Vanquish?"

48. Kaplinsky, "IDF in the Years before the Second Lebanon War," 29.

49. Winograd Commission, final report, chap. 7, n. 6.

50. Ibid., para. 18.

51. Author interview with Roni Amir.

52. Winograd Commission, final report, chap. 7, para. 27.

53. Ibid., n. 14.

54. Naveh, interview, November 1, 2007, 8.

55. Hanan Greenberg, "Interim Report: 91st Division Didn't See It as War," *Yediot Ahronoth*, October 15, 2006.

56. Yaakov Katz, "IDF Think-Tank Chief: Better Tactical Language Needed," *Jerusalem Post*, December 20, 2006.

57. Winograd Commission, final report, chap. 7, para. 29.

58. Nir Hasson, "Hirsch: MI Warning Would Have Prevented Kidnapping," *Haaretz*, November 15, 2006.

59. Maj. Gen. Doron Almog, interview, November 21, 2006.

60. See his memoir, Hirsch, *Defensive Shield*, chaps. 12–13.

61. Ibid., 199–202; Amir Oren, "In Lebanon, Government Hamstrung Troubled Division," *Haaretz*, October 15, 2006.

62. Naveh, interview, November 1, 2007, 7.

63. Amos Harel, "Settling Accounts," *Haaretz*, August 6, 2009.

64. Author interview with Meir Elran.

65. Author interview with Shlomo Brom.

66. For Hirsch's side of the story regarding the Yair Committee and the Almog Committee, see Hirsch, *Defensive Shield*, chap. 23.

67. "Eye on the Enemy: Israel Not Ready for War, Eyes to North, to Syria and Hezbollah," Al-Ahed News, February 11, 2012.

68. Hirsch, *Defensive Shield*, 435.

69. Author interview with Ron Tira.

70. Graicer, lecture, June 20, 2008.

71. Author interview with Zvi Lanir.

72. Author interview with Ofra Graicer.

73. Author interview with Shimon Naveh.

74. Author interview with Zvi Lanir.

75. Author interview with Shimon Naveh.

76. Naveh, *Operational Art and the IDF*, 3–4.

77. Ibid., 12.

78. Naveh, interview, October 25, 2007.

79. Naveh, *Operational Art and the IDF*, 2–3.

80. Ibid., 97.

81. Author interview with Ofra Graicer.

82. Winograd Commission, final report, chap. 9, paras. 8–9 and 26.

83. Author interview with Amos Granit.

84. Cohen, *Israel and Its Army*, 50–52.

85. Peretz, interview, June 6, 2013.

86. Winograd Commission, final report, chap. 7, para. 4.

87. Ibid., para. 20.

88. Gantz, interview, December 26, 2007.

89. For example, see Winograd Commission, final report, chap. 9, paras. 1–64, 337–50.

90. For more on the disastrous incident in Debel, the village west of Bint Jbayl, see Marcus, "Military Innovation and Tactical Adaptation," 519–21.

91. Winograd Commission, final report, chap. 11, para. 58.

92. Farquhar, *Back to Basics*.

93. Matthews, "Hard Lessons Learned," 21–24.

94. Author interview with Ofra Graicer.

95. Ryan, "Applications of Complex Systems to Operational Design."

96. Department of the Army, *Full Spectrum Operations*, 38–44.

97. Graves and Stanley, "Design and Operational Art"; Watts, *US Combat Training*, 48–52; Wass de Czege, "Systemic Operational Design"; Naveh, Schneider, and Challans, *Structure of Operational Revolution*; Zweibelson, "To Design or Not to Design"; Zweibelson, "Application of Theory." See also dozens of monographs on SOD from SAMS, Fort Leavenworth, KS.

98. For example, see SAMS, *Art of Design*, 1–7; Department of the Army, *Operations Process*, chaps. 2–3; and Department of the Army, *Operations*, chap. 7.

99. Anderson, "Systemic Operational Design"; Lauder, "Systemic Operational Design." For a broader perspective, see Beaulieu-B. and Dufort, "Conclusion." For Australian examples, see Scott, "Adapt or Die," and other articles in the same issue of the *Australian Army Journal*.

100. Swain, *Fundamentals of Operational Design*, iii–iv.

101. Paz, *Transforming Israel's Security Establishment*, 26.

102. Author interview with Shimon Naveh.

103. Ibid. For context, see Graicer, lecture, February 15, 2016; Graicer, "Self Disruption."

104. Author interview with Shimon Naveh.

105. Ibid.

106. Ibid.

CONCLUSION TO PART II

Part II has illustrated the trials and tribulations of military innovation and transformation. The IDF incorporated conceptual and technological elements of the RMA as part of a decades-long process to adapt its warfighting concept originally sparked by changes to the external strategic environment regarding the proliferation of long-range, unconventional threats and following the internal shock at the IDF's failures during the 1973 war. Innovative weaponry and technology pioneered by the IDF in the 1980s were generally adopted into the army's traditional organizational structures after its successful utilization during the 1982 Bekaa Valley air battle against Syria. The winds of change affected parts of the IDF as it adapted and slowly became "slimmer and smarter," but troops in Lebanon throughout the 1980s and 1990s remained in a conceptual black hole. While sectors of the IDF partially benefited from the technological advances, troops on the ground generally remained in a quagmire in regard to adapting their operational understanding or order of battle to deal with Hezbollah.

The first attempts to solidify some sort of operational concept amid the evolving strategic environment were spearheaded by the cohorts of Maj. Gen. Doron Rubin's "intellectual insurgency." Because of the charisma of Brig. Gen. Shimon Naveh and the associated prestige and promotions it brought proponents and followers, OTRI attempted with partial success to provide commanders with thinking tools and methodologies to deal with the complex new operational reality. The intellectual atmosphere fostered by OTRI permeated segments of the IDF throughout the 1990s and 2000s and successfully encouraged officers to creatively challenge their preexisting conceptions about war and command, despite the fact that some officers lacked the formal education or intellectual stamina to do so.

The IDF's action-oriented, anti-intellectual culture seems to have partially hindered the effective implementation of SOD. The 2006 Israeli state comptroller's report astonishingly noted that three out of every four senior officers who served during the 2006 war had not enrolled in any military college education in the four years prior to the war. A leading military pundit accurately faulted the IDF educational system for some of the shortcomings of 2006 because of large-scale neglect and lack of oversight, which he likened to a "military circus."[1] OTRI cofounder Brig. Gen. (Ret.) Dov Tamari reflected that the IDF's organizational culture and lack of "intellectual process" contributed to its failure to implement a coherent operational concept, owing to an obsession with the "current system" and a failure to look beyond the prevailing paradigm.[2]

While SOD is an eloquent and intellectually impressive methodology, it was said to have failed the test of reality during the 2006 war. The preceding chapters have illustrated that SOD was only utilized on the margins in 2006 and was not mature enough to be implemented on the battlefield. While this does not detract from valid criticisms of SOD regarding its theoretical complexity, its complicated vocabulary, and the confusion it generated regarding command responsibility, the postwar blame game that sought to pin culpability for the IDF's mediocre performance on a specific theoretical concept, operational blunder, or leadership of a specific general is therefore not justified or accurate.[3]

Upon becoming COS in 2004, Lt. Gen. Dan Halutz inherited an army in the midst of a two-decade process of institutional transformation, whose seeds were first planted by COS Lt. Gen. Dan Shomron's "slimmer and smarter" plan and nurtured by successors under the banner of the RMA. The IDF's inability to devise a theoretical or conceptual construct to harness the long-term benefits brought by this technological revolution left the IDF in a conceptual mess.[4] One of the "fathers" of the RMA in Israel, Maj. Gen. (Ret.) Isaac Ben-Israel, recently reflected on the efficacy of the IDF's technological capabilities and lack of coherent doctrine: "This entire aspect of weapons is worthless if it is not integrated within the combat doctrine because the two reinforce each other. The combat doctrine must nurture weapons development, which in turn allows for fulfillment of that doctrine."[5]

The RMA remained ill defined and subject to divergent interpretation by various sectors of the IDF, partially as a result of the IDF's tendency to improvise and its lack of a "culture of writing" to formally outline doctrinal concepts. One colonel involved in doctrine development quipped that the IDF's pre-2006 operational doctrine was a "jungle of concepts."[6] Many diverse and conflicting opinions whizzed around the IDF. For example, many generals active in Lebanon during the 1990s, including the head of the IDF Strategic Planning Division, argued that the IDF never fully utilized the

RMA against Hezbollah during the 1993 or 1996 operations.[7] On the other hand, IDF weapon experts argued that the IDF was too reliant on RMA-inspired technology, held false hopes throughout the 1990s for its effective use against a guerrilla opponent, and questioned the relevance of the US military's transformation for the IDF.[8] IAF brigadier general Itai Brun, former head of research in MI, argued that the 1993 and 1996 operations were carried out dominantly by airpower, less because of the influence of the RMA but more because of societal risk aversion.[9] Another senior general with deep experience in Lebanon argued that the RMA focus led the IDF to emphasize standoff firepower and technology there at the expense of ground maneuver and lamented that capturing and holding Lebanese territory should have been an essential element.[10] Intelligence officers in Lebanon argued that the IDF became too reliant on the RMA and neglected to consider Hezbollah's learning and counteradaptations throughout previous decades.[11] Even within OTRI there were differing views about the impact of the RMA on the development of SOD and whether SOD was "ripe" enough to be utilized on the battlefield.[12]

Despite these views and the IDF's evident shortcomings in 2006, RMA supporters still remain in Israel, such as IAF reserve colonel Shmuel Gordon, the proponent of "counterguerrilla air warfare" in the 1990s who argued that the RMA was validated by the air force and special forces in the first week of the 2006 war and urged continuing the "revolutionary process" inspired by the RMA by "avoiding the massive deployment of armored and ground forces, and emphasizing the integration of the Air Force, Special Forces, and real-time intelligence."[13] As seen from the Winograd Commission and debates within the Israeli defense community today, the efficacy and utility of the RMA and associated elements have not been resolved.

In General Halutz's postwar letter of resignation, he reflected on the transformative processes under way in the years prior to the 2006 war: "One of the main things we learned was that the IDF is deeply influenced by long-term processes. Sometimes, this influence isn't felt, and we aren't aware of its ramifications. These processes have an effect on Israeli society and on the army's ability in particular."[14]

Long-term societal shifts that emerged in the 1980s related to increased casualty aversion, especially in asymmetrical wars and wars launched without national consensus, weakened the role of the IDF as the "people's army." Muddied by societal discontentment with Israel's involvement in the "Lebanese swamp," these trends deeply shaped the IDF's propensity to emphasize standoff firepower and airpower over large-scale ground operations under the banner of the RMA.[15] Defense Minister Amir Peretz reflected on the psychological impact of Israel's historical experience in Lebanon on the top brass's decision-making in 2006:

The army viewed the air campaign as the central instrument of decision, of that there is no doubt. The Chief of Staff led this thinking. If it had worked, he would have been praised to the skies. No one was eager to send in ground forces, especially not with the Lebanese trauma hanging over everyone's head. The truth has to be told: the trauma of the withdrawal from Lebanon hung over the heads of the security cabinet ministers and over the heads of some of the army chiefs.[16]

General Brun noted that much of the early academic scholarship that concluded that the IDF's doctrine signed by Israel's first COS from the air force resulted in an overreliance on airpower and technology provides "superficial analysis to a question that demands much more serious analysis." Brig. Gen. (Res.) Gal Hirsch, who has no love for Halutz, concurred that it is "nonsense" to blame Halutz's air force background and that doing so actually reflects an "immaturity of understanding" the deeper issues.[17] General Brun concluded that "the priority accorded to airpower did not reflect adoption of either EBO or strategic bombing as a foundation. Instead it was, first and foremost, the outcome of a long process of increasing societal and political restraint on military operations."[18] The Winograd Commission added that these postheroic trends were exacerbated "during the long years of hope that there would be no 'real' war anymore and as a result of social processes that are deeply rooted in Western and Israeli societies, which have seeped into the army."[19] In response to such suggestions that he was overly influenced by his air force background, General Halutz adamantly argued in a 2008 interview, "I never said—not as the chief of staff and definitely not during the Second Lebanon War—that the Air Force would decide the campaign. On the contrary, I was asked by the government what would be considered a victory, I told them that there wouldn't be a 'knockout.'"[20]

Halutz was not alone in his hope to avoid a large-scale ground operation. As Benjamin Lambeth has noted, an air operation was viewed by all of Israel's leadership as the best available option for an initial military response. Former COS Lt. Gen. Shaul Mofaz stated in his testimony to the Winograd Commission that "if you can do it from the air, it is better. I do not believe any of us would want to use ground forces if you can attain [objectives] otherwise," while the late former COS Lt. Gen. Amnon Lipkin-Shahak remarked, "I am not sure that any other Chief of Staff would have used the [IAF] less."[21]

The two decades prior to 2006 were marked by uncoordinated efforts to adapt the IDF in an attempt to cope with the changing operational environment, societal shifts related to casualty aversion, and budgetary constraints. A plethora of clashing personalities and different reformist streams percolated relating to officer education, operational art, SOD, Limited Conflict, and effects-based concepts. The IDF was infused with technology-minded officers influenced by the perceived American successes of the RMA during the 1991 Gulf War and the 1999 Kosovo operation and sought to rely on airpower, standoff firepower, and technical solutions for Israel's diverse challenges. Despite such well-intentioned efforts, these different streams of innovation remained uncoordinated and unsystematic and lacked unifying direction from senior staff who themselves were often split between where to focus their efforts and where to give support.

In contrast, the late 1990s marked a transition period in the IDF from its focus on high-intensity RMA-inspired warfare to an era of disproportionate operational focus on counterterrorism and Limited Conflict. General Halutz described the impact on the IDF: "The IDF's state of preparedness didn't manifest itself by a lack of water or a lack of bullets. There is something deeper there that stems from, among other things, the fact that the IDF has been involved in missions that are not purely military ones for the past 20 years. Twenty years is a generation. The commanders of today were born into this reality."[22]

Given the rising threat from Hezbollah and Palestinian terrorism, the pendulum had swung heavily toward LIC as the IDF's RMA programs were not relevant to solving its day-to-day operational predicaments. Paradoxically, in the run-up to 2006, the IDF's force structure, force size, and weapons procurement was focused on RMA-inspired warfare, but the army itself had been operationally focused on LIC, policing, and counterterrorism through much of the previous decade. Defense Minister Peretz reflected on the "erosion" of the IDF's conventional ground-warfare capabilities during this period, especially after the Lebanon withdrawal: "Six years we didn't train. . . . Did someone think the IDF could be put on ice? That everything was OK? I think that since the withdrawal from Lebanon there was a theory that the threats around us had decreased. . . . [Ehud] Barak forged the first conception that the threats had diminished dramatically and therefore greater risks could be taken."[23]

Peretz said elsewhere that in 2006 "Halutz set a new norm while all the others, primarily Mofaz and Yaalon, were looking for a way to dive into the depths in order for people to forget the fact that they were overwhelmingly responsible for the atrophying process of the IDF."[24] He recalled the state of the IDF upon his appointment prior to the war in 2006 and criticized the damaging impact of the RMA-related budgetary diversions away from ground forces training.

> All those experienced people who sat here [in the Defense Ministry prior to 2006] left me an army with no training, no reserves, no budget backing, no technological development against rockets, no feeling of emergency that war would break out. . . . They went with the trend of making cuts in the defense establishment. . . . They continued with the conception of the unfeasibility of war, which created a long process of a decline in the level of training. . . . That

is why we found ourselves with brigades that had not undergone training for five years and with much missing equipment in very sensitive spheres.[25]

There is much validity to these claims, confirmed by the Winograd Commission, as SOD was only one piece of the much greater (albeit muddled) process of innovation and change.[26] Indeed, the IDF was in a conceptual mess for much of the 1990s and early 2000s, grappling with various RMA concepts and how to synthesize and adapt them for use in various operational arenas, while also attempting to mitigate the impact of increased societal sensitivity to casualties and risk aversion. The RMA became Israel's preferred way of war to cope with these challenges. Unfortunately for Israel, the success of the air force, RMA-inspired sensor-to-shooter capabilities, and precision targeting ultimately did not adequately factor in the adaptability of Hezbollah and the group's ability to dampen the IDF's technological prowess.[27]

Hezbollah challenged the IDF's RMA-inspired, technocentric way of war by devising a military approach uniquely tailored to its operational context and utilizing a relatively simple but effective mode of warfare. Hezbollah southern commander Sheikh Nabil Qawook elucidated the group's fundamental ability to circumvent IDF conventional superiority: "The issue was not the technology of our missiles as some Israelis claimed after the war. The issue was determination, creativity, and innovation in the battlefield."[28]

The IDF was prepared to fight a totally different type of war than the one it faced in 2006, as Hezbollah's unconventional guerrilla paradigm, based on lessons learned over previous decades, utilized concealment, camouflaged bunkers, deception, and fighting in low-signature cells among the local population. This mode of warfare denied the IDF the opportunity to target its centers of gravity and limited the effectiveness of the IDF's air strikes and precision targeting. Hezbollah prevented the IDF from achieving anything resembling decisive victory in 2006 by emphasizing its own organizational survivability ("victory by not losing") and adopting an attritional paradigm centered on the resilient and persistent concentration of rocket fire against Israeli population centers.[29] This "rocket doctrine" was enhanced throughout the preceding decade based on critical lessons learned during the 1993 and 1996 operations regarding the importance of expanding the range and redundancy of its rocket arsenal.

Hezbollah's operational approach in 2006 included irregular elements, asymmetrical tactics, and hit-and-run guerrilla attacks, coupled with uniformed conventional elements that used offensive and defensive tactics whose primary mission was to hold ground in an attempt to prevent, or at least delay, the IDF from capturing Hezbollah's rocket-launching areas.[30] Hezbollah avoided playing into the IDF's strengths through its mastery of an effective mode of warfare that resembled, in the words of Sec.-Gen. Hassan Nasrallah, "an unparalleled new school that functions as a combination of a regular army and guerrilla fighters."[31] Summing up the IDF's greatest mistake, General Brun lamented that "the collection of understandings developed in the decade preceding the war did not represent an alternative doctrine that could have served as a solid basis for responding to the challenge presented by Hezbollah."[32] Hence, as the scholar Eliot Cohen has written, "the enemy never really figured very much into the RMA debate, and this may have been the worst mistake of all."[33]

NOTES

1. Alex Fishman, "A Military Circus," *Yediot Ahronoth*, December 6, 2006.
2. Tamari, "Operation Danny."
3. For example, see Winograd Commission, final report, chap. 11, paras. 7–8.
4. Adamsky, *Culture of Military Innovation*, 108–9.
5. Ben-Israel, "Use of Weapons in Densely Populated Areas," 22.
6. Author interview with Giora Segal.
7. Author interview with Shlomo Brom.
8. Bonen, "Sophisticated Conventional War."
9. Brun, "Second Lebanon War," 307.
10. Eitam, lecture, July 12, 2012.
11. Author interview with Ronen Cohen.
12. Author interview with Zvi Lanir.
13. Gordon, "Why Is the IDF Failing?"
14. Haloutz, "Letter of Resignation."
15. Brun, lecture, September 16, 2008.
16. Peretz, interview, May 3, 2007.
17. Hirsch, *Defensive Shield*, 376.
18. Brun, "Second Lebanon War," 306. For an example of blaming airpower, see Kreps, "2006 Lebanon War." For insightful rebuttals of such assertions, see Lambeth, *Air Operations*, 282–98; Berman, "Beyond the Basics," 4–5.
19. Winograd Commission, final report, chap. 11, para. 31.
20. Halutz, interview, February 15, 2008.
21. Quoted in Lambeth, *Air Operations*, 294–95.
22. Halutz, interview, February 15, 2008.
23. Peretz, interview, May 3, 2007.
24. Peretz, interview, February 17, 2008.
25. Peretz, interview, May 3, 2007.
26. Winograd Commission, final report, chap. 7, paras. 40–41.
27. Marcus, "Israeli Revolution in Military Affairs," 107–8.
28. Quoted in part 2 of the two-part documentary *God's Chariot*, Al-Jazeera English, May 14, 2007.
29. Tira, *Nature of War*, 115.

30. Author interview with senior IDF officers, November 2015. For two perspectives on Hezbollah's mode of warfare, see Hoffman, *Conflict in the 21st Century*; Biddle and Friedman, *2006 Lebanon Campaign*.

31. Nasrallah, speech, February 22, 2008.

32. Brun, "Second Lebanon War," 323.

33. Cohen, "Change and Transformation in Military Affairs," 402.

CONCLUSIONS

The most dangerous enemy of Israel's security is the conceptual inertia of those responsible for its security.

—David Ben-Gurion

The trajectory of the IDF's odyssey in Lebanon and its strategic and operational decision-making throughout the security zone period, the 2000 withdrawal, and the 2006 war were shaped by the army's (in)ability to adapt. This book explains the complexity and "messiness" of military adaptation related to the IDF's conceptualization of the threat in Lebanon, its strategic approach to confront Hezbollah, and the IDF's operational concept for warfighting. It tells the story of slow strategic adaptation and disjointed operational adaptation, in which civilian-military relations, geostrategic context, institutional dynamics, domestic pressures, and organizational culture each shaped the IDF's adaptation in Lebanon.[1] This conclusion thematically summarizes the major factors that promoted or hindered adaptation in the IDF related to the central strategic and operational milestones of the conflict. A dynamic interplay of the main schools of thought of military innovation—civil-military relations, rivalry and competition (including emulation), and organizational culture—had an overarching and nuanced effect on processes of change on both sides of the Israel-Hezbollah conflict. An examination of the drivers and shapers of change illustrates the complementary and interdependent effects these factors had on IDF adaptation in Lebanon and highlights the inherent challenges of adapting under fire in protracted conflict.

THE IDF AND HEZBOLLAH: DUELING RIVALS
IN PROTRACTED CONFLICT

As Clausewitz wrote, "war is a nothing but a duel on a larger scale," and the underlying trigger for much of the adaptation in the IDF was the threat from and lethality of Hezbollah's guerrilla warfare as part of the "duel" between competing adversaries. The grinding attritional impact of Hezbollah's guerrilla warfare contributed to a strategic and operational reevaluation in the IDF that deeply affected its modus operandi in Lebanon throughout the decades. The IDF's own adaptation caused major strategic and operational innovation in Hezbollah that engaged in its own sophisticated organizational learning and adaptation. Hezbollah benefited from the lack of attention the IDF devoted to Lebanon in the 1980s and early 1990s, which granted Hezbollah the strategic space to adapt and refine its modus operandi as it moved away from suicide bombings and frontal hill-storming toward night assaults and guerrilla ambushes (see chapter 1). The assassination of Sec.-Gen. Abbas Mussawi in 1992 acted as an impetus for Hezbollah to improve its organizational security and command structure and led to the increased utilization of short-range rocket fire against the Israeli home front.

Hezbollah's learning experiences with the IDF throughout the 1990s led to its refinement and mastery of guerrilla warfare, IED attacks, and antitank operations. Hezbollah's observations of Israeli societal casualty aversion, sensitivity to rocket fire, and the IDF's increased preference for RMA-inspired airpower and standoff firepower during the 1993 and 1996 operations (see chapter 6) led Hezbollah to refine its military paradigm put into play in 2006, which emphasized organizational survivability, a strategy of "winning by not losing," resilience through its sophisticated network of bunkers, and a versatile and redundant rocket capability to target Israeli population centers that increased its own deterrent strength.

Lt. Col. (Res.) Ron Tira has perceptively described the IDF and Hezbollah as having fought "parallel wars" during the 2006 war, in which each adopted a conflicting war paradigm that mirrored the weaknesses of the opponent. As described in chapter 8, in 2006 the IDF fought to achieve military decision based on the decisive use of airpower, limited ground engagements, and destruction of Hezbollah targets using RMA-inspired firepower, while Hezbollah fought to survive and wear down the resilience of the IDF and Israeli society through persistent rocket fire and guerrilla warfare. The IDF operated within the framework of Hezbollah's military paradigm and "played the part scripted by Hezbollah" by exchanging standoff firepower for an extended period of time and delaying a larger ground campaign. Meanwhile, Hezbollah was able to target IDF troops operating in the Lebanese villages and strike the Israeli home front with rockets that acted as Israel's center of gravity and dramatically shaped early perceptions of disappointment with the war in Israel. Notably, the IDF was still able to achieve its operational goals of destroying thousands of Hezbollah targets and killing hundreds of Hezbollah fighters (but not the overly lofty strategic goals set by Prime Minister Ehud Olmert) yet was unable to prevent Hezbollah from achieving its own limited war goals.[2]

Former deputy head of the IAF Maj. Gen. (Ret.) Giora Romm has argued that the 2006 war "reflected two strategies with practically no intersecting points," as the IDF's strategy was based on air superiority with the hopes of a rapid culmination of victory, while Hezbollah's strategy was based on steadfastness, attrition, and persistent rocket fire. In an apt metaphor, the rival strategies resembled "two ships passing in the night," as each side was able to achieve its operational goals without overly affecting or preventing the achievement of the goals of its adversary.[3] This posed a direct challenge to the IDF, which historically sought rapid and overwhelming military decision, and ultimately proves that "classical" military decision is not possible for the IDF in protracted conflict.

This realization contributed to the development of the IDF's Dahiya doctrine and its 2015 official document *IDF Strategy*, which reconceptualized strategic success as the achievement of deterrence to delay the next round of fighting. This in turn led Hezbollah to threaten Israel's critical infrastructure with rocket fire and Israel's northern villages with commando incursions in its own effort to instill deterrence (see chapter 4). Israel and Hezbollah continue to engage in a dialectical cycle of learning and adaptation just as in Clausewitz's famously described "wrestling match," as each attempts to render its adversary incapable of further resistance by adapting a warfighting concept built on its traditional strengths while circumventing the strengths of the rival. This complex "duel" of innovation and adaptation was affected by several drivers and shapers of change.

A DYSFUNCTIONAL CIVIL-MILITARY DYNAMIC

The IDF's evolving conceptualization of Hezbollah and the strategic adaptation of its use of deterrence was deeply affected by the dysfunctional civil-military dynamic in Israel. The most damning aspect of the IDF's involvement in Lebanon was the poor articulation of strategy during the security zone period (1985–2000) by both civilian and military leaders. As chapter 1 demonstrated, after the opening phases of the 1982 Lebanon War and the haphazard establishment of the security zone in 1985, the Lebanon conflict was sidelined strategically because of a lack of a significant threat to the IDF. Throughout most of the IDF's eighteen-year occupation of the security zone, Lebanon was not the main strategic focus of the IDF. In the late 1980s and 1990s, the IDF was primarily concerned with Syria's bellicose military, long-range and nonconventional threats from Iraq, and Palestinian militancy. The political echelon was busy containing blowback from the First Intifada and was later deeply engaged in the peace process with the Palestinian Authority throughout the 1990s. The conflict in Lebanon was allowed to fester and was sidelined strategically, which often led to the IDF's being more reactive than proactive on the strategic and operational levels there.

Throughout the 1990s, the IDF had only a limited ability to shape Israel's broader strategy in Lebanon because of the civilian echelon's involvement in peace negotiations with Syria (Hezbollah's patron), which indirectly restrained the IDF and forced the army to cyclically engage Hezbollah on the tactical level, without clear strategic goals or objectives. This resulted in the "tactical-ization of strategy" for the IDF, which allowed Hezbollah's tactical achieve-ments vis-à-vis the IDF to resonate on the strategic level because of the IDF's inability to change the fundamental strategic equation of the conflict while remaining an occupying power. The IDF's goal elusively became "maintain-ing the quiet" for Israel's northern communities while also attempting to ensure the political and strategic space for the political echelon carrying out sensitive negotiations with Syria. The lack of overall direction and the restraint imposed on the IDF from the civilian echelon forced the army to fight Hezbollah with "one hand tied behind its back," leading to the slow attrition of the IDF by Hezbollah, which inflicted a relatively low but steady number of combat deaths (averaging twenty per year). The strategic mandate confined IDF activities to reactive and restrained operations and forced the IDF to assume a relatively defensive posture vis-à-vis Hezbollah that slowly eroded Israeli deterrence and societal morale.

The political echelon's lack of strategic clarity obfuscated the IDF's goals in Lebanon, as commanders there had different perceptions and priorities than the politicians, who were more concerned with keeping the quiet in order not to jeopardize ongoing negotiations with Syria or elicit a barrage of Hezbollah rocket fire on the Israeli home front that might jeopardize their political standing. As discussed in chapter 2, Hezbollah's incessant guerrilla warfare did eventually force military commanders facing the difficult opera-tional reality in Lebanon to push back against the restraint of the politicians. Notably, upon becoming head of Northern Command, Maj. Gen. Amiram Levin created new benchmarks for success and adapted the IDF's previously static, defensive modus operandi in Lebanon. General Levin's appointment marked the first time a military commander significantly adapted the IDF's tempo of operations and reshaped operational goals and priorities, by attempting to regain initiative and enhance IDF deterrence with offensive commando strikes against Hezbollah.

Visionary officers such as General Levin changed the IDF's conceptual-ization of Hezbollah from a "terrorist group" to a "guerrilla army," created a new mission focus and operational responsibilities, and developed a new unit—the Egoz counterguerrilla battalion—to develop innovative tactics for Lebanon. The IDF's adaptation of its approach toward Hezbollah was profoundly influenced by processes of bottom-up innovation carried out by the Egoz unit, which received autonomy and operational freedom from the senior command to devise new counterguerrilla warfare tactics. The shapers of Levin's innovative reorientation were the rising threat from Hezbollah, his receptivity to officers in Lebanon who lamented their lack of tactical know-how for counterguerrilla warfare, and the eventual support of key figures in the top brass, illustrating the dynamic interplay between top-down and bottom-up processes of change.[4]

With very little input from civilian leaders, General Levin successfully changed the operational realities on the ground, having influenced like-minded military officers, including COS Lt. Gen. Amnon Lipkin-Shahak, to grant him leeway to take a more assertive and resourceful approach in Lebanon. Levin did not enjoy smooth relations with the political echelon and engaged in several high-profile disagreements with Prime Minister Yitzhak Rabin in the mid-1990s, characterized by Rabin's office publicly rebuking him "to simply shut up" in 1995. In the late 1990s, other senior military officers publicly pushed back against the civilian echelon for the constraints imposed on the IDF by the "rules of the game." Civilian leaders clung to the "understandings" with Hezbollah established after the 1993 and 1996 operations and exerted restraint on the IDF top brass, which was forced to toe the line and abide by the rules. Ultimately, the civilian echelon inhibited the IDF's ability to adapt strategically, as the understandings with Hezbollah limited the IDF's means to respond and eroded deterrence.

While the civilian echelon in the security zone period generally acted as an inhibitor of military adaptation, determined civilian leaders from outside the military establishment, such as Defense Minister Moshe Arens during his brief tenure in 1999, made a concerted effort to adapt the IDF's strategy for containing Hezbollah and had a nuanced effect on shaping IDF deterrence, as recounted in chapter 3. In contrast to the IDF's policy of attempting to leverage Hezbollah's support base (with standoff firepower) to pressure the governments of Lebanon and Syria to rein in Hezbollah, Defense Minister Arens sought to shift away from Israel's abidance of the rules of the game toward a strategy of applying direct pressure against those who allowed Hezbollah to operate with impunity (the Lebanese government) and supply it militarily (Syria). Arens, in his role as a determined civilian leader concerned with impending strategic failure, attempted with mixed success to adapt IDF policies. While Arens's tenure in 1999 as defense minister was short-lived, his efforts to reshape Israeli deterrence toward the state-on-state sphere did indirectly influence elements of its deterrence approach in the early 2000s, as well as the IDF's Dahiya doctrine in the post-2006 period discussed in chapter 4, which involved directly targeting Lebanese infrastructure with massive displays of destructive firepower to drive home the high price of Hezbollah provocations.

The most important episode of strategic change was Prime Minister Ehud Barak's decision to withdraw from Lebanon after eighteen years, carried out as a result of a combination of military, political, and domestic factors. Highlighted in chapter 3, the grinding effects of occupying the security zone, eroding societal morale, domestic pressures from protest movements, and the subtle discontent of some IDF officers led to the realization by Barak that remaining in the "Lebanese mud" was not serving Israel's strategic goals. This led to the eventual unilateral withdrawal in 2000 under the pretext that it would improve Israel's bargaining position in Syrian peace negotiations. Notably, Prime Minister Barak, who was also acting defense minister at the time, overcame the disapproval of nearly all eighteen senior generals to carry out a unilateral withdrawal from Lebanon. The IDF was not opposed to a withdrawal per se under a negotiated agreement with Syria and Lebanon but was opposed to a unilateral withdrawal, fearing the symbolic effect it would have on the IDF's deterrent posture.[5] The decision marks a major strategic adaptation driven primarily by domestic concerns and civilian leader perseverance in the face of IDF opposition and highlights the critical role that civilian leaders have on changing the strategic equation. However, an improvisational decision-making process, an unrealistic assessment of postwithdrawal scenarios (Barak downplayed army assessments that a withdrawal would not placate Hezbollah), and a lack of other options seriously considered by the civilian echelon except those offered by the IDF ultimately highlight the deep effect the dysfunctional civil-military dynamic had on hindering processes of change and obfuscating adaptation. As described in chapter 8, these same pathologies reemerged during the 2006 war and again plagued the IDF's wartime decision-making cycle, especially pertaining to the formulation of militarily achievable objectives and the torturous deliberations on if and when to launch a large-scale ground offensive.[6]

THE MILITARY AS THE ENGINE OF OPERATIONAL CHANGE

Given the clout the IDF enjoys compared to the civilian establishment regarding security issues, military leaders dominated the major processes of operational and organizational change. The strength of the military establishment and the abundance of retired generals in the political establishment have historically allowed the IDF to rapidly implement innovative programs without significant bureaucratic wrangling or red tape. While the civilian echelon had an important role in influencing strategic elements of the conflict and restraining the IDF, it had almost no influence on initiating major operational innovation regarding the IDF's warfighting concept. The drivers of change that led the IDF to adapt its way of war were related to sociological shifts in Israeli society linked to "postheroism" and casualty aversion, the advent of new technologies, and perceived operational necessity related to the changing nature of the enemy following the 1973 war. As noted in chapter 5, the IDF was the first to utilize the technologies and methods associated with the RMA but slow to develop a theoretical or conceptual framework for their use. The successes of the "revolutionary" technologies tested and battle-proven by the IDF in the 1982 Bekaa Valley air battle against Syria led to the enthusiastic adoption of the associated means and methods. This contributed to the IDF's transformation influenced by the RMA, a process originally spearheaded from the top down in the late 1980s by COS Lt. Gen. Dan Shomron and his "slimmer and smarter" plan and promoted by Lt. Gen. Ehud Barak after the IDF witnessed external validation of the RMA in the 1991 Gulf War. The IDF was the engine for operational change, and the enthusiastic embrace of RMA capabilities and the concerted focus of the top brass over the ensuing two decades led to the relatively rapid adaptation of the IDF's force structure and operational preferences (see chapters 5 and 6). The IDF's "doer" ethos and its cultural proclivity for action led to the development, implementation, and utilization of these innovative technologies (even before the American military), despite warnings from some Israeli civilian defense officials of the need to carefully adopt these technologies into a suitable conceptual framework.[7]

Chapter 7 told the story of the innovative operational concepts that were developed by the military mavericks at OTRI, which also acted as an institutional engine for change in the IDF. Visionary officers such as Brig. Gen. Shimon Naveh defined new ways and means of understanding war and created means for professional prestige and promotion by adherence to OTRI's methodologies. SOD diffused through processes internal to the military, facilitated by midlevel officers identified as rising stars. The quintessential maverick, General Naveh, "championed his product," and his personal role as a charismatic and determined military leader was essential to advancing the process. Institutional support he received from key IDF officials, including the COS and the deputy COS, helped accelerate the innovation process within the original incubator of Central Command. However, as discussed in chapters 8 and 9, the immediate prestige offered to adopters of SOD led many to adopt the methodology and operational vocabulary in a piecemeal or superficial fashion, which led to inconsistent, idiosyncratic interpretation and inappropriate application in the 2006 war. Civilian leaders had no discernible effect on the operational innovations associated with OTRI other than to eventually order its closure via a state comptroller's report in 2005, though with the backing of COS Lt. Gen. Dan Halutz.

THE TOXIC EFFECT OF
INTRAORGANIZATIONAL COMPETITION

Intraorganizational competition led to the development of a cleavage between the better-funded and better-equipped IAF and the neglected ground forces (especially reserve units), which were devoid of serious training and adequate resources in the years prior to the 2006 war. This schism was largely because of the trajectory of the RMA and its impact on the IDF defense budget and technological acquisitions and the perceived (rather than actual) operational priorities. As illustrated in chapters 5 and 6, the IAF and special forces were given prioritization by the top brass and were allocated disproportionate resources and technologies as the RMA took hold. A chasm developed between the capabilities and resources of the IAF and the ground forces, who competed for funds, with the IAF ultimately prevailing. The IAF invested in expensive air and space platforms, precision and standoff technology, and network-centric systems. Ground units suffered large training, supply, and acquisition cuts, the disastrous repercussions of which were highlighted in chapter 8 with the sloppy tactical performances and numerous logistical short-comings (e.g., a shortage of basic supplies for reserve soldiers), which resulted in strategically damaging errors in the 2006 war. This prioritization by the defense establishment of the IAF resulted in internal competition between the two services and led to polarization between highly trained and well-equipped "chosen" units that enjoyed the full benefits of the RMA and a large number of neglected, ill-equipped ground units, especially in the reserves.[8]

From an operational perspective, significant rivalry and intraorganizational competition between OTRI and the rest of the IDF hindered a thorough or systematic implementation of SOD. Highlighted in the OTRI saga in chapter 7, friction between those in the IDF establishment inherently resis-tant to change and ingrained in their battle-tested norms and the mavericks in OTRI pushing dramatically different methodologies acted as a major institutional impediment to the more systematic application of SOD. General Naveh's rambunctious and crass command style undoubtedly caused friction between OTRI "insiders" and "outsiders," and, because rivalries within the IDF were never pacified, when several key protectors of OTRI were eventu-ally forced out, OTRI was left vulnerable to its opponents who were able to systematically purge OTRI from the IDF.

Owing to the intimate nature of the IDF, interservice rivalry in wartime tends to be less of an inhibitor of adaptation because those in the General Staff are actively encouraged to lose their distinct service identity. However, it has been suggested that there may have been some "natural inner resent-ment" from the General Staff regarding the appointment of General Halutz as the first COS in IDF history to come from the air force, which may have caused friction and internal rivalry. Halutz dubiously claimed in 2015 that he felt he was a "blue" airman in a "green" military during the war and that "the General Staff would have done anything to see me fail."[9] The ground forces commanders in the General Staff may have perceived and assumed (with only partial accuracy) that Halutz's command style and operational proclivities as a former IAF fighter pilot would be airpower-centric. However, as discussed in chapter 8, there is no evidence to indicate that ground forces generals actively worked against Halutz during the war, especially as they too had an initial preference for standoff operations and no keen desire to wage a large-scale ground offensive against Hezbollah in which ground troops would inevitably incur casualties.[10] Petty rivalry did exist between individual commanders in the 2006 war, such as the head of Northern Command, Maj. Gen. Udi Adam, squabbling concurrently with General Halutz and OTRI confidante Brig. Gen. Gal Hirsch, the Ninety-First Division's commander. Eventually Halutz replaced Adam for his incompetence midwar with his confidante Maj. Gen. Moshe Kaplinsky, another opponent of Hirsch.[11] While interpersonal rivalry and egoism did affect the IDF command, it seems that other shapers of adaptation had a more profound effect on the overall trajectory of the war and innovation processes.

DOMESTIC PRESSURE AS A KEY DRIVER OF CHANGE

Domestic pressure had a profound impact on the strategic trajectory of the conflict as the Israeli public became increasingly averse to the IDF's continued occupation of Lebanon, with its mounting casualties and several high-profile military blunders. As is the case in other protracted conflicts, the gap between set goals and the actual degree of progression in Israeli-Syrian negotiations amid ongoing guerrilla warfare in Lebanon led to disillusionment in increasingly large sectors of society and fueled calls for withdrawal. In a way, the domestic population entered into fierce competition with the IDF in the late 1990s to shape Israel's Lebanon policy. As described in chapter 3, political leaders were forced to navigate the treacherous rivalry between increasingly vocal domestic protest groups and the IDF, while attempting to avoid demoralizing troops and angering commanders in the field. Senior officers such as Brig. Gen. Erez Gerstein, head of the Lebanon Liaison Unit, often publicly castigated the protesting social movements that were pushing for a withdrawal, while the Four Mothers Movement intensely lobbied the political echelon to withdraw the IDF from Lebanon.

With the election of Barak, the Four Mothers Movement, in effect, "won" in its competition with the IDF, as domestic pressures and internal politics were central drivers in facilitating the IDF's withdrawal in 2000. The withdrawal occurred at a time when the IDF had assumed an increasingly defensive posture, which had actually resulted in a significant reduction in IDF losses over the two years prior to withdrawal (i.e., in 1998, there were twenty-four killed, which dropped to thirteen in 1999, and nine in the first half of 2000). This exemplifies the strength of domestic pressures on civilian leaders but also how external perceptions and domestic considerations affect strategic change and the overall trajectory of conflict, regardless of facts on the ground.

THE DANGERS OF UNCRITICAL EMULATION

A major theme within the IDF over the last two decades is its overreliance on lessons learned from the experiences of the American military. The IDF's close relationship with the US and other Western militaries has brought many intellectual, technological, and practical advantages but has sometimes resulted in "automatic" emulation or institutional imitation without sufficiently balancing local sources of knowledge and learning. The former head of the IDF Concept Development and Doctrine Department noted in an article in the IDF's journal that the IDF maintained an overreliance on the US military and uncritically adopted many strategic and operational principles, especially related to the transformational concepts associated with the RMA.[12] Contrary to the diverse sources of knowledge that the IDF drew from in its formative decades, which it synthesized into its local context, after the 1973 war the IDF tended to overly focus on learning from the US military, part of a larger trend of Americanization in the IDF and in Israeli society more broadly.[13] Partially because the US military became the IDF's chief weapon supplier after 1973, and also because Arab states largely adopted Soviet doctrine and weaponry, the IDF looked with aspiration to the US military for "verified" lessons.

The US military underwent its transformation based on the revolutionary operational concepts seemingly validated in the Gulf War, the Kosovo campaign, and during the earliest stages of the Afghanistan and Iraq Wars. The enthusiastic embrace of these concepts by the US military had a profound effect on the trajectory and acceleration of the RMA globally, and, as discussed in chapter 5, the IDF was quick to emulate the Americans and adopt these principles, which validated its own budding operational concepts. However, as seen in chapters 6 and 8, the IDF's overreliance on standoff firepower and precision technology for use in Lebanon did not take into account the fact that Hezbollah had dug in and was able to strike the Israeli home front throughout the duration of conflict, a key variable that did not exist in any of the American campaigns.[14] Socially, the Americanization of Israeli society and its shift toward individualization and self-realization over national sacrifice and collective responsibility has affected IDF risk-taking and casualty aversion and contributed to the adoption of aspects of the RMA related to reducing the need for large ground formations.[15] Such societal shifts exacerbated domestic concerns related to casualty aversion and utilizing a greater number of ground troops, which deeply affected the IDF's hesitant decision to launch a large-scale ground campaign during the 2006 war.

Additionally, with General Naveh having already shown interest in the Americans' AirLand Battle conceptual framework in the 1980s, the successes of the Gulf War demonstrated the US military's mastery of operational art and reaffirmed the need for the IDF to embrace such modes of operational thinking. Because of their close cooperation, OTRI adopted (and adapted) some elements of the conceptual revolution being spearheaded by the DOD's Office of Net Assessment throughout the 1990s and 2000s. This brought OTRI greater intellectual and reputational prestige, opened doors to the US defense community, and accelerated the implementation of SOD into the IDF.

The IDF did not sufficiently internalize the limits of learning and adaptation from foreign experiences and did not adequately factor in Israel's unique circumstances, culture, and operational environment before carrying out uncritical emulation. The US military's dominant status—its size, resources, freedom of maneuver internationally, and geographic distance from enemies—should inform Israel's more discerning adoption of American concepts. The IDF's experiences in 2006 should act as a cautionary tale for military organizations worldwide before they adopt foreign concepts in a blanket fashion. Uncritical emulation inadvertently reduced the overall depth of knowledge in the IDF, limited available operational options, and, in many cases, resulted in learning that was not relevant to the IDF's unique strategic circumstances and operational requirements in Lebanon.

The overly enthusiastic adoption of the US military's technocentric principles led the former head of the IDF's Concept Development and Doctrine Department to write in the IDF journal *Maarachot* that the IDF seemed to have overemphasized RMA-inspired technology, contrary to its traditional focus on its qualitative military edge based on the personal characteristics of its creative and adaptable commanders. He argued that the IDF must reembrace its traditional cultural strengths related to the quality, creativity, flexibility, and autonomy of its soldiers rather than the reflexive reliance on advanced technological weapon systems.[16] The Winograd Commission reiterated this point: "The investment in the quality and competence of the commanders and troops is sometimes more important than the investment in the quality of the equipment at their disposal, and it is essential for the purpose of making the optimal use of the sophisticated and expensive equipment that the IDF needs."[17]

THE IMPORTANCE OF ORGANIZATIONAL CULTURE

The open and dynamic nature of Israeli military culture that emphasizes action and improvisation deeply affected all aspects of innovation, adaptation, and the IDF's modus operandi in Lebanon. The IDF's overarching strategic approach throughout its experience in Lebanon was to respond to major Hezbollah provocations with large displays of force to exact a "high price." It has been suggested that the IDF's assertive use of deterrent strikes resembles a long-cultivated strategic reflex.[18] This proclivity is partially shaped by the IDF's historical experience using deterrence by punishment in its early history, exemplified by David Ben-Gurion, who declared in 1953, "Unless we show the Arabs that there is a high price to pay for murdering Jews, we won't survive."[19] The IDF's earliest combat experiences had a formative effect on the military's modus operandi in ensuing decades that is deeply imbued in the strategic culture of the organization. The preference for rapid retaliation to instill deterrence resembles a culturally compatible strategy for action, as elements of the IDF's traditional use of deterrence are evident in the 1993 Operation Accountability and the 1996 Operation Grapes of Wrath (see chapter 2). Reflecting historical continuity, highlighted in chapter 4, the IDF's emphasis on deterrence since the 2006 war has again been articulated in its Dahiya doctrine, meant to inflict massive damage on Hezbollah areas in response to any provocation.

The IDF's relatively informal and open organizational culture enabled commanders on the ground to initiate processes of significant change from the bottom up. In chapter 2, Maj. Gen. Amiram Levin's reconceptualization of Hezbollah was shaped by his openness as a commander, where soldiers felt free to engage and raise concerns with senior officers, as IDF soldiers traditionally maintain a certain amount of "chutzpah" that enables them to confront superiors. IDF culture granted soldiers autonomy and enabled those "on the bottom" to confront General Levin, whom they viewed as more responsive than his predecessor in Northern Command. Levin alerted the top brass to a problem and convinced them of the need to delegate autonomy and authority to battle-hardened mavericks in the field who would develop tactical solutions as part of the newly created Egoz unit. The rapid operationalization of the unit, whose task was centered on promoting tactical adaptation and bottom-up learning to bring the rest of the army up to speed, was enabled by IDF culture and resembles a culturally compatible pattern of Israeli military adaptation.[20]

The culturally enabled pattern of innovation was also seen in chapter 7 in the drive to improve operational-level thinking in the IDF. Reform-minded officers such as Maj. Gen. Doron Rubin and General Naveh encouraged the top brass to delegate authority to OTRI to solve the specific problem relating to the dearth of operational-level knowledge in the IDF. Once OTRI was delegated autonomy to develop solutions in response to perceived shortcomings related to operational art, it was able to devise innovative methodologies that diffused relatively rapidly throughout army echelons. Just as the Egoz unit developed innovative tactics to improve the army's ability to wage counterguerrilla warfare, OTRI attempted to bring the army up to speed by developing methodologies to improve operational art in the IDF. A similar pattern was apparent in chapter 6 with the rise of the Limited Conflict doctrine, where, in response to a lack of utility of the IDF's methods against Hezbollah and in an attempt to solve the IDF's problem with Hezbollah's attritional warfare, in just a few years a small number of intelligence officers in Lebanon led by Col. Shmuel Nir were able to rapidly shift the IDF's operational concept toward an emphasis on "fatiguing" Hezbollah.

This pattern of innovation, where change and adaptation is spearheaded by a specialized unit whose task is to solve the IDF's specific problem, led scholars in one seminal article to write, "Israeli operational concepts often resemble keys carefully crafted to fit particular locks, rather than a general approach to the problem of opening doors."[21] Shaped by the IDF's earliest combat experiences of flexibly learning and improvising under fire, this paradigm led to an ingrained emphasis on innovative tactical problem solving and organic lesson learning in the army's lower echelons, often by hyperspecialized units.[22] The cultural proclivity for action and immediate tactical solutions sometimes led to short-term, superficial responses and a general dearth of deep strategic thinking.[23] However, if changes to the fundamental or underlying strategic equation are not possible (barring an Arab-Israeli peace agreement), rapid innovation and improvisation on lower levels of the organization can be considered a major strength of the IDF and an essential element to buy time and space for strategic-level solutions.[24]

Israeli strategic culture has an ingrained casualty aversion owing to the influence of Jewish values and the collective trauma inherent in Israel's founding in the aftermath of the Holocaust, which led to heightened sensitivity to casualties by the IDF and Israeli society. The small and intimate culture of the IDF, the strong sense of trust, purpose, and shared values within units, and the perception that the IDF fights wars of survival out of "no choice" historically led to maintaining high troop morale and cohesion. Notably, the 1982 Lebanon War marked Israel's first "war of choice" and badly dented Israel's favorable perceptions of the military and its role in society in ensuing decades.[25] The slow, grinding attrition in Lebanon contributed to the increasing societal pressure that weighed on the shoulders of Prime Minister Barak, who advocated for a withdrawal as part of his election campaign. In the years occupying the security zone, IDF combat deaths averaged twenty per year, hardly a high number for a country with hundreds of fatal road accidents every year. However, the sacrosanct value of IDF soldiers and the cultural importance of the army in society as the guarantors of Jewish survival, combined with the personal nature of Israeli society "where everyone knows everyone," led social protest movements comprising mothers of soldiers serving in Lebanon to mobilize a large portion of society, which eventually culminated in the strategically significant 2000 withdrawal discussed in chapter 3. The intimate nature of Israeli society, sensitivity to casualties, and the societal importance of reservists who are drafted from the general population greatly influenced the IDF's hesitant decision-making in 2006 over the launching of a ground operation and mobilizing reserve units for ground combat.

The IDF's cultural sensitivity to casualties contributed to the enthusiastic embrace of the RMA and standoff precision technology that could be used to replace soldiers on the battlefield and avoid messy ground operations. The IDF's postheroism in Lebanon was exacerbated by the low existential danger of LIC and the rise of sophisticated RMA technology, which made casualty avoidance more feasible.[26] Furthermore, personnel downsizing to create a slimmer and smarter IDF as part of the budgetary cutbacks of the RMA era affected IDF culture by damaging "the psychological contract between an organization and its downsizing survivors." Training cuts, especially to reserve units, reduced opportunities for confidence building in their battle skills and also affected unit cohesion and morale.[27]

From an operational perspective, the IDF's open and informal culture, its relatively flat organizational structures, and its small, intimate nature facilitated experimentation and the rapid operationalization of innovative RMA technologies in the 1980s and 1990s (see chapters 5 and 6). It enabled the rapid institutionalization and transmission of SOD and related ideas between informal networks in the IDF (see chapter 7). As Dima Adamsky has noted, the IDF was the first to use RMA technology in the 1980s because of its action-oriented, "doer" ethos and emphasis on field experience, initiative, and rapid results but was notably slow in developing a systematic theoretical construct or plan for harnessing the full potential of the RMA.[28] These cultural tendencies have been reflected in the IDF's characterization as an army of doers rather than thinkers.[29] The historical lack of formalized doctrine, an absence of a "culture of writing," nonemphasis on formal military education, and a tendency to prefer action over theory ultimately contributed to the haphazard implementation of the RMA and the institutional shortfalls regarding implementing OTRI's ideas, as too few officers critically challenged SOD intellectually and led to the superficial adoption of the jargon and concepts.[30] As discussed in chapter 9, this contributed to the inconsistent interpretation and piecemeal adoption of SOD and related ideas, which greatly confounded the IDF's operational concept in 2006.

The IDF's experience in Lebanon highlights the importance of a delicate cultural balance between encouraging initiative, improvisation, flexibility, and agility on the one hand and, on the other, institutionalizing theoretical insights, encouraging systematic decision-making processes, and adhering to organizational norms, procedures, and regulations. The IDF's informal organizational culture and action-oriented ethos acted as a double-edged sword, often resulting in tactical audacity and operational ingenuity throughout its involvement in Lebanon, while occasionally resulting in flawed decision-making processes and haphazard institutional and organizational dynamics.

Strategically, from the origins of the conflict, IDF organizational culture inhibited long-term thinking and systematic planning about its strategic goals throughout the security zone period. It also led to the IDF's overly reactive rather than proactive application of force regarding its deterrent strikes in response to Hezbollah's guerrilla warfare throughout the 1990s and in 2006. Operationally, the IDF's cultural strengths allowed it to rapidly develop and institutionalize many innovative RMA-inspired programs but also hindered the thorough development of a new conceptual framework for its application. Tactically, IDF culture emphasizes mission command and operational autonomy of its soldiers; hence, specialized units in Lebanon in the 1990s were encouraged to seize the initiative and autonomously develop innovative battlefield solutions to specific operational problems that were then effectively diffused more widely throughout the army. However, non-conformity with protocols and lax training amid budgetary cuts contributed to some of the tactical blunders in the 1990s and in the 2006 war, as the IDF's improvisational and informal culture occasionally backfired without adequate training, oversight, and generalship and sometimes had disastrous and fatal consequences on the battlefield. The Winograd Commission noted:

> There is nothing appealing or appropriate in the anti-intellectual tendency among parts of the senior military-command echelon in the IDF. Such a tendency is not conducive to the indispensable deep thinking or strategic conception. . . .
>
> [Operational] disciplinary problems reflected a flawed organizational culture that simultaneously also causes failure. . . . We highly recommend that the IDF devote renewed thinking to the way in which discipline can be enforced in the IDF . . . *without hampering personal initiative when the circumstances demand it*, together with an assumption of responsibility on the part of the commanders.[31]

The commission noted the benefits inherent in the IDF's flexible organizational culture but warned about dangerous tendencies that can backfire on the battlefield: "We did not find in the IDF—not even in the top-most echelons—the internalization of the supreme importance of a methodical, systematic action in accordance with a common set of rules and principles that is exercised, checked, and updated. *We discovered a strong tendency to improvise and to minimize the importance of careful early preparedness (which is the essential basis for the improvisation required during action)*."[32]

The IDF has since made important efforts to institutionalize its ad hoc learning and tactical adaptation by developing a formal lesson-learning system. The ground forces have institutionalized a battlefield "knowledge management" system that diffuses tactical lessons learned to other units on the ground in real time. This formal system did not exist during the Lebanon security zone period; instead, the IDF relied on improvised tactical learning as the innovative solutions devised by the Egoz unit were diffused horizontally to other ground units largely through informal channels. Throughout much of the Lebanon conflict, there was limited institutionalization of lessons learned, which was compounded by the aforementioned "tacticalization" of strategy. The IDF's recent institutionalization of a culturally compatible mechanism for tactical lesson-learning implemented during the 2006 war (and refined in the 2008 Gaza War) positively contributes to formalizing and rectifying the IDF's traditional cultural pattern of improvisational learning.[33]

In an attempt to improve the IDF's cultural nonemphasis on formal education or theoretical learning and to compensate for the lack of professionalism of certain IDF commanders during the 2006 war, the IDF has revamped the curriculum at the IDF Command and General Staff College. In an effort to instill a greater appreciation of theory and history, the IDF has created an interservice command and staff course based on that of the United Kingdom's Joint Services Staff College. The IDF's course has incorporated several full-time academic positions into the IDF Staff College (as opposed to the past marginal use of academics as mere adjuncts). The new curriculum has bolstered academic and theoretical aspects of the curriculum by having military staff and academic lecturers coinstruct courses. Partially based on the short-comings revealed in the 2006 war, the new curriculum emphasizes force development, jointness, force planning, training exercises, multibranch logistics, supply chain management, and other traditional weak points of the IDF.[34] The course has improved professionalism in the IDF to a degree, and further improvements to the educational curriculum in the staff colleges may contribute to slowly balancing the IDF's cultural preference for action and quick results. The IDF has also taken organizational measures to improve the quality of the action-oriented officer corps by increasing professionalization and "academization" of the force, institutionalizing enhanced professional officer training, and adjusting officer length of service and patterns of posting.[35]

In an effort to improve strategic thinking and long-term planning, Israel has bolstered the role of the long-marginalized National Security Council.[36] While its establishment was originally recommended in 1974 by Israel's official post–Yom Kippur War commission, the NSC was finally formed in 1999 in an effort to improve Israel's strategic policymaking. In the aftermath of the 2006 war, the Winograd Commission implored Israel to better utilize and integrate the NSC to consolidate and integrate political, military, and intelligence assessments.[37] The civilian-run NSC has been given a greater mandate in the aftermath of the 2006 war to engage in high-level contacts with Israel's closest allies, handle high-priority policy issues, and enhance Israel's long-term planning and strategy development. With the passing of the 2008 National Security Law, the NSC was given a refreshed mandate and enjoys greater influence than in previous years, when it had been historically side-lined by the defense and army establishments. The NSC is meant to improve professional staff work and decision-making in the government, synthesize divergent opinions from the government, prepare briefings and policy recommendations, and sit in close proximity to the prime minister's office.[38] While the IDF and MI still dominate planning and assessment processes, increasing the strength of the NSC is a step in the right direction to reforming Israel's pathology of improvisational and short-term strategic thinking.

The IDF's efforts to eradicate the detrimental organizational pathologies that hinder innovation demonstrate the concerted institutional focus by the IDF to improve its strategic, operational, and tactical capacity to learn and adapt. The experiences of the IDF throughout the conflict with Hezbollah illustrate the trials and tribulations of adaptation under fire in protracted conflict, as Israel faced both internal and external friction while attempting to carry out innovative processes of strategic and operational change. Ultimately, the IDF's experiences do show how organizations effectively master aspects of the adaptation process as part of a grueling learning competition between dueling adversaries. Going forward, the IDF would do well to heed Lawrence of Arabia's famous warning: "I hope you have kept the enemy always in the picture. War books so often leave them out."[39]

NOTES

Epigraph: Quoted in Levite, *Offense and Defense*, 25.

1. This chapter's framework draws from Osinga and Russell, "Conclusion: Military Adaptation and the War in Afghanistan."

2. Tira, *Nature of War*, 85–107.

3. Romm, "Test of Rival Strategies."

4. Marcus, "Military Innovation and Tactical Adaptation."

5. Freilich, *Zion's Dilemma*, chap. 5.

6. Freilich, "Israel in Lebanon"; Rapaport, *Friendly Fire*, chap. 1.

7. Bonen, "Sophisticated Conventional War."

8. Cohen, *Israel and Its Army*, 50–51.

9. Halutz, interview, May 5, 2015.

10. Lambeth, *Air Operations*, 340–41.

11. Hirsch, *Defensive Shield*, 267–70; Harel and Issacharoff, *34 Days*, 125–27; Rapaport, *Friendly Fire*, chap. 15.

12. Finkel and Shamir, "From Whom Does the IDF Need to Learn?"

13. Shamir, "When Did a Big Mac?"

14. Tira, *Nature of War*, 22–25.

15. Cohen, "Israel after Heroism."

16. Finkel, "Qualitative Edge of the IDF."

17. Winograd Commission, final report, chap. 12, para. 31.

18. Henriksen, "Deterrence by Default?"

19. Byman, *High Price*, 21.

20. Marcus, "Military Innovation and Tactical Adaptation."

21. Cohen, Eisenstadt, and Bacevich, *Knives, Tank, and Missiles*, 125.

22. Marcus, "Military Innovation and Tactical Adaptation," 504–8; Marcus, "Learning 'Under Fire.'"

23. Vardi, "Pounding Their Feet."

24. Author interview with Eitan Shamir.

25. Horowitz, "Israel's War in Lebanon."

26. Kober, "Heroic to Post-Heroic Warfare."

27. Catignani, "Motivating Soldiers."

28. Adamsky, *Culture of Military Innovation*.

29. Hasdai, "'Doers' and 'Thinkers' in the IDF."

30. Kober, "Israeli Military Thought."

31. Winograd Commission, final report, chap. 11, para. 19 (emphasis added).

32. Ibid., chap. 12, paras. 5 and 6 (emphasis added).

33. Marcus, "Military Innovation and Tactical Adaptation"; Ariely, "Learning while Fighting."

34. Libel, "David's Shield," 72–73.

35. Bazak, "IDF and the Road to a More Professional Military."

36. Freilich, *Zion's Dilemma*, 231–46.

37. Winograd Commission, final report, chap. 18, para. 20.

38. Arad, "Future for Israel's National Security Council." For an alternative view, see Even, "National Security Staff."

39. T. E. Lawrence, letter to Col. A. P. Wavell, February 9, 1928.

AFTERWORD

Back to the Future: IDF Force Planning and Hezbollah's Military Adaptation in Syria

Here, both sides danced a precarious ballet on a floor littered with shards of glass.

— Maj. Gen. Yair Naveh, IDF Deputy Chief of Staff

From the very beginning, we knew that our battle in Syria will be long and tough.

— Sec.-Gen. Hassan Nasrallah

This afterword discusses strategic and operational adaptation that has occurred between Israel and Hezbollah since the outbreak of the Syrian Civil War in 2011. As part of the learning process triggered by the 2006 Lebanon War, recent experiences fighting Hamas in Gaza, and the ongoing Syria conflict, the IDF has implemented two multiyear plans that have impacted its force structure and operational focus. The internal deliberations surrounding the IDF's operational adaptation echo past debates of the RMA era. Hezbollah has learned militarily as it adapts to the strategic and operational environment, overshadowed by its intervention in the Syrian conflict in 2012. It has gained significant battlefield experiences fighting against the Islamic State of Iraq and Syria (ISIS) and Sunni groups in Syria at a bloody cost, while it concurrently attempts to maintain its long-standing focus on Israel. Hezbollah has made efforts to establish a foothold on the Syrian side of the Golan Heights as the ongoing tit-for-tat border clashes between Israel and Hezbollah resemble the six-year period that preceded the 2006 war. Both sides continue to learn and adapt as the fragile equation of mutual deterrence is maintained amid the increased chaos and complexity of the Syrian conflict.

THE IDF'S "REVOLUTIONARY" FORCE PLANS

As the IDF grows increasingly confident as a result of twelve years of quiet since 2006, internal debates have reemerged that call for downsizing the IDF and echo past deliberations during the 1980s "slimmer and smarter" era. Shaped by budgetary constraints, domestic pressure to cut the size of the army, and the weakening of neighboring Arab state militaries during the Arab Spring, the central priority of the IDF's 2013 five-year plan called Teuza (translation: Daring) was the trimming of excess units and outdated weaponry as part of a transformation into a lighter, more flexible, technological force. In much the same way that top generals carried out RMA-inspired force cuts in the 1980s and 1990s to make the IDF slimmer and smarter to help compensate for reductions and offset downsizing, the IDF has put a greater emphasis on interoperability and "jointness" while doubling-down investments in digital, networked command-and-control systems to improve real-time battlefield awareness.[1] Many of the force reduction priorities included in Teuza were included in the IDF's RMA-era 2003 Kela plan a decade earlier, in which many of the same personalities were involved in defense planning, albeit in different roles (see chapter 5).[2]

To subsidize the shift toward becoming a "smarter army," amid civil-military wrangling and domestic pressure to cut the defense budget, the IDF was forced to improvise, which resulted in the cutting of several large-scale reservist-training drills, since training is viewed as one of the few "flexible" components of the budget.[3] COS Lt. Gen. Benny Gantz lamented the budget constraints and yearlong training cuts, which he noted are intricately tied to increased postheroism in Israeli society and sliding professionalization of the IDF: "National priorities are changing, and with it, unfortunately, decisions on defense. As a result, we are dealing with a complicated resource challenge."[4]

While the IDF's traditional strengths of airpower, intelligence, and technology remained well resourced and well funded under the Teuza Plan, vast differences have grown more pronounced between professional and reserve units, as a gap developed with the air force and special forces on one side and reserve units on the other. This widening gap in capabilities is because professional soldiers are deemed more suitable than conscripts to operate hi-tech weapon systems. This mirrors the dangerous division that developed in the RMA era in the 1990s, which contributed to the slow erosion of ground forces' capabilities over the decade and their poor performance during the 2006 war (see chapter 9).

In an effort to compensate for force cuts, much like during the RMA period the military is heavily investing in expensive air force systems, such as fighter jets, precision firepower, stealth technologies, and drones. The IDF aims to reduce the need for large-scale ground forces by emphasizing its superior technology and surgical firepower. Accordingly, the IAF has revamped its headquarters to support a tenfold increase in the number of targets it can simultaneously detect and destroy and has enhanced its sensor-to-shooter capability for time-sensitive targets. It is believed that precision strikes will increase IDF deterrence and expedite a diplomatic endgame to a future conflict through rapid destruction of enemy targets and minimal harm to uninvolved civilians. In statements that mirror the same postheroic affinity for airpower that emerged in the 1990s and 2000s during the RMA era, Maj. Gen. Amikam Norkin, the former head of IAF operations who was promoted to head of the IAF in 2017, explained: "Air power assumes enormous added value in our defensive concept and in all Western cultures that are less tolerant of the heavy casualties that come from big maneuvering ground wars. . . . Air power can be controlled in a very calibrated, surgical manner. It's like a thermostat that you can direct as hard or as soft as needed or turned off entirely when it's time to stop."[5]

Despite the apparent damage being done to ground forces' training programs, Defense Minister Moshe Yaalon (2013–16), who was a big supporter of the RMA as COS in the mid-2000s, praised the IDF's "revolutionary multi-year plan" with strikingly similar enthusiasm and emphasized that "the IDF's technological superiority . . . with less heavy equipment and increasing use of sophisticated and unmanned weapons will give us a substantial advantage over any enemy."[6] Defense Minister Yaalon's statements demonstrate an increasing reliance on technology and airpower at the expense of large-scale ground maneuver and resembles the IDF's misguided thinking before the 2006 war.[7] Former head of Northern Command Maj. Gen. Yair Golan (2011–15) warned of possible repercussions:

> We are repeating the same mistakes that were made in 2003 [in the Kela plan]. . . . One year of not training adequately is enough for us to see a drastic fall-off in our preparedness. . . . Even today, reservist training is not some extravaganza. It's at its bare minimum. . . . Ultimately, the army is not a cheap organization to run, and I don't think that the strategic situation is such that the state of Israel can afford to slash the defense budget, to shrink defense expenditures, and to exhale and say that we are in the clear.[8]

Brig. Gen. (Ret.) Chico Tamir, one of the IDF's top field commanders and a former commander of the Egoz unit who spent much of his career based in Lebanon, slammed the plan because it is slowly atrophying the ground forces and eroding their ability to carry out a focused, decisive ground maneuver: "The war in 2006 should have acted as a warning light. It was a warning not only in regard to the thesis that land-maneuver capability is no longer needed in this era, but primarily about the strategic danger inherent in atrophying the IDF's ability to decide a war by ground means. . . . In the long-term it is impossible to rely only on our excellent firepower, intelligence gathering and the air force."[9]

The IDF must ensure the proper balance between light, adaptable, agile forces and ground formations capable of large-scale maneuver, or it risks setting up "the next missed opportunity."[10] IDF precision firepower is able to hit Hezbollah's strategic weaponry, such as long-range missiles, but short-range rockets will continue unabated unless the IDF displays the willingness and capability to launch a large, decisive ground invasion with a well-equipped and well-trained force. As deterrence is a central pillar to Israel's security, two IDF insiders quipped, "He who wants to avoid a full-scale ground war should exhibit his readiness to conduct one successfully."[11]

In another strange twist that echoes the past, Brig. Gen. (Res.) Gal Hirsch, the scapegoated OTRI disciple and brigade commander during the 2006 war, has on several occasions since his appointment as deputy head of the IDF Depth Corps in 2012 incredulously declared the arrival of a "Second RMA." Hirsch proclaimed that "we must bring about the new Revolution in Military Affairs" by harnessing the technological potential of the current era by emphasizing the synchronization of precision technology and firepower with the effective use of networked special forces units.[12] These decentralized commando forces would operate with a light footprint and maintain the ability to liaise in real time with air support, precision weaponry, and other special assets, which avoids the risk of larger ground formations getting bogged down in casualty-heavy operations.[13] His proposal bears a striking resemblance to elements of the Northern Storm battleplan designed in the 2000s using SOD in Northern Command for war in Lebanon and also draws on the OTRI-related Diffused Warfare concept of the same period, which sought to use networked commando units ("dynamic molecules") and simultaneous "diffused" precision strikes to damage networked enemies such as Hezbollah (see chapter 7). While the ideas are certainly innovative, because General Hirsch's command of the IDF Depth Corps (2012–15) oversaw deep operations in enemy territory, his creative plan can be viewed as an attempt to gain greater organizational attention, intellectual prestige, and operational action for his corps. It also highlights the enduring imprint OTRI's theoretical teachings had on many of its disciples, even years later. The saga of OTRI and the difficulty of implementing SOD more widely in the military should inform the IDF's cautious engagement with such ideas beyond a specific operational context.

Despite ominous cuts during the tenure of COS General Gantz, the IDF implemented several programs to ensure an appropriate balance in its mission orientation and training regimen between offense and defense and between firepower and ground maneuver. To be able to fight effectively in both major combat operations and low-intensity warfare, the IDF adopted an innovative training regimen for ground forces that emphasized flexibility, adaptation, and learning "under fire." Instead of futilely attempting to predict the nature of future war or devise contingency plans based on (imperfect) intelligence, the IDF developed a training regimen to challenge commanders on mental, cognitive, and physical issues related to responding to inevitable battlefield surprise.[14] The IDF has emphasized a flexible, nonmonolithic doctrine, weapon diversity, technological versatility, and decentralized networked command and has institutionalized a real-time lesson-learning system to improve learning and adaptation.[15] Previously in charge of this process, Col. Meir Finkel, former head of the Concept Development and Doctrine Department, explained that "I'm responsible for lesson learning in the ground forces and for balancing training. . . . The 2006 war balanced us. . . . We were too focused on counterinsurgency and standoff fire, and now we are more balanced on both fronts today."[16]

The new COS appointed in 2015, Lt. Gen. Gadi Eizenkot, has significantly boosted the training of the ground forces and reserves, which has become a "central priority" in the IDF.[17] Gen. Eizenkot doubled down on the IDF's focus on ground warfare training because of perceived shortcomings in the recent 2012 and 2014 Gaza campaigns and sought to rectify some of the dangerous cuts of his predecessor and slow down the process of making the army slimmer and smarter.

Gen. Eizenkot released the IDF's multiyear Gideon plan in late 2015, which calls for significantly increasing the power of wartime multiarena combat divisions, restructuring the army to create specialized brigades that focus exclusively on "routine security" while leaving the main fighting to professional divisions, and improving ground forces' training and weaponry. The conceptual framework for the Gideon plan is the *IDF Strategy* document (see chapter 4), and it reinforces the importance of ground maneuver, the diversification of operational capabilities, air superiority, and improvements in cyber and intelligence assets.[18] With its implementation, Gideon ultimately augments the IDF's capacity to fight in multiple theaters, bolsters home-front defense, enhances air, sea, ground, cyber, and tunnel warfare capabilities, and streamlines several noncombat-related programs.[19] It cuts several reserve battalions and various career positions, which should be viewed as an attempt to balance domestic pressure to downsize the army's budget while avoiding larger cuts that would damage the IDF's capabilities (and avoid the same mistakes made prior to the 2006 war). It is an effective response to balancing the IDF's operational priorities in an era of persistent conflict against diverse threats and also reconciles the IDF's slow shift toward becoming a career "professional" army and the decreasing utility of reservists.[20]

HEZBOLLAH'S "VIETNAM"? THE SYRIAN CIVIL WAR
AND THE RISE OF ISIS

Hezbollah's involvement in the Syrian Civil War in 2012 on the side of President Bashar al-Assad has acted as a major unforeseen challenge for the group. It has led to bloody fighting against ISIS and Sunni militant groups and has also resulted in deep domestic dissatisfaction in Lebanon. Hezbollah's ability to adapt and rearm has also been indirectly impacted by the nuclear deal and associated sanctions between the West and Hezbollah's chief patron, Iran.

Hezbollah secretary-general Hassan Nasrallah reaffirmed in a May 2017 speech that Hezbollah entered the Syrian conflict out of loyalty to the Iranian and Syrian regimes, which, as this book has discussed, provided weaponry, military assistance, financing, and political backing throughout the decades.[21] Nasrallah publicly confirmed Hezbollah's involvement in the fighting in Syria on the side of Assad in a speech in 2013, though Hezbollah had been clandestinely active in Syria since early 2012. Nasrallah explained Hezbollah's rationale for intervention in Syria: "Obviously Syria has been the cherisher of the Resistance, so the Resistance can't stand still while that cherisher is being ruined! Acting otherwise would mean we're absolutely dumb because it's only someone dumb who does nothing in times of conspiracy, death, and besiegement! . . . Through the stance we're making today, we see that we are defending Lebanon, Palestine, and Syria."[22]

Nasrallah has adapted Hezbollah's strategic orientation by focusing on the fight against ISIS and Sunni groups while still maintaining a consistent focus on Israel. Hezbollah MP Mohammad Raad explained Hezbollah's order of priorities and stressed that the group's fight in Syria does not detract from its fight with Israel:

> When it comes to being prepared to confront the threats and aggressions of the Israeli enemy, this falls outside the scope of calculations for intervention in other places [Syria]. This preparation has its own equipment, training, provisions, weapons and ammunition. It has its own allocations that continue night and day. We monitor any movement the enemy makes at all times, because the primary enemy that we are concerned with confronting is the Israeli enemy. . . . We joke with each other, saying that anyone who works on something not involved in the direct confrontation with Israel is an apprentice.[23]

Hezbollah's Syria adventure has proven to be a double-edged sword. One the one hand, Hezbollah has gained significant operational experience in Syria and has learned valuable military lessons during fierce fighting against Sunni militant groups. It has provided Hezbollah fighters with deep battlefield experience in ground operations and urban warfare and has offered commanders the opportunity to improve battle planning, command and control, and decision-making under fire. On the other hand, Hezbollah has no exit strategy from Syria, its military adventure has elicited severe domestic criticism in Lebanon, and it has provoked reprisals from groups such as ISIS that have waged a terrorist campaign against Hezbollah's areas of support throughout Lebanon.

Hezbollah officials have boasted of the increased operational skills and capabilities that its battle-hardened fighters have mastered in Syria. Hezbollah MP Mohammad Raad explained: "The enemy knows that the experience gained by the Resistance members via their participation in Syria, for example, has doubled the Resistance's horizons—not only on the geographical level, but in terms of fighting, the quality of weapons and the means of tactical combat they have learned. Perhaps this makes the [Israeli] enemy more afraid to make a stupid move."[24]

Brig. Gen. Meir Finkel, who became head of the IDF's military studies center in 2014, noted in an author interview that Hezbollah has developed greater military and fighting experience during its operations in Syria and better unit coordination, especially in urban areas.[25] Highlighting the operational experiences gained by Hezbollah, a fighter in Syria during the lengthy battle of Qusayr in 2015 said, "After Qusayr, it doesn't matter where we are sent. We are trained for everything."[26] Another Hezbollah fighter in Syria stated, "We have gained huge experience in Syria. I know what it's like to shoot and kill and to be shot at. And I know how I behave in this situation. The more times I go to Syria, the better I become as a fighter."[27]

The involvement of Russian forces in Syria on the side of President Assad in 2015 has provided Hezbollah a potentially monumental opportunity to learn, adapt, and improve core fighting skills, particularly related to conducting large-scale, offensive operations. Brig. Gen. Muni Katz, head of the Ninety-First "Galilee" Division until 2015, noted that in Syria Hezbollah has engaged in complex offensive maneuver warfare in urban areas involving hundreds of fighters, honing a vital skill Hezbollah rarely used in the decades fighting Israel. During the Israeli security zone period, Hezbollah evolved militarily from an ineffective militia that engaged in "hill-storming" (see chapter 1) to a versatile guerrilla army (see chapter 2). It engaged in two decades of defensive, attritional guerrilla warfare against the IDF, and during the 2006 war Hezbollah utilized offensive operations and small-unit commando operations on a limited scale in the southern Lebanese villages (see chapter 8). By its direct cooperation with Russian advisers and military officers in Syria, Hezbollah has been exposed to high-level strategic planning, sophisticated operational concepts, advanced intelligence-collection methods, electronic warfare capabilities, and large-scale command-and-control methods for urban warfare.[28] Hezbollah may also have benefited from learning how to use advanced Russian weapon systems, including the SA-22 surface-to-air missile and the Yakhont surface-to-sea missile, which Israel views as potential "game-changers." Ominously, a Hezbollah fighter on the battlefield in 2017 boasted, "What the world saw from Hezbollah in 2006 is 3 percent of what we are now. Especially after the experience we've gained in Syria."[29] General Katz wrote, "In previous conflicts, Hezbollah tactics focused on guerrilla warfare, with small units responsible for defending their villages or blocking IDF movements. This approach does not apply to many battles in Syria, where Hezbollah has often had to deploy much larger units in offensive operations in tandem with artillery and aerial assets. . . . The group will learn important lessons."[30]

General Katz argued that Hezbollah's "Russian military education" and its enhanced ability to seize and hold territory and wage high-tempo ground warfare in Syria may contribute to Hezbollah's shifting its operational paradigm away from its traditional defensive guerrilla approach of "winning by not losing" toward a greater emphasis on offensive maneuver warfare. Adding greater cause for concern in the IDF, recent reports emerged in 2016 that Russian air strikes were directly assisting Hezbollah and that Russian special forces were operating alongside Hezbollah in the Latakia region.[31] A Hezbollah fighter with field experience in Syria said, "Around Latakia was very difficult for us" but "the intervention of the Russians made it much easier. . . . Without their air force we can't advance and they couldn't give us air support without our information from the ground." Another Hezbollah fighter claimed he had been assigned to guard Russian arms depots and that after learning the know-how from the Russians, "Hezbollah is teaching the Syrian army how to use many of these new weapons."[32] Reflecting the alarm this revelation caused in Israel, the Israeli ambassador to Russia said in a leaked classified briefing that "we made our red lines regarding Syria and the involvement by Iran and Hezbollah clear to the Russians, and when we have any concerns, we discuss them." He also revealed that the Russian Foreign Ministry reached out to the IDF in 2016 on its own initiative to notify them that a Russian army investigation found no cases of Russian weaponry being passed to Hezbollah.[33]

Highlighting the less rosy aspect of the conflict for Hezbollah, the group sustained at least 360 verified military deaths and hundreds wounded by April 2014, including senior commanders who were veterans of the fighting with Israel in the 1980s and 1990s.[34] Following the bloody battles with ISIS in Qusayr, Qalamoun, Zabadani, Aleppo, and elsewhere, by early 2018 Hezbollah's casualty count was estimated to be seventeen hundred dead and five thousand wounded. Creeping casualties in Hezbollah's ranks have also caused grumbling within its base of support. Hezbollah has made greater efforts to recruit new fighters with money and perks and has even reportedly lowered the age for recruitment of fighters to sixteen owing to stresses on the group and losses in clashes against Sunni militant groups.[35]

Hezbollah's involvement in Syria has elicited a string of suicide bombings, ambushes, and car bombs by Sunni jihadists against both Hezbollah and Iranian targets in Hezbollah strongholds in Beirut and the Bekaa Valley. Hussein Laqees, one of Hezbollah's most senior military commanders, with close ties to Iran and expertise in missiles, drone technology, and logistics, was assassinated under murky circumstances in Beirut in 2013 and was publicly eulogized by Nasrallah.[36] In May 2016, Mustafa Badreddine, the most senior commander in Hezbollah's external security apparatus, was killed in a blast outside the Damascus airport. The death of Badreddine, who was revealed by Nasrallah to have personally commanded fighters during the 1996 Grapes of Wrath and 1997 Ansariya Operations, marked a major blow for Hezbollah. He was eulogized by Nasrallah as "one of the first members of the Resistance" and the "great jihadi commander" who succeeded Imad Mughniyeh, the group's chief of external operations (assassinated by Israel in Damascus in 2008).[37] In October 2016, Hatem Hamade, another senior Hezbollah commander in Syria, was killed in Aleppo, and it was noted by Nasrallah in his eulogy that Hamade had "joined as a young man and became white haired until martyrdom."[38] The loss of senior commanders with deep expertise, knowledge, and experience may hinder Hezbollah's ability to innovate and adapt in the future.

The organizational capital Hezbollah is expending to deal with the threat from ISIS and Sunni jihadist groups at home also detracts from their capabilities to fight Israel. Signifying the precarious strategic situation in which Hezbollah now finds itself, Nasrallah spoke in August 2014 of "a true existential threat confronting us" in Syria.[39] He proclaimed in 2015 that "the danger that threatens us is an existential threat similar to 1982" but also attempted to paint a brighter picture by noting that because of significant military expenditures, "there is no time since the Resistance was born in 1982 when Hezbollah has been larger, better equipped and more determined than it is today!"[40]

As the Syrian war grinds into its eighth year and despite significant operational losses, Hezbollah leaders continue to reaffirm steadfastness in the fight. In October 2016, Deputy Sec.-Gen. Naim Qassem proclaimed, "Whatever the price, we will continue!" and "If people are betting on our tiredness, we are a people who do not become tired," while Hassan Nasrallah proclaimed later that month, "We will continue in Syria until the end!"[41] While Hezbollah and Assad's forces have made moderate gains in 2018 and Nasrallah has spoken of Hezbollah's "second liberation day" in Syria and a "semifinal victory," Hezbollah shows few signs of significantly limiting its role there.[42]

Domestic Tensions in Lebanon

The general instability in Lebanon since the beginning of the Syrian conflict has put Hezbollah in a precarious domestic situation. Hezbollah, which refused to lay down its weapons after the Lebanese Civil War in contravention of the 1989 Taif Accord, historically vowed to utilize them "only" against Israel. However, Hezbollah's bloody battles against Sunni militant groups in Syria have resulted in the deaths of thousands of fellow Muslims. Fierce domestic criticism has emerged, as former Lebanese president Michel Suleiman decried Hezbollah's involvement in Syria and sharply criticized Hezbollah's professed contribution to the security of Lebanon and its so-called unifying role in Lebanon: "The army-people-Resistance formula is no longer appropriate for any ministerial statement, because the Resistance unilaterally decided to get involved in Syria without consulting the army and the people. . . . It has therefore violated the conditions of this political formula."[43] In 2012, a Lebanese opposition MP declared, "The battle in al-Qusayr will act as Hezbollah's Vietnam and it will have repercussions on the whole of Lebanon!"[44]

The domestic pressures have been reflected in Nasrallah's increasingly defensive speeches about Hezbollah's presence in Syria.[45] Hezbollah's contribution to the blockade of the Syrian town of Madaya in January 2016 implicated the group in the systematic starvation of many Syrian civilians.[46] Sensing the severity of the domestic dismay and regional criticism, Hezbollah issued numerous statements rejecting such claims, and its official mouthpiece Al-Manar TV released a report about the "fabrications" of starvation in the town, despite UN reports to the contrary.[47] In response to its involvement in Syria, the Arab League blacklisted Hezbollah in 2016 as a terrorist organization. Interestingly, disgruntled former Hezbollah secretary-general Subhi Tufayli, booted from Hezbollah in the mid-1990s over disagreements with the group's political participation, criticized Hezbollah's divisive involvement in Syria in a 2013 interview. He proclaimed that Hassan Nasrallah "provoked the whole world" when he challenged those who disagreed with him to fight against Hezbollah in Syria: "We asked those who differ with us to fight against us in Syria, [which is] as if we are inviting 1.3 billion [Sunni Muslims] to fight against us." Tufayli added that "Hezbollah's project as a Resistance party that works to unify the Islamic world has fallen."[48]

Implications of Sanctions against Iran

Owing to this loss of legitimacy suffered by Hezbollah for its engagement in Syria, it is less likely that the international community will attempt to inhibit the IDF in a future war with the group. International scrutiny of Syrian armaments limits any assistance Syria could offer Hezbollah in the event of war. Iran, Hezbollah's chief patron, is engaged with the West regarding the nuclear agreement, which could potentially limit the level of support Iran could offer if an escalation erupted. The adoption of the Joint Comprehensive Plan of Action in October 2015 by the West and Iran put increased scrutiny on Iran's foreign meddling in Syria and Lebanon and has increased Western attention on Hezbollah's global activities. In an effort to reassure Israel following the Iran deal, the US government took several noteworthy steps to target Iran's nefarious foreign activities, including its material and military support for Hezbollah. In 2015, President Barack Obama signed into law the Hezbollah International Financing Prevention Act, meant to impose tough sanctions against banks or institutions that do business with Hezbollah, sanctions satellite companies that broadcast Hezbollah's Al-Manar programming, prevents Hezbollah's global logistical and financial networks from operating, and curtails funding of Hezbollah's international and domestic activities.[49]

The global scrutiny on Iran's activities and the remaining sanctions against Iran's proxies will likely impact Hezbollah's material strength, weapons supply, and organizational ability to adapt. Adam Szubin, then the US Treasury Department's top terrorism-sanctions official, summed up the deep effect such measures are having on Hezbollah, noting in 2016 that "today, the group is in its worst financial shape in decades."[50] He said elsewhere in a speech: "Hizballah's leader, Hassan Nasrallah, recently took a very unusual step. He spent about half of a speech he gave—a long speech on July 25 [2015]—specifically speaking about sanctions and decrying our sanctions. . . . We read this speech, in fact, as an indication that our designations are having an impact at the highest levels on Hizballah's thinking, as well as their ability to conduct business and finance even in places like southern Lebanon."[51]

Under the Donald J. Trump administration, scrutiny on Iran's global activities and Hezbollah has intensified dramatically, as exemplified by the May 2017 addition of Hashem Safieddine, head of Hezbollah's executive council, to the Treasury Department's sanctions blacklist, the February 2018 blacklisting of several Hezbollah financiers, and the strengthening of the Hezbollah International Financial Act. Trump's new sanctions in October 2017 against Iran and the IRGC over its support for terrorism have also heightened scrutiny on Hezbollah. Illustrating Hezbollah's perseverance, Nasrallah retorted, "We are not worried, but very optimistic, for [he] who resides in the White House is an idiot."[52] Nevertheless, Hezbollah's ability to adapt will likely be hindered to an extent by this increased pressure.

THE FUTURE OUTLOOK OF THE CONFLICT

An IDF MI officer recently assessed in *Maarachot* that Hezbollah's current operational concept is based on a deep "understanding of the benefits of Israeli supremacy in technology, intelligence, air, and precision capabilities, as well as Israel's vulnerabilities: high sensitivity to casualties, clear reluctance to conduct extended campaigns, and the need for clear victory."[53] In response to Hezbollah's rocketing in 2006 and the vulnerability of Israel's population centers, Israel made a concerted effort to enhance its passive and active defense systems. In a major strategic and operational game-changer, Israel has developed the Iron Dome missile-defense system that has acted as a stunning counter to short-range rockets. Iron Dome provides mobile missile-defense coverage that launches countermeasures at incoming rockets whose trajectory is predicted to strike Israeli population centers (and allows other incoming rockets to fall harmlessly in open areas). Iron Dome was successfully operationalized in 2011 and 2012 in Israel's conflict with Hamas, where it enjoyed an 84 percent success rate, and by the 2014 Gaza conflict it enjoyed a more than 90 percent success rate.[54] Israel also unveiled its "David's Sling" medium-range missile-defense system in 2017, which adds another layer of protection against Hezbollah's versatile arsenal.

IDF Home Front Command has made significant efforts to increase public fortified bomb shelters and improve the IDF's early warning siren systems to alert only those residents within a missile's immediate trajectory to seek cover (thereby limiting disruption to the general population). Only six civilians were killed by rockets in the fifty-one-day 2014 Gaza conflict with Hamas, which illustrates the fruits of the IDF's learning and innovation since 2006. This dramatically dampens the deterrent threat posed by Hezbollah's rockets and suggests Israel's willingness to embark on a significant military campaign while concurrently absorbing sustained rocket fire.

According to a colonel in IDF Home Front Command, Hezbollah's effective use of rockets against the Israeli civilian front triggered the IDF's adaptation and enhancement of its absorptive capacity and resilience: "We are preparing for a massive and highly concentrated fire strike [from Hezbollah] within a small radius in the central region [of Israel]. . . . The story of 2006 must not repeat itself. . . . The name of the game is the civilian population. . . . We must help the people maintain their resilience and strength."[55]

Hezbollah's central pillar of organizational survivability and societal resilience in the face of the IDF's damaging strikes has been mirrored by Israel, which internalized that, since the shock of 2006, national and societal resilience are important elements regarding buying time and strategic space for the military to operate effectively.[56] Defense Minister Yaalon summed up the impact of Israel's resilience after the 2014 war with Hamas: "I think that during [2014] Operation Protective Edge [in Gaza] we placed exclamation points, as a society, in such a way that Hassan Nasrallah today will not repeat the 'spider web' speech. . . . We projected strength particularly in our ability to stand and take it."[57]

The central pillar of Hezbollah's military paradigm is the maintenance of its rocket fire capability, which has acted as a significant deterrent against Israel for much of the four-decade conflict. Brig. Gen. Itai Brun, head of research in MI in 2014, stated that Hezbollah had more than a hundred thousand rockets able to hit Haifa (a 28-mile range), "a few thousand missiles" able to hit Tel Aviv (a 155-mile range), and "a few hundred missiles" able to hit the entirety of Israel.[58] The IDF top brass assess that Hezbollah plans to fire a thousand rockets a day in an attempt to overwhelm and saturate the Iron Dome system and demonstrate the group's strength in an attempt to shorten any future war.[59]

To counteract Hezbollah's warfighting concept, the IDF has sought to advance its abilities to hit more targets with greater firepower, accuracy, precision, and speed. According to an IDF colonel in Home Front Command, Hezbollah is seemingly aware that in a future war, as in 2006, the IDF's opening air strikes will severely damage the group's arsenal:

> [Hezbollah] realized they should have concentrated their barrages and launched everything they had to maximum effect right at the outset [of the 2006 war], rather than wasting away the effect by launching their arsenal "bit by bit"—that a dramatic opening move would have been more effective. This is a rational conclusion: what they fail to launch during the initial stages, they would no longer have for the final stages.[60]

Reflecting adherence to the IDF's cumulative deterrence policy related to "mowing the grass," the IDF has indicated that in future conflict it may attempt to carry out a longer-term, punishing campaign of attrition against Hezbollah, as there seems to be an apparent interest in the IDF of mirroring Hezbollah's strategy of attrition. Brig. Gen. (Res.) Udi Dekel, head of the IDF Center for Strategic Planning, wrote, "Attrition need not be the exclusive weapon of the weaker party. Israel could also make use of this course of action, given its superiority in regard to resources, its ability to provide a satisfactory protective solution [Iron Dome], and its ability to erode [the group's capabilities]."[61] In what seems to be a remarkable adoption of Hezbollah's long-held strategic orientation of attrition, Maj. Gen. (Ret.) Amos Yadlin, former MI head, described how Israel has adapted its strategic posture for future conflict against Hezbollah: "Israel basically turned it upside down and said, 'You want attrition? You are welcome. You lost your strategic military tools against Israel. Our firepower and our intelligence and our capability to sustain more days is much bigger than yours.' This is the strategy."[62] Israel's utilization of attrition against nonstate adversaries represents an adaptation of Israel's policy of cumulative deterrence, which is enabled by the IDF's superior firepower, the success of Iron Dome, and the resilience of the Israeli population (evident in the 2014 war against Hamas).[63]

To counter the IDF's strategy, instead of reactively absorbing IDF strikes by relying on its organizational endurance and fortified bunkers, Hezbollah has hinted it will seek ways to *shorten* a future war by launching short, sharp offensive operations against Israeli targets in the Galilee.[64] Hezbollah has come to the realization that a long, drawn-out attritional war with Israel would yield unsustainable destruction of Hezbollah strongholds in Lebanon. Given Hezbollah's newfound precarious geopolitical situation, ground incursions would allow it to take a greater role in shaping the outcome of a conflict and gain important initiative in the fighting. As IDF MI noted, instead of Hezbollah being forced to absorb punishing Israeli firepower from bunkers in southern Lebanese villages, Hezbollah could attempt to attack important strategic targets within Israel proper to "nip the [IDF's] attack in the bud."[65]

Hezbollah alluded to this adaptation toward offensive ground operations as early as 2011 when Nasrallah threatened to invade the Galilee in future confrontation (see chapter 4) and repeated the threat numerous times since then in an effort to bolster Hezbollah's deterrence.[66] After the 2006 wake-up call and witnessing the operational experiences Hezbollah has obtained in Syria, the IDF now views Hezbollah "as an army fighting with modern assets" in every sense, so the IDF is preparing and training for high-intensity ground warfare accordingly.[67] The IDF launched its largest drill in nineteen years in October 2017, which simulated a war with Hezbollah sparked by a large-scale Hezbollah incursion into northern Israel, reflecting the severity of the perceived threat from the group's offensive ground operations.[68]

Military adaptation by Hezbollah toward offensive ground operations mirrors the IDF's own traditional approach of using preemptive, rapid force to gain initiative, deter its opponents, and heavily erode enemy capabilities in the opening phases of war. A ground invasion by Hezbollah into Israel would shorten the war and allow it to deviate from its current reactive role where it is forced to absorb damaging Israeli air strikes. Hezbollah's combat experience in Syria carrying out offensive urban warfare and seizing and holding terrain has also enhanced its ability to militarily adapt to this new approach.[69] Brig. Gen. Itai Brun of IDF MI believes that Hezbollah will launch "pinpoint" terrorist strikes against Israel's northern towns, as well as "other more substantive operations to grab territory inside Israel. . . . There is a deep seated idea here—to undermine Israel's sense of security. . . . When it happens, we will be deeply shocked. In Nasrallah's view, that deep shock is something that can help him in the long term."[70] Another IDF MI officer noted, "The question that should be asked here is not whether Hezbollah could carry out an attack or raid on an Israeli target, but what it tells us that they are engaging with such ideas."[71]

Hezbollah has also learned many lessons from Hamas's learning experiences during the Gaza conflicts.[72] Hassan Nasrallah gave a masterful analysis of the IDF's recent Gaza campaigns and its relevance for Hezbollah militarily and politically.[73] One central lesson Hezbollah learned was related to the effectiveness of Hamas's underground tunnel infiltrations and offensive commando assaults into Israel during the 2014 Gaza War, which may represent a precursor of what Hezbollah has in store for Israel.[74] General Brun noted,

"We haven't found any [tunnels from Lebanon], but we are always looking. The basic assumption is that they exist and we have to find them."[75] Forebodingly, as part of its deterrence posture, Hezbollah gave an exclusive tour of its tunnel network to the sympathetic *Al-Safir* newspaper in May 2015, which revealed their extensive system of offensive tunnels and defensive fortifications with twenty-four-hour generators, ventilation systems, stocks of supplies, escape shafts, and advanced rocketry aimed at Israel.[76]

Israel learned a bloody lesson in 2006 regarding the vulnerability of its famed Merkava tanks to Hezbollah's ATMs, with notable calamities like the Wadi Saluki ambush (see chapter 8) seared into collective memory. In response to Hezbollah's prowess with ATMs, perfected over the decades, the IDF developed an innovative protective system for its tanks and armored vehicles. The IDF Trophy system provides 360-degree active protection from ATMs and/or projectiles that are fired simultaneously from any elevation. Trophy fires explosive defensive countermeasures to deflect the incoming projectiles, acting as a "personal Iron Dome" for each vehicle.[77] This technological innovation, battle-tested during the IDF's 2012 and 2014 Gaza campaigns, is a significant game-changer in the IDF's arsenal as a means to counteradapt to the threat from Hezbollah's mobile ATM squads.

Though Hezbollah would ideally prefer to repeat its successful battle-proven model focused on survivability and attrition utilized in 2006, the IDF's own adaptations may lead Hezbollah to combine these new operational methods with its existing military paradigm to leverage its "basket of tools." In addition to offensive ground raids, Hezbollah may launch UAVs and explosive-laden drones into Israel, which they have done a number of times since the 2006 war, or, in the words of Nasrallah, fire "qualitative weapons" such as cruise missiles or surface-to-air missiles that Hezbollah may have acquired from Syria amid the chaos.[78] Nasrallah even threatened to fire rockets at industrial ammonia-storage facilities in Haifa, which he claimed would be the equivalent of a "nuclear bomb" explosion that would deter Israel, designed to send the IDF a message "that a clear, decisive, and quick victory is not assured!"[79] General Brun summed up:

> In the past we had a monopoly on precision capabilities, and now the other side [Hezbollah] is also developing this capability. . . . [It is] leading the other side to thoughts regarding the concept of the ability to move from attrition of long wars with numerous casualties *to shortening the war.*
>
> This is based on their negative experiences in 2006 . . . and they are looking for a way to attack massively with firepower to cause us considerable pain and damage and *cause us to stop the fighting before we are able to express our capabilities.* . . . They are trying to infiltrate fighters into our territory, some by using tunnels, and create confusion, fear, and panic in order to have a major effect on our side.[80]

Hezbollah's "traditional" focus targeting the Israeli home front with their newly augmented, versatile, and redundant long-range rocket arsenal, coupled with damaging ground incursions or tunnel operations into Israel, offers Hezbollah a wider range of options during war and could yield a surprisingly devastating result.

DÉJÀ VU: BORDER SKIRMISHES AND THE DANGER OF MISCALCULATION

The "balance of deterrence" between Israel and Hezbollah, as described recently by a former head of Mossad, has contributed to the relative calm amid the tumultuous Arab Spring and the Syrian Civil War next door.[81] Illustrating historical continuity, Israel and Hezbollah have maintained throughout the Syrian conflict a set of tacit understandings and have revised the "rules of the game" that seek to prevent unintended escalations. Having learned a lesson in 2006 about the gap between Israel's "declared deterrence" and the level of deterrence perceived by its adversaries (see chapter 4), Israeli leaders have clearly displayed Israel's red lines in Syria: First, the IDF will prevent the transfer of advanced, unconventional, "game-changing" weapons from Syria and Iran to Hezbollah, and, second, a Hezbollah presence near the Israeli-Syrian border or in the Golan Heights is unacceptable. The IDF has shown that violations of these red lines elicit a lethal counterreaction.

Resembling the fragile tit-for-tat period from 2000 to 2006, recent years have seen Israel's red lines tested several times. In a suspected (but never officially confirmed) IAF air strike in early 2014, a Hezbollah base on the Syrian border suspected of "game-changing" weapon procurement was hit. In response, Hezbollah launched a rare roadside bomb attack against the IDF in the Shebaa Farms area. General Brun explained the IDF's intelligence assessment of the incident and the ongoing deterrence equation: "In January 2014 he [Nasrallah] identified what he viewed for the first time as an [Israeli] attack on Lebanese soil. . . . I think that he felt that we were testing him, starting out small in efforts to open up Lebanon to our attacks. . . . In his eyes, he had to respond. In my opinion, he didn't do it with a happy heart. Only to signal to us that he had enough."[82]

The attack, which caused no injuries, was the first claimed publicly by Hezbollah since 2006, and Israel assessed that it was not meant to spark a violent confrontation but rather to show that there is a tacit understanding to keep the balance of deterrence against Israel.[83] Nasrallah explained his perceptions: "Following the operation in Shebaa Farms, the message was clear: We retaliate, and we do not tolerate any change in the rules of engagement to the interest of the enemy because the story here is not rules of engagement; it is rather deterrence."[84]

In the clearest example of the deterrence equation in the context of the Syrian conflict, Nasrallah explained Hezbollah's current strategic approach and the need for the group to keep boosting its deterrence in a calculated manner:

> The Resistance works around the clock to develop its deterrence capability, and this is what keeps the enemy worried, as they talk about this constantly. . . . This is one of the points that haunt the Israeli enemy who is always looking at Syria, Iran, and all our friends as to what they might offer or have offered to this Resistance.
>
> As far as deterrence power is concerned, you cannot reach a point and say this is enough. . . . I will be precise: if we reach a point which requires the intervention of the Resistance, the Resistance will not remain silent toward any insult, offense, or aggression. . . . Everything is being tackled relatively and in a proportional way."[85]

The mutual deterrence equation was tested again in January 2015, when Israel was forced to act because of violations of its red line. A two-vehicle convoy carrying high-ranking Hezbollah fighters and top Iranian military officers was targeted by the IAF on the Syrian side of the Golan Heights, an action that killed six Hezbollah fighters, including high-ranking commanders involved in operations on the Israel-Syria border. Six Iranian military officers were also killed, including Gen. Mohammad Allahdadi, a top IRGC commander responsible for coordinating Iranian military support with the Syrian regime. Hezbollah's actions were deemed outside the rules of the game by brazenly operating within Syria so close to the Golan Heights, especially in conjunction with Iranian military officers. Defense Minister Yaalon seemed to confirm this, hinting on Israeli radio at the time that "if Hezbollah say their people were hurt in the targeted killing, let them explain what they were doing in Syria," noting that "two days ago, we heard Nasrallah say that Hezbollah's elements are not present in the Golan, can he explain to us what happened?"[86]

Hezbollah publicly claimed responsibility for a payback attack one week later that killed two IDF soldiers, and Nasrallah later proclaimed that the attack, as part of its deterrence, represented "more than vengeance, but less than a war."[87] While this operation marked the deadliest attack on Israel's northern border since the 2006 war, Hezbollah's smaller-scale retaliatory attack should be viewed as a signal of Hezbollah's apparent reluctance to engage in an all-out war with Israel. After the attack, Hezbollah apparently signaled via UNIFIL that it sought calm and was content not to escalate further, indicating that it viewed the latest border attack as having fulfilled their criteria for retaliation for the Israeli strike.[88]

The mayhem in Syria and the four-decade conflict between Israel and Hezbollah precariously converged in December 2015. Samir Kuntar, a

Hezbollah commander with a long history of terrorist and militant involvement, was killed in an Israeli air strike in Damascus. Kuntar, originally imprisoned in Israel for a notorious 1979 attack that killed four Israelis, including two children, had been released in 2008 after thirty years in prison, as part of the prisoner exchange for the IDF soldiers kidnapped in Hezbollah's opening operation of the 2006 war. Hassan Nasrallah recounted in a speech that after Kuntar's release and return to Lebanon, Kuntar sought a place in Hezbollah's military command.[89] Upon Hezbollah's involvement in the Syrian conflict, Kuntar was delegated by Nasrallah to help organize Hezbollah's operations in the Golan Heights. In September 2015, the US State Department described him as a "specially designated global terrorist" for his "operational role, with assistance of Iran and Syria, in building up Hezbollah's terrorist infrastructure in the Golan."[90] Hezbollah's bold effort with Iran to establish military infrastructure in the Golan was viewed by Israel as passing a red line and violating the rules of the game. Kuntar was one of Hezbollah's key commanders who continued its military efforts in the Golan, and he paid the price. The IDF has sustained efforts to prevent Iran's military buildup in Syria, and there have been several suspected Israeli airstrikes and mysterious explosions at Iranian military sites throughout 2017 and 2018.

The outgoing head of the IAF admitted in August 2017 that Israel has launched more than one hundred air strikes over the last five years against Syrian and Hezbollah weapon convoys that were deemed violations of Israel's red lines.[91] In response to a recent IAF strike against a Syrian weapon factory, Deputy Sec.-Gen. Naim Qassem signaled that the strike was not a reason for Hezbollah to spark a war with Israel and that there were other ways to respond.[92] Hezbollah, which has lost hundreds of fighters in Syria, is not in a strong enough position to engage in a two-front conflict with Syrian rebels and ISIS on one front and Israel on another.[93] Israel will likely tolerate low-level responses from Hezbollah as long as it does not cause significant casualties or violate the rules of the game. Israel does not want a major war that would elicit Hezbollah's rocket fire against the Israeli home front, nor does it want to get sucked further into the messy Syrian conflict. Former Deputy-COS Maj. Gen. (Res.) Yair Naveh poetically described the dangerous situation: "Here, both sides dance a precarious ballet on a floor littered with shards of glass."[94]

While neither Israel nor Hezbollah seeks escalation, the danger of miscalculation remains ever present, especially within the context of the volatile Syrian Civil War. Hence, understanding the history and lessons of the last four decades is essential to understanding the evolution of the conflict and its possible future trajectories. As Hassan Nasrallah reflected in a 2012 "Martyrs Day" speech, "we adhere to this past and to this part of our history. That's because the present is the outcome of the past, and it sets the foundations of the future."[95]

NOTES

Epigraphs: Navah, interview, *Jerusalem Post*, March 28, 2015; Nasrallah interview, Al-Ikhbariya TV, April 6, 2015.

1. Yaakov Lapin, "Ground Forces Undergo Communications Revolution," *Jerusalem Post*, December 18, 2012; Barbara Opall-Rome, "Israel Boosts C4I to Compensate for Downsized Force," *Defense News*, January 10, 2014.

2. Rapaport, "Where Is the Israeli Army Heading?"

3. Amos Harel, "When an Army Cries Wolf," *Haaretz*, May 21, 2014.

4. "Gantz Cancels Training for Reserves Amidst Battle over Defense Budget," *Jerusalem Post*, May 19, 2014.

5. Norkin, interview, October 27, 2013.

6. Quoted in Ben Hartman, "Yaalon: IDF Cuts Revolutionary, Will Recreate Army," *Jerusalem Post*, July 11, 2013; Amos Harel and Gili Cohen, "With Budget Cuts, the IDF Is Taking a Calculated Risk to Israel's Security," *Haaretz*, July 11, 2013.

7. Segal, "Threat to Ground Maneuver as a Deciding Element."

8. Golan, interview, April 6, 2012.

9. Tamir, interview, July 20, 2013.

10. Shamir and Hecht, "Building the Next Missed Opportunity."

11. Shamir and Hecht, "Neglect of IDF Ground Forces."

12. Hirsch, "Sixth Dimension Has Taken Off."

13. Such ideas were repeated in Hirsch, "Other Boots on the Ground"; and Hirsch, *Defensive Shield*, 426–33.

14. Author interview with Meir Finkel. See also Marcus, "Learning 'Under Fire,'" 13.

15. Finkel, "Flexible Force Structure"; Marcus, "Military Innovation and Tactical Adaptation."

16. Author interview with Meir Finkel.

17. Ibid.

18. Even, "IDF Strategy and Responsibility of Political Leadership."

19. Barbara Opall-Rome, "Israel's 5-Year Plan Bulks Up Combat Capabilities, Cuts Manpower," *Defense News*, January 7, 2016.

20. Gili Cohen, "IDF Proposes 7.8 Billion Budget, Highest in Israel's History," *Haaretz*, July 21, 2015.

21. Nasrallah, speech, May 25, 2017.

22. Nasrallah, speech, May 25, 2013.

23. Raad, interview, May 22, 2015.

24. Ibid.

25. Author interview with Meir Finkel.

26. Quoted in Nicholas Blanford, "Syria as Vietnam?," *Christian Science Monitor*, March 12, 2015.

27. Quoted in Nicholas Blanford and Elhanan Miller, "Hezbollah-Israel Conflict: Two Young Fighter Assess It from Opposite Sides," *Christian Science Monitor*, July 12, 2016.

28. Katz and Pollak, "Hezbollah's Russian Military Education in Syria."

29. Quoted in Sulome Anderson, "The Next Middle East War?," *Newsweek*, July 3, 2017.

30. Katz and Pollak, "Hezbollah's Russian Military Education in Syria."

31. "Russian Special Forces Are Aiding Hezbollah in Latakia," *Now Lebanon*, January 28, 2016.

32. Quoted in Jesse Rosenfeld, "Russia Is Arming Hezbollah, Says Two of the Group's Field Commanders," *Daily Beast*, January 16, 2016.

33. Barak Ravid, "Russia Assured Israel It Isn't Transferring Arms to Syria," *Haaretz*, February 1, 2016.

34. Intelligence and Terrorism Information Center, *Hezbollah's Involvement*; Hisham Ashkar, "Infographic: Hezbollah Fighters Killed in Syria," *Al-Akhbar*, March 31, 2014.

35. AP, "Suffering Heavy Losses in Syria, Hezbollah Entices New Recruits with Money and Perks," *Haaretz*, December 19, 2015; Nicholas Blanford, "Hezbollah Lowers Fighting Age as It Takes on Islamic State," *Christian Science Monitor*, August 18, 2014.

36. Nasrallah, speech, December 20, 2013.

37. Nasrallah, speech, May 20, 2016; "Senior Hezbollah Leader Mustafa Badreddine Martyred," Al-Manar TV, May 13, 2016; Nasrallah, speech, May 11, 2017.

38. Nasrallah, speech, October 23, 2016.

39. Nasrallah, speech, August 15, 2014.

40. Nasrallah, speech, May 24, 2015.

41. Qassem, interview, October 19, 2016; Nasrallah, speech, October 23, 2016.

42. For example, see Nasrallah, speech, August 28, 2017; Nasrallah, speech, January 19, 2018.

43. "Suleiman: Army-People-Resistance Formula No Longer Valid," *Now Lebanon*, August 7, 2013; "Lebanese President Urges Hezbollah to Pull Out of Syria," Reuters, June 20, 2013.

44. "Mouawad: Hezbollah's Battle in al-Qusayr Aimed at Fragmenting Syria," *Naharnet*, May 26, 2013.

45. For example, see Nasrallah, speech, March 29, 2014.

46. Nicholas Blanford, "Starvation in Madaya,'" *Christian Science Monitor*, January 8, 2016.

47. Khalil Moussa, "Al-Manar Camera Unfolds Fabrications in Madaya," Al-Manar TV, January 16, 2016; "Syria: UN and Partners Get Relief Convoy into Besieged Town of Madaya," UN News Centre, January 11, 2016.

48. Tufayli, interview, June 8, 2013.

49. US Congress, H.R. 2297.

50. Szubin, testimony, May 25, 2016.

51. Szubin, "Beyond the Vote."

52. Nasrallah, speech, February 12, 2017.

53. Lt. Col. N., "Third Lebanon War," 5.

54. Amos Harel, "Iron Dome Racks Up 90% Success Rate So Far," *Haaretz*, July 9, 2014.

55. Lardo, interview, April 5, 2015.

56. Elran, "Civilian Front in the Second Lebanon War"; Reut Institute, *National Resilience*; Elran, Israeli, Padan, and Altshuler, "Social Resilience."

57. Yaalon, lecture, September 30, 2014.

58. Brun, lecture, June 9, 2014.

59. Brun, interview, January 16, 2015. See also author interview with Meir Finkel.

60. Lardo, interview, April 5, 2015.

61. Dekel, "Is Israel Facing a War of Attrition against Hamas?"

62. Quoted in Jodi Rudoren, "Israel Kills 3 Hamas Leaders as Latest Fighting Turns Its Way," *New York Times*, August 21, 2014.

63. Naveh, interview, March 27, 2015; Shamir and Hecht, "Gaza 2014."

64. Lt. Col. N., "Third Lebanon War."

65. Ibid., 7.

66. Nasrallah, interview, January 15, 2015.

67. Author interview with Meir Finkel.

68. Judah Ari Gross, "Simulating War with Hezbollah, IDF Looks to Avoid Past Mistakes," *Times of Israel*, September 12, 2017.

69. Katz and Pollak, "Hezbollah's Russian Military Education in Syria."

70. Brun, interview, January 16, 2015.

71. Lt. Col. N., "Third Lebanon War," 6.

72. Author interview with Meir Finkel.

73. For example, see Nasrallah, speech, November 23, 2012; Nasrallah, interview, August 14, 2014.

74. On the IDF's response to Hamas tunnel warfare, see Marcus, "Learning 'Under Fire.'"

75. Brun, interview, January 16, 2015. See also Adiv Sternman, "IDF Combs North for Possible Attack Tunnels," *Times of Israel*, January 28, 2015.

76. Roi Kais, "Hezbollah Shows Off Its Tunnels, Claims It Is Prepared for War with Israel," *Yediot Ahronoth*, May 23, 2015.

77. Rafael Advanced Defense Systems, "Trophy Active-Protection System"; Amos Harel "IDF Armor-Defense System Foils Attack on Tank for First Time," *Haaretz*, March 1, 2011.

78. Lt. Col. N., "Third Lebanon War," 7–8; on Hezbollah's UAVs: Nasrallah, speech, October 11, 2012; on cruise missiles: Nasrallah, speech, May 9, 2013.

79. Nasrallah, speech, February 16, 2016.

80. Brun, lecture, June 9, 2014 (emphasis added).

81. Halevy, lecture, May 12, 2014. See also Dekel, Siboni, and Einav, *Quiet Decade*.

82. Brun, interview, January 16, 2015.

83. Internal Israeli briefing to the author, November 2014.

84. Nasrallah, interview, April 7, 2014.

85. Nasrallah, speech, May 25, 2014.

86. Raphael D. Marcus, "Are Israel and Hizbollah on the Brink of War?," *The Telegraph*, January 20, 2015.

87. Nasrallah, speech, January 30, 2015.

88. Raphael D. Marcus, "Are Israel and Hizbollah Prepared for War?," *The Telegraph*, January 29, 2015.

89. Nasrallah, speech, December 21, 2015.

90. US State Department, "Terrorist Designation of Samir Kuntar."

91. Eshel, interview, August 17, 2017.

92. Qassem, interview, September 10, 2017.

93. Raphael D. Marcus, "How Will Hizbollah Respond to the Assassination of One of Its Commanders in Syria?," *The Telegraph*, December 22, 2015.

94. Naveh, interview, March 27, 2015.

95. Nasrallah, speech, November 11, 2012.

CHRONOLOGY

1975	Start of Lebanese Civil War.
1975	Formation of Amal militia marks rise of Shi'ite militancy in Lebanon.
1976	Syria's military enters Lebanon amid civil war.
1978	March 14–21: IDF launches Operation Litani in Lebanon.
1978	August 31: Disappearance of iconic cleric Musa al-Sadr while on trip to Libya reverberates deeply throughout Lebanon's Shi'ite population.
1979	Islamic revolution in Iran leads to rise of Ayatollah Khomeini.
1982	June 3: Palestinian militants critically wound Israeli ambassador Shlomo Argov in London, which serves as justification by Defense Minister Ariel Sharon to launch Operation Peace for Galilee against PLO in Lebanon.
1982	June 6: Operation Peace for Galilee launched, and IDF enters Lebanon.
1982	June 9: Air battle between IAF and Syrian air force in Bekaa Valley marks first large-scale use of Israel's precision weaponry and advanced technology.
1982	August 30: Israel's main goal of Operation Peace for Galilee is achieved as PLO leadership is expelled from Lebanon to Tunisia.
1982–85	Hezbollah emerges in Lebanon as loose umbrella for radical Shi'ite militancy.
1983	September: IDF begins phased withdrawal south of Lebanon's Awali River.
1985	January 14: Israel pledges to withdraw from Lebanon and establishes "temporary" security zone in southern Lebanon in collaboration with SLA.
1985	February 16: Hezbollah declares its formal existence and publishes "Open Letter" manifesto.

1987–91	COS Lt. Gen. Dan Shomron formulates plan to make IDF "slimmer and smarter."
Late 1980s– early 1990s	Reformist officers form "intellectual insurgency" in wake of IDF's mediocre performance in Lebanon and internally develop new conceptual agenda for IDF.
1989	Subhi Tufayli officially assumes position of first secretary-general of Hezbollah.
1989	October 22: Taif Accord signed, ending Lebanese Civil War.
1991	January–February: Success of US-led coalition during Gulf War leads to formal proclamation by US defense community of "Revolution in Military Affairs."
1991	Abbas Mussawi assumes control of Hezbollah as second secretary-general and leads program of reform to improve Hezbollah's military capabilities.
1992	February 16: Abbas Mussawi assassinated in southern Lebanon by IDF helicopter strike.
1992	February: Hassan Nasrallah assumes control of Hezbollah as its third secretary-general and leads sustained program to improve Hezbollah's operational security and guerrilla capabilities.
1992	October: IDF initiates aggressive new targeting policy under Northern Command head Maj. Gen. Yitzhak Mordechai.
1993	July 25–31: IDF launches Operation Accountability, which results in establishment of tacit "understanding" between Israel and Hezbollah outlining "rules of the game."
1994	Maj. Gen. Amiram Levin becomes head of Northern Command and pushes IDF to adapt its conceptualization of Hezbollah from terrorist group to guerrilla army.
1995	January: Egoz Reconnaissance Battalion, specializing in counterguerrilla warfare, established in Northern Command.
1995	April 27: IDF Operational Theory Research Institute (OTRI) officially established, co-led by Brig. Gen. Shimon Naveh, and innovative concept of Systemic Operational Design (SOD) begins to diffuse in small pockets of the military.
1996	April 11–27: IDF launches Operation Grapes of Wrath, resulting in establishment of written set of "understandings" between Israel and Hezbollah, formulating tacit 1993 agreement.
1997	February 4: Two IDF helicopters collide in northern Israel, killing seventy-three soldiers en route to Lebanon.
1997	Establishment of Four Mothers Movement.

1998–99	Development of Limited Conflict doctrine by Col. Shmuel Nir as alternative solution to deal with Hezbollah's asymmetrical warfare.
1999	January: Moshe Arens reassumes position of defense minister and encourages IDF to directly target Lebanese government infrastructure as way of pressuring Hezbollah.
2000	May 24: Prime Minister Ehud Barak defies military recommendations and orders a unilateral IDF withdrawal from Lebanon.
2000–2005	IDF adopts several RMA-inspired multiyear plans that result in large-scale investment in air force, precision munitions, and surveillance capabilities.
2000–2005	Recurrent meetings between IDF and US Department of Defense's Office of Net Assessment result in exchange of ideas regarding SOD and RMA.
2000–2005	High-profile border attacks by Hezbollah erode IDF deterrence and pave road to war.
2001	April 16: IDF targets Syrian installations in Lebanon for first time since 1982 in response to Hezbollah attack, in attempt to directly pressure Syria to restrain Hezbollah. Syrian installations are targeted again on July 1.
2002	March–April: Israel launches Operation Defense Shield in West Bank against Palestinian militant groups, marking first operational utilization of SOD on battlefield.
2002	IDF Northern Command and OTRI begin developing Northern Storm plan using SOD, for war with Hezbollah.
2005	OTRI formally shut down after critical state comptroller report.
2005	April: Syrian military withdraws from Lebanon after twenty-nine years, in response to Lebanon's Cedar Revolution.
2006	April: COS Lt. Gen. Dan Halutz signs new "operational concept" document, distributed to IDF in May.
2006	July 12: Outbreak of thirty-four-day Lebanon War.
2006	August 14: UN Resolution 1701 goes into effect, establishing cease-fire between Israel and Hezbollah and formally ending war.
2007	April: Publication of Winograd Commission Interim Report.
2008	January: Publication of Winograd Commission Final Report.
2008	IDF's Dahiya doctrine unofficially elucidated by Maj. Gen. Gadi Eizenkot, head of Northern Command.
2011	March: Outbreak of violence in Syria between forces of President Bashar al-Assad and rebel groups.

2013   May 25: Hassan Nasrallah publicly admits Hezbollah
            militarily operating in Syria alongside Syrian military.
2015   October: Russia launches military operations in Syria in
            support of President Assad and begins coordination with
            Hezbollah.
2013–18   Border skirmishes occur intermittently between Israel and
            Hezbollah over group's violation of Israel's "red lines"
            regarding transfer of weapons from Syria and Hezbollah's
            presence in the Golan Heights.

SELECTED BIBLIOGRAPHY

AUTHOR INTERVIEWS

Amir, Lt. Col. (Ret.) Roni, IDF. Head of the IAF Doctrine Branch. Ramat Gan, January 29, 2013; June 15, 2015.

Arens, Moshe. Minister of defense (1983–84, 1990–92, 1999). By telephone, June 12, 2017.

Azani, Col. (Res.) Eitan, IDF. Head of Intelligence, Lebanon Liaison Division. Herzliya, July 5, 2012.

Blanford, Nicholas. Lebanon correspondent, *Christian Science Monitor*. Beirut, August 19, 2011.

Brom, Brig. Gen. (Ret.) Shlomo, IDF. Head of IDF Strategic Planning Division, IDF Planning Directorate (1995–98); Deputy head, IDF Strategic Planning Division (1990–94). Ramat Aviv, January 18, 2012.

C., IDF Military Intelligence. Tel Aviv, January 19, 2012; July 4, 2012.

Cohen, Col. (Ret.) Ronen, IDF. Deputy head, Research and Production Division, IDF Military Intelligence (2006–7); head of Terrorism Desk, IDF Military Intelligence (2003–6); head of Intelligence, Thirty-Sixth Division, Northern Command (1999–2001); head of IAF Special Operations Intelligence Branch, Lebanon (1997–99); intelligence officer in Lebanon (1983–97). Ramat Aviv, January 27, 2013.

E., Lt. Col. (Ret.), IDF. Northern Command, served in Lebanon. Ramat Gan, July 2, 2012; February 4, 2015; November 17, 2015; November 20, 2015.

Eiland, Maj. Gen. (Ret.) Giora, IDF. Head of National Security Council (2004–6); head of IDF Planning Directorate (2001–3); head of IDF Operations Directorate (1999–2001); head of IDF Operations Division (1996–99). Ranana, July 10, 2012.

Eiran, Maj. (Res.) Ehud, IDF. Golani Brigade; served in Lebanon (1988–92). Netanya, January 30, 2013.

Elran, Brig. Gen. (Ret.) Meir, IDF. Special consultant to the Winograd Commission (2006–7); deputy head, IDF Military Intelligence (1987–89). Ramat Aviv, January 12, 2012.

Erlich, Col. (Ret.) Reuven, IDF. Deputy head, Government Coordinator for Lebanese Affairs, Ministry of Defense (1985–2000); IDF Military Intelligence (1964–94). Glilot, January 30, 2013.

Finkel, Brig. Gen. (Res.) Meir, IDF. Head (as colonel), commander, IDF Dado Center for Interdisciplinary Military Studies (2014–); Concept Development and Doctrine Department, IDF Ground Forces (2008–14). Tsrifin, July 1, 2012; Glilot, November 2, 2015.

G., Lt. Col. (Ret.), IDF. Officer in an IDF special forces unit. Afula, January 31, 2013.

Gal, Orit. Analyst, IDF Operational Theory Research Institute (2004–5). London, March 22, 2012.

Goksel, Timur. Spokesperson, United Nations Interim Force in Lebanon (UNIFIL) (1979–2003); senior adviser, UNIFIL (1995–2003). Beirut, August 6, 2011.

Graicer, Ofra. Senior researcher, IDF Operational Theory Research Institute (1999–2005). Tel Aviv, January 17, 2012; June 26, 2012.

Granit, Lt. Col. (Ret.) Amos, IDF. Senior researcher, Operational Theory Research Institute (1996–2004). Ramat HaSharon, July 10, 2012.

Guy, Frances. UK ambassador to Lebanon (2006–11). London, November 3, 2011.

Henkin, Yagil. Lecturer, IDF Command and General Staff College (2007–). Glilot, June 25, 2012.

I. Hezbollah official spokesperson. Hezbollah Public Relations Office; former official, Al-Manar TV. September 16, 2014.

Lanir, Col. (Ret.) Zvi, IDF. Cohead, Operational Theory Research Institute (1995–2002). Tel Aviv, January 12, 2012.

Levy, Michael. UK special envoy to the Middle East (1998–2007). London, March 11, 2013.

Naveh, Brig. Gen. (Ret.) Shimon, IDF. Cohead, Operational Theory Research Institute (1995–2005). By email, May 31, 2012; Glilot, June 14–15, 2015.

Raveh, Lt. Col. (Ret.) Saar, IDF. IDF Behavioral Science Unit, Personnel Directorate (1997–2009); Golani Brigade, served in Lebanon (1984–88). Shoham, July 9, 2012.

Saleh, Mohsen. Director, Al-Zaytouna Center for Research and Documentation. Beirut, July 28, 2011.

Segal, Col. (Res.) Giora, IDF. Director, IDF Institute for the Study of the Tactical Environment. Herzliya, June 26, 2012.

Shamir, Eitan. Head, National Security Doctrine Department, Israel Ministry of Strategic Affairs (2011–12); research fellow, IDF Dado Center for Interdisciplinary Military Studies (2009–11). Jerusalem, January 11, 2012; Ramat Aviv, January 28, 2013.

Siboni, Col. (Ret.) Gabi, IDF. Chief of staff, Golani Brigade; deputy head, IDF Research Center for Force Utilization and Buildup Experimentation Laboratory. Ramat Aviv, January 17, 2012.

Sneh, Brig. Gen. (Ret.) Ephraim, IDF. Member of Knesset (1992–2008); deputy defense minister (1999–2000, 2006–7); commander of the Lebanon Security Zone (1981–82). Herzliya, June 11, 2015.

Tira, Lt. Col. (Res.) Ron, IDF. Fighter pilot; head of IAF Lahak Intelligence Unit; IAF Campaign Planning Department. Herzliya, January 21, 2013.

Williams, Michael. UN undersecretary-general for the Middle East and special coordinator for Lebanon (2008–11); UK special envoy to the Middle East (2007–8); UN special coordinator for the Middle East (2006–7). London, March 19, 2014.

Y., Maj. (Ret.), IDF. IDF Military Intelligence. January 30, 2013.

Yadlin, Maj. Gen. (Ret.) Amos, IDF. Head of IDF Military Intelligence Directorate (2006–10); head of IDF National Defense College (2002–4); former deputy commander of the IAF. By email, February 15, 2018.

PUBLISHED OR BROADCAST INTERVIEWS, SPEECHES, LECTURES, AND TESTIMONY

Adam, Maj. Gen. Udi. Interview by Hanan Greenberg. "Northern Command Chief: Ground Forces Entered Late." *Yediot Ahronoth*, August 16, 2006.

Al-Khalil, Hussein. Interview. *Al-Hayah*, November 30, 1995. FBIS.

Almog, Maj. Gen. Doron. "Interview with Maj. Gen. Doron Almog: The Israeli Military Is in a Crisis of Leadership." By Christoph Schult. *Der Spiegel*, November 21, 2006.

Arens, Moshe. Interview by Zeev Schiff. *Haaretz*, July 4, 1999.

———. Interview. Israel Channel 2 Television, June 25, 1999. In *BBC Summary of World Broadcasts*, June 28, 1999.

———. Interview by Charlie Rose. *Charlie Rose* on PBS, April 30, 1999.

———. Interview. Jerusalem Television, February 16, 1992. FBIS.

———. Lecture. "The Lebanese Border: Between Deterrence and Decision." The Lebanon Wars and Israel's Security Concept Conference, Institute for National Security Studies (INSS), Tel Aviv, July 12, 2012 (Hebrew).

Barak, Ehud. Interview by Lisa Beyer. "The Time Has Come to End a Tragedy." *Time*, June 5, 2000.

———. Interview. Voice of Israel Radio, March 2, 1999. In *BBC Monitoring Middle East*, March 3, 1999.

———. Interview. Qol Yisrael Radio, December 15, 1994. FBIS.

———. Interview. Jerusalem Television Service, October 16, 1985. FBIS.

———. Speech. "Israel Completes Pull-Out from Lebanon." Israel Ministry of Foreign Affairs, May 24, 2000.

Ben-Israel, Maj. Gen. (Ret.) Isaac. Interview by Amnon Barzilai. "A Perceptual Change." *Haaretz*, December 18, 2001.

———. Lecture. "Israel's Security Concept." Tel Aviv University, April 4, 2013.

Biran, Maj. Gen. (Ret.) Ilan. Lecture. Twelfth Annual Herzliya Conference, Herzliya, Israel, February 2, 2012.

Brun, Brig. Gen. Itai. Interview by Yoav Limor. "Attacks in the Golan Heights Are a Matter of Time." *Israel HaYom*, January 16, 2015.

———. Lecture. "Middle East Intelligence Assessment." Fourteenth Annual Herzliya Conference, Herzliya, Israel, June 9, 2014.

———. Lecture. "Trends in the IDF Maneuver Concept." Land Warfare in the 21st Century Conference, Institute for Land Warfare Studies, Latrun, Israel, September 16, 2008.

Drori, Maj. Gen. Amir. Interview by Zeev Schiff. "The Ground Forces as an Example." *Haaretz*, May 16, 1986. FBIS.

Eitam, Brig. Gen. Effie. Lecture. "Israel's Extended Presence in Lebanon." The Lebanon Wars and Israel's Security Concept Conference, INSS, Tel Aviv, July 12, 2012 (Hebrew).

Eizenkot, Maj. Gen. Gadi. Interview. "Israel Warns Hezbollah War Will Invite Destruction." *Yediot Ahronoth*, October 3, 2008.

———. "IDF Press Conference following the Kfar Qana Incident." Israel Ministry of Foreign Affairs, July 30, 2006.

Eshel, Maj. Gen. Amir. Interview by Amos Harel. "We Prevented Israel from Going to War." *Haaretz*, August 17, 2017.

Fadlallah, Mohammad Hussein. Interview. "Islamic Unity and Political Change." *Journal of Palestine Studies* 25, no. 1 (Autumn 1995): 61–75.

———. Interview. *Monday Morning*, December 16–22, 1985. FBIS.

Gantz, Lt. Gen. Benny. Interview by Alon Ben-David. *Jane's Defence Weekly*, December 26, 2007.

———. Interview by Barbara Opall-Rome. "Mideast Crisis to Drive Future Needs." *Defense News*, August 15, 2006.

———. Speech. "Challenges to Israel's National Security." Thirteenth Annual Herzliya Conference, Herzliya, Israel, March 11, 2013.

Golan, Maj. Gen. Yair. Interview by Yoav Limor. "Iran, Hezbollah Are 'Up to Their Necks' in Syria, Says Israeli General." *Israel Hayom*, April 6, 2012.

———. Speech. "Chief of IDF Northern Command: Hezbollah Is Better Armed, Better Trained and More Cautious." IDF official website, August 1, 2013.

Graicer, Ofra. TEDx Lecture. "Why Generals Need to Forget before They Can Be Generals." Tel Aviv University, February 15, 2016.

———. Lecture. "Session II: Lessons for Doctrine and Force Structure." The Second Lebanon War: Lessons for Modern Militaries Conference. Royal United Services Institute (hereafter RUSI), London, June 20, 2008.

Halevy, Ephraim. Lecture. "Between Shifting Sovereignties and Shifty Actors: Quo Vadis for the Middle East?" RUSI, London, May 12, 2014.

Halutz, Lt. Gen. Dan. Interview by Raviv Drucker. *Hamakor*, Israel Channel 10 Television, May 5, 2015 (Hebrew).

———. Interview by Barbara Opall-Rome. "Israel's Lebanon War Chief Defends Strategy." *Defense News*, February 22, 2010.

———. Interview by Sima Kadmon. "Halutz: Not Calling Up Reserves Was a Mistake." *Yediot Ahronoth*, February 15, 2008.

———. Lecture. "A Perspective on Then and Now." INSS, Tel Aviv, July 14, 2016 (Hebrew).

———. Testimony to the Winograd Commission, January 28, 2007 (Hebrew).

Hashem, Col. Akel. Interview by Ronen Bergman. "Thanks for Your Cooperation." *Haaretz*, October 29, 1999.

Inbar, Brig. Gen. Giora. Press statement, Qol Yisrael Radio, April 17, 1996. FBIS.

———. Press statement. IDF Radio, April 16, 1996. FBIS.

Kitri, Brig. Gen. Ron. Interview. IDF Radio, April 16, 2001. In *BBC Monitoring Middle East*, April 16, 2001.

Komati, Mahmoud. Interview by Sheherezade Faramarzi. "Hezbollah: We Didn't Expect Such Strong Reaction from Israel." Associated Press, July 25, 2006.

Kuperwasser, Brig. Gen. Yossi. Interview by Gidi Weitz. "To Beirut if Necessary." *Haaretz*, August 10, 2006.

Lahd, Gen. Antoine. Interview by Beni Issembert. Infolive TV, March 5, 2007.

———. Interview by Roee Nahmias. "Lahad: Syria behind Gemayel's Murder." *Yediot Ahronoth*, November 26, 2006.

Lardo, Col. Yoram. Interview by Or Heller. "The Next War Will Not Be a Brief Event." *Israel Defense Magazine*, April 5, 2015.

Levin, Maj. Gen. Amiram. Briefing. *Al HaMishmar*, February 20, 1995. FBIS.

———. Interview. Qol Yisrael Radio, August 25, 1995. FBIS.

———. News conference. Qol Yisrael Radio, April 13, 1996. FBIS.

———. Press statement. Israel Channel 1 TV, August 18, 1997. In *BBC Summary of World Broadcasts*, August 20, 1997.

———. Press statement. Qol Yisrael Radio, August 6, 1996. FBIS.

———. Press statement. IDF Radio, June 16, 1995. FBIS.

———. Speech. Qol Yisrael Radio, January 28, 1996. FBIS.

Levy, David. Press briefing. "Withdrawal from Lebanon." Israel Ministry of Foreign Affairs, May 23, 2000.

Lubrani, Uri. Interview by Yoav Limor. *Bamahane*, October 5, 1988. FBIS.

Mofaz, Lt. Gen. Shaul. Interview by Arieh O'Sullivan. "The IDF in 2000: Smarter, Newer and Stronger." *Jerusalem Post*, April 20, 1999.

Mordechai, Maj. Gen. Yitzhak. Interview. IDF Radio, July 26, 1993. FBIS.

———. Interview by Alex Fishman and Aharon Klein. *Hadashot*, May 6, 1992. FBIS.

Musawi, Ammar. "Interview: Ammar Musawi." *Lebanon Report* 5, no. 12 (December 1994): 10.

Mussawi, Sec.-Gen. Abbas. Interview. Voice of the Oppressed (clandestine), September 6, 1991. FBIS.

———. Interview. AFP, July 10, 1985. FBIS.

Nasrallah, Hassan. Interview. Al-Ikhbariya TV (Syria), April 6, 2015. Transcript on Al-Ahed News.

———. Interview. Al-Mayadeen TV, January 15, 2015. Also aired on Al-Manar TV.

———. Interview. *Al-Akhbar*, August 14, 2014.

———. Interview. *Al-Safir*, April 7, 2014. Translation on Al-Ahed News.

———. Interview. Al-Mayadeen TV, August 14, 2013. Transcript on Al-Ahed News.

———. Interview by Julian Assange, RT Television, April 17, 2012.

———. Interview. Al-Jazeera TV, July 23, 2007. Middle East Media Research Institute.

———. Interview. Al-Alam TV, May 6, 2007. In *BBC Monitoring Middle East*, May 10, 2007.

———. Interview. Al-Manar TV, May 2, 2007. In *BBC Monitoring Middle East*, May 2, 2007.

———. Interview. New TV, August 27, 2006. In Noe, *Voice of Hezbollah*.

———. Interview. Al-Jazeera TV, July 20, 2006. Excerpted transcript in *Journal of Palestine Studies* 36, no. 1 (2006): 178–83.

———. Interview by Ambassador Edward Peck. Council for the National Interest, February 2006 (full date unknown). Available in three parts on YouTube.

———. Interview. Al-Jazeera TV, May 27, 2003.

———. Interview. *Teshreen*, June 21, 1999. In Noe, *Voice of Hezbollah*.

———. Interview. *Al-Hawadaith*, March 19, 1999.

———. Interview. *Al-Shira'*, March 30, 1998.

———. Interview. *Al-Moharrer*, March 29, 1998. In Noe, *Voice of Hezbollah*.

———. Interview. *Al-Safir*, April 30, 1996. In Noe, *Voice of Hezbollah*.

———. Interview. *Nida al-Watan*, August 31, 1993. In Noe, *Voice of Hezbollah*.

———. Interview. *Al-Safir*, August 27, 1993. In Noe, *Voice of Hezbollah*.

———. Interview. *Ettela'at*, February 13, 1993. FBIS.

———. Interview. *Al-Safir*, November 14, 1992. FBIS.

———. Interview. Voice of the Mountain, June 25, 1992. FBIS.

———. Interview. *Al-Safir*, February 27, 1992. FBIS.

———. Interview. *Al-Khaleej*, March 11, 1986. In Noe, *Voice of Hezbollah*.

———. Speech. Al-Ahed News, January 19, 2018.

———. Speech. Al-Manar TV, August 28, 2017.

———. Speech. Press TV, May 25, 2017.

———. Speech. Al-Ahed News, May 11, 2017.

————. Speech. Al-Ahed News, February 12, 2017.

————. Speech. Al-Ahed News, October 23, 2016.

————. Speech. Al-Ahed News, May 20, 2016.

————. Speech. Al-Ahed News, March 21, 2016.

————. Speech. Al-Ahed News, February 16, 2016.

————. Speech. Eulogy for Samir Kuntar. Al-Ahed News, December 21, 2015.

————. Speech. Al-Ahed News, May 24, 2015.

————. Speech. Al-Ahed News, January 30, 2015.

————. Speech. Al-Manar TV, August 15, 2014. Transcript on Al-Ahed News.

————. Speech. Al-Ahed News, May 25, 2014.

————. Speech. Al-Ahed News, March 29, 2014.

————. Speech. Anniversary of the martyrdom of Abbas Mussawi. Al-Manar TV, February 16, 2014. Transcript on Al-Ahed News.

————. Speech. Eulogy for Hassan Laqees. Al-Ahed News, December 20, 2013.

————. Speech. Press TV, August 16, 2013.

————. Speech. Al-Ahed News, May 25, 2013.

————. Speech. Twenty-fifth anniversary of Al-Nour radio station. Press TV, May 9, 2013.

————. Speech. Tenth night of Ashura. November 23, 2012. Excerpts in Al-Ahed News, November 24, 2012.

————. Speech. Martyrs Day. Hezbollah official website, November 11, 2012.

————. Speech. Press TV, October 11, 2012.

————. Speech. Martyrs Day. Hezbollah official website, November 11, 2011.

————. Speech. Al-Manar TV, February 16, 2011. Middle East Media Research Institute.

————. Speech. Al-Manar TV, February 16, 2010. In *BBC Monitoring Middle East*, February 18, 2010.

————. Speech. Islamic Resistance Week. Al-Manar TV, February 22, 2008.

————. Speech. Al-Manar TV, August 3, 2006.

————. Speech. Al-Manar TV, July 17, 2006. Excerpted transcript in *Journal of Palestine Studies* 36, no. 1 (2006): 176–77.

————. Speech. Hezbollah official website, July 14, 2006.

————. Speech. Anniversary of the death of Ayatollah Khomeini. June 4, 2002. In Noe, *Voice of Hezbollah*.

————. Speech. "Resistance and Liberation Day." Hezbollah official website, May 26, 2000.

————. Speech. Baalbek Voice of the Oppressed, July 31, 1993. FBIS.

————. Speech. Elegy for Abbas Mussawi. February 18, 1992. In Noe, *Voice of Hezbollah*.

Naveh, Brig. Gen. Shimon. Interview by Ofra Graicer. "Beware the Power of the Dark Side: The Inevitable Coupling of Design and Doctrine." *Experticia Militar* no. 2 (July–October 2017): 30–37.

————. Interview by Matt Matthews. "Interview with BG (Ret.) Shimon Naveh." Operational Leadership Experiences. Combat Studies Institute, November 1, 2007.

————. Interview by Yotam Feldman. "Dr. Naveh, or How I Learned to Stop Worrying and Walk through Walls." *Haaretz*, October 25, 2007.

————. Interview by Stephen Johnson. "Retired Israeli General Recalls Days of Unrest." *Houston Chronicle*, November 20, 1993.

Naveh, Maj. Gen. Yair. Interview by Yaakov Lapin. "Deterring Hezbollah: The Ex-IDF Deputy Chief of Staff Shares His Vision for Israeli Security." *Jerusalem Post*, March 28, 2015.

————. Interview by Amir Rapaport. "IDF Must Regain Its Maneuvering Capabilities." *Israel Defense Magazine*, March 27, 2015.

Netanyahu, Benjamin. Interview. Voice of Israel Radio, January 1, 1999. In *BBC Summary of World Broadcasts*, January 4, 1999.

Norkin, Brig. Gen. Amikam. Interview by Barbara Opall-Rome. "Israel Air Force Plan Shoots for 10-Fold Boost in Bombs on Target." *Defense News*, October 27, 2013.

Olmert, Ehud. Interview by Raviv Drucker. *Hamakor*, Israel Channel 10 Television, May 5, 2015 (Hebrew).

———. Lecture. "The Second Lebanon War: The Test of Time." The Lebanon Wars and Israel's Security Concept Conference, INSS, Tel Aviv, July 12, 2012 (Hebrew).

———. Speech to the Knesset. Knesset Official Release. "Prime Minister Ehud Olmert's Address to the Knesset during the Conflict in the North." July 17, 2006.

Orr, Brig. Gen. Ori. Interview. IDF Radio, April 13, 1985. FBIS.

Peled, Maj. Gen. Yossi. Interview. IDF Radio, June 18, 1987. FBIS.

Peres, Shimon. Speech to the Knesset. Qol Yisrael Radio, April 22, 1996. FBIS.

Peretz, Amir. Interview by Raviv Drucker. *HaMakor*, Israel Channel 10 Television, May 5, 2015 (Hebrew).

———. Interview by Mazal Mualem. "Former Israeli Defense Minister: IDF Must Cut Its Ground Forces." Al-Monitor, June 6, 2013.

———. Interview by Atilla Somfalvi. "Peretz Says Halutz Brave, Fit for Politics." *Yediot Ahronoth*, February 17, 2008.

———. Interview by Ari Shavit. "Looking Back in Satisfaction." *Haaretz*, May 3, 2007.

Qassem, Naim. Interview. Al-Mayadeen TV, September 10, 2017.

———. Interview. "Sheikh Qassem: Hezbollah Will Not Leave Syria as Long as There Is Need to Fight Takfiris." Al-Manar TV, October 19, 2016.

———. Interview. Hezbollah official website, February 12, 2010.

———. Interview by Borzou Daragahi. "Lebanon's Hezbollah Savors Increasing Legitimacy." *Los Angeles Times*, April 13, 2009.

———. Interview. *Monday Morning*, November 20, 2000.

———. Interview. Radio Monte Carlo, December 12, 1994. FBIS.

Raad, Mohammad. Interview by Ali Hashem. "Senior Hezbollah Official Speaks Out." Al-Monitor, May 22, 2015.

———. Interview. *Mideast Mirror*, December 13, 1994. FBIS.

Rabin, Yitzhak. Interview. Jerusalem Television Service, April 3, 1985. FBIS.

———. Lecture. "After the Gulf War: Israel Defense and Its Security Policy." BESA Center for Strategic Studies, Ramat Gan, Israel, June 10, 1991.

———. Speech to the Knesset. Channel 2 Television, July 28, 1993. FBIS.

———. Speech. Jaffee Center for Strategic Studies, Tel Aviv, February 15, 1985.

Shomron, Lt. Gen. Dan. Interview by Yaakov Erez and Immanuel Rosen. *Maariv*, September 23, 1987. FBIS.

———. Interview by Robert Lacontre. *Le Figaro*, October 28, 1988. FBIS.

———. Interview. Jerusalem Television Service, May 4, 1988. FBIS.

———. Interview. IDF Radio, June 4, 1986. In *BBC Summary of World Broadcasts*, June 6, 1986.

———. Press statement. IDF Radio, August 30, 1987. FBIS.

———. Speech. IDF Radio, March 9, 1988. FBIS.

Szubin, Adam. "Testimony of Acting Under Secretary for Terrorism and Financial Intelligence before the House Committee on Foreign Affairs." US Department of the Treasury Press Center, May 25, 2016.

Tamir, Brig. Gen. Chico. Interview by Amos Harel. "For Army Reform Plan, an Authoritative Voice of Dissent." *Haaretz*, July 20, 2013.

Tufayli, Subhi. Interview. "Hezbollah Provoking the World, Ex-Militia Chief Says." Al-Arabiya TV, June 8, 2013.

———. Interview. *Monday Morning*, April 22, 1991.

———. Interview. *Al-Nahar al-Arabi wa al-Duwali*, December 21–27, 1987. FBIS.

———. Interview. *Al-Majallah*, June 15–21, 1987. FBIS.

———. Interview. *Al-Ittihad al-Usbu'I*, December 4, 1986. FBIS.

———. Speech. Radio Free Lebanon (clandestine), September 4, 1987. FBIS.

Yaalon, Moshe. Interview by Ari Shavit. "The Enemy Within." *Haaretz*, August 29, 2002.

———. Lecture. The Lessons of Operation Protective Edge Conference, INSS, Tel Aviv, September 30, 2014.

Yaari, Adm. Yedidya. Lecture. "Session IV: Technology and Counter-Insurgency." The Second Lebanon War: Lessons for Modern Militaries Conference, RUSI, London, June 20, 2008.

BOOKS, PERIODICALS, AND OTHER SOURCES

Adamsky, Dima. "From Israel with Deterrence: Strategic Culture, Intra-war Coercion and Brute Force." *Security Studies* 26, no. 1 (2016): 157–84.

———. *The Culture of Military Innovation*. Stanford, CA: Stanford University Press, 2010.

———. "Jihadi Operational Art and the Coming Wave of Jihadi Strategic Studies." *Studies in Conflict and Terrorism* 33, no. 1 (2009): 1–19.

Ajami, Fouad. *The Vanished Imam: Musa al-Sadr and the Shia of Lebanon*. Ithaca, NY: Cornell University Press, 1986.

Alagha, Joseph. *Hizbullah's Identity Construction*. Amsterdam: Amsterdam University Press, 2011.

———. *The Shifts in Hizbullah's Ideology*. Leiden: Amsterdam University Press, 2006.

Allon, Yigal. "The Case for Defensible Borders." *Foreign Affairs* 55, no. 1 (1976): 38–53.

Al-Manar Group. *Hajj Khaled Bazzi: Prince of the Battlefield*. Hezbollah official documentary. Al-Manar TV, 2010 (Arabic).

Almog, Maj. Gen. Doron. "Cumulative Deterrence and the War on Terrorism." *Parameters* 34, no. 4 (2004): 4–19.

Amidror, Maj. Gen. Yaakov. *Winning Counterinsurgency War: The Israeli Experience*. Jerusalem: Jerusalem Center for Public Affairs, 2008.

———. "Can a Conventional Army Vanquish a Terrorist Insurgency?" Jerusalem Viewpoints no. 550, Jerusalem Center for Public Affairs, January 1, 2007.

———. "The Military Strike as a Cognitive Paradigm of Effects." *Maarachot* 403–4 (2005): 54–57 (Hebrew).

Amnesty International. *Unlawful Killings during "Operation Grapes of Wrath."* London: Amnesty International, July 23, 1996.

Anderson, Lt. Col. John. "From Systemic Operational Design (SOD) to a Systemic Approach to Design and Planning: A Canadian Experience." *Canadian Military Journal* 12, no. 3 (2012): 35–44.

Arad, Uzi. "Is There a Future for Israel's National Security Council?" BESA Perspectives Paper no. 180, BESA Center for Strategic Studies, Ramat Gan, Israel, September 5, 2012.

———. "A Cumulative Deterrence Deficit." *Yediot Ahronoth*, September 22, 2006.

Arens, Moshe. "Hezbollah 2 Israel 0." *Haaretz*, February 3, 2004.

Arian, Asher. "Public Opinion on Lebanon and Syria, 1999." *Strategic Assessment* 2, no. 1 (1999): 19–23.

Ariely, Lt. Col. Gil. "Learning while Fighting." *Maarachot* 412 (May 2007): 4–13 (Hebrew).

Arkin, William. *Divine Victory: Airpower in the 2006 Israel-Hezbollah War*. Maxwell AFB, AL: Air University Press, 2007.

Avant, Deborah. "The Institutional Sources of Military Doctrine: Hegemons in Peripheral Wars." *International Studies Quarterly* 37, no. 4 (1993): 409–30.

Azani, Col. Eitan. *Hezbollah: The Story of the Party of God; From Revolution to Institutionalization*. New York: Palgrave Macmillan, 2011.

Bar, Shmuel. "Deterring Nonstate Terrorist Groups: The Case of Hezbollah." *Comparative Strategy* 26, no. 5 (2007): 469–93.

Bar-Joseph, Uri. "The Hubris of Initial Victory: The IDF and the Second Lebanon War." In Jones and Catignani, *Israel and Hezbollah*, 147–61.

———. "RMA: The View from Israel." Paper presented at the conference Modern Military Thought in the Post-Cold War Era: A Critical Approach, Norwegian Defence University College, Oslo, July 25, 2009.

———. "Introduction." In *Israel's National Security towards the 21st Century*, edited by Uri Bar-Joseph. London: Frank Cass, 2001. Also in *Journal of Strategic Studies* 24, no. 2.

———. "Variations on a Theme: The Conceptualization of Deterrence in Israeli Strategic Thinking." *Security Studies* 7, no. 3 (1998): 145–81.

Barak, Oren, and Gabriel Sheffer. "Israel's 'Security Network' and Its Impact: An Exploration of a New Approach." *International Journal of Middle East Studies* 38, no. 2 (2006): 235–61.

Bazak, Col. Yuval. "The IDF and the Road to a More Professional Military." *Military and Strategic Affairs* 1, no. 3 (2009): 51–68.

Beaulieu-B., Philippe, and Philippe Dufort. "Conclusion: Researching the Reflexive Turn in Military and Strategic Studies." *Journal of Military and Strategic Studies* 17, no. 4 (2017): 273–89.

Belfer Center for Science and International Affairs. *Deterring Terror: How Israel Confronts the Next Generation of Threats; English Translation of the Official Strategy of the Israel Defense Forces*. Cambridge, MA: Harvard University, 2016.

Ben-Horin, Yoav, and Barry Posen. *Israel's Strategic Doctrine*. Santa Monica, CA: RAND Corp., 1981.

Ben-Israel, Maj. Gen. Isaac. "The Use of Weapons in Densely Populated Areas." *Military and Strategic Affairs* 5 (special issue, April 2014): 17–22.

———. "The Revolution in Military Affairs and the Operation in Iraq." In *After the War in Iraq: Defining the New Strategic Balance*, edited by Shai Feldman, 55–74. Eastbourne, UK: Sussex Academic Press, 2003.

Ben-Shalom, Uzi, and Eitan Shamir. "Mission Command between Theory and Practice: The Case of the IDF." *Defense and Security Analysis* 27, no. 2 (June 2011): 101–17.

Bennet, Naftali. "Hezbollah Is Lebanon in Hezbollah." *Times of Israel*, April 2, 2017.

Berman, Lazar. "Capturing Contemporary Innovation: Studying IDF Innovation against Hamas and Hizbullah." *Journal of Strategic Studies* 35, no. 1 (2012): 121–47.

———. "Beyond the Basics: Looking beyond the Conventional Wisdom Surrounding the IDF Campaigns against Hizbullah and Hamas." *Small Wars Journal*, April 28, 2011.

Biddle, Stephen. "Victory Misunderstood: What the Gulf War Tells Us about the Future of Conflict." *International Security* 21, no. 2 (1996): 139–79.

Biddle, Stephen, and Jeffrey Friedman. *The 2006 Lebanon Campaign and the Future of Warfare: Implications for Army and Defense Policy.* Carlisle, PA: Strategic Studies Institute, 2008.

Bilmyer, Maj. John. *The IDF: Tactical Success-Strategic Failure, SOD, the Second Intifada, and Beyond.* Fort Leavenworth, KS: School of Advanced Military Studies (SAMS), 2011.

Blanford, Nicholas. *Warriors of God: Inside Hezbollah's Thirty-Year Struggle against Israel.* New York: Random House, 2011.

Bolton, Amb. John. *Surrender Is Not an Option.* New York: Simon & Schuster, 2007.

Bond, Brian. "Liddell Hart's Influence on Israeli Military Theory and Practice." *RUSI Journal* 121, no. 2 (1976): 83–89.

Bonen, Zeev. "Sophisticated Conventional War." In *Advanced Technology and Future Warfare,* edited by Zeev Bonen and Eliot Cohen, 19–30. Mideast Security and Policy Studies no. 28. Ramat Gan, Israel: BESA Center for Strategic Studies, 1996.

———. "The Technological Arms Race: An Economic Dead End?" In *Israeli Security Planning in the 1980s,* edited by Zvi Lanir, 108–27. New York: Praeger, 1984.

Bregman, Ahron. *Israel's Wars: A History since 1947.* London: Routledge, 2010.

Brom, Brig. Gen. Shlomo. "Political and Military Objectives in a Limited War against a Guerilla Organization." In Brom and Elran, *Second Lebanon War,* 13–23.

———. "The Withdrawal from Southern Lebanon: One Year Later." *Strategic Assessment* 4, no. 2 (2001): 22–27.

———. "After the Withdrawal: Three Scenarios." *Strategic Assessment* 3 no. 1 (2000): 10–13.

Brom, Shlomo, and Meir Elran, eds. *The Second Lebanon War: Strategic Perspectives.* Tel Aviv: INSS, 2007.

Brun, Brig. Gen. Itai. "The Second Lebanon War, 2006." In *A History of Air Warfare,* edited by John Andreas Olsen, 297–324. Washington, DC: Potomac Books, 2010.

———. "While You're Busy Making Other Plans: The 'Other RMA.'" *Journal of Strategic Studies* 33, no. 4 (2010): 535–65.

Brun, Itai, and Itamar Rabinovich. *Israel Facing a New Middle East: In Search of a National Security Strategy.* Stanford, CA: Hoover Institution, 2017.

Byman, Dan. *A High Price: The Triumphs and Failures of Israel Counterterrorism.* New York: Oxford University Press, 2011.

Cambanis, Thanassis. *A Privilege to Die: Inside Hezbollah's Legions and Their Endless War against Israel.* New York: Free Press, 2010.

Catignani, Sergio. "Coping with Knowledge: Organizational Learning in the British Military?" *Journal of Strategic Studies* 37, no. 1 (2013): 30–64.

———. "'Getting COIN' at the Tactical Level in Afghanistan: Reassessing Counter-Insurgency Adaptation in the British Army." *Journal of Strategic Studies* 35, no. 4 (2012): 513–39.

———. "Israeli Counterinsurgency Strategy and the Quest for Security in the Israeli-Lebanese Conflict Arena." In Jones and Catignani, *Israel and Hezbollah,* 67–88.

———. *Israeli Counter-Insurgency and the Intifadas.* London: Routledge, 2008.

———. "Israel Defence Forces Organizational Changes in an Era of Budgetary Cutbacks." *RUSI Journal* 149, no. 5 (2004): 72–76.

———. "Motivating Soldiers: The Example of the Israeli Defense Forces." *Parameters* 34, no. 3 (2004): 108–21.

Cedar, Joseph, dir. *Beaufort.* United King Films, 2007 (Hebrew).

Challans, Lt. Col. Tim. "Tipping Sacred Cows: Moral Potential through Operational Art." *Military Review* 89, no. 5 (2009): 19–28.

Chasnoff, Joel. *The 188th Crybaby Brigade: A Skinny Jewish Kid from Chicago Fights Hezbollah*. New York: Free Press, 2010.

Clausewitz, Carl von. *On War*. Edited by Michael Howard and Peter Paret. Princeton, NJ: Princeton University Press, 1976.

Cohen, Eliot. "Change and Transformation in Military Affairs." *Journal of Strategic Studies* 27, no. 3 (2004): 395–407.

———. "Israel after Heroism." *Foreign Affairs* 77, no. 6 (1998): 112–28.

Cohen, Eliot, Michael Eisenstadt, and Andrew J. Bacevich. "Israel's Revolution in Security Affairs." *Survival* 40, no. 1 (1998): 48–67.

———. *Knives, Tanks, and Missiles: Israel's Security Revolution*. Washington, DC: Washington Institute for Near Eastern Policy, 1998.

Cohen, Stuart A. *Israel and Its Army: From Cohesion to Confusion*. London: Routledge, 2008.

———. "Israel's Three Strategic Challenges." *Middle East Quarterly* 6, no. 4 (1999): 41–49.

———. "Small States and Their Armies: Restructuring the Militia Framework of the Israel Defense Forces." *Journal of Strategic Studies* 18, no. 4 (1995): 78–93.

———. "The Peace Process and Its Impact on the Development of a 'Slimmer and Smarter' Israel Defence Force." *Israel Affairs* 1, no. 4 (1995): 1–21.

———. "Changing Emphases on Israel's Military Commitments, 1981–1991." *Journal of Strategic Studies* 15, no. 3 (1992): 330–50.

Collins, Jeffrey, and Andrew Futter, eds. *Reassessing the Revolution in Military Affairs: Transformation, Evolution, and Lesson Learnt*. Basingstoke, UK: Palgrave Macmillan, 2015.

Cordesman, Anthony. *Lessons of the 2006 Israeli-Hezbollah War*. Washington, DC: Center for Strategic and International Studies, 2007.

———. *Arab-Israeli Military Forces in an Era of Asymmetric Wars*. Westport, CT: Praeger, 2006.

———. *Peace and War: The Arab-Israeli Military Balance Enters the 21st Century*. Westport, CT: Praeger, 2002.

Correll, John. "The Assault on EBO." *Air Force Magazine* 96, no. 1 (January 2013): 50–54.

Cragin, Kim. "Hizballah, the Party of God." In Jackson et al., *Aptitude for Destruction: Volume 2*, 37–54.

Dayan, Moshe. "Israel's Border and Security Problems." *Foreign Affairs* 33, no. 2 (1955): 250–67.

Deeb, Marius. "Shi'a Movements in Lebanon: Their Formation, Ideology, Social Basis, and Links with Iran and Syria." *Third World Quarterly* 10, no. 2 (1988): 683–98.

Dekel, Brig. Gen. Udi. "Is Israel Facing a War of Attrition against Hamas?" INSS Insight no. 588, INSS, August 13, 2014.

Dekel, Udi, Gabi Siboni, and Omer Einav, eds. *The Quiet Decade: In the Aftermath of the Second Lebanon War, 2006–2016*. Memorandum no. 167. Tel Aviv: INSS, July 2017.

Demchak, Chris. "Technology's Knowledge Burden, the RMA and the IDF: Organizing Hypertext Organization for Future 'Wars of Disruption'?" *Journal of Strategic Studies* 24, no. 2 (2001): 77–146.

———. "Numbers or Networks: Social Construction of Technology and Organizational Dilemmas in IDF Modernization." *Armed Forces and Society* 23, no. 2 (1996): 179–208.

———. "Coping, Copying, and Concentrating: Organizational Learning and Modernization in Militaries (Case Studies of Israel, Germany, and Britain)." *Journal of Public Administration Research and Theory* 5, no. 3 (1995): 345–76.

Department of the Army (US). *Operations: Field Manual 3–0*, February 2011.

————. *The Operations Process: Field Manual 5–0*, March 2010.

————. *The Army Capstone Concept*. TRADOC Pam. 525–3-0. Training and Doctrine Command, December 21, 2009.

————. *Full Spectrum Operations: Unified Quest '07*. TRADOC Pam. 525–5-300. Training and Doctrine Command, August 2008.

Department of Defense (US). *Quadrennial Defense Review*. Washington, DC: Department of Defense, 2014.

————. *Military Transformation: A Strategic Approach*. Washington, DC: Office of Force Transformation, Fall 2003.

Deptula, Brig. Gen. David. *Effects-Based Operations: Change in the Nature of Warfare*. Arlington, VA: Aerospace Education Foundation, 2001.

Dolnik, Adam. *Understanding Terrorist Innovation: Technology, Tactics, and Global Trends*. London: Routledge, 2007.

Eiland, Maj. Gen. Giora. "Think before You Act: On the IDF Withdrawal from Lebanon in 2000." *Military and Strategic Affairs* 3, no. 3 (2011): 75–81.

————. "The Foundations of Israel's Response to Threats." *Military and Strategic Affairs* 2, no. 1 (2010): 69–79.

————. "The Second Lebanon War: Lessons on the Strategic Level." *Military and Strategic Affairs* 1, no. 2 (2009): 9–24.

————. "The IDF: Addressing the Failures of the Second Lebanon War." In *Middle East Strategic Balance, 2007–2008*, edited by Mark Heller and Zvi Shtauber. Tel Aviv: INSS, 2008, 31–37.

————. "The Third Lebanon War: Target Lebanon." *Strategic Assessment* 11, no. 2 (2008): 9–17.

————. "The Decision-Making Process in Israel." In Brom and Elran, *Second Lebanon War*, 25–31.

Eiran, Ehud. *The Essence of Longing: General Erez Gerstein and the War in Lebanon*. Tel Aviv: Yediot Books, 2007 (Hebrew).

Eisenberg, Laurie. "History Revisited or Revamped? The Maronite Factor in Israel's Invasion of Lebanon." *Israel Studies* 15, no. 4 (2009): 372–96.

Eisenstadt, Michael. "Hizballah Operations: Past Patterns, Future Prospects." *Policy Watch* no. 197. Washington Institute for Near Eastern Policy, May 7, 1996.

Eizenkot, Lt. Gen. Gadi. *IDF Strategy*. Bureau of the Chief of Staff, IDF: August 2015 (Hebrew).

————. "A Changed Threat? The Response on the Northern Arena." *Military and Strategic Affairs* 2, no. 1 (2010): 29–40.

Elran, Brig. Gen. (Ret.) Meir. "The Civilian Front in the Second Lebanon War." In Brom and Elran, *Second Lebanon War*, 103–19.

Elran, Brig. Gen. (Ret.) Meir, Zipi Israeli, Carmit Padan, and Alex Altshuler. "Social Resilience in the Jewish Communities around the Gaza Strip Envelope during and after Operation Protective Edge." *Military and Strategic Affairs* 7, no. 2 (2015): 5–31.

Erlich, Col. (Ret.) Reuven. "When Did the First Lebanon War End?" Lecture given at the Israeli Center for Defense Studies, Intelligence and Terrorism Information Center, June 12, 2014.

————. *The Road to the First Lebanon War*. Glilot, Israel: Intelligence and Terrorism Information Center. August 1, 2012.

————. *Hezbollah's Use of Lebanese Civilians as Human Shields*. Glilot, Israel: Intelligence and Terrorism Information Center, November 2006.

Eshel, Col. (Ret.) David. "Armored Anti-Guerilla Combat in South Lebanon." *Armor* 106, no. 4 (July/August 1997): 26–29.

Etzioni-Halevy, Eva. "Civil-Military Relations and Democracy: The Case of the Military-Political Elites Connection in Israel." *Armed Forces and Society* 22, no. 3 (1996): 401–17.

Even, Shmuel. "The IDF Strategy and the Responsibility of the Political Leadership." INSS Insight no. 736, INSS, August 19, 2015.

———. "The National Security Staff: Will the New Law Bring About Change?" *Strategic Assessment* 11, no. 3 (2009): 85–101.

Evron, Yair. "Deterrence and Its Limitations." In Brom and Elran, *Second Lebanon War*, 35–47.

———. *War and Intervention in Lebanon: The Israeli-Syrian Deterrence Dialogue*. New York: Routledge Revivals, 1987.

Exum, Andrew. "Hizballah at War: A Military Assessment." Policy Focus no. 63, Washington Institute for Near Eastern Policy, December 2006.

Farkash, Maj. Gen. Aharon Zeevi. "Intelligence in the War: Observations and Insights." In Brom and Elran, *Second Lebanon War*, 77–86.

Farquhar, Lt. Col. Scott, ed. *Back to Basics: A Study of the Second Lebanon War and Operation Cast Lead*. Fort Leavenworth, KS: Combat Studies Institute, 2009.

Farrell, Theo. "Introduction: Military Adaptation in War." In Farrell, Osinga, and Russell, *Military Adaptation in Afghanistan*, 1–23.

———. "Improving in War: Military Adaptation and the British in Helmand Province, Afghanistan, 2006–2009." *Journal of Strategic Studies* 33, no. 4 (2010): 567–94.

———. "The Dynamics of British Military Transformation." *International Affairs* 84, no. 4 (2008): 777–807.

———. "World Culture and Military Power." *Security Studies* 14, no. 3 (2005): 448–88.

———. "Culture and Military Power." *Review of International Studies* 24, no. 3 (1998): 407–16.

———. "Figuring Out Fighting Organisations: The New Organisational Analysis in Strategic Studies." *Journal of Strategic Studies* 19, no. 1 (1996): 122–35.

Farrell, Theo, Frans Osinga, and James Russell, eds. *Military Adaptation in Afghanistan*. Stanford, CA: Stanford University Press, 2013.

Farrell, Theo, and Terry Terriff. "Sources of Military Change." In *The Sources of Military Change: Culture, Politics, Technology*, edited by Theo Farrell and Terry Terriff, 3–20. Boulder, CO: Lynne Rienner, 2002.

Fayyad, Ali. "Hezbollah and the Lebanese State: Reconciling a National Strategy." Arab Reform Brief no. 11, Arab Reform Initiative, August 2006.

Feldman, Shai. "Deterrence and the Israel-Hezbollah War: Summer 2006." In *Deterrence in the Twenty-First Century* (conference proceedings), 279–89. Maxwell AFB, AL: Air Force Research Institute, 2010.

———. "Israel's Deterrent Power after Its Withdrawal from Lebanon." *Strategic Assessment* 3, no. 1 (2000): 1–5.

Finaud, Marc. "The 1996 Grapes of Wrath Ceasefire Agreement and the Israel-Lebanon Monitoring Group: A Model of Successful Negotiations in Conflict Management." In *Negotiating in Times of Conflict*, edited by Gilead Sher and Anat Kurz, 173–91. Tel Aviv: INSS, 2015.

Finkel, Col. Meir. *On Flexibility: Recovery from Technological and Doctrinal Surprise on the Battlefield*. Stanford, CA: Stanford University Press, 2012.

———. "The Qualitative Edge of the IDF: Not on Technology Alone." *Maarachot* 439 (2009): 33–39 (Hebrew).

———. "Flexible Force Structure: A Flexibility Oriented Force Design and Development Process for Israel." *Israel Affairs* 12, no. 4 (2006): 789–800.

Finkel, Col. Meir, and Eitan Shamir. "From Whom Does the IDF Need to Learn?" *Maarachot* 433 (2010): 28–35 (Hebrew).

Foley, Robert. "A Case Study in Horizontal Military Innovation: The German Army, 1916–1918." *Journal of Strategic Studies* 35, no. 6 (2012): 799–827.

Foley, Robert, Stuart Griffin, and Helen McCartney. "Transformation in Contact: Learning the Lessons of Modern War." *International Affairs* 87, no. 2 (2011): 253–70.

Folman, Ari, dir. *Waltz with Bashir.* Sony Picture Classics, 2008 (Hebrew).

Four Mothers Movement. "Leaving Lebanon in Peace." Official press release, n.d.

Freedman, Lawrence. *Strategy: A History.* New York: Oxford University Press, 2013.

———. *The Transformation of Strategic Affairs.* Adelphi Paper no. 379. London: IISS, 2006.

———. *The Revolution in Strategic Affairs.* Adelphi Paper no. 318. London: IISS, 1998.

Freilich, Charles. *Zion's Dilemma: How Israel Makes National Security Policy.* Ithaca, NY: Cornell University Press, 2012.

———. "Israel in Lebanon—Getting It Wrong: The 1982 Invasion, 2000 Withdrawal, and 2006 War." *Israel Journal of Foreign Affairs* 6, no. 3 (2012): 41–75.

———. "National Security Decision-Making in Israel: Processes, Pathologies, and Strengths." *Middle East Journal* 60, no. 4 (2006): 635–63.

Friedman, Matti. *Pumpkin Flowers: A Soldier's Story.* Chapel Hill, NC: Algonquin Books, 2016.

Friedman, Thomas. *From Beirut to Jerusalem.* New York: Random House, 1989.

Gambill, Gary. "Sharon Ends Moratorium on Striking Syrian Forces in Lebanon." *Middle East Intelligence Bulletin* 3, no. 4 (April 2001).

Gazit, Orit. "Nonstate Actors, Identity, and Change: The Southern Lebanese Army between Lebanon and Israel." Leonard Davis Institute for International Relations Working Paper Series, Hebrew University of Jerusalem, 2013.

Gazit, Maj. Gen. (Ret.) Shlomo. "The Security Zone Has Served Us Faithfully but Its Time Has Passed." *Maariv,* September 8, 1997.

Geraghty, Col. Timothy. *Peacekeepers at War: Beirut 1983; The Marine Commander Tells His Story.* Washington, DC: Potomac Books, 2009.

Ghrorayeb, Amal Saad. *Hizbullah: Politics and Religion.* London: Pluto, 2002.

Gilboa, Brig. Gen. (Ret.) Amos. *"Morning Dawn": The True Story of the IDF's Departure from Lebanon.* Glilot, Israel: Intelligence and Terrorism Information Center, 2016 (Hebrew).

Giustozzi, Antonio. "Military Adaptation by the Taliban 2002–2011." In Farrell, Osinga, and Russell, *Military Adaptation in Afghanistan,* 242–62.

Golan, Haggai, and Shaul Shai, eds. *The Limited Conflict.* Tel Aviv: Maarachot, 2004 (Hebrew).

Goldman, Emily. "Cultural Foundations of Military Diffusion." *Review of International Studies* 32, no. 1 (2006): 69–91.

———. "New Threats, New Identities, and New Ways of War: The Sources of Change in National Security Doctrine." *Journal of Strategic Studies* 24, no. 2 (2001): 43–76.

Goldman, Emily, and Leslie Eliason. "Introduction." In *The Diffusion of Military Technology and Ideas,* edited by Emily Goldman and Leslie Eliason, 1–30. Stanford, CA: Stanford University Press, 2003.

Gordon, Col. Shmuel. "Why Is the IDF Failing?" *Yediot Ahronoth,* March 2, 2010.

———. *The Vulture and the Snake: Counter-Guerrilla Air Warfare; The War in Southern Lebanon.* Mideast Security and Policy Studies no. 39, BESA Center for Strategic Studies, Ramat Gan, Israel, 1998.

Graicer, Ofra. "Between Teaching and Learning: What Lessons Could the Israeli Doctrine Learn from the 2006 Lebanon War." *Experticia Militar* no. 2 (July–October 2017): 22–29.

———. "Self Disruption: Seizing the High Ground of Systemic Operational Design (SOD)." *Journal of Military and Strategic Studies* 17, no. 4 (2017): 21–37.

———. *Two Steps Ahead: From Deep Ops to Special Ops; Wingate the General.* Tel Aviv: Maarachot, 2015 (Hebrew).

———. "Between Teaching and Learning: IDF Doctrine and the Unfolding of the Second Lebanon War." Unpublished paper, June 2008.

Grant, Rebecca. "The Bekaa Valley War." *Air Force Magazine* 85, no. 6 (2002): 58–62.

Graves, Col. Thomas, and Bruce Stanley. "Design and Operational Art: A Practical Approach to Teaching the Army Design Methodology." *Military Review* (July/August 2013): 53–59.

Griffin, Stuart. "Military Innovation Studies: Multidisciplinary or Lacking Discipline?" *Journal of Strategic Studies* 40, nos. 1–2 (2017): 196–224.

Grissom, Adam. "The Future of Military Innovation Studies." *Journal of Strategic Studies* 29, no. 5 (2006): 905–34.

Haloutz, Lt. Gen. Dan. *At Eye Level.* Tel Aviv: Yediot Books, 2010 (Hebrew).

———. "The Second Lebanon War: Achievements and Failures." *Military and Strategic Affairs* 1, no. 2 (2009): 61–71.

———. "Halutz's Full Letter of Resignation." *Yediot Ahronoth*, January 17, 2007.

———. "21st Century Threats Facing Israel." *Jerusalem Issue Brief* 3, no. 16, Jerusalem Center for Public Affairs, February 3, 2004.

———. "Air and Space Strategy for Small Powers: Needs and Opportunities." In *Towards Fusion of Air and Space* (conference proceedings), edited by Dana J. Johnson and Ariel Levite, 147–57. Santa Monica, CA: RAND Corp., 2003.

Hamzeh, Ahmed Nizar. *In the Path of Hizbullah.* Syracuse, NY: Syracuse University Press, 2004.

———. "Lebanon's Islamists and Local Politics: A New Reality." *Third World Quarterly* 21, no. 5 (2000): 739–59.

———. "Lebanon's Hizbullah: From Islamic Revolution to Parliamentary Accommodation." *Third World Quarterly* 14, no. 2 (1993): 321–37.

Harel, Amos, and Avi Issacharoff. *34 Days: Israel, Hezbollah, and the War in Lebanon.* New York: Palgrave Macmillan, 2008.

Harris, William. "Lebanon." In *Middle East Contemporary Survey.* Vol. 23 (1999), edited by Bruce Maddy-Weitzman, 379–404. Tel Aviv: Tel Aviv University, 2001.

———. "Lebanon." In *Middle East Contemporary Survey.* Vol. 12 (1988), edited by Ami Ayalon and Haim Shaked, 615–41. Boulder, CO: Westview Press, 1990.

Hasdai, Yaakov. "'Doers' and 'Thinkers' in the IDF." *Jerusalem Quarterly* no. 24 (1982): 13–25.

Hecht, Eado. "Low-Intensity Wars: Some Characteristics of a Unique Conflict." In Golan and Shai, *Limited Conflict*, 45–68.

Helmer, Daniel I. *Flipside of the COIN: Israel's Lebanese Incursions between 1982–2000.* Long War Series. Occasional Paper no. 21. Fort Leavenworth, KS: Combat Studies Institute, 2007.

————. "Hezbollah's Employment of Suicide Bombing during the 1980s." *Military Review* 86, no. 4 (July/August 2006): 71–82.

Henkin, Yagil. "On Swarming: Success and Failure in Multi-Directional Warfare from Normandy to the Second Lebanon War." *Defence Studies* 14, no. 3 (2014): 310–32.

————. "Confused Warfare." *Azure* no. 25 (2006): 130–34.

————. "How Great Nations Can Win Small Wars." *Azure* no. 24 (2006): 39–81.

Henriksen, Dag. "Deterrence by Default? Israel's Military Strategy in the 2006 War against Hizballah." *Journal of Strategic Studies* 35, no. 1 (2012): 95–120.

————. "A Misapplied and Overextended Example: Gen. Mattis's Criticism of Effects-Based Operations." *Air and Space Power Journal* (September/October 2012): 118–31.

Hirsch, Brig. Gen. Gal. *Defensive Shield: An Israeli Special Forces Commander on the Front Lines of Counterterrorism.* Jerusalem: Gefen, 2016.

————. "Other Boots on the Ground." *Israel Defense Magazine*, February 11, 2016.

————. "Urban Warfare." *Military and Strategic Affairs* 5 (special issue, April 2014): 23–30.

————. "The Sixth Dimension Has Taken Off." *Israel Defense Magazine*, December 2, 2013.

————. *War Story, Love Story.* Tel Aviv: Yediot Books, 2009 (Hebrew).

————. "The Development of the Campaign in the Central Military District 2000–2003." In Golan and Shai, *Limited Conflict*, 239–51.

————. "On Dinosaurs and Hornets: A Critical View on Operational Moulds in Asymmetric Conflicts." *RUSI Journal* 148, no. 4 (2003): 60–63.

Hoffman, Frank G. "How We Bridged a Wartime 'Learning Gap.'" *Proceedings* 142, no. 5 (May 2016): 22–29.

————. *Conflict in the 21st Century: The Rise of Hybrid Wars.* Arlington, VA: Potomac Institute for Policy Studies, 2007.

————. "Complex Irregular Warfare: The Next Revolution in Military Affairs." *Orbis* 50, no. 3 (2006): 395–411.

Horowitz, Dan. "Strategic Limitations of 'a Nation in Arms.'" *Armed Forces and Society* 13, no. 2 (1987): 277–94.

————. "Israel's War in Lebanon: New Patterns of Strategic Thinking and Civilian-Military Relations." *Journal of Strategic Studies* 6, no. 3 (1983): 83–102.

————. "Flexible Responsiveness and Military Strategy: The Case of the Israeli Army." *Policy Sciences* 1, no. 2 (1970): 191–205.

Horowitz, Michael. *The Diffusion of Military Power: Causes and Consequences for International Politics.* Princeton, NJ: Princeton University Press, 2010.

Hoyt, Timothy. "Revolution and Counter-Revolution: The Role of the Periphery in Technological and Conceptual Innovation." In *The Diffusion of Military Technology and Ideas*, edited by Emily Goldman and Leslie Eliason, 179–201. Stanford, CA: Stanford University Press, 2003.

Human Rights Watch. *Why They Died: Civilian Casualties in Lebanon during the 2006 War.* New York: Human Rights Watch, September 2007.

————. *Civilians under Assault: Hezbollah Rockets Attacks on Israel in the 2006 War.* New York: Human Rights Watch, August 2007.

————. *Operation Grapes of Wrath: The Civilian Victims.* New York: Human Rights Watch, September 1, 1997.

————. *Civilian Pawns: Laws of War Violations and the Use of Weapons on the Israel–Lebanon Border.* New York: Human Rights Watch, May 1, 1996.

Hurley, Matthew. "The Bekaa Valley Air Battle, June 1982: Lessons Mislearned?" *Airpower Journal* 3, no. 4 (Winter 1989): 60–70.

IDF Spokesperson. "IDF Special Ops Raid on Hezbollah Hospital HQ Deep inside Lebanon." Video. August 4, 2006.

Inbar, Efraim, and Eitan Shamir. "Mowing the Grass: Israel's Strategy for Protracted Intractable Conflict." *Journal of Strategic Studies* 37, no. 1 (2014): 65–90.

Inbar, Col. Giora. *Decisive Factors in the Gulf War from the IDF Lesson Learning Perspective.* Carlisle, PA: US Army War College, 1993.

Intelligence and Terrorism Information Center. *Hezbollah's Involvement in the Civil War in Syria.* Glilot, Israel: Intelligence and Terrorism Information Center, April 22, 2014.

Israel Ministry of Foreign Affairs. "English Summary of the Winograd Commission Report." Press conference of Judge Eliyahu Winograd, January 30, 2008.

——. "Winograd Commission Submits Interim Report." Press release, April 30, 2007.

——. *Preserving Humanitarian Principles while Combating Terrorism: Israel's Struggle with Hizbullah in the Lebanon War.* April 1, 2007.

——. "IDF Apprehends Hizbullah Terrorist Involved in July 12 Kidnapping." Press release by IDF Spokesperson, August 8, 2006.

——. "Completion of Inquiry into the July 30 Incident in Qana." Press release by IDF Spokesperson, August 2, 2006.

——. "Hizbullah's Exploitation of Lebanese Population Centers and Civilians: Photographic Evidence." Press release, July 12, 2006.

——. "Hizbullah Attacks along Israel's Northern Border May 2000–June 2006." Press release, June 1, 2006.

——. "Main Events on the Israel-Lebanese Border since the IDF Withdrawal." Press release, August 10, 2003.

——. "Ceasefire Understanding in Lebanon, and Remarks by Prime Minister Peres and Secretary of State Christopher." Press release, April 26, 1996.

Jaber, Hala. *Hezbollah: Born with a Vengeance.* New York: Columbia University Press, 1997.

Jackson, Brian A., John C. Baker, Peter Chalk, Kim Cragin, John Parachini, and Horacio R. Trujillo. *Aptitude for Destruction, Volume 1: Organizational Learning in Terrorist Groups and Its Implications for Combating Terrorism.* Santa Monica, CA: RAND Corp., 2005.

——. *Aptitude for Destruction, Volume 2: Case Studies of Organizational Learning in Five Terrorist Groups.* Santa Monica, CA: RAND Corp., 2005.

Johnson, David E. *Hard Fighting: Israel in Lebanon and Gaza.* Santa Monica, CA: RAND Corp., 2011.

Jones, Clive. "'A Reach Greater Than the Grasp': Israeli Intelligence and the Conflict in South Lebanon, 1990–2000." *Intelligence and National Security* 16, no. 3 (2001): 1–26.

——. "Israeli Counter-Insurgency Strategy and the War in South Lebanon, 1985–97." *Small Wars and Insurgencies* 8, no. 3 (1997): 82–108.

Jones, Clive, and Sergio Catignani, eds. *Israel and Hezbollah: An Asymmetric Conflict in Historical and Comparative Perspective.* London: Routledge, 2009.

Kaplinsky, Maj. Gen. Moshe. "The IDF in the Years before the Second Lebanon War." *Military and Strategic Affairs* 1, no. 2 (2009): 25–37.

Katz, Brig. Gen. Muni, and Nadav Pollak. "Hezbollah's Russian Military Education in Syria." Policy Watch no. 2541, Washington Institute for Near Eastern Policy, December 24, 2015.

Katz, Yaakov, and Amir Bohbot. *Weapon Wizards.* New York: St. Martin's, 2017.

Kauffman, Asher. "Who Owns the Shebaa Farms? Chronicle of a Territorial Dispute." *Middle East Journal* 56, no. 4 (2002): 576–95.

Kaye, Dalia Dassa. "The Israeli Decision to Withdraw from Southern Lebanon: Political Leadership and Security Policy." *Political Science Quarterly* 117, no. 4 (2002): 561–85.

Khatib, Lina, Dina Matar, and Atef Alshaer. *The Hizbullah Phenomenon: Politics and Communication.* London: Hurst, 2014.

Kier, Elizabeth. "Culture and Military Doctrine: France between the Wars." *International Security* 19, no. 4 (1995): 67–69.

Kober, Avi. *Practical Soldiers: Israel's Military Thought and Its Formative Factors.* Leiden: Brill, 2016.

———. "From Heroic to Post-Heroic Warfare: Israel's Way of War in Asymmetric Conflicts." *Armed Forces and Society* 41, no. 1 (2015): 96–122.

———. "What Happened to Israeli Military Thought?" *Journal of Strategic Studies* 34, no. 5 (2011): 707–32.

———. "The Rise and Fall of Israeli Operational Art, 1948–2008." In *The Evolution of Operational Art: From Napoleon to the Present,* edited by John Andreas Olsen and Martin Van Creveld. Oxford: Oxford University Press, 2011, 166–94.

———. *Israel's Wars of Attrition: Attrition Challenges to Democratic States.* London: Routledge, 2009.

———. "The Israel Defense Forces in the Second Lebanon War: Why the Poor Performance?" *Journal of Strategic Studies* 31, no. 1 (2008): 3–40.

———. "Israel's Wars of Attrition: Operational and Moral Dilemmas." *Israel Affairs* 12, no. 4 (2006): 801–22.

———. "From *Blitzkrieg* to Attrition: Israel's Attrition Strategy and Staying Power." *Small Wars and Insurgencies* 16, no. 2 (2005): 216–40.

———. "The Intellectual and Modern Focus in Israeli Military Thinking as Reflected in *Ma'arachot* Articles, 1948–2000." *Armed Forces and Society* 30, no. 1 (2003): 141–60.

———. "Western Democracies in Low Intensity Conflict: Some Postmodern Aspects." In *Democracies and Small Wars,* edited by Efraim Inbar, 3–20. London: Frank Cass, 2003. Also in *Review of International Affairs* 2, no. 3.

———. "Has Battlefield Decision Become Obsolete? The Commitment to the Achievement of Battlefield Decision Revisited." *Contemporary Security Policy* 22, no. 2 (2001): 96–120.

———. "Israeli War Objectives into an Era of Negativism." *Journal of Strategic Studies* 24, no. 2 (2001): 176–201.

Kramer, Martin. "The Oracle of Hizbullah: Sayyid Muhammad Husayn Fadlallah." In *Spokesmen of the Despised: Fundamentalist Leaders in the Middle East,* edited by Scott Appleby, 83–181. Chicago: University of Chicago Press, 1997.

———. "Hizbullah: The Calculus of Jihad." In *Fundamentalisms and the State: Remaking Polities, Economies, and Militance,* edited by Martin E. Marty and R. Scott Appleby, 539–56. Chicago: University of Chicago Press, 1993.

Kreps, Sarah. "The 2006 Lebanon War: Lessons Learned." *Parameters* (Spring 2007): 72–84.

Kulick, Amir. "Hizbollah vs. the IDF: The Operational Dimension." *Strategic Assessment* 9, no. 3 (2006): 29–33.

Kuperwasser, Brig. Gen. Yossi. "The Next War with Hizbollah: Should Lebanon Be the Target?" *Strategic Assessment* 11, no. 2 (2008): 19–28.

———. *Lessons from Israel's Intelligence Reforms.* Analysis Paper no. 14. Saban Center, Brookings Institution, 2007.

Lahd, Antoine. *In the Midst of a Storm: An Autobiography.* Tel Aviv: Yediot Books, 2004 (Hebrew).

Lambeth, Benjamin. "Israel's Second Lebanon War Reconsidered." *Military and Strategic Affairs* 4, no. 2 (2012): 45–63.

———. "Israel's War in Gaza: A Paradigm of Effective Military Learning and Adaptation." *International Security* 37, no. 2 (2012): 81–118.

———. *Air Operations in Israel's War against Hezbollah: Learning from Lebanon and Getting It Right in Gaza.* Santa Monica, CA: RAND Corp., 2011.

Lanir, Zvi. *Reframing Strategy in the Knowledge Age.* Praxis White Paper. Tel Aviv: Praxis, 2001.

———. *Reframer: A New Generation of Thinking Software.* Tel Aviv: Praxis, 2001.

———. *Fundamental Surprises.* Tel Aviv: Center for Security Studies, 1983.

Lanir, Zvi, and Gad Sneh. *Beyond Post-Modern Deconstruction.* Tel Aviv: Praxis, 2000.

Lauder, Matthew. "Systemic Operational Design: Freeing Operational Planning from the Shackles of Linearity." *Canadian Military Journal* 9, no. 4 (2009): 41–49.

Legro, Jeffrey. "Military Culture and Inadvertent Escalation in World War II." *International Security* 18, no. 4 (1994): 108–42.

Levite, Ariel, "Changes of the Guard in Israel." *Armed Forces Journal International* (June 1987): 50–51.

———. *Offense and Defense in Israeli Military Doctrine.* Jaffee Center for Strategic Studies, study no. 12. Boulder, CO: Westview Press, 1990.

Levitt, Matthew. *Hezbollah: The Global Footprint of the Party of God.* Washington, DC: Georgetown University Press, 2013.

Libel, Tamir. "Crossing the Lebanese Swamp: Structural and Doctrinal Implications on the Israeli Defense Forces Engagement in the Southern Lebanon Security Zone, 1985–2000." *Marine Corps University Journal* 2, no. 1 (2011): 67–80.

———. "David's Shield: The Decline and Partial Rise of the IDF Command and General Staff College." *Baltic Security and Defence Review* 12, no. 2 (2010): 50–80.

Lieberfeld, Daniel. "Media Coverage and Israel's Four Mothers Movement: Agenda, Tactics, and Political Context in Movement Success." *Media, War, and Conflict* 2, no. 3 (2009): 317–38.

———. "Parental Protest, Public Opinion, and War Termination: Israel's Four Mothers Movement." *Social Movement Studies* 8, no. 4 (2009): 375–92.

Lubotzky, Asael. *From the Wilderness and Lebanon: An Israeli Soldier's Story of War and Recovery.* Milton, CT: Toby Press, 2016.

Luft, Gal. "Israel's Security Zone in Lebanon: A Tragedy?" *Middle East Quarterly* 7, no. 3 (2000): 13–20.

Luttwak, Edward. "Towards Post-Heroic Warfare." *Foreign Affairs* 74, no. 3 (1995): 109–22.

Luttwak, Edward, and Dan Horowitz. *The Israeli Army.* London: Allen Lane, 1975.

Mains, Steven, and Gil Ariely. "Learning while Fighting: Operational Knowledge Management That Makes a Difference." *Prism* 2, no. 3 (2011): 165–76.

Makovsky, David, and Jeffrey White. "Lessons and Implications of the Israel-Hizballah War: A Preliminary Assessment." Policy Focus no. 60, Washington Institute for Near Eastern Policy, October 2006.

Malka, Maj. Gen. Amos. "Israel and Asymmetrical Deterrence." *Comparative Strategy* 27, no. 1 (2008): 1–19.

Maoz, Samuel, dir. *Levanon.* Ariel Films, 2009 (Hebrew).

Maoz, Zeev. "Evaluating Israel's Strategy of Low-Intensity Warfare, 1949–2006." *Security Studies* 16, no. 3 (2007): 319–49.

Marcus, Raphael D. "Hizbullah." In *Routledge Handbook of Terrorism and Counterterrorism*, edited by Andrew Silke, chap. 26. London: Routledge, forthcoming.

———. "Learning 'Under Fire': Israel's Improvised Military Adaptation to Hamas Tunnel Warfare." *Journal of Strategic Studies* (2017): 1–27.

———. "Military Innovation and Tactical Adaptation in the Israel-Hizballah Conflict: The Institutionalization of Lesson-Learning in the IDF." *Journal of Strategic Studies* 38, no. 4 (2015): 500–528.

———. "The Israeli Revolution in Military Affairs and the Road to the 2006 Lebanon War." In Collins and Futter, *Reassessing the Revolution in Military Affairs*, 92–111.

Matthews, Matt. "Hard Lessons Learned." In Farquhar, *Back to Basics*, 5–44.

———. *We Were Caught Unprepared: The 2006 Hezbollah-Israeli War*. Long War Series: Occasional Paper no. 26. Fort Leavenworth, KS: Combat Studies Institute, 2008.

Mattis, Gen. James. "USJFCOM Commander's Guidance for Effects-Based Operations." *Joint Forces Quarterly* 51, no. 4 (2008): 105–8.

McMaster, H. R. "On War: Lessons to Be Learned." *Survival* 50, no. 1 (2008): 19–30.

Meilinger, Phillip. "The Origins of Effects-Based Operations." *Joint Forces Quarterly* 35 (2003): 116–22.

Merom, Gil. "The Second Lebanon War: Democratic Lessons Imperfectly Applied." *Democracy and Security* 4, no. 1 (2008): 5–33.

———. *How Democracies Lose Small Wars*. Cambridge: Cambridge University Press, 2003.

Metz, Steven, and James Kievet. *Strategy and the Revolution in Military Affairs: From Theory to Practice*. Carlisle, PA: Strategic Studies Institute, June 1995.

Michael, Kobi. "Military Knowledge and Weak Civilian Control in the Reality of Low Intensity Conflict: The Israeli Case." *Israel Studies* 12, no. 1 (2007): 28–52.

———. "The Dilemma behind the Classical Dilemma of Civil-Military Relations: The 'Discourse Space' Model and the Israeli Case during the Oslo Process." *Armed Forces and Society* 33, no. 4 (2007): 518–46.

———. "The Israel Defense Forces as an Epistemic Authority: An Intellectual Challenge in the Reality of the Israeli-Palestinian Conflict." *Journal of Strategic Studies* 30, no. 3 (2007): 421–46.

Ministry of Defence (UK). *Army Doctrine Publication: Operations*. Shrivenham, UK: Development, Concepts and Doctrine Centre (DCDC), November 2010.

———. *Future Character of Conflict*. Shrivenham, UK: DCDC, February 2010.

Mofaz, Lt. Gen. Shaul. "The IDF toward the Year 2000." *Strategic Assessment* 2, no. 2 (1999): 9–11.

———. "Spring of Youth: The Revolution in IDF Organizational Culture." *Maarachot* 358 (1998): 1 (Hebrew).

Moghadam, Assaf. "How Al-Qaeda Innovates." *Security Studies* 22, no. 3 (2013): 466–97.

Murden, Simon. "Understanding Israel's Long Conflict in Lebanon: The Search for an Alternative Approach to Security during the Peace Process." *British Journal of Middle Eastern Studies* 27, no. 1 (2000): 25–47.

Murray, Williamson. *Military Adaptation in War: With Fear of Change*. Cambridge: Cambridge University Press, 2011.

———. "Innovation: Past and Future." *Joint Forces Quarterly* 12 (1996): 51–60.

N., Lt. Col. "The Third Lebanon War: Towards the Changing Operational Design of Hezbollah." *Maarachot* 454 (April 2014): 4–8 (Hebrew).

Nagl, John. *Learning to Eat Soup with a Knife: Counterinsurgency Lessons from Malaya and Vietnam*. Chicago: University of Chicago Press, 2005.

Nakash, Yitzhak. *Reaching for Power: The Shi'a in the Modern Arab World*. Princeton, NJ: Princeton University Press, 2006.

Naveh, Brig. Gen. Shimon. *Operational Art and the IDF: A Critical Study of a Command Culture*. Washington, DC: Center for Strategic and Budgetary Assessment, 2007.

———. "Operational Art, Operational Command, Systemic Operational Design: Transforming the Triad, Extending the Potential." Powerpoint for Unified Quest '07, Fort Leavenworth, KS, January 2007.

———. "Between the Striated and the Smooth: Urban Enclaves and Fractal Maneuvers." Paper presented at the symposium "Archipelago of Exceptions: Sovereignties of Extraterritoriality," Centre de Cultura Contemporània, Barcelona, November 10–11, 2005.

———. "Asymmetric Conflict: Reflections on Hegemonic Strategies." In Golan and Shai, *Limited Conflict*, 101–45.

———. "Mikhail Nikolayevich Tukhachevsky." In *Stalin's Generals*, edited by Harold Shukman, 255–73. London: Phoenix Giant Press, 1997.

———. *In Pursuit of Military Excellence: The Evolution of Operational Theory*. London: Frank Cass, 1997.

———. "The Cult of the Offensive Preemption and Future Challenges for Israeli Operational Thought." In *Between War and Peace: Dilemmas of Israeli Security*, edited by Ephraim Karsh, 168–87. London: Frank Cass, 1995. Also in *Israel Affairs* 2, no. 1.

———. "From *Vernichtungsschlacht* to AirLand Battle: The Evolution of Operational Theory." PhD dissertation, Department of War Studies, King's College London, 1995.

Naveh, Brig. Gen. Shimon, Jim Schneider, and Tim Challans. *The Structure of Operational Revolution: A Prolegomena*. Fort Leavenworth, KS: Booz Allen Hamilton, 2009.

Nir, Col. Shmuel. "The Nature of the Limited Conflict." In Golan and Shai, *Limited Conflict*, 19–45.

———. "Attrition and the Test of Adaptation." In *The Strategy of Attrition in Limited Conflict*, 163–74. Perspectives in National Security no. 4. Glilot, Israel: IDF National Defense College: March 2003 (Hebrew).

———. "Intelligence in Limited Conflict between Asymmetric Rivals." *Maarachot* 380–81 (2001): 72–77 (Hebrew).

———. "The Fighting in the Lebanese Arena as a Conflict between Unbalanced Forces: Simple Truths." *Zarkor* no. 1, February 1999 (Hebrew).

Noe, Nicholas, ed. *Voice of Hezbollah: The Statements of Sayyed Hassan Nasrallah*. London: Verso, 2007.

Norton, Augustus R. *Hezbollah: A Short History*. Princeton, NJ: Princeton University Press, 2007.

———. "Hizballah and the Israeli Withdrawal from Southern Lebanon." *Journal of Palestine Studies* 30, no. 1 (2000): 22–35.

———. *Hizballah in Lebanon: Extremist Ideals versus Mundane Politics*. Council on Foreign Relations, 1999.

———. *Amal and the Shi'a: Struggle for the Soul of Lebanon*. Austin: University of Texas Press, 1987.

Opall-Rome, Barbara. "Hoisted by Its Own PR." *Armed Forced Journal*, April 2008.

O'Shea, Brendan. "Israel's Vietnam?" *Studies in Conflict and Terrorism* 21, no. 3 (1998): 307–19.

Olmert, Ehud. "In Retrospect: The Second Lebanon War." *Military and Strategic Affairs* 6, no. 1 (2014): 3–18.

Osinga, Frans, and James Russell. "Conclusion: Military Adaptation and the War in Afghanistan." In Farrell, Osinga, and Russell, *Military Adaptation in Afghanistan*, 288–326.

Pahlavi, Pierre, and Eric Ouellet. "Institutional Analysis and Irregular Warfare: Israel Defense Forces during the 33-Day War of 2006." *Small Wars and Insurgencies* 23, no. 1 (2012): 32–55.

Palmer-Harik, Judith. *Hezbollah: The Changing Face of Terrorism*. New York: I. B. Tauris, 2005.

———. "Between Islam and the System: Sources and Implications of Popular Support for Lebanon's Hizballah." *Journal of Conflict Resolution* 40, no. 1 (1996): 41–67.

Paz, Col. Alon. *Transforming Israel's Security Establishment*. Policy Focus no. 140, Washington Institute for Near Eastern Policy, 2015.

Peri, Yoram. *Generals in the Cabinet Room: How the Military Shapes Israeli Policy*. Washington, DC: United States Institute of Peace, 2006.

Posen, Barry. *The Sources of Military Doctrine: France, Britain, and Germany between the World Wars*. Ithaca, NY: Cornell University Press, 1984.

Qassem, Naim. *Hizbullah: The Story from Within*. London: Saqi, 2010.

Rabi, Uzi, and Joshua Teitelbaum. "Armed Operations." In *Middle East Contemporary Survey*. Vol. 12 (1988), edited by Ami Ayalon and Haim Shaked, 120–35. Boulder, CO: Westview Press, 1990.

Rabinovich, Itamar. *The Brink of Peace: The Israeli-Syrian Negotiations*. Princeton, NJ: Princeton University Press, 1998.

———. *The War for Lebanon, 1970–1985*. Ithaca, NY: Cornell University Press, 1985.

Rafael Advanced Defense Systems. "Trophy Active-Protection System." Promotional video, n.d.

Ranstorp, Magnus. "The Hizballah Training Camps of Lebanon." In *The Making of a Terrorist: Recruitment, Training, and Root Causes*. Vol. 2, edited by James Forest, 243–62. Westport, CT: Praeger, 2005.

———. "The Strategy and Tactics of Hizbullah's Current 'Lebanonization Process.'" *Mediterranean Studies* 3, no. 1 (1998): 103–34.

———. *Hizballah in Lebanon: Politics of the Western Hostage Crisis*. Basingstoke, UK: Palgrave Macmillan, 1997.

———. "Hizbollah's Command Leadership: Its Structure, Decision-Making and Relationship with Iranian Clergy and Institutions." *Terrorism and Political Violence* 6, no. 3 (1994): 303–39.

Ranstorp, Magnus, and Magnus Normark, eds. *Understanding Terrorist Innovation and Learning: Al-Qaeda and Beyond*. London: Routledge, 2015.

Rapaport, Amir. "Where Is the Israeli Army Heading?" BESA Perspectives Paper no. 210, BESA Center for Strategic Studies, Ramat Gan, Israel, August 7, 2013.

———. *Friendly Fire: How We Defeated Ourselves in Lebanon*. Tel Aviv: Maariv, 2007. (Hebrew). Selected chapters also in English in *Israel Defense Magazine*, July 2011.

Rasmussen, Maria, and Mohammed Hafez, eds. *Terrorist Innovations in Weapons of Mass Effect: Preconditions, Causes, and Predicative Indicators*. Workshop report. Fort Belvoir, VA: Defense Threat Reduction Agency, August 2010.

Reut Institute. *National Resilience: Victory on the Home Front*. Tel Aviv: Reut Institute, November 2008.

Rice, Condoleezza. "Secretary Rice Holds a News Conference." Transcript. *Congressional Quarterly*, July 21, 2006.

Rid, Thomas. "Deterrence beyond the State: The Israeli Experience." *Contemporary Security Policy* 33, no. 1 (2012): 4–19.

Romjue, John. "The Evolution of the AirLand Battle Concept." *Air University Review* 35, no. 4 (May/June 1984): 4–15.

Romm, Maj. Gen. Giora. "A Test of Rival Strategies: Two Ships Passing in the Night." In Brom and Elran, *Second Lebanon War*, 49–60.

Rosen, Stephen P. *Winning the Next War: Innovation and the Modern Military.* Ithaca, NY: Cornell University Press, 1991.

———. "New Ways of War: Understanding Military Innovation." *International Security* 13, no. 1 (1988): 134–68.

Ross, Dennis. *The Missing Peace: The Inside Story of the Fight for Middle East Peace.* New York: Farrar, Strauss and Giroux, 2004.

Rubin, Uzi. *The Rocket Campaign against Israel during the 2006 Lebanon War.* Mideast Security and Policy Studies no. 71. BESA Center for Strategic Studies, Ramat Gan, Israel, 2007.

———. "Hizballah's Rocket Campaign against Northern Israel: A Preliminary Report." Jerusalem Issue Brief 6, no. 10, Jerusalem Center for Public Affairs, August 31, 2006.

Rumsfeld, Donald. "Transforming the Military." *Foreign Affairs* 81, no. 3 (2002): 20–32.

Russell, James. *Innovation, Transformation, and War: Counterinsurgency Operations in Anbar and Ninewa Provinces, Iraq, 2005–2007.* Stanford, CA: Stanford University Press, 2011.

———. "Innovation in War: Counterinsurgency Operations in Anbar and Ninewa Provinces, Iraq, 2005–2007." *Journal of Strategic Studies* 33, no. 4 (2010): 595–624.

Ryan, Alex J. "Applications of Complex Systems to Operational Design." In *Unifying Themes of Complex Systems.* Conference proceedings. Vol. 8, 1252–66. Quincy, MA: NECSI Press, 2011.

Samaan, Jean-Loup. *From War to Deterrence: Israel-Hezbollah Conflict since 2006.* Carlisle, PA: Strategic Studies Institute, 2014.

Scales, Robert. "Adaptive Enemies: Achieving Victory by Avoiding Defeat." *Joint Forces Quarterly* 23 (1999): 7–14.

Schiff, Zeev. *A History of the Israeli Army.* London: Sidgwick & Jackson, 1987.

Schiff, Zeev, and Ehud Yaari. *Israel's Lebanon War.* London: George Allen & Unwin, 1985.

Schmitt, John F. *A Systemic Concept for Operational Design.* Quantico, VA: Marine Corps Warfighting Lab, August 2006.

School of Advanced Military Studies. *Art of Design: Student Text.* Version 2.0. Fort Leavenworth, KS: SAMS, 2010.

Scott, Lt. Col. Trent. "Adapt or Die: Operational Design and Adaptation." *Australian Army Journal* 6, no. 3 (2009): 107–32.

Segal, Col. Giora. "The Threat to Ground Maneuver as a Deciding Element." *Strategic Assessment* 10, no. 4 (2008): 27–35.

Sela, Avraham. "Civil Society, the Military, and National Security: The Case of Israel's Security Zone in South Lebanon." In *Militarism and Israeli Society*, edited by Gabriel Sheffer and Oren Barak, 67–94. Bloomington: Indiana University Press, 2010.

Serena, Chad. *It Takes More Than a Network: The Iraqi Insurgency and Organizational Adaptation.* Stanford, CA: Stanford University Press, 2014.

———. *A Revolution in Military Adaptation: The US Army in the Iraq War.* Washington, DC: Georgetown University Press, 2011.

Shalom, Zaki, and Yoaz Hendel. "Conceptual Flaws on the Road to the Second Lebanon War." *Strategic Assessment* 10, no. 1 (2007): 23–30.

Shapira, Brig. Gen. (Ret.) Shimon. "Hizbullah Discusses Its Operational Plan for War with Israel." *Jerusalem Issue Brief* 11, no. 18, Jerusalem Center for Public Affairs, November 2, 2011.

Sheaito, Ahmad. "Seven Years on July War: Israel's Day of Grief." Al-Manar, July 13, 2013.

Siboni, Col. (Ret.) Gabi. "Victims of Friendly Fire: The Winograd Commission vs. the Citizens of Israel." *Strategic Assessment* 11, no. 1 (2008): 84–88.

———. "Disproportionate Force: Israel's Concept of Response in Light of the Second Lebanon War." INSS Insight no. 74, INSS, October 2, 2008.

———. "The Military Campaign in Lebanon." In Brom and Elran, *Second Lebanon War*, 61–76.

Shamir, Eitan. *Transforming Command: The Pursuit of Mission Command in the US, British, and Israeli Armies.* Stanford, CA: Stanford University Press, 2011.

———. "Coping with Nonstate Rivals." *Infinity Journal* 1, no. 2 (2011): 8–11.

———. "When Did a Big Mac Become Better Than a Falafel? The Americanization of the IDF (1973–2006)." Paper presented at the International Studies Association Annual Conference, Montreal, March 16, 2011.

Shamir, Eitan, and Eado Hecht. "Gaza 2014: Israel's Attrition vs Hamas Exhaustion." *Parameters* 44, no. 4 (2014): 82–90.

———. "Building the Next Missed Opportunity." *Maarachot* 454 (April 2014): 9–13 (Hebrew).

———. "Neglect of IDF Ground Forces: A Risk to Israel's Security." BESA Perspectives Paper no. 225. BESA Center for Strategic Studies, Ramat Gan, Israel, December 4, 2013.

Shanahan, Rodger. *The Shi'a of Lebanon: Clans, Parties, and Clerics.* London: I. B. Tauris, 2005.

Shelah, Ofer, and Yoav Limor. *Captives of Lebanon.* Tel Aviv: Yediot Books, 2007 (Hebrew).

Smith, Rupert. *The Utility of Force: The Art of War in the Modern World.* London: Vintage Books, 2008.

Sneh, Ephraim. "Why I Opposed Israel's Withdrawal from Lebanon." *Haaretz*, May 21, 2010.

Sobelman, Daniel. "Learning to Deter: Deterrence Failure and Success in the Israel-Hezbollah Conflict, 2006–16." *International Security* 41, no. 3 (2017): 151–96.

———. "Lebanon 2007: Old Realities, New Uncertainties." *Strategic Assessment* 10, no. 3 (2007).

———. *New Rules of the Game: Israel and Hizbollah after the Withdrawal from Lebanon.* Memorandum no. 69. Tel Aviv: JCSS, 2004.

Sorrells, Lt. Col. William T., Lt. Col. Glen Downing, Maj. Paul Blaksley, Maj. David Pendall, Maj. Jason Walk, and Maj. Richard Wallwork. *Systemic Operational Design: An Introduction.* Fort Leavenworth, KS: SAMS, 2005.

Swain, Richard. *Fundamentals of Operational Design.* Fort Leavenworth, KS: Booz Allen Hamilton, 2009.

Szubin, Adam. "Beyond the Vote: Implications for the Sanctions Regime on Iran." Speech given at the Washington Institute for Near Eastern Policy, Washington, DC, September 16, 2015.

Tal, Maj. Gen. Israel. *National Security: The Israeli Experience.* Westport, CT: Praeger, 2000.

———. "The Offensive and Defensive in Israel's Campaigns." *Jerusalem Quarterly* no. 51 (1989): 41–47.

———. "Israel's Doctrine of National Security: Background and Dynamics." *Jerusalem Quarterly* no. 4 (1977): 45–57.

Tamari, Brig. Gen. Dov. "Operation Danny." *Haaretz*, February 24, 2010 (Hebrew).

Tamir, Brig. Gen. Moshe "Chico." *Undeclared War*. Tel Aviv: Maarachot, 2005 (Hebrew).

Terriff, Terry. "Warriors and Innovators: Military Change and Organizational Culture in the US Marine Corps." *Defence Studies* 6, no. 2 (2006): 215–47.

Tira, Lt. Col. Ron. *The Nature of War: Conflicting Paradigms of Israeli Military Effectiveness*. Eastbourne, UK: Sussex Academic Press, 2010.

———. *The Limitations of Standoff Firepower-Based Operations: On Standoff Warfare, Maneuver, and Decision*. Memorandum no. 89, Tel Aviv: INSS, 2007.

———. "Breaking the Amoeba's Bones." *Strategic Assessment* 9, no. 3 (2006): 7–15.

Tsur, Nadir. "The Test of Consciousness: The Crisis of Signification in the IDF." *Military and Strategic Affairs* 2, no. 2 (2010): 3–18.

Ucko, David. *The New Counterinsurgency Era*. Washington, DC: Georgetown University Press, 2009.

United Nations. "Security Council Calls for Immediate End to Hostilities in Lebanon, Expresses Support for Diplomatic Effort." Press release SC/6208. April 18, 1996.

US Congress. H.R. 2297: Hizbullah International Financing Prevention Act of 2015, December 2015.

US State Department. "Terrorist Designation of Samir Kuntar." Office of the Spokesperson, September 8, 2015.

Valensi, Carmit, and Brig. Gen. Itai Brun. "The Revolution in Military Affairs of the Radical Axis." *Maarachot* 432 (2010): 4–17 (Hebrew).

Van Creveld, Martin. *The Sword and the Olive: A Critical History of the Israeli Defense Force*. New York: PublicAffairs, 2002.

Vardi, Gil-li. "Pounding Their Feet: Israeli Military Culture as Reflected in Early IDF Combat History." *Journal of Strategic Studies* 31, no. 2 (2008): 295–324.

Vego, Milan. "Systems versus Classical Approach to Warfare." *Joint Forces Quarterly* 52 (2009): 40–48.

———. "A Case against Systemic Operational Design." *Joint Forces Quarterly* 53 (2009): 69–75.

Wald, Col. Emanuel. *The Wald Report: The Decline of Israeli National Security since 1967*. Boulder, CO: Westview Press, 1992.

Wass de Czege, Brig. Gen. Huba. "Systemic Operational Design: Learning and Adapting in Complex Missions." *Military Review* 89, no. 1 (2009): 2–12.

Watts, Barry. *US Combat Training, Operational Art, and Strategic Competence: Problems and Opportunities*. Center for Strategic and Budgetary Assessment, 2008.

Wegman, Col. Yehuda. "A Distorted Self-Image: On the IDF and Its Responsibility for Civilians." *Strategic Assessment* 10, no. 2 (2007): 23–30.

———. "Israel's Security Doctrine and the Trap of 'Limited Conflict.'" *Military Technology* 29, no. 3 (March 2005): 88–96.

———. "Israel's Security Doctrine and the Trap of 'Limited Conflict.'" Jerusalem Viewpoints no. 514, Jerusalem Center for Publics Affairs, March 1, 2004.

Weizman, Eyal. "The Art of War." *Frieze* no. 99 (May 2006).

———. "Lethal Theory." *Log* no. 7 (Winter/Spring 2006): 53–78.

———. "Walking through Walls: Soldiers as Architects in the Israeli-Palestinian Conflict." *Radical Philosophy* no. 136 (March/April 2006): 8–22.

Whitson, Sarah Leah. "Hezbollah Needs to Answer." *Human Rights Watch*, October 6, 2006.

Winograd Commission. *The Commission to Examine the Events of the 2006 Campaign in Lebanon: The Second Lebanon War* (final report). State of Israel, January 2008

(Hebrew). Author's translations from Hebrew; selected chapters translated to English by the Open Source Center.

Yaalon, Moshe. "Lessons from the Palestinian 'War' against Israel." Policy Focus no. 64, Washington Institute for Near Eastern Policy, 2007.

———. "Preparing the Forces for the Limited Conflict." *Maarachot* nos. 380–81 (2001): 24–29 (Hebrew).

Yaari, Adm. Yedidia, and Haim Assa. *Diffused Warfare: The Concept of Virtual Mass.* Haifa: University of Haifa, February 2007.

———. "Dynamic Molecules: The Theory of Diffused Warfare." *Pointer: Journal of the Singapore Armed Forces* 31, no. 3 (2005): 5–15.

Yadlin, Maj. Gen. Amos. "How Israel Created Deterrence in the Lebanon War." *Yediot Ahronoth*, May 22, 2015.

———. "Confronting Enemy Force Buildup: The Case of Advanced Weaponry for Hizbollah." INSS Insight no. 401, February 7, 2013.

Yaniv, Avner. *Dilemmas of Israeli Security: Politics, Strategy, and the Israeli Experience in Lebanon.* New York: Oxford University Press, 1987.

Yaniv, Avner, and Robert Lieber. "Personal Whim or Strategic Imperative? The Israeli Invasion of Lebanon." *International Security* 8, no. 2 (Fall 1983): 117–42.

Zisk, Kimberly M. *Engaging the Enemy: Organization Theory and Soviet Military Innovation.* Princeton, NJ: Princeton University Press, 1993.

Zisser, Eyal. "Israelis Confront the Second Lebanon War." *Bustan: Middle East Book Review* 1, no. 1 (2010): 29–43.

———. "Hizballah and Israel: Strategic Threat on the Northern Border." *Israel Affairs* 12, no. 1 (2006): 86–106.

———. "Hizballah: New Course or Continued Warfare." *Middle East Review of International Affairs* 4, no. 3 (2000).

———. "Hizballah in Lebanon: At the Crossroads." *Terrorism and Political Violence* 8, no. 2 (1996): 90–110.

———. "Maronites, Lebanon, and the State of Israel: Early Contacts." *Middle East Studies* 31, no. 4 (1995): 889–918.

Zweibelson, Ben. "The Application of Theory." *Small Wars Journal*, February 19, 2017.

———. "To Design or Not to Design." *Small Wars Journal*, March 4, 2011.

INDEX

Abu Nidal Organization, 18
Adamsky, Dima, 134, 258
Adam, Udi: Bint Jbayl directives of, 195–96;
on deterrence, erosion of, 93; on ground
offensive, slow launching of, 199; on
ground operations, actions on, 193;
Halutz and Hirsch, clashes with, 198,
253; on Ice Breaker battle plan, 179;
replacement of, 223
adaptation. See military adaptation
Advanced Operational Command Course,
166, 170
Advanced Operational Group. See Opera-
tional Theory Research Institute
Afghanistan War (2001), 136–137, 254
Afwaj al-Muqawama al-Lubnaniya (Amal,
"Lebanese Resistance Detachments,"
Shi'ite militia), 19, 22, 44, 46
AirLand Battle doctrine (US), 125, 133,
163, 255
airpower: IDF's reliance on, 44, 45, 142–44,
145, 186, 191, 202, 229, 239–40; nature
of, 206. See also Israeli Air Force
Allahdadi, Mohammad, 279
allies, emulation among, 8, 254–55
Al-Manar (Hezbollah television station):
Hezbollah end-of-year statement on, 68;
Hezbollah statement on Syria, involve-
ment in, 272
Almog, Doron, 224–25
Alon, Nitzan, 170, 173, 233
Amal (Afwaj al-Muqawama al-Lubnaniya,
"Lebanese Resistance Detachments,"
Shi'ite militia), 19, 22, 44, 46

Americanization (of IDF), 254
Amidror, Yaakov, 156, 222
Amir, Roni: on EBO, 216–17; on Halutz,
189–90, 216–17; on Hezbollah's rocket
doctrine, 148, 203; on Mussawi assassi-
nation, 47; on RMA, 147, 151–52; on
targeting challenges, 206
Ansariya operation, 78
antitank missiles (ATMs), 42, 68, 93, 95,
194, 230, 277
Aoun, Michel, 104
April 2006 operational doctrine. See Israel
Defense Forces, reappraisal of 2006
operational concept
April understandings (1996), 64–66, 79,
80, 249
Arab guerrillas (fedayeen), 34
Arab-Israeli War (Yom Kippur War,
1973), 17, 38, 51, 128, 130
Arab League, 272
Arab Spring, 264
Arad, Uzi, 95
Arafat, Yasser, 19
Arens, Moshe: Ghaddar, talks with, 19–20;
IDF strategy under, 87; influence of, 91,
92, 249; on military approach to south-
ern Lebanon, 79–80, 82, 84; on
Mussawi assassination, 47; overall policy
goals of, 79; state-on-state wars and,
103, 104, 114; strategic adaptation
under, 75; on strikes against Lebanese
government, 94
Argov, Shlomo, 18
artillery, IDF's use of, 44, 142–43

Asad, Hafez al-. *See* Assad, Hafez al-
Ashkenazi, Gabi, 83, 85, 178, 180, 231
Assad, Bashar al-, 91, 268
Assad, Hafez al-, 56, 63, 79
Assa, Haim, 173
asymmetrical conflict, 122, 142, 154–57, 167, 207
ATMs (antitank missiles), 42, 68, 93, 95, 194, 230, 277
attrition, 84–85, 115, 242, 275
Aviv Neurim ("Spring of Youth") program, 135
Azani, Eitan, 42

Baalbek, raid on, 197
Badreddine, Mustafa, 271
Bagnall, Nigel, 164
Baidatz, Yossi, 232
Barak, Ehud: election of, 80–87, 253, 257; Hezbollah pressure on, 115; IDF, impact on, 133, 134; on Israel's new strategic rationale, 91; on Lebanon, Israeli presence in, 23; on Lebanon, withdrawal from, 20–21, 250; muddled Lebanon policies of, 115; on operational complexities, 57; operational concept of, 241; on political-military disputes, 61; as promoter of IDF transformation, 251; security zone and, 81
Bar-Kochba, Moshe, 20
basic security (fundamental security, *bitachon yisodi*), 34, 37
Bazzi, Khaled, 186
Beaufort Castle, assault on, 42
Begin, Menachem, 19
Beirut: siege of, 19; suicide bombing in, 40
"Beirut for Tel Aviv" equation, 106, 107, 116
Bekaa Valley air operation (1982), 128–29, 130, 137, 237, 251
Ben-Eliezer, Benjamin, 61
Ben-Gurion, David, 245, 256
Ben-Israel, Isaac, 102, 108, 133, 153, 238
Bennett, Naftali, 105, 159n21
Bertalanffy, Ludwig von, 167
Bint Jbayl, Lebanon, 193–98, 224, 230
Biran, Ilan, 101
bitachon shotef. See routine security

bitachon yisodi (basic security, fundamental security), 34, 37. *See* fundamental security
blame game. *See* Israel Defense Forces, reappraisal of 2006 operational concept
Blanford, Nicholas, 14
Blue Line (Israel-Lebanon border), 91
Bodinger, Herzl, 145
Bolton, John, 199
Bonen, Zeev, 137–38, 158
border skirmishes, 278–80
bottom-up military adaptation, 9–10, 71, 249, 256
Boyd, John, 166
Brigade 401, 162nd Division, 200
Britain, *Future Character of Conflict*, 4
Broken Telephone game, 220
Brom, Shlomo: on April understandings, 64; on counterguerrilla warfare, threat toward, 59; on deterrence policy, 63; on First Gulf War, 132; on Hezbollah's adaptability, 153; on military adaptation, post–Yom Kippur War, 128; on OTRI and Hirsch, scapegoating of, 225; on RMA, 129, 134, 143
Brun, Itai: on airpower, use of, 239; on April 2006 operational document, 217, 218; on Halutz, criticisms of, 240; on Hezbollah rocket power, 274–75; on Hezbollah's future tactics, 276, 277; on IDF's mistakes, 243; on IDF's strategic concept, 101; on operational plans, 186; on Shebaa Farms roadside bomb attack, 278; on tunnels, 276–77
Buckley, William, 40
budget cuts. *See* training budget cuts
bunkers, Hezbollah use of, 149, 193, 204, 206
bush warfare, 60

casualties: aversion to, 72, 82, 86, 122, 132, 142–43, 158, 179, 189, 193, 195, 196, 201–2, 239, 254–55, 257–58; casualty ratios, 60, 69; Hezbollah's, 69, 270–71; IDF's, 58, 69, 253–54, 257; during Lebanon War, 200, 201, 203; 1982 to 1999, 70, 248; Sneh on, 75
cease-fire agreement (July 1981), 18

cease-fire agreement (2006 Lebanon War), 190, 199, 200, 201
Cedar Revolution, 94, 178
Central Command (IDF), SOD and, 170–72, 180
change. *See* military adaptation; military adaptation, operational; military adaptation, strategic
chief of staff (COS, IDF); *and individual generals*
Christians (Maronites), in Lebanon, 17
chronology, 285–88
civilian contractors, 175
civilians: as casualties during 2006 Lebanon War, 186, 197, 201; civilian areas, Hezbollah's concealment in, 145, 146; civilian homeland defense system (Israel), 35; erroneous IDF strike against, 146; Hezbollah's continued targeting of, 64–65; during Operation Accountability, 55–56, 143; understandings on, in 1996 cease-fire agreement, 64. *See also* political leaders (Israel)
civil-military relations, 6–8, 114, 247–50. *See also* political leaders
Clausewitz, Carl von, 2, 31, 124, 246
cognitive failures, 165
Cohen, Eliot, 243
Cohen, Ronen, 49, 50, 60–61, 144
commando forces, Hezbollah as, 67–68, 72
competition, military change and, 6, 8–9
containment policy (Israel), 55, 98, 115
contextual history, importance of, 32
COS (chief of staff, IDF). *See* Halutz, Dan; Lipkin-Shahak, Amnon
counterguerrilla warfare, 55, 59–62, 71, 72, 151
culture: IDF culture, 11, 255–61; organizational culture, conclusions on, 255–61; organizational culture, military change and, 6, 8–12

Dagan, Meir, 188
Dahiya doctrine, 101–6, 109, 116, 247, 249–50, 256
David's Sling medium-range missile-defense system, 274
Dayan, Moshe, 11, 133

Dayan, Uzi, 170, 171
Defense Department (DOD, US), 163, 174–75, 176
Defense of the Land (Magen Haaretz) battle plan, 178, 192
Dekel, Udi, 275
Deleuze, Gilles, 167
denial, deterrence by, 35
Department of ___. *See name of specific department, e.g., State Department*
Depth Corps (IDF), 226
DePuy, William, 125
deterrence: balance of, 278–79; cumulative deterrence, 34–35, 102, 275; by denial, 35; determining factors in, 98; deterrence equation, strategic adaptation to, 78–80; IDF concept of, 31, 256; importance to Hezbollah, 279; 2006 Lebanon War, lessons learned from, 99, 101–2; Lubrani on, 45; mutual deterrence, 50–51, 107–8, 247, 263; preparation for war as, 266; by punishment, 35, 104, 116; role in Israeli strategic thinking, 34
deterrence, erosion of (2000–2017), 90–109; conclusions on, 108–9; Dahiya doctrine, 101–5; Hezbollah's post-2006 deterrence, 106–8; *IDF Strategy* document and, 105; introduction to, 90; post-2000 shifts in, 90–94; 2006 war, IDF strategy in, 98–100; 2006 war, road to, 94–98
deterrence, guerrilla warfare and (1993–99), 54–72; April Understandings, 64–66; conclusions on, 71–72; counterguerrilla warfare, 59–62; Hezbollah's guerrilla warfare, shift in, 66–71, 114, 269; introduction to, 54–55; July understandings, 56–57; Northern Command, new head of, 57–59; operational accountability, 55–56; Operation Grapes of Wrath, 62–63. *See also* Israel Defense Forces, operations in Lebanon (1990s)
Diffused Warfare concept, 173–74, 176–77, 194, 266
disproportional firepower, 100
disproportional responses, 104, 109
Doctrine Division (IDF Operations Directorate), 219

DOD (Defense Department, US), 163, 174–75, 176
domestic pressure, as driver of change, 253–54
Drori, Amir, 20, 21, 81

Effects-Based Operations (EBO), 169, 205, 216–17
Effects Doctrine. *See* Effects-Based Operations (EBO)
Egeland, Jan, 206
Egoz Reconnaissance Battalion (counterguerrilla warfare unit, IDF), 59–62, 71, 72, 192–93, 249, 256
890th Paratrooper Battalion, 193–94
Eiland, Giora: on Arens, 79; on casualties, impact of, 70–71; on Hezbollah, misunderstandings of, 38; on IDF's ineffective learning, 70, 114; on IDF's opinion on security zone, 78–79; on Lebanon War objectives, 99; on postwithdrawal strategy, 115; on state-on-state war with Lebanon, 103; on Winograd Commission, 2
Eisenberg, Eyal, 192
Eitan, Itzik, 170
Eitan, Rafael, 19
Eizenkot, Gadi: on Dahiya doctrine, 103, 104–5; on ground operations during Lebanon War, 196; Halutz and, 180, 198–99; on Hezbollah, restraining elements on, 102–3; Lebanon War, actions during, 187; as postwar analysis committee leader, 215; training, support for, 267
Elevated Waters (Mai Marom) battle plan, 178, 186, 192
Elran, Meir, 225
emergency situations, as described in *IDF Strategy*, 105
emulation, uncritical, 254–55
Erlich, Reuven, 20, 40, 84
erosion of deterrence. *See* deterrence, erosion of
expensive innovations, preferences for, 8

Fadlallah, Mohammad Hussein, 22, 40, 62
Fajr arsenal, 190–91
Fayyad, Ali, 96–97

fedayeen (Arab guerrillas), 34
field security (Hezbollah), 48–49
field units (Hezbollah), operational autonomy of, 206
find-fix-kill chain process, 141
Finkel, Meir, 220, 267, 269
First Intifada, 248
First Lebanon War (1982), 14, 18–19, 128–29
Fneish, Muhammad, 81
force, IDF's use of, 35
fortifications, Hezbollah's, 144, 149–50
Four Mothers Movement, 76–77, 253
Free Lebanon Army, 17
fundamental security (basic security, *bitachon yisodi*), 34, 37
Future Character of Conflict (British Ministry of Defence), 4

Galilee: Hezbollah threats to, 107; security zone protecting, 21
Gal, Orit, 170–71
Gantz, Benny: cuts under, 266–67; on deterrence, 104; on ground forces, neglect of, 230; on ground offensive, slow launching of, 199; Halutz, defense of, 188; as head of Northern Command, 176; Lebanon, battle plans for, 178; on 2006 Lebanon War, 185, 187–88; Naveh and, 232; SOD and, 179; on training budget cuts, 264; Winograd letter on Hirsch to, 226; withdrawal from Lebanon, opposition to, 83
Gaza conflict (2014), 274, 276
Gaza War (2008), 13, 231
Gazit, Shlomo, 77
Gemayel, Amin, 19
Gemayel, Bashir, 19
General Staff (IDF), 136, 228, 252–53
Gerstein, Erez, 60, 76–77, 78, 253
Ghaddar, Muhammad, 19–20
Gideon multiyear plan, 267
Gilad, Amos, 83
Goksel, Timur: on 2006 Hezbollah attack, 96; on Hezbollah adaptation, 48–49, 147–48, 205; on Hezbollah rocket fire, 204–5; on Hezbollah's activities, 43; on Hezbollah's early development, 41; on

IDF defensive posture (late 1990s), 69; on security zone withdrawal, 84; on Wadi Saluki battle, 201

Golan Heights, 66, 280

Golan, Yair, 265

Goldwasser, Ehud, 185

Gordon, Shmuel, 151, 239

Graicer, Ofra: on Gantz, 176; on Halutz's operational concept document, 215–16; on Ice Breaker battle plan, 179; officer leadership course, development of, 232–33; on OTRI, 164, 166, 175, 226; on SOD implementation, 173, 228

Granit, Amos: on Ice Breaker battle plan, 179; on IDF's focus on precision firepower, 229; in MI, 231; operational plans developed by, 178, 187; SOD and, 164, 173, 179

ground forces and ground operations: ground incursions, 107–8; Hezbollah's adaptation of use of, 276; IAF, competition with, 252–53; neglect of, 137, 228–31, 233, 241–42, 265–66; problems with, during Lebanon War, 191–202

Ground Forces Command (GFC, Mazi), 135–36

guardianship of the Islamic jurist *(wilayat al-faqih)*, 23

Guattari, Félix, 167

guerrilla warfare: counter-guerrilla air warfare, 151; guerrilla war of attrition, 115, 242; Hezbollah's, impact on IDF through, 242, 246; Hezbollah's preference for, 150; rise of, in Lebanon, 129; RMA's lack of applicability to, 137–38. *See also* deterrence, guerrilla warfare and

Gulf War (1991): influence on RMA, 127, 132–34, 137, 241; as model for IDF, 125, 144, 254, 255; preparedness for, lack of, 163

HaCohen, Gershon, 170, 174

Haddad, Saad, 17

Haifa, Hezbollah rocket attacks on, 191

Halevy, Herzi, 233

Halutz, Dan: Adam, clash with, 198; Bint Jbayl operation and, 194, 195–96; COS, appointment as, 252–53; 2006 Lebanon War, actions during, 186–92, 195, 197–202; military reforms, support for, 136–37; Naveh on, 227; operational doctrine under, 181, 215; OTRI and, 179–80, 251; Peretz and, 191; as signer of operational concept document and, 214; spelling of name of, 26n73

Halutz, Dan: on containment policy, 115; on EBO, 216; on Hezbollah, 90; on IDF's deterrence policies, 99–100; on IDF transformation, 239; on Lebanese government, targeting of, 103; on Lebanon War, 108; on lever strategy, 102; on Limited Conflict, 157; on success, definition of, 240

Hamade, Hatem, 271

Hamas, 96, 274, 276

Hanit (Israeli navy corvette), destruction of, 191, 230

Harakat al-Mahrumin (Movement for the Deprived), 22

Harb, Khalil, 66

Harb Tammuz. *See* Lebanon War (2006)

Harel, Yitzhak, 180, 189

Hashem, Akel, 78

Hawn, Goldie, 76

helicopter collisions, 78

Hezbollah: as archetypical adversary, 4; during Bint Jbayl operation, 194; ceasefire (1996), agreement to, 64; as commando force, evolution into, 67–68, 72; creation of, 46; deterrence (post-2006) strategy of, 106–8; emergence of, 21–23; as guerrilla army (*See* deterrence, guerrilla warfare and); IDF as rival of, 246–47; IDF's initial understanding of, 37, 39; initial weakness of, 37–38; kidnappings by, 39–40, 93, 96–97, 98–99, 185–86; Lebanonization of, 14–15; military approaches, successes of, 4; Mussawi assassination, reaction to, 47–50, 51; operational adaptation of, 147–51, 158, 202–8; operational concepts of, 123–24, 154, 158, 242, 273; operations, numbers of, 58, 68, 92–93; organizational survivability of, 205–6; scholarly literature on, 14; Syrian Civil War as challenge to,

Hezbollah *(continued)*
268–73. *See also* Katyusha rockets;
Nasrallah, Hassan
Hezbollah, evolution of (1985–92), 37–51;
in 1980s, 39–45; conclusions on, 50–51;
IDF in 1980s, 38–39; innovative developments (early 1990s), 45–50;
introduction to, 37
Hezbollah International Financing Prevention Act (2015), 273
Higgins, William, 40
hill-storming operations, 42–43
Hirsch, Gal: Adam, clash with, 193, 198;
criticisms of, 224–25, 226–27; as division leader, 192; on Halutz, scapegoating
of, 240; IAF precision strikes, support
for, 145; Lebanon War and, 177; on
Maydun operation, 44; scapegoating of,
194, 223–28; on Second RMA, 266;
SOD and, 170, 172; vindication of, 226;
on Web of Steel operation, 193, 194–95
Home Front Command (IDF), 7, 133, 274
horizontal learning, 10
human-wave attacks, 42–43
Hussein, Saddam, 125, 133, 163

IAF. *See* Israeli Air Force
Ice Breaker (Shoveret Kerach) battle plan,
179, 186, 196
Idan 2010 plan, 135
IDF. *See* Israel Defense Forces
IDF Strategy document, 105, 109, 247,
267
improvised explosive devices (IEDs), 42, 43
Inbar, Giora, 63, 77
initiative, IDF policy of, 57–58
Institute for Systemic Intelligence Analysis
(MI), 231
insurgent-group learning, 12, 246–47
intraorganizational competition, 8–9,
252–53
Iran: Hezbollah, assistance to, 45–46; Hez-
bollah's commitment to, 41; Iranian
Revolution (1979), 22; sanctions against,
272–73; suicide bombings and, 40. *See
also* Islamic Revolutionary Guard Corps
Iraq War (2003), 136–37, 218, 254
IRGC (Islamic Revolutionary Guard
Corps, Iran), 41, 44, 273, 279

Iron Dome missile defense system, 7, 197,
274, 275
irregular adversaries, adaptive nature of, 4
ISIS (Islamic State of Iraq and Syria), 263,
268, 269
Islamic Resistance. *See* Hezbollah
Islamic Revolutionary Guard Corps
(IRGC, Iran), 41, 44, 273, 279
Islamic State of Iraq and Syria (ISIS), 263,
268, 269
Israel: cease-fire (1996), agreement to, 64;
civil-military relations, nature of, 7–8;
defense systems, improvements to, 274;
dysfunctional civil-military dynamic in,
247–50; electoral debates, Hezbollah
influence on, 81; Lebanon, 1982 invasion of, 18–21; society, role of IDF in, 9;
strategic doctrine of, 33–35. *See also*
Israel Defense Forces; Israeli Air Force;
political leaders
Israel, war with Hezbollah: conclusions
on, 245–61; deterrence, erosion of
(2000–2017), 90–109; deterrence, guerrilla warfare and (1993–99), 54–72;
future outlook on, 273–78; Hezbollah,
evolution of (1985–92), 37–51; IDF
2006 operational concept, reappraisal of,
214–33; IDF operations in Lebanon
(1990s), 141–58; IDF withdrawal from
Lebanon (2000), 75–87; introduction
to, 1–28; Lebanon War (2006), military
adaptation and counteradaptation in,
185–209; Operational Theory Research
Institute, 162–81; RMA in Israel, origins of, 127–38. *See also* Hezbollah;
Israel Defense Forces
Israel Defense Forces (IDF): budget,
changes to, 136; deterrence policy, 2–3;
as engine of operational adaptation,
250–51; force plans in Syria, 264–67;
fundamental strategic mistake of, 113;
General Staff discussions on withdrawal
from Lebanon and, 20; Hezbollah as
rival of, 246–47; Hezbollah, conceptual
understanding of, 37, 67–68; Israeli
society, role in, 7–8; in Lebanon, actions
against, 19; in 1980s, 37–39; operational
art, 163, 164, 165, 166, 168; organizational culture of, 11, 255–61; OTRI's

effects-based operations, impact of, 168–69; as people's army, 21, 122, 131, 162, 239; popular perceptions of, 21; RMA and, 237, 239; security zone, map of, x; strategic doctrine of, 33–34; suicide vehicle-bombs, responses to, 43; uncritical emulation by, dangers of, 254–55. *See also* deterrence; low-intensity conflict; military adaptation, operational; military adaptation, strategic; Northern Command; security zone; "slimmer and smarter" era; way of war, IDF's; Winograd Commission Final Report

Israel Defense Forces, operations in Lebanon (1990s), 141–58; conclusions on, 157–58; Hezbollah, operational adaptation of (1990s), 147–51; introduction to, 141–42; limited conflict doctrine, 154–57; Operation Accountability (1993), 142–44; Operation Grapes of Wrath (1996), 145–47; RMA in Lebanon (late 1990s), 151–54. *See also* deterrence, guerrilla warfare and

Israel Defense Forces, reappraisal of 2006 operational concept, 214–33; conclusions on, 231–33; ground forces, neglect of, 228–31; Hirsch, scapegoating of, 223–28; introduction to, 214–15; nebulous concepts, diffusion of, 220–22; SOD, critical assessment of, 222–23; SOD, survival of, 231–33; 2006 operational concept, discussion of, 215–20

Israel Defense Forces, withdrawal from Lebanon (2000), 75–87; Barak, election of, 80–87; conclusions on, 87; deterrence equation, strategic adaptation to, 78–80; introduction to, 75; run-up to withdrawal, 75–78

Israel-Hezbollah War (2006). *See* Lebanon War (2006)

Israeli Air Force (IAF): ground forces, competition with, 229–30, 252–53; helicopter collisions, 78; Lebanon, offensive sorties in, 152; Mussawi, assassination of, 46–47; Operation Specific Weight, 186; RMA, use of, 128–29, 143, 151–52, 158; Syria, strikes against, 280; technological changes in, 265; Yom Kippur War, failures of, 128

Israel-Lebanon border ("Blue Line"), 91
Israel-Lebanon Monitoring Group, 64

jargon, 166–68, 177, 226, 231
Joint Comprehensive Plan of Action (2015), 272–73
Joint Forces Command (US), 169
Jordan, expulsion of PLO from, 17
Joyous Festivals (Moadim L'Simcha, military policy), 49–50
July understandings (1993), 56–57, 62, 63, 64, 79, 80, 249
July War. *See* Lebanon War (2006)

Kahalani, Avigdor, 77
Kaplinsky, Moshe: appointment of, 253; on Egoz Reconnaissance Battalion, 59; Halutz and, 180; on Halutz, opposition to, 198–99; on IDF's operational approach, 93, 198, 223; on Israel's misunderstanding of Hezbollah capabilities, 48; Lebanon War, actions during, 187
Katyusha rockets: al-Khalil on, 62; Hezbollah's success with, 50, 51, 148–49; during 2006 Lebanon War, 188, 197; Nasrallah on, 54; during Operation Accountability, 56, 144; Peretz on Hezbollah use of, 100
Katz, Muni, 269, 270
Kela 2008 plan, 136, 264
Khalil, Hussein al-, 62
Khomeini, Ayatollah Ruhollah, 22, 23, 40, 41
kidnappings: by Hamas, 96; by Hezbollah, 39–40, 93, 96–97, 98–99, 185–86; Hirsch's responses to, 224–25
Kiryat Shmona, 18, 148
Kitri, Ron, 92
Kochavi, Aviv, 170, 172, 173, 231, 233
Komati, Mahmoud, 96
Kuntar, Samir, 279–80
Kuperwasser, Yossi, 96, 170, 173, 208

Lahd, Antoine, 21, 84, 86–87
Lambeth, Benjamin, 240
language: Hezbollah's use of, 207; jargon, 166–68, 177, 226, 231
Lanir, Zvi, 164–65, 167, 226, 227
Laqees, Hussein, 271

Lawrence, T. E. (Lawrence of Arabia), 261
leadership. *See* political leaders (Israel)
learning. *See* military adaptation
Lebanese Resistance Detachments (Afwaj
    al-Muqawama al-Lubnaniya, Amal,
    Shi'ite militia), 19, 22, 44, 46
Lebanon and Lebanon conflict: Cedar
    Revolution, 94, 178; domestic tensions
    in, 271–72; Hezbollah, cooperation
    with, 104; Hezbollah presence in gov-
    ernment of, 103; infrastructure, planned
    attacks on, 103–4, 106, 109, 114, 116,
    145, 188–91, 202; Lebanese Civil War,
    17; Lebanese, relationship with Hezbol-
    lah, 41, 55–56, 63, 65, 71, 77, 100–102,
    114, 142, 205; Lebanese, Syria and, 91;
    limitations of scholarship on, 12–13; as
    proxy for Syria, 79–80; Sharon's aspira-
    tion for, 19; Shi'ites in, 22. *See also* Israel
    Defense Forces, withdrawal from Leba-
    non; Lebanon War; lever strategy;
    security zone; southern Lebanon, Israeli
    occupation of; South Lebanon Army
Lebanon Liaison Unit, 76
Lebanon War (1982), 128–29, 257
Lebanon War (2006) (Second Lebanon
    War, July War, Harb Tammuz): begin-
    nings of, 1; as harbinger of future
    conflict, 3–4; IDF strategy in, 98–100;
    impact of RMA on, 158; origins of, 94,
    115; road to, 94–98; SOD and planning
    for, 172, 176–79; successes of, 108. *See
    also* Israel Defense Forces, reappraisal of
    2006 operational concept
Lebanon War (2006), military adaptation
    and counteradaptation in, 185–209; air
    campaign, 186–91; conclusions on,
    208–9; ground offensive, 199–202;
    Hezbollah's military adaptation in,
    202–8; IDF, limited ground operations
    of, 191–99; introduction to, 185–86
lever strategy: Arens' strategy versus, 87,
    249; disuse of, after 2006, 101–2; Halutz's
    reliance on, 189, 190, 202; ineffectiveness
    of, 114, 205, 217; international opinion
    and, 190; Yaalon's preference for, 177
Levi, Moshe, 81
Levin, Amiram: on April understandings,
    Hezbollah and, 65; as change enabler,

113, 256; conclusions on, 71; as head of
    Northern Command, 57–62, 248–49; on
    Hezbollah, response to, 54; on Hezbol-
    lah's strategic changes, 68; on IDF
    defensive posture (late 1990s), 69–70;
    increased operations under, 68; on
    Operation Grapes of Wrath, 63, 145; as
    postwar analysis committee leader, 215;
    on security zone, withdrawal from, 77;
    wife of, political activism of, 77
Levy, David, 85
Levy, Michael, 80
LIC. *See* low-intensity conflict
Limited Conflict doctrine: creation of, 142;
    discussion of, 154–57; influence of, 220,
    230, 241, 257; remnants of, 217; repudi-
    ation of, 172–73
Lipkin-Shahak, Amnon: on airpower, 240;
    on Four Mothers Movement, 77; on
    Inbar, 63; influence of, 59; Levin's influ-
    ence on, 249; military think-tank group,
    recognition of, 165; OTRI and, 171;
    reform, tepid support for, 134–35
long-range missile capabilities, Hezbol-
    lah's, 106
low-intensity conflict (LIC): challenges of,
    241; deterrence as strategic doctrine
    against, 34; Diffused Warfare and, 173;
    lack of research on, 12; Limited Conflict
    doctrine and, 154–57; misunderstand-
    ings of, 221; as operational focus, during
    Second Intifada, 230; as operational
    focus of IDF in Lebanon, 37; status of,
    after Arab-Israeli War, 38. *See also* rou-
    tine security
Lubrani, Uri, 45, 84
Luwayza (Hezbollah stronghold), IDF
    assault on, 45

Maarachot ("Campaigns," military journal):
    on Hezbollah's current operational con-
    cept, 273; IDF doctrinal documents in,
    15–16; on RMA-inspired technology,
    255
Magen Haaretz (Defense of the Land)
    battle plan, 178, 192
Mai Marom (Elevated Waters) battle plan,
    178, 186, 192
Main Commandment (Hezbollah), 149

Malka, Amos, 83, 94, 98
Maltam. *See* Operational Theory Research Institute
Mao Tse Tung, 67
maps, of IDF security zone, x
marjah al-taqlid (source of emulation), 23
Maronites (Christians), in Lebanon, 17
Maroun al-Ras, Lebanon, battle in, 192–93, 198
Marshall, Andrew, 174–76
Mattis, James, 221
maverick military officers, 6–7, 11, 60, 71, 164
Maydun (Hezbollah stronghold), IDF assault on, 44
media, criticisms of, 78
memoirs, on Lebanon conflict, 13
Merkava tanks, 200–201, 277
MI (Military Intelligence Directorate), 97, 173, 186, 231, 276
midlevel officers, SOD diffusion and, 170
militaries: conservative nature of, 5, 6, 50; as engines of operational change, 250–51; military-civil dynamic, dysfunctional nature of, 247–50; military cognition, 165; military innovation, studies of, 4–5; military intelligence, limitations of, 188; military learning institutions, characteristics of, 11; US and Western, IDF relationship with, 254; Western, incompetence of, 168. *See also* ground forces and ground operations; Hezbollah; Israel Defense Forces; Israeli Air Force
military adaptation: definition of, 5; domestic pressure as driver of, 253; under fire, 267; IDF's and Hezbollah's interrelated, 246; implementation of, 9; importance of, 4; learning and, 197, 206, 259–60; top-down versus bottom-up, 9–10, 71, 113. *See also* Syria, IDF and Hezbollah in
military adaptation, operational: conclusions on, 237–43; IDF 2006 operational concept, reappraisal of, 214–33; IDF operations in Lebanon (1990s), 141–58; introduction to, 121–26; Lebanon War (2006), military adaptation and counteradaptation in, 185–209; militaries as engines of, 250–51; Operational Theory

Research Institute, 162–81; RMA in Israel, origins of, 127–38
military adaptation, strategic: conclusions on, 113–16; deterrence, erosion of (2000–2017), 90–109; deterrence, guerrilla warfare and (1993–99), 54–72; Hezbollah, evolution of (1985–92), 37–51; IDF withdrawal from Lebanon (2000), 75–87; introduction to, 31
Military Intelligence Directorate (MI), 97, 173, 186, 231, 276
military think tanks. *See* Operational Theory Research Institute
Ministry of Defence (Britain), 4
miscalculations, dangers of, 280
missile-defense technology, 133, 274. *See also* Katyusha rockets; rocket fire
mission command, bottom-up innovation and, 10
Mofaz, Shaul: on airpower, 152, 240; Barak, secret discussions with, 83; on Hezbollah successes, 152; IDF reform under, 135; Naveh and, 171; on rules of the game, 79; on security zone withdrawal, 76, 77, 82
Mordechai, Yitzhak, 49–50, 55, 57, 58
Moussawi, Nawaf, 65
Movement for the Deprived (Harakat al-Mahrumin), 22
"mowing the grass" (military actions), 101, 105, 275
Mughniyeh, Imad, 271
Musawi, Ammar, 56
Mussawi, Abbas: assassination of, 46–50, 51, 141, 246; Hezbollah, improvements to organizational capabilities of, 46; and Hezbollah, organizational adaptation of, 113; on IDF escalations, 45; as information source, 15; on Khomeini, 41; Nasrallah on, 46
mutual deterrence, 50–51, 247, 263

Nagl, John, 11
Nasrallah, Hassan: deterrence, overconfidence in, 95; Galilee, threats against, 276; genius leadership of, 48; *Hanit* attack and, 191; Kuperwasser on, 96; MI's assessments of, 187; restraints on, 104; spider web speech, 75, 86, 87, 193, 274;

Nasrallah, Hassan *(continued)*
successes of, 147; Szubin on, 273; Tufayli on, 272; 2006 Lebanon War, surprise at, 97

Nasrallah, Hassan, general views of: on April understandings, 65; on Badreddine, 271; on concealment, benefits of, 150; on deterrence, essence of, 109; on guerrilla warfare, 150; on Hamade, 271; on information, importance of, 185; on Katyusha bombardments, 56–57; on Kuntar, 280; on Laqees, 271; on learning, 214; on 2006 Lebanon War, 100; on Mofaz's comments, 152; on Mussawi assassination, 47–48; on operational autonomy, 206; on the past, 280; on popular resistance, 127; on reminder operations, 93; on rules of the game, 54; on security zone, 77, 78; on Syria, battle with, 263; on Trump, 273; on Winograd Commission Final Report, 32, 115–16

Nasrallah, Hassan, on Hezbollah: adaptation by, 2, 46, 113, 202–3, 207, 276; attritional strategy, 84–85; current strategic approach, 279; deterrence strategies, 90, 106–7, 108; early stages of, 39, 41; operational changes to, 48–49; operational concepts of, 208, 243; organizational adaptation of, 113, 202–3; politics, entry into, 15; rocket-fire power, 56, 203; successes of, 147; Syrian Civil War, Hezbollah involvement in, 268, 271

Nasrallah, Hassan, on Israel and IDF: airpower, IDF preference for, 142; bombing Israel, 277; IDF actions, 42, 153–54; IDF actions against Syrian targets in Lebanon, 92; IDF defensive posture (late 1990s), 70; IDF security zone withdrawal, 86; Israel, characterization of, 87; Israeli military strength, 75; Israeli military technology, 141; Israeli understanding of Hezbollah, 37, 48; Israel's containment policy, 98; Operation Accountability, 144; Shebaa Farms operation, 278; shocking Israel, 276

National Security Council (NSC), 8, 260–61

National Security Law (2008), 261

Naveh, Shimon: AirLand Battle doctrine, interest in, 163, 255; command style, 237, 252, 256; as consultant to US military, 231–32; Granit on, 229; IDF reform plan, 175; IDF, return to, 232–33; influence of, 251; Marshall and, 174, 176; as military maverick, 164; OTRI creation and, 162, 164–66, 180; perceptions of, 228; Rubin and, 163–64; SOD and, 167–68, 171

Naveh, Shimon, views of: on Dayan, 170; on Halutz, 180, 195, 215–16, 227; on Hirsch, 195, 225, 226–27; on Ice Breaker battle plan, 179; on learning, 162; on Limited Conflict concepts, 220; on military forces, reductions in, 134; on Mofaz, 171; on OTRI's relationship with Marshall, 174; on planning process for anti-Hezbollah campaigns, 176–77; on RMA, 130; on SOD, 169, 227–28; on Tamari, 167

Naveh, Yair, 263, 280

navy, 136, 173

Nehushtan, Ido, 180

Netanyahu, Benjamin, 75, 76, 80

Night of the Fajrs, 186, 204

Ninety-Eighth Division, 192, 200

Ninety-First Division, 192, 196, 200

Nir, Shmuel "Samo," 154–55, 220

non-state groups, Israeli wars against, 103

Norkin, Amikam, 265

Northern Command (IDF): Defense of the Land battle plan, 178; divisions operating in, during 2006 Lebanon War, 192; ineffectiveness of, 57, 198; new head of, 57–59; SOD and, 176–79, 180; targeting policy, changes to, 49

Northern Storm (operational contingency plan), 176, 177–78, 194

NSC (National Security Council), 8, 260–61

Numa, Roni, 233

Obama, Barack, 273

observe, orient, decide, act (OODA) loop, 166–67

Office of Net Assessment (US DOD), 174–75, 176, 255

Olmert, Ehud: on deterrence, loss of, 94–95; Granit on, 229; on Lebanon War objectives, 98–99, 105, 108, 247; Peretz and, 191; Rice and, 103

162nd Division, 192, 200

ongoing security. *See* routine security

On Guerilla Warfare (Mao Tse Tung), 67

OODA (observe, orient, decide, act) loop, 166–67

"Open Letter Addressed by Hezbollah to the Downtrodden in Lebanon and in the World" (Hezbollah manifesto), 23

Operation Accountability (1993), 55–56, 142–44, 256

operational adaptation. *See* military adaptation, operational

operational concepts: Hezbollah's, 123–24, 154, 158, 273; IDF's new, 162; IDF's operational art, 163–66, 168; importance of, 238; Winograd Commission on, 123. *See also* Israel Defense Forces, reappraisal of 2006 operational concept; *specific operational plans*

Operational Mediation, 232–33

operational shocks (udar), 167, 168

Operational Theory Research Institute (OTRI, Maltam, IDF), 162–81; activities of, 256–57; on American EBO, IDF reliance on, 221–22; authorization for, 134–35; conclusions on, 180–81, 251; continuing influence of, 266; criticisms and scapegoating of, 215, 219, 222, 225; downfall of, 179–80; effects-based operations, impact on IDF, 168–69; introduction to, 162–63; origins of, 163–66; partial successes of, 237; RMA, meeting point with, 174–76; on SOD, 220; Systemic Operational Design, about, 166–67; Systemic Operational Design, conceptual sources of, 167–68; Systemic Operational Design, diffusion of, 170–74; Systemic Operational Design, pre-2006 war planning and, 176–79; terminology of, 195

Operation Change of Direction-11, 199–201

Operation Defensive Shield, 157, 172–73

Operation Desert Storm (US), 132–34

Operation Grapes of Wrath (1996), 62–63, 142, 145–47, 203, 256

Operation Law and Order, 44

Operation Litani, 17–18

Operation Morning Dawn, 83

Operation New Horizon, 83

Operation Peace for Galilee (1982), 18–21

Operation Protective Edge (2014), 274

Operations Directorate (General Staff), 136

Operation Specific Weight, 186

Operation Web of Steel, 193–94, 196

organizations: organizational culture, conclusions on, 255–61; organizational culture, military change and, 6, 8–12; organizational learning capacity, 10

Orr, Ori, 20, 21

Orr, Yaakov, 165

OTRI. *See* Operational Theory Research Institute

Palestinians and Palestine Liberation Organization (PLO): expulsion from Jordan, 17; First Intifada, 248; in Lebanon, 17–18; Operation Litani and, 18; Palestinian Authority, peace process with, 248; Palestinian suicide terrorism, impact of, 12; Second Intifada, 13, 93, 156, 172, 230

parallel wars, 246–47

paratroopers (IDF), innovation and, 171

peace process (1990s), impact on IDF, 54–55

Peled, Yossi, 42, 43

people's army, IDF as, 21, 122, 131, 162, 239

Peres, Shimon, 63, 146

Peretz, Amir: Bint Jbayl operation and, 194; Granit on, 229; Halutz and, 99; on IDF decision-making, 239–40; on IDF's ground-warfare capabilities, 241; on Lebanon War, 100, 191, 214; Lebanon War, actions during, 190, 201; on reserve units, 230

persistent firepower, 203

Phalange, 19

pinpoint operations, 61

PLO. *See* Palestinians and Palestine Liberation Organization political leaders (Israel): aggressive operations, lack of will for, 61; casualties and, 86; IDF's accusations against, 57; military, disagreements with, 63, 189; military, poor communications with, 187, 199; military, relationship with, 6, 7; strategic adaptation, hindering of, 71; on withdrawal from Lebanon, 82. *See also* civil-military relations

politics, Hezbollah's participation in, 14–15, 103

Posen, Barry, 6

postheroism and postheroic warfare, 142, 152, 189, 221, 264, 265

potentiation, 168–69

Praxis Institute, 164–65, 167, 172, 227

precision firepower, 123, 146–47, 150, 217, 229

preemptive offensive operations, 34

prisoner swaps, 93, 280

professionalization, of IDF, 131, 137, 175, 260, 267

promotions (in rank), influence on innovations, 7, 170, 228

public opinion: on IDF operations, 61; on Lebanon campaign, 64, 70, 72; on remaining in Lebanon, 81–82; on security zone, 75–76, 78; on security zone, casualties and, 84

punishment, deterrence by, 35

Qana, Lebanon, civilian casualties in, 146–47, 197

Qassem, Naim: on April understandings, violations of, 65; assessment of military situation (1990s), 62; on Hezbollah leadership, 15; on Hezbollah's successes, 150; on IDF's assassination of Mussawi, 47; on IDF's inaction after Shebaa Farms kidnapping, 92; on IDF's use of airpower, 143; on Operation Grapes of Wrath, impact of, 149; on strike against Syrian weapon factory, 280; on Syrian Civil War, Hezbollah involvement in, 271

Qawook, Nabil, 49, 62, 65, 84, 200–201, 242

Raad, Mohammad, 61–62, 80, 92, 268, 269

Rabin, Yitzhak: Barak and, 81; on Gulf War, 132; on Lebanon, Israeli involvement in, 20–21, 23, 37, 61; Levin, relationship with, 61, 249; Nasrallah on, 48; Netanyahu, comparison with, 76; on Operation Accountability, 55–56; security concept, actions on, 130; on security zone, withdrawal to, 38–39; on Syria, 54

raids, 191–92, 196, 198, 224

Raveh, Saar, 172

red lines (Israel's): Hezbollah's understanding of, 90, 98; poor communication of, 115; reestablishment of, 108; setting of, 35; for Syria, 270, 278; violations of, 279, 280

reformist-traditionalist argument, over Israeli security doctrine, 129–30

Reframer (software), 165

Regev, Eldad, 185

reminder operations, 93, 115

reservists (IDF): expense of, 131; during Lebanon War (2006), 186–87, 189, 191; neglect of, 230, 264; reduction in forces of, 135

residential areas, Hezbollah's use of, 206–7

Resistance. *See* Hezbollah

retaliation, IDF preference for, 256

Revolution in Military Affairs (RMA): adoption of, 258; description of, 125–26; influence of, 122–23, 189, 202, 252, 254; in Lebanon (late 1990s), 151–54; operational uses of (*See* Israel Defense Forces, operations in Lebanon (1990s)); OTRI meeting point with, 174–76, 180; post-Lebanon War assessments of, 229–30; problems with, 238–39, 242; Second RMA, 266

Revolution in Military Affairs (RMA), in Israel: origins of, 127–38; conclusions on, 137–38; Gulf War and, 132–34; introduction to, 127; RMA, implementation of, 134–37; Shomron's impact on IDF, 130–32; sources and origins of, 128–30

Rice, Condoleezza, 103

rivalry (competition), military change and, 6, 8–9

RMA. *See* Revolution in Military Affairs

rocket fire: Hezbollah's capabilities of, 202–3, 212n102, 242, 274–75; Hezbollah's rocket doctrine, 148–49; "rocket war," during Lebanon war, 188. *See also* Katyusha rockets

Romm, Giora, 247

Rosen, Stephen, 7

Ross, Dennis, 56, 63, 64, 65–66

routine security (ongoing security, *bitachon shotef*), 34. *See also* Hezbollah, evolution of; low-intensity conflict

routine situations, as described in *IDF Strategy*, 105

Rubin, Doron, 163–64, 237, 256

Rubin, Uzi, 204

rules of the game: establishment of, 55, 71, 113; favorable to Hezbollah, 147; futility of, 79; goals of Lebanon War and, 99; Hezbollah's understandings of, 98; Israeli adherence to, 65; Katyusha bombardments and, 56–57; revisions to, after security zone withdrawal, 91, 115; during Syrian Civil War, 278. *See also* deterrence, guerrilla warfare and

Rumsfeld, Donald, 175

Russia and Soviet Union: involvement in Syria, 269–70; Military Technical Revolution, 125; operational shock theory, 167, 168

SA-22 surface-to-air missile, 269–70

Sadr, Musa al-, 22

Safa, Wafiq, 97

Safieddine, Hashem, 273

Saliman, Ali Hassan, 95, 96

sanctions, against Iran, implications of, 272–73

School of Advanced Military Studies (SAMS, Fort Leavenworth, Kansas), 175, 176, 232

Schwarzkopf, H. Norman, 133

Second Intifada, 13, 93, 156, 172, 230

Second Lebanon War. *See* Lebanon War (2006)

security concept/doctrine (Israel), 99, 128, 129–30, 133. *See also* deterrence

security zone (in southern Lebanon): criticisms of, 76–77; establishment of, 50; impact on IDF strategy, 114; limitations

of, 66; map of, x; Netanyahu on, 80; origins of, 17; public opinion on, 75–76; purpose of, 21; Sneh and, 20; strategy for, poor articulation of, 247–48. *See also* Israel Defense Forces, withdrawal from Lebanon

Segal, Giora, 46

Shaldag aerial commando unit (IDF), 145

Shalit, Gilad, 96

Shara, Farouk al-, 56

Sharon, Ariel: on Bekaa Valley air operation, 129; IDF actions under, 92; ill health of, 94; Lebanon, initiation of invasion of, 18–19; muddled Lebanon policies of, 115

Shebaa Farms / Mount Dov area, 91–92, 93, 115, 278

Shi'ites, 19, 22–23, 44

Shkedy, Eliezer, 188

Shomron, Dan: IDF, influence on, 127, 130–32, 133, 134, 137; on IDF in security zone, 39; on Maydun operation, 44–45; on real threats to Israel, 38; Rubin and, 163; "slimmer and smarter" plan, 238, 251

short-range rockets, Hezbollah's, 43, 68, 142–43, 149, 154, 188, 197, 198, 200, 204, 208, 246, 266

Shoveret Kerach (Ice Breaker) battle plan, 179, 186, 196

Siboni, Gabi, 104

siege of Beirut, 19

Simpkin, Richard, 164, 167, 168

Siniora, Fouad, 103

"sit and wait" principle, 93

skyjackings, 40

SLA. *See* South Lebanon Army

"slimmer and smarter" era: Barak's support for, 133; elite units versus reserve units during, 229–30; Halutz and results of, 238; IDF culture, impact on, 258; IDF force structure adaptation during, 123, 127; Naveh's plan mirroring, 175; problems of, 134, 201, 237; Shomron's plan for, 130–32, 238, 251; Teuza five-year plan, comparison with, 264

Smith, Rupert, 4

Sneh, Ephraim: Barak and, 82, 84, 91; on casualties, 75; conceptual rigidity of, 115; on Free Lebanon Army, 17; on IDF strikes against Lebanese infrastructure, 80; on Netanyahu, 76; on security zone, 20, 21, 81, 84; on SLA, abandonment of, 86; on technology use in Lebanon, 153

Sobelman, Daniel, 108

social protest movements, 76

societal shifts (Israel), challenges of, 122, 239–40

SOCOM (United States Special Operations Command), 232

SOD. *See* Systemic Operational Design

source of emulation *(marjah al-taqlid),* 23

southern Lebanon, Israeli occupation of: IDF in, lack of research on, 12–13; overview of, 16–23; responses to, 21–23. *See also* Israel Defense Forces, operations in Lebanon; Israel Defense Forces, withdrawal from Lebanon; security zone

South Lebanon Army (SLA): attacks against, rise in, 61; capabilities of, 20; casualties, 70; IDF embedment in, 82; Israeli security zone withdrawal and, 85–86; origins of, 17; problems of, 78; security zone, manning of, 21

Soviet Union. *See* Russia and Soviet Union

special intelligence evaluations, 83

specialized commando units (IDF), 60–61

Special Operations Command (SOCOM, US), 232

Staff College (IDF), 260

standoff firepower: Hezbollah's, 188; IDF emphasis on, 124–25, 129–30, 142–43, 147, 151, 158, 173–74, 177, 179, 189, 190, 202, 205, 239; United States' use of, 216

Starry, Donn, 125

State Department (US), on Kuntar, 280

state-on-state wars, 103, 104, 114, 249

steadfastness, 149, 205, 208

strategic adaptation. *See* military adaptation, strategic

strategic raiding, 168, 194

strategy and strategic learning: Barak election and, 81, 85; conclusions on, 113–16; introduction to, 31–36; lack of deep thinking on, 257; strategic doctrine (Israel's), 33–35; strategic failures, of IDF, 59; strategy of fatigue, 154–57; tacticalization of, 114, 248, 260. *See also* military adaptation; military adaptation, strategic

Streisand, Barbara, 76

structural adaptations, of IDF (1980s and 1990s), 123

suicide bombings, 40, 43, 45, 271

Suleiman, Michel, 272

Sunni militant groups, in Syria, 263, 268, 271, 272

Sun Tzu, 169

surveillance, improvements in, 60

swarming operations, 172, 193–95, 224

Syria: antiaircraft missile batteries, in Lebanon, 18; Arens on, 79; Bekaa Valley air operation, 128–29, 130, 137, 237, 251; cease-fire (1996), agreement to, 64; Israeli air strikes against, 280; peace negotiations with, 55, 56, 58, 61, 63, 71, 72, 248; Rabin on, 54; US precision-guided firepower, witnessing of, 141; Zeevi on, 57

Syria, IDF and Hezbollah in, 263–80; future outlook for, 273–78; IDF's force plans, 264–67; introduction to, 263; miscalculations, dangers of, 278–80; Syrian Civil War as challenge to Hezbollah, 268–73

Syria, in Lebanon: control of, 65–66; invasion of, 17; Lebanon as proxy, 79–80; responsibility for, 90–91; Syrian targets in, IDF actions against, 92; use of, as bargaining chip, 76; withdrawal from, 94, 178

Systemic Operational Design (SOD): about, 166–67; assessments of, 222–23, 238; challenges to implementation of, 238, 252; conceptual sources of, 167–68; continued attention to, 231–33; diffusion of, 170–74, 251; effects-based operations and, 168–69; in Halutz's

operational concept document, 215–16; Hirsch's use of, 194–95; introduction to, 123; OTRI development of, 163; pre-2006 war planning and, 176–79; superficial adoption of, 258
Systemic Reframing Thinking, 165
Szubin, Adam, 273

tacticalization of strategy, 72, 114, 248
tactical reconnaissance, 60
Taif Accord (1989), 46, 272
Tal, Israel, 33, 127, 129–30
Tamari, Dov, 164–65, 167, 174, 238
Tamir, Moshe "Chico," 59, 114, 265
tank units, during Lebanon War (2006), 200
targeting policy (IDF), changes to, 49–50
technology: homemade Israeli RMA, 136, 251; IDF's increasing reliance on, 264–65; impact of, 130–32; precision firepower, 123, 146–47, 150, 217, 229. See also Revolution in Military Affairs
Teffen operational plan, 231
Tel Aviv University, 164
Teuza (Daring) five-year plan, 264–66
theological seminaries (Shi'ite), 22
Think-Tank for Operational Studies. See Operational Theory Research Institute
13 principles of warfare, 66
366th "Pillar of Fire" Division, 192, 200
Tira, Ron, 218, 219, 246
top-down adaptation, 9, 10, 71, 113, 180, 249
traditionalist-reformist argument, over Israeli security doctrine, 129–30
TRADOC (Training and Doctrine Command, US Army), 175, 231–32
Training and Doctrine Command (IDF), 164
Training and Doctrine Command (TRADOC, US Army), 175, 231–32
training budget cuts, impact of, 135–37, 158, 192, 194–95, 201, 258, 264
Treasury Department (US), sanctions blacklist, 273
Trophy system (tank protective system), 277
Trump, Donald J., 273

Tufayli, Subhi, 15, 40–41, 44, 45, 272
Tukhachevsky, Mikhail N., 167, 168
tunnel networks, 149–50, 206, 276–77, 278
TWA Flight 847, 40
2006 war. See Lebanon War (2006)
2006 operational doctrine. See Israel Defense Forces, reappraisal of 2006 operational concept
Tyre, suicide bombing in, 40
Tzahal 2000 plan, 135
Tzur, Guy, 192

udar (operational shock), 167, 168
uncritical emulation, dangers of, 254–55
understandings: April understandings (1996), 64–66, 79, 80, 249; July understandings (1993), 56–57, 62, 63, 64, 79, 80, 249
Unified Quest exercises, 231
United Nations (UN): Israel-Lebanon Monitoring Group, 64–65; Resolution 425, Israel's fulfillment of, 90; Resolution 1559, 98; Resolution 1701, 201; Resolutions 425 and 426, 18; United Nations Interim Force in Lebanon (UNIFIL), 18, 201
United States: AirLand Battle doctrine, 125, 133, 255; EBO, discarding of, 221; IDF's overreliance on US military, 254; Iran, actions against, 273; Israel, military aid to, 129, 136, 151; 2006 Lebanon War cease-fire and, 199; political pressure on Israel, during 2006 Lebanon War, 190; Special Operations Command (SOCOM), 232; strategic agenda, post–Cold War, 125; US Army, 4, 176, 231
urban warfare skills, Hezbollah's improvements in, 44, 269

van Creveld, Martin, 222
Van Riper, Paul, 232
victory (winning) by not losing, 150, 178, 207–8, 242, 270
Vietnam War, 128, 272
Vilnai, Matan, 141, 146, 165, 171
violent bargaining, 113
Virilio, Paul, 167
visionary (military) officers, 7, 248, 251

Wadi Saluki, battle at, 200–201, 230, 277
war: Clausewitz on, 2, 31; as described in
    IDF Strategy, 105; parallel wars, 246–47;
    postheroic warfare, 142, 221, 240; wars
    of choice, 21, 70, 76, 257; Western way
    of war, 132. *See also* Israel, war with
    Hezbollah
War between Brothers, 44
war of the brains, 48
Wass de Czege, Huba, 232
way of war, 132, 175
way of war, IDF's: April 2006 operational
    document and, 215, 218; characteristics
    of, 175; drives of changes to, 251;
    Halutz on, 136; Hezbollah response to,
    138, 202, 207, 209; Limited Conflict
    document and, 154; operational concept
    as, 123; precision weapons as preferred,
    146; RMA and, 122, 242; during secu-
    rity zone era, 153–54; Winograd
    Commission on, 229. *See also* Israel
    Defense Forces, reappraisal of 2006
    operational concept; operational
    concepts
Wegman, Yehuda, 156, 222
Western way of war, 132
wilayat al-faqih ("guardianship of the
    Islamic jurist"), 23
Williams, Michael, 97
Wingate, Orde, 168, 177
winning (victory) by not losing, 150, 178,
    207–8, 242, 270
Winograd Commission Final Report: on
    battle plans, 186; on Bint Jbayl opera-
    tions, 196; on Defense of the Land
    campaign plan, 178; description of, 1–2;
    on ground forces, neglect of, 230; Halutz
    and, 200; on Hirsch, 194, 195, 224; on
    IAF, limitations of, 188; IDF, critiques
    of, 31, 32, 255, 259; on IDF's opera-
    tional concepts, 121, 230–31; on Israel's
    strategic failures, 101; on 2006 Lebanon
    War, origins of, 115; on Limited Con-
    flict concept, 221; on National Security
    Council, 260; on operational concept
    document, 214–15, 217, 218–19; on
    operational concepts, 123, 162; on
    OTRI, language used by, 223–24; on
    postheroic trends, 240; on prewar army
    intelligence estimates, 188; raids, criti-
    cisms of, 198; on training deficiencies,
    192; on trends influencing IDF's war-
    fighting concepts, 122
Winograd, Eliyahu, 1, 226
World War II, Chindit commandos, 168

Yaalon, Moshe "Bogie": budget cuts under,
    136; on deterrence against Hezbollah,
    94; on Hezbollah actions in Syria, 279;
    on Israeli resilience, 274; on Limited
    Conflict doctrine, 157; OTRI and,
    171–72, 177–78, 179–80; Teuza plan,
    support for, 265
Yaari, Yedidia, 172–73
Yadlin, Amos: on attrition, 275; on deter-
    rence, 101; Halutz and, 180; on
    Hezbollah tactics, 96; in internal mili-
    tary deliberations, on 2006 Lebanon
    War, 190; on 2006 Lebanon War, 100,
    103, 187, 188
Yair, Yoram, 224
Yakhont surface-to-sea missile, 270
Yom Kippur War (Arab-Israeli War, 1973),
    17, 38, 51, 128, 130

Zeevi-Farkash, Aharon, 97, 180, 188
Zeevi, Rehavam, 57
Ziv, Israel, 180
zu'ama (feudal leaders in Lebanon), 22
Zuckerman, Erez, 192

ABOUT THE AUTHOR

RAPHAEL D. MARCUS is a nonresident fellow at the Insurgency Research Group in the Department of War Studies, King's College London, where he received his PhD. His research interests include Middle East security issues, terrorism, military affairs, and organizational learning. He is currently working as an intelligence and counterterrorism analyst at a law-enforcement agency.

CPSIA information can be obtained
at www.ICGtesting.com
Printed in the USA
BVHW071611161218
535509BV00002B/34/P